Management of Child Development Centers

FOURTH EDITION

VERNA HILDEBRAND
Michigan State University

PATRICIA F. HEARRON
Appalachian State University

Merrill,
an imprint of Prentice Hall
Upper Saddle River, New Jersey   Columbus, Ohio

Library of Congress Cataloging-in-Publication Data

Hildebrand, Verna.
    Management of child development centers / Verna Hildebrand and
    Patricia F. Hearron—4th ed.
      p.   cm.
    Includes bibliographical references and indexes.
    ISBN 0-13-238635-6
      1. Nursery schools—United States—Administration. 2. Day care centers—
United States—Administration. 3. Early childhood education—United States
I. Hearron, Patricia F. II. Title.
LB2822.7.H55   1997
372.21′6′0973—dc20
                                        96-11463
                                          CIP

Cover photo: © Lawrence Migdale
Editor: Ann Castel Davis
Production Editor: Linda Hillis Bayma
Copy Editor: Laura Larson
Design Coordinator: Jill E. Bonar
Text Designer: STELLARViSIONs
Production Manager: Laura Messerly
Electronic Text Management: Marilyn Wilson Phelps, Matthew Williams, Karen L. Bretz,
    Tracey Ward
Illustrations: Tracey Ward

This book was set in New Baskerville BT by Prentice Hall and was printed and bound by
R.R. Donnelley & Sons Company. The cover was printed by Phoenix Color Corp.

 © 1997 by Prentice-Hall, Inc.
Simon & Schuster/A Viacom Company
Upper Saddle River, New Jersey 07458

Printed in the United States of America

10 9 8 7 6 5 4 3 2

ISBN: 0-13-238635-6

Prentice-Hall International (UK) Limited, *London*
Prentice-Hall of Australia Pty. Limited, *Sydney*
Prentice-Hall of Canada, Inc., *Toronto*
Prentice-Hall Hispanoamericana, S. A., *Mexico*
Prentice-Hall of India Private Limited, *New Delhi*
Prentice-Hall of Japan, Inc., *Tokyo*
Simon & Schuster Asia Pte. Ltd., *Singapore*
Editora Prentice-Hall do Brasil, Ltda., *Rio de Janeiro*

We dedicate Management of Child Development Centers *to all the*
young children who share our small spaceship Earth,
to the families and caregivers who nurture them,
and to the managers of child development centers
whose commitment to high-quality programs
helps make that nurturing possible.

Preface

● ●

M*anagement of Child Development Centers* is based on the premise that high-quality programs for young children are an essential support for families in today's world. Maintaining the quality of those programs requires a sound knowledge of child development and a thorough understanding of the management process. Today's managers face additional challenges as well: as our child development programs reflect the increasing diversity of our society, managers must strive to provide services that are culturally responsive and sensitive to a variety of family needs. The inclusion of children with disabilities in centers, a recent and growing phenomenon, can benefit us all—if the managers and staff members of those centers are prepared to collaborate with families and health professionals to help each child fulfill his or her potential.

Management of Child Development Centers addresses each phase of the management process and provides specific examples of how that process applies to programs for young children and their families. In addition to providing a variety of practical tools, such as menu planning and evaluation forms, this edition integrates discussions of special needs and a multicultural perspective throughout the text. Photographs enliven each chapter, illustrating significant aspects of high-quality programs for young children.

Resources at the end of each chapter have been extensively updated so that readers will be able to pursue topics of particular interest. The "Decisions, Decisions . . . " sections in each chapter have been revised or augmented to stimulate readers to think more deeply and apply the information provided.

This book is suitable for use in a variety of settings: in formal classes in 2- or 4-year college programs, in child development associate training or inservice programs for practicing early childhood professionals, and for independent study by individuals contemplating a move from classroom teacher or caregiver to center manager.

Management of Child Development Centers is the product of the authors' combined experience over several decades, in which we have worked with children and their families, with young people anticipating a career in the early childhood profession, and with practicing professionals at many levels. Previous editions have been field-tested in university classrooms, and the present edition incorporates much of what has been learned in that process. Managers who apply the information in the book will be well positioned to meet the growing demand for high-quality programs that are capable of serving *all* children.

Acknowledgments

Acknowledgment is due the late Dr. Beatrice Paolucci, specialist in management, who challenged the author about management and decision-making concepts; other Michigan State University colleagues Jeanne Brown, Margaret Bubolz, Eileen Earhart, Betty Garlick, Marjory Kostelnik, Lois Lund, Linda Nelson, Lillian Phenice, Lawrence Schiamberg, Ann Soderman, Marilyn Waters, and Alice Whiren, with whom I have been associated for many years in planning our demonstration early childhood program; Joan Raven, Cathy Moore, Debbie Nickel, and Cynthia Fairchild Karimullah, who helped me in numerous ways as graduate assistants.

I gratefully acknowledge the helpful suggestions of Dorothy Hewes of San Diego State University; Sherrill Richardz of Washington State University; Joan Raven Robison of Cloud County (Kansas) Community College; and Julia Miller, Robert Griffore, Kathy Woehrle, and Linda Herring of Michigan State University. Also, acknowledgment is due to the National Association for the Education of Young Children (NAEYC) for granting permission to reprint the nomenclature and Sue Bredekamp of NAEYC headquarters for helping me more fully understand the center accreditation process. Acknowledgment for photos is stated with each photo. In addition, recognition for assistance with photos goes to Ruth Davis, Oakwood College; Joan Raven Robison and Jennifer Nading, Cloud County Community College; Rebecca Hines, Bethany Weekday School; Mary Gray, University of Missouri at Columbia; Beverly Briggs and Faye Persnal, Kansas State University; Betty Larson, San Antonio College; Phyllis Klein, Bay-Arenac Skill Center; Theda Connell, Southeast Oakland Vocational Technical Center; Joan Wilson, Howard University; Elizabeth Seelhoff Byrum, Calhoun School; Karen Lui, University of Minnesota at Waseca; Craig Hart, Louisiana State University; Carolyn Rafter and Frank Fortune, Georgia Southern College; Deborah Steinberg, Division of Human Resources and Family Ecology, School of Human Resources and Family Studies, University of Illinois; Methodist Hospital Child Care Center, Lubbock, Texas; and especially the children, parents, and teachers who cooperated.

Verna Hildebrand

I am indebted to several people who offered support and assistance in the preparation of this fourth edition. Margaret Bubolz and M. Suzanne Sontag generously shared their conceptualization of family ecosystems. Plenum Press granted permission to use the diagram of the family ecosystem, and the American Public Health Association gave permission to reprint the chart, "Food Components for Infants." My colleagues at Appalachian State University, Ellen Carpenter and Mary Etta Reeves, and Whitney Danhof of the North Carolina Cooperative Extension Service, all provided useful information. Becky DeHart, Beckie Fuller, and Connie Green graciously welcomed me in their classrooms to observe and photograph the children in action. Special thanks are also due to the children in those classrooms, as well as their parents.

I gratefully acknowledge the skillful assistance of Laura Larson, copy editor, and Linda Bayma, production editor, as well as the helpful suggestions of the reviewers for this fourth edition: Craig H. Hart, Brigham Young University; Pat Kellogg, Northeast Louisiana University; Kim A. Madsen, Chadron State College, and Ramona E. Patterson, Southern University.

Patricia F. Hearron

Contents

● ●

PART I
Introduction   1

● ●

CHAPTER 1   **Managing Children's Centers
in Today's World   2**
Child Development Centers: A Support
          System for Families   4
Early Childhood Education Data   4
Types of Child Development Centers   12
Institutional Cooperation   22
Conclusion   25
Applications   25
Study Questions   25
Suggested Readings   26

CHAPTER 2   **Applying Theories in Managing a Child
Development Center   28**
Developmental Theory   29
The Ecological System Framework   35
Management Theory   43
Managing Requires a Systems
          Approach   45
Conclusion   46
Applications   46
Study Questions   47
Suggested Readings   47

CHAPTER 3   **Management Processes and Approaches   50**
The Managerial Processes   50
Accreditation   58
What Will Be Your Style of Managing?   59
Decision Making   61
The Decision Process   62
Rationality in Decision Making   65
Time Management   66
Knowing Yourself   68
Conclusion   69
Applications   69
Study Questions   70
Suggested Readings   70

PART II
Management Principles and Tasks   73

CHAPTER 4   **Planning   74**
The Policy Board   75
Advisory Boards   76
Why Planning Is Important   79
Time for Planning   80
Steps in the Planning Process   82
Types of Planning   87
Policies, Procedures, and Rules   90
Time, Scope, and Cycling of Plans   91
Planning Categories   92
Conclusion   93
Applications   93
Study Questions   93
Suggested Readings   94

CHAPTER 5   **Organizing   96**
Task Analysis   97
Authority and Responsibility   100
Span of Control   102
Organizing Classrooms or Groups   104
Organizing Services   107
Conclusion   112
Applications   112
Study Questions   112
Suggested Readings   113

CHAPTER 6   **Staffing   114**
Human Capital in the Child Development Center   114
The Manager's Role in Staffing   115
Hiring New Staff   119
The Staffing Shortage   120
Job Analysis, Description, and Specification   123
Fringe Benefits   131
Educational Preparation of Teachers   131
Experienced or Inexperienced?   135
Supervisory Staff   136
Professional Services Staff   137
Listing the Job   138
The Job Application   139
References   142
Legal Aspects of Staffing   142
The Interview   144
The Offer   147
Informing Unsuccessful Candidates   148
On-the-Job Orientation   148
On-the-Job Performance   150
Dismissing Staff Members   151
Employee-Employer Relations   151
Staff Communication   153
Evaluation Conferences   156
Staff Meetings   156
Professional Development   156
Volunteers   160
Conclusion   162
Applications   162
Study Questions   163
Suggested Readings   163

CHAPTER 7   **Leading   166**
Managing and Leading Differ   166
Leadership and Accreditation   168
Leadership in a Child Development Center   171
Values   171
Developmentally Appropriate Practice   178
Communicating   181
Professional Support   182
The Professional Library   183
Professional Research and Writing   183
Conclusion   184
Professional Organizations and Their Journals   184
Early Childhood Discussion Groups on the Internet   187

Applications   187
Study Questions   188
Suggested Readings   188

CHAPTER 8   **Monitoring and Controlling
for Quality   190**
Standards   191
Accreditation   192
Monitoring and Controlling Defined   193
Program Evaluation   193
Monitoring Other Units   203
Evaluation of Management   207
Conclusion   207
Applications   209
Study Questions   209
Suggested Readings   210

PART III
Managing Resources   213
• •

CHAPTER 9   **Managing Monetary Resources   214**
Funding Child Development Centers   214
Fund-Raising   220
Starting a New Business   222
Types of Resources   224
Resources Required   226
Monetary Decisions   229
The Efficiency Rule   232
Control of Funds and Expenses   232
Conclusion   239
Applications   239
Study Questions   240
Suggested Readings   241

CHAPTER 10   **Child Care in the Corporate
World   242**
Child Care Provisions   242
Motivation for Supporting Child Care   243
Ways Companies Are Involved   244
Labor-Management and Child Care   247
Church-Sponsored Child Care   250
College- and University-Sponsored Child Care   250

Hospital-Sponsored Child Care   251
Military Child Care   251
Conclusion   251
Applications   252
Study Questions   252
Suggested Readings   253

CHAPTER 11 **Managing Spatial Resources   254**
Managing Space   255
Classroom Arrangements   271
Conclusion   278
Equipment Suppliers   278
Other Useful Addresses   279
Applications   279
Study Questions   280
Suggested Readings   280

CHAPTER 12 **Managing Health and Safety Needs of Children   283**
Policies and Practices   283
Planning for a Healthful Environment   284
Individual Records   286
Child Care for Sick Children   287
Organizing a System for Meeting Health Requirements   289
Employees' Health   292
Children with Disabilities and Chronic Medical Problems   293
Parental Responsibility for Children's Health   295
Confidential Family Information   297
Prescription Medications and Diets   298
Meeting Children's Physiological Needs   299
Diapering Infants   300
Toilet Training   301
Resting and Sleeping   302
Health Education for Children   303
Safe Arrival and Departure   304
Safety Protection for Children   306
Child Abuse   307
Transporting Children   308
Monitoring Health and Safety Conditions   309
Conclusion   311
Resources   311
Applications   312

Study Questions   312
Suggested Readings   312

CHAPTER 13 Managing Food Service   315

Planning Meal Service   316
Federal Subsidies for Food Programs   316
Cultural Diversity   320
Facilities for Preparation and Serving   320
Food Service Personnel   321
Prevention of Food Poisoning   322
Menu Planning   324
Seating and Serving Children   331
Planning the Midmorning or Midafternoon Snack   333
Food and Curriculum   333
Communicating with Parents on Food Matters   336
Monitoring and Controlling Food Programs   337
Conclusion   337
Applications   340
Study Questions   340
Suggested Readings   341

CHAPTER 14 Children's Programs: The Manager's Role   343

Center Accreditation   343
Manager's Role in Program Development   344
Group Size   344
Preliminary Organization   345
Developmental Principles to Know   347
Basic Guides to Program Development   349
Teachers' Planning and Scheduling   351
Parental Concern for Quality   356
A Manager's Inputs into Curriculum and Interaction   357
Conclusion   367
Applications   368
Study Questions   368
Suggested Readings   369

CHAPTER 15 Communicating with Parents and the Public   371

Communication with Parents   371
Communication with Community Members   385
The NAEYC's Child Care Information Service   389
Double Duty in Public Relations   389

Conclusion   390
Applications   390
Study Questions   391
Suggested Readings   391

CHAPTER 16 **Advocacy and Professionalism**   394
Goals of Child Advocates   394
Work of the Advocate   395
Steps in Advocacy   396
Examples of Advocacy   396
Reaching Decision Makers   402
Linking Advocacy to Other Professional Roles   402
Conclusion   405
Applications   405
Study Questions   406
Suggested Readings   406

PART IV
Conclusions   409
• •

CHAPTER 17 **Children: Our Future**   410
Dedication . . . and Enlightened Self-Interest   410
Humility . . . and Professional Pride   411
Patience . . . and Righteous Impatience   413
Thoughtfulness . . . and Thoughtful Action   413
Service Orientation . . . and Healthy Assertiveness   414
A Global View . . . and a Local Agenda   415
Applications   416
Study Questions   417
Suggested Readings   417

Appendix A   Comparison of State Licensing Requirements for Child Care Centers   419

Appendix B   State Agencies Responsible for Licensing Child Care Centers   422

Name Index   426

Subject Index   431

PART I

Introduction

CHAPTER 1

Managing Children's Centers in Today's World

A re you a person who has always dreamed of owning and managing a
school for young children? Or do you expect to move up to managing the
center where you now work? Or would you like to be the principal at the
elementary school where you now teach kindergarten or prekindergarten?

What do you need to know to perform the manager's role adequately and efficiently? Will your experience as a successful teacher make a difference in your
ability to manage a center? If you have an MBA (master of business administration) yet have never been a teacher, could you manage a group of classrooms in a
school or center? Are similar managerial skills and knowledge required in other
human service organizations, such as a child care referral service or a family
counseling agency?

This book focuses on management as applied in child development centers.
Agreeing on key definitions is essential.

Management is the science of (a) setting goals, (b) allocating human and material resources judiciously for achieving the goals, (c) carrying out the work or
action required in the goals, (d) monitoring the outcome or product of the work
or action based on established standards, and (e) making necessary adjustments
or improvements to assure that performance reaches or exceeds goals.

Child development center will be used to refer to the out-of-home education
and care of a young child within a group of young children, a service that supplements the education and care parents are giving their child.

The term **child development center** refers to programs that are full- or part-
day, profit or nonprofit, and programs known as preschools, child care or day

care centers, kindergarten, prekindergarten, cooperative, Head Start, or variations of any of these. Though the main focus in this book is on center- or school-based programs, many of the principles discussed will be applicable to home-based family day care providers. Significant in the definition of child development centers is the linking of education and care. Research and experience of parents and early childhood authorities indicate that, for young children, it is inappropriate to think of care without including education or vice versa.

Management is a science; some individuals spend their careers perfecting this science. Management has a background of theory, research, experience, applications, and knowledge that must be brought together by an individual who assumes the managerial role in any enterprise. Management of a center is complex—more complex than operating a single entity such as a home or a classroom. Many individuals are likely to have a stake in the outcome of a decision or action. President Harry S Truman had a sign on his desk that read, "The buck stops here." In other words, as president, he was the ultimate decision maker, the manager.

Would you like being a manager? How will you know? Can someone else tell you whether you would like being a manager? What experience have you had that could make you a good manager? How many managers have you worked for? Were these "good" managers? What makes a manager good? What things that a manager does are especially enjoyable? What things are difficult? As you read this chapter, take some time to reflect on all these questions and to answer them for yourself.

DECISIONS, DECISIONS . . .

 What parts of the manager's job do you think you would enjoy? What parts do you think you would find difficult? Does it take a certain type of personality to do well in the manager's role?

Where are you on your time line of professional development? Management of a school or center can give your professional life new challenges after you have had a number of years of successful experiences in teaching. Or you may feel that you will need more teaching experience before taking on a managerial role.

DECISIONS, DECISIONS . . .

 Imagine yourself 5 or 10 years from now. Where would you like to be working? What would you like to be doing? What steps can you take now to achieve those dreams?

You may be like some people who look for quick management courses and advice when they are pressed into the manager's role, perhaps without adequate preparation when the manager leaves suddenly. Of course, certain management skills are required in a single classroom and in the home. Therefore, whether you are already a manager, expect to become a manager soon, or have management as a future goal, learning about the intricacies of child development center management can add a new dimension to your professional career. Knowledge of managerial principles can make you more appreciative and supportive of managers with whom you work, even when you are happy that the buck still stops at their desk.

CHILD DEVELOPMENT CENTERS: A SUPPORT SYSTEM FOR FAMILIES

Families throughout the world hold the primary responsibility for nurturing children. Nurturing may be done by the natural or adoptive parent or parents, extended family systems, or institutions. Families often desire and decide to supplement the care and education they can give with assistance from institutions outside the family. Historical, cultural, political, and economic factors within each society affect their decisions. The demand for child development services is very high in the industrialized world, but it is not universal. Some cultural groups would prefer to care for and educate their children of all ages within the family circle. Some parents may even refuse to send any of their children or, more likely, their children of a certain age or gender out of the home to school unless compulsory school attendance is enforced.

The child development centers considered here, including public school kindergarten, generally will be optional services for families. Families may choose to use such a center or to provide child care and education in their homes for their young children. Understanding the context within which families in today's world are living and rearing their children is essential if we are to be able most effectively to manage or administer such services as child development centers or any social service for families.

EARLY CHILDHOOD EDUCATION DATA

Knowing the current situation and trends in one's field of business is part of wise management.[1] Each manager makes a concerted effort to keep abreast of

---

[1] Several sources of U.S. government statistics are used in this section. Each was the latest available as the book went to press. Included are U.S. Department of Labor, Bureau of Labor Statistics, *Employment in Perspective: Women in the Labor Force*, Report 879, Second Quarter 1994; U.S. Department of Commerce, Current Population Reports, Series P-70, No. 36, *Who's Minding the Kids? Child Care Arrangements: Fall 1991* (Washington, DC: U.S. Government Printing Office, 1994); U.S. Department of Commerce, Statistical Brief No. 91-6, *The Shifting Fertility Patterns of American Women* (Washington, DC: U.S. Government Printing Office, January 1992); U.S. Department of Commerce, Statistical Brief No. 92-13, *Family Life Today and How It Has Changed* (Washington, DC: U.S. Government Printing Office, November 1992); Children's Defense Fund, *The State of America's Children Yearbook 1995* (Washington, DC: Children's Defense Fund, 1995); U.S. Department of Commerce, Statistical Brief No 94-1, *Americans with Disabilities* (Washington, DC: U.S. Government Printing Office, January 1994).

A goal of managers of early childhood programs is for children to be relaxed, happy, and friendly.
Child Care Center, Haslett, MI

national statistics and collects similar data covering his or her local community and state. Information on local employment trends is needed in addition to data showing needs for children's services. A local licensing agency or the chamber of commerce can suggest the best source of local and state statistics.

Numbers and Characteristics of Children

Today there are about 19.5 million children under 5 years of age and 36.6 million who are ages 5–14. Each family averages 2.1 children, a slight increase after a long-term downward trend in family size in the United States. However, the post–World War II baby boomers have grown to become the parents of today's young children. Thus, large numbers of parents are in the childbearing years, and, even though they are having fewer children than their parents, there are, overall, more children for our concern. Many of today's couples are delaying parenthood. Over 14% of the first-time mothers are over age 30—mature parents who know what they want for their child or children. As their age would indicate, older parents generally have completed several levels of education and have served in the working world for some time.

Several other groups of children are of special concern for the manager of children's programs in today's world. According to the U.S. Census Bureau, 11% of all births in 1988 were to women born in other countries. The increasing immigrant population means that many children will be entering centers where the dominant language and customs are dramatically different from those they experience at home. Other U.S. government statistics estimate that 2% of all children under 3 years of age and 5% of those from 3 to 5 years of age have some sort of disability. There is a growing movement, supported by federal legislation, toward inclusion of these children in programs for all children. These trends mean that center managers will be challenged to find ways to accommodate diverse needs and view differences as potential strengths rather than deficits.

Problems experienced by society at large will also impact children's programs. Homelessness afflicts a growing number of families with children; in some cities, child care facilities have been established to provide some measure of stability for young children in this stressful situation. Rising rates of teen pregnancy mean that centers may need to meet the needs of very young parents as well as those of their children. Fathers, grandparents, and others as primary caregivers of children give new meanings to our ideas about involving family in programs for children. Children may enter early childhood programs having been exposed to drugs in utero or with HIV-positive status. The manager of children's programs in today's world will need a broad knowledge base and access to many resources to serve a wide range of family needs.

Demand Increasing

A perusal of U.S. government statistics shows that the demand for children's services has steadily increased since the 1950s. Parents who are more highly educated tend to enroll their children in early childhood schools and centers at a higher rate than parents with less education. Nursery schools were considered of higher quality ("more educational") than (day) child care centers, and during the 1960s and 1970s, many working parents pieced together half-day nursery school programs, family day care, and baby-sitting to get enough hours to enable parents to manage their work and family responsibilities. As more and more mothers joined the workforce, the demand for full-time high-quality child care also increased. By the year 2000, the workforce is expected to be 48% women (see Figure 1–1 for the historical and projected trends for women in the workforce).

Figure 1–2 shows the rates women with children under 6 participated in the workforce from 1950 to 1991. These charts show a steadily increasing trend for women to participate in the workforce. Many working women have already experienced divorce or realize that divorce is a possibility and, once they are in a satisfactory work situation, prefer to remain there for the security it offers in salary and health, vacation, advancement, and retirement benefits.

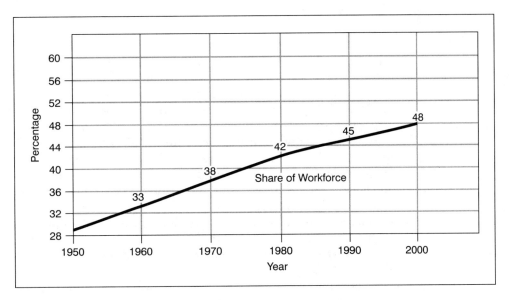

Figure 1–1
Women are a growing share of the total workforce.
Source: Bureau of Labor Statistics, November 1991.

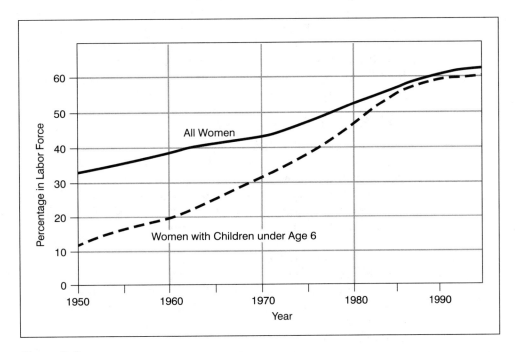

Figure 1–2
Labor force participation for all women and women with children under age 6 (1950–1990)
Source: Bureau of Labor Statistics, November 1991.

Cutbacks, layoffs, and plant closings affected many working families during the 1980s and 1990s. With uncertainty in men's jobs, women became hesitant about giving up any job for more than a short maternity leave. Thus, the demand for infant and toddler care increased during the period. The recent era shows some fathers gaining shared or total custody of their children and some fathers as primary caregivers of their children while their wives work full-time. (The Bureau of Labor Statistics reports that 357,000, or 0.5%, of fathers with children under 6 maintain families without a spouse.) Thus, managers will deal with some fathers who have total or partial responsibility for their young children.

Historically, child care centers were used primarily by poor parents and were considered a last resort in the choice of care of children away from home. Affluent families who wished sent their children to nursery school for a few hours a week. However, as more educated and moderate- to upper-income mothers began working, more affluent families began seeking full-day child care. They expected the high-quality education they would receive in a nursery school. The increase in numbers and shift in the child care centers' clientele have created the demand for improvement in the quality of child care. Table 1–1 shows the types of care employed mothers use for children under 5 and for those 5–14 years old.

Organized child care, according to governmental statisticians, is defined as enrollment in a child care center or participation in nursery school and is differentiated from in-home care by relatives or family day care. Significantly, mothers with the most education and who work in managerial-professional jobs are most likely to enroll their children under 5 in organized child care facilities. One suggested reason for service workers and laborers not using organized child care is that the hours of operation of centers typically are daytime hours, which may not coordinate with the worker's schedule.

Working Parents

Only 10% of families today are considered what was once called "traditional"; that is, the father works outside the home and the mother stays home to do child care and other homemaking duties.

Nearly three-quarters of all married mothers with children under 6 worked sometime during 1992, according to a report by the U.S. Department of Labor. About half of that number worked full-time, year-round. Both parents worked in 65% of two-parent families with children under 5. These figures represent a sharp rise since 1970. Over that period, the types of child care used by working parents have changed. U.S. Census records show that the use of organized child care facilities increased dramatically between 1977 and 1985 (going from 13% to 23%) and has remained fairly constant since then. Table 1–1 is based on data gathered by the U.S. Census Bureau in 1991 and illustrates the types of care used by employed mothers of children in various age groups in 1991. Principal findings of the 1991 survey indicate a slight decrease in the percentage of young children in organized child care facilities (23% in 1991 versus 26% in 1988) as well as

Table 1–1

Percentage primary child care arrangements used by employed mothers for children under 15, by age of child: Fall 1991

Type of Arrangement	All Children	Less Than 1 Year	1 and 2 Years	3 and 4 Years	5 to 14 Years
Care in child's home	35.7	40.5	38.7	31.1	10.7
By father	20.0	21.6	21.2	18.3	6.6
By grandparent	7.2	8.7	8.0	5.8	1.2
By other relative	3.2	2.7	3.9	2.7	1.9
By nonrelative	5.4	7.5	5.5	4.3	0.9
Care in another home	31.0	40.5	33.8	24.5	3.6
By grandparent	8.6	14.3	8.6	6.3	1.2
By other relative	4.5	5.6	4.7	3.8	1.0
By nonrelative	17.9	20.5	20.4	14.4	1.4
Organized child care facilities	23.0	11.5	17.5	32.9	1.9
Day/group care center	15.8	9.8	15.2	18.6	1.4
Nursery/preschool	7.3	1.7	2.3	14.2	0.5
School-based activity	0.5	0	0.1	1.1	3.0
Kindergarten/grade school	1.1	0	0	2.5	76.2
Child cares for self	0	0	0	0	2.7
Mother cares for child at work*	8.7	7.6	9.9	7.9	2.0

*Includes women working at home or away from home

Source: U.S. Department of Commerce, Current Population Reports, Series P-70, No. 36, *Who's Minding the Kids? Child Care Arrangements: Fall 1991* (Washington, DC: U.S. Government Printing Office, 1994).

a decline from 24% to 18% for children under 5 in family day care settings over the same period. On the other hand, more young children were cared for by their fathers while their mothers worked (20% in 1991, as opposed to 15% in 1988). Married mothers were more likely to rely on fathers for child care, while the children of lone mothers were more often cared for by grandparents.

The Demand and Supply of Child Care in 1990 is a research study published in 1991. Using a nationwide sample of households, the researchers interviewed by telephone a representative sample of parents with a child under 13. They found that the types of supplemental care arrangements varied according to the child's age. They learned that more children over age 3 were in supplemental care than were children under 3. Children whose mothers were employed were more likely to be in care, though in the 3- and 4-year-old groups nearly half of the children were enrolled whether or not their mothers were working. The older the children were, the less likely they were to be enrolled in family child care. Most of the school-age children enrolled were children of working mothers and were enrolled in centers, with only a few in family child care.[2]

Kindergartens

Kindergartens today enroll over 95% of the 5-year-olds. A few states have made kindergarten a prerequisite to entering first grade; thus, the previously optional nature of kindergarten has been removed. The kindergartens in many states now have the longer day equal to that of elementary school children. This change has doubled the demand for kindergarten teachers because one teacher no longer teaches two groups of children. The programs for before- and after-school care for elementary-age children have been increasing around the country.

Four-Year-Olds

Four-year-olds and a few 3-year-olds have been added to the public school rolls in a number of states. According to a study conducted by the Children's Defense Fund, 32 states provided such programs in 1992, almost three times the number existing in 1979.[3] Many of these are children "at risk" of school failure as selected by often complex criteria. The programs are part-day and thus do not fulfill the needs for child care when parents are working. Some require the parents to pay tuition. Managers of these programs in the public schools are being challenged to make the programs developmentally appropriate. Managers of other centers will be alert to the trends of serving "at-risk" children in the public schools of their communities, because these children are a large portion of the clientele of many nonpublic school centers.

---

[2] B. Willer, S. L. Hofferth, E. E. Kisker, P. Divine-Hawkins, E. Farquhar, and F. B. Glantz, *The Demand and Supply of Child Care in 1990* (Washington, DC: National Association for the Education of Young Children, 1991), p. 10.

[3] Children's Defense Fund, *The State of America's Children Yearbook 1995* (Washington, DC: Author, 1995), p. 39.

Head Start

The popular U.S. government–sponsored Head Start program has continued under several presidents since 1965. It does not yet enroll all the eligible children of families who are in poverty, earning less than $15,000 yearly. Head Start has been authorized to be increased to a full-day program and to include care for children of working parents. For fiscal year 1995, $3.5 billion was authorized for Head Start.

Infant and Toddler Programs

The 1980s saw a steady increase in the number of infant and toddler programs. The need was clear as many mothers were required to return to their jobs to preserve their right to the job or desired to return to the workforce for financial and personal reasons. In 1991, 189,000 infants under 1 year and 705,000 1- and 2-year-olds were in organized child care facilities, according to the U.S. Bureau of the Census.[4] Standards for licensing and staffing these centers were widely debated. Protection of the children was of primary importance to many child development specialists.

Care for Mildly Ill Children

In the typical half-day nursery school of many years ago, a child with even a minor illness was routinely required to stay home. Full-day programs adopted the same policies even though this meant financial hardship and a threat to the livelihood of parents who had to stay home from work when their children were sick. In the 1980s, this pressure created a demand for child development centers to establish facilities for the care of mildly ill children. Some communities created entire centers for this specific purpose. The American Public Health Association and the American Academy of Pediatrics have established standards for this type of care.[5] (The health and safety needs of children are further discussed in Chapter 12.)

The Family and Medical Leave Act of 1993 may decrease the need for this type of care and have an impact on infant care as well. Under this act, a worker may take up to 12 weeks per year, without pay but with job protection and continued insurance benefits, to care for a sick child, a newborn, or a newly adopted baby.[6]

Employer-Assisted Child Care

The trend for businesses to enter the child care arena for their employees' children is a steadily increasing one. From 1978 to 1988, the rise in employer-assisted child

---

[4] U.S Department of Commerce, Current Population Reports, Series P-70, No. 36, *Who's Minding the Kids? Child Care Arrangements: Fall 1991* (Washington, DC: U.S. Government Printing Office, 1994), p. 5.

[5] *Caring for Our Children: National Health and Safety Performance Standards: Guidelines for Out-of-Home Child Care Programs* (Washington, DC: American Public Health Association, and Elk Grove Village, IL: American Academy of Pediatrics, 1992).

[6] Verna Hildebrand, Lillian Phenice, Mary Gray, and Rebecca Hines, *Knowing and Serving Diverse Families* (Upper Saddle River, NJ: Prentice Hall, 1996), p. 57.

care centers and programs was 2,000%—from 105 to 2,500 centers and programs.[7] In addition to on-site centers, programs include child care referral services, flexible scheduling, job sharing, and so forth. Although this trend toward more employer involvement has leveled off in recent years, in 1993 child care subsidies remained a benefit for 7% of full-time employees in medium and large private firms.[8]

Child care has become a part of the smorgasbord of employee benefits from which employees can choose. Some collective-bargaining contracts spell out child care provisions. Managers of already established centers often contract with an industry to provide the spaces for that company's employees' children. Center managers who are not alert to these opportunities could see their numbers dwindle when an employer institutes an on-site child care program. (Employer-assisted centers are discussed further in Chapter 10.)

Child Care for Children of Poor Mothers

The 1988 Congress passed the Welfare Reform Act, which provided grants to welfare recipients to encourage them to enter training programs to improve their skills for a good job and to help them get off welfare. Health benefits and child care were provided for welfare mothers and children. A number of states already sponsor similar programs. Clearly, these programs affect the demand for child care. According to the U.S. Department of Labor, this legislation affects 3.1 million children below 6 years of age and 2.9 million children between ages 6 and 13. Teenage mothers are expected to be eligible for education and child care benefits, adding additional children to eligible groups. Changes proposed by a new congress in 1994 will shift responsibility for these services to individual states while reducing the overall federal funding levels available to provide them. Child advocates fear that, as a result, many children and families in need will be denied services.

TYPES OF CHILD DEVELOPMENT CENTERS

What do all types of child development centers have in common? First, they serve young children. Second, the children are served outside their homes on less than a 24-hour-a-day basis. Third, they must be managed by an appropriate set of principles to protect children and deliver the needed services of the quality promised.

Child development centers are organized as part of the public social service system, the education system, the philanthropic system, and the business system. Breadth and depth of service vary considerably among the centers, and such philosophical differences will guide management decisions. Though the breadth and depth of programs differ, the principles of managing the centers remain substantially the same. Child development centers offer families child care and education services that they need and want for their young children—services that

---

[7] U.S. Department of Labor, *Child Care: A Workforce Issue* (Washington, DC: U.S. Government Printing Office, 1988), p. 125.

[8] Roger Neugebauer, "Employer Child Care Growing and Consolidating," *Child Care Information Exchange* 103 (May/June 1995), p. 67.

will enhance life for both children and parents. Generally speaking, the various philosophies have as common elements a stress on nurturing and educating young children and on accepting their individual differences in development. Parents selecting a program for their child may find six basic program types available. Depending on their primary needs and interests, parents may choose one rather than others. The six basic program types are as follows:

1. Investment in human capital
2. A consumer good
3. Supplemental care
4. Remedial
5. Substitution
6. Research and teacher preparation

Type 1: Investment in Human Capital

Skills, talents, knowledge, and abilities are a person's **human capital**. When enrolling a child in a child development center with the objectives of enhancing the child's abilities or human capital, parents expect that this investment will have a payoff later on—a payoff in terms of better performance through school and better job performance beyond school. Probably most public kindergartens have been supported because patrons believed that an investment in children's education has future payoffs.

Project Head Start, which was initiated by the U.S. government in 1965, was developed as an investment in children's human capital. Head Start was designed for disadvantaged children as part of President Lyndon Johnson's War on Poverty. The emphasis on giving young children a "head start" arose when it was observed that children of the poor had more difficulties with later school performance than more advantaged children—particularly when many of the advantaged children had had a preprimary school experience or had parents who provided many types of intellectual stimulation. The argument for Project Head Start was that an earlier start in preprimary school with more educationally oriented programs would decrease the number of later school dropouts and also decrease the number of children entering special education. Such a desirable outcome would indicate a wise investment.

Studies of the outcomes of Head Start indicate that the hopes of the early planners did materialize.[9] Gains for parents and older siblings of Head Start children also resulted.[10] An analysis of studies conducted over time has found that low-income children with preprimary experience were less likely to be held back a grade or placed in

---

[9] Sally Ryan, *A Report on Longitudinal Evaluations of Preschool Programs* (Washington, DC: Department of Health, Education, and Welfare, 1974), pp. 1–13.

[10] Irving Lazar et al., *Summary Report: Lasting Effects after Preschool* (Washington, DC: Department of Health, Education, and Welfare, 1979), pp. 19–20; Ruth Hubbell McKay, Larry Condelli, Harriet Ganson, Barbara Barrett, Catherine McConkey, and Margaret Plantz, *The Impact of Head Start on Children, Families and Communities* (Washington, DC: U.S. Department of Health and Human Services, 1985).

special education than children from similar backgrounds with no early education. Managers will find this information helpful in gaining support for their programs from public agencies, private organizations, parents, and the general public.

Until the time of Head Start, public school kindergartens were generally confined to some northern and western states. Therefore, these states generally used their federal funds for Head Start programs for 3- and 4-year-olds because their 5-year-olds were already being served with public funds. In the southern states, however, where few state-supported public kindergartens existed in 1965, the federal Head Start programs initially served mostly 5-year-olds. Since 1970 most southern states have started funding public school kindergartens, increasing to more than 96.1% the proportion of 5-year-olds in the country's kindergartens. As the states assumed responsibility for kindergartens for the 5-year-olds in the public school system, the federal Head Start monies began serving more 3- and 4-year-olds. Some half-day programs are now becoming full-day.

A movement in a number of states is arising now toward providing public support for 3- and 4-year-olds in the public schools—clearly an investment in human capital. This approach increases public educational services to children of the middle and upper classes rather than confining it to the poor children eligible under Head Start programs. This educational opportunity is now facilitated because classrooms stand empty owing to decreased birthrates and residence shifts within cities.

Type 2: A Consumer Good

Early private nursery schools and kindergartens were used by parents as a consumer good, which is "nice to have if one can afford it." Private early childhood programs were the province of the middle and upper classes. Evidence of elitism surfaced when parents took pride in having a child enrolled in a prestigious school. Occasionally parents were required to reserve a place for their child during infancy to be assured of a space when the child was ready at age 3 or 4. One early childhood professional indicated that some of these private schools were analogous to the private clubs of the parents. They were complete with everything for the child's entertainment.

Parent cooperative nursery schools grew out of parents' desire for a nursery school experience for their children—at a price they could afford. Parents pooled their money and hired a professional teacher. All other labor was provided by parents. These schools flourished during 1945–1975. After about 1975, mothers in greater numbers began entering the labor force. Work interfered with the mothers' participation in the co-ops, and most working mothers needed more hours of child care than the co-op offered. The number of cooperatives declined as a result.

The middle-class families that were served by co-ops were future oriented and upwardly mobile. Many parents likely saw this schooling as an investment in their children's future educational success. Thus, there is an obvious overlap with type 1 schools. Parents enjoyed and learned from the co-op situation. With few children at home and with more labor-saving devices in their homes, the mothers, and occasionally fathers, had time to contribute to the organization and operation of the cooperative nursery or kindergarten. Parents liked the social group of friends they built around the co-op experience. Thus, co-ops served a valuable function for children and parents in highly mobile communities where grandparents or other support groups were unavailable to the family. The co-op model is one that managers can turn to for help in welcoming and encouraging parent involvement in child development centers.

In some foreign countries, private school systems fall into this consumer good category. Affluent parents rarely consider a public preprimary school. They support the prestigious private schools not only for preprimary but for elementary and secondary schooling as well.

Type 3: Supplemental Care

Supplemental care extends the strengths and talents that parents have for caring for and educating their children. All early childhood education and care should be considered a support service for families. Supplemental care arrangements support parents by nurturing and educating their children in the hours during the day

A goal of managers of every early childhood program is to provide the nurturing children need, when they need it.
Nazarene Child Care Center, Lansing, MI

when they must be at work using their time, energy, and talent to provide material resources for the family. Child care teachers and caregivers must firmly grasp the idea that they simply do for the child the nurturing that a good parent would do if she or he were available and make every effort to serve as a support for each family system. Parents can learn a great deal from their contacts with qualified caregivers and teachers, increasing their levels of parenting competence.

Managers and staff involved in supplemental care programs must value highly parent-child bonding and attachment and work to strengthen, never to undermine, these crucial emotional relationships. Supplemental care must never become a substitute for parental nurturing and educating. Staff members must always keep this bonding and attachment aspect clearly in mind as they interact with parents. Supplemental care is not a substitute for parents' care or education.

As indicated in earlier discussion, the need for supplemental care for children has grown with the increasing participation of women in the workforce over the past several decades. Between 1977 and 1985, the proportion of children under 5 in organized care facilities nearly doubled, going from 13% to 23%; it has remained at or near that percentage since 1985. Figure 1–3 shows the enrollment of infants, toddlers, and preschoolers in child care programs. Programs for infants and toddlers are in short supply and expensive in most localities.

Table 1–2 shows the caring arrangements for children of school age. These children are often called **latchkey children** because of the key to their houses

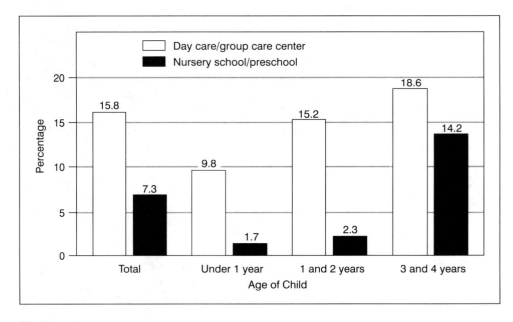

Figure 1–3
Children under age 5 in organized child care facilities (1991)
Source: U.S. Department of Commerce, Current Population Reports, Series P-70, No. 36, *Who's Minding the Kids? Child Care Arrangements: Fall 1991* (Washington, DC: U.S. Government Printing Office, 1994).

they carry on a string around their necks and use to let themselves into their empty homes. Many accounts of fires and other mishaps during a child's self-care periods have alerted the country to the problems resulting from children having several hours a day alone at home. Programs are increasing for before- and after-school care and summer care of elementary-age children.

Employers have been encouraged to become more responsive to the family needs faced by their employees. There has been a large increase in employer involvement—from funding of on-site child care to organizing referral sources for appropriate child care to flextime and shared jobs. By allowing individuals to select a benefit that helps them meet their child care obligations, employers have reduced job-related stress and increased productivity. Positive results have occurred in labor-management relations and family relationships as well.

Child care centers developed in the early 1800s to protect children while their mothers and siblings worked in factories. These were custodial situations giving primarily physical care. Child care centers continued to have a second-class status compared with the consumer-good programs discussed earlier. Certainly in recent years a concerted effort has been made to incorporate an appropriate educational component into child care programs. State and federal regulations have been designed to improve the quality of full-day care, which may run to 10 hours daily for some 260–300 days yearly for a child, compared with about 3 hours for 180 days in kindergartens and other short-day programs.

Many educated and affluent parents are using child care today. Several of these parents are well aware that prolonged nonstimulating environments might have negative effects on their child. Many of them consciously monitor their child's child care center to be sure good care is provided, education is stimulating, and regulations are followed. Even with limited time (most work an 8-hour day), such parents attempt to keep interested and involved in their child's education rather than merely accept whatever services the center provides. Supplemental care extends the strengths and talents that parents have for child care and education.

According to studies of European child care programs, the French have concluded that child care with appropriate educational components is a **social utility** essential for improving the well-being of society as a whole.[11] The United States has not reached such a conclusion yet. The establishment of 4C (community coordinated child care) organizations, the CDA (child development associate) certificate for child care workers, and federal initiatives for more tax support for increased and improved child care services may be steps toward our country's acknowledgment that child care is an essential educational necessity—that is, that it yields needed social utility.

Managers and staffs of these supplemental child care centers must explore ways to respond to parents' needs, perhaps through extending hours; allowing drop-ins, irregular, or half-day enrollees; arranging after-school kindergarten child care; and so on. For example, in response to parental demand, centers have

---

[11] S. Kammerman and A. Kahn, *Mothers Alone: Strategies for a Time of Change* (Dover, MA: Auburn House, 1988).

Table 1-2
Child care arrangements used by employed mothers for children 5–14 years: Fall 1991 (numbers in thousands)

Type of Arrangement	5 to 14 Years		5 Years		6 to 11 Years		12 to 14 Years	
	Total	Percentage	Total	Percentage	Total	Percentage	Total	Percentage
Primary arrangement:								
Total	21,220	100.0	2,072	100.0	12,841	100.0	6,307	100.0
Care in child's home	2,263	10.7	419	20.2	1,351	10.5	493	7.8
By father	1,411	6.6	278	13.4	865	6.7	267	4.2
By grandparent	263	1.2	54	2.6	144	1.1	65	1.0
By other relative	396	1.9	32	1.6	222	1.7	142	2.2
By nonrelative	193	0.9	55	2.6	119	0.9	18	0.3
Care in another home	757	3.6	237	11.4	413	3.2	107	1.7
By grandparent	249	1.2	93	4.5	106	0.8	49	0.8
By other relative	203	1.0	38	1.8	131	1.0	33	0.5
By nonrelative	305	1.4	105	5.1	176	1.4	25	0.4
Organized child care facilities	405	1.9	336	16.2	69	0.5	0	0
Day/group care center	299	1.4	230	11.1	69	0.5	0	0
Nursery/preschool	106	0.5	106	5.1	0	0	0	0
School-based activity	638	3.0	63	3.0	456	3.5	119	1.9
Kindergarten/grade school	16,176	76.2	900	43.4	10,187	79.3	5,089	80.7
Child cares for self	566	2.7	0	0	133	1.0	433	6.9
Mother cares for child at work*	416	2.0	117	5.6	232	1.8	66	1.1

Primary arrangement, excluding child's time in school:

	Number	Percent	Number	Percent	Number	Percent	Number	Percent
Total	21,220	100.0	2,072	100.0	12,841	100.0	6,307	100.0
Care in child's home	4,966	23.4	570	27.5	3,299	25.7	1,098	17.4
By father	2,607	12.3	346	16.7	1,733	13.5	529	8.4
By grandparent	616	2.9	82	3.9	418	3.3	116	1.8
By other relative	1,222	5.8	47	2.2	788	6.1	388	6.2
By nonrelative	521	2.5	96	4.6	361	2.8	65	1.0
Care in another home	2,647	12.5	492	23.7	1,832	14.3	324	5.1
By grandparent	961	4.5	184	8.9	628	4.9	149	2.4
By other relative	543	2.6	55	2.6	384	3.0	105	1.7
By nonrelative	1,143	5.4	253	12.2	820	6.4	69	1.1
Organized child care facilities	1,023	4.8	423	20.4	585	4.6	14	0.2
Day/group care center	906	4.3	306	14.8	585	4.6	14	0.2
Nursery/preschool	117	0.5	117	5.6	0	0	0	0
School-based activity†	1,082	5.1	76	3.7	787	6.1	219	3.5
Child cares for self	1,562	7.4	0	0	524	4.1	1,038	16.5
No care mentioned	9,322	43.9	378	18.2	5,450	42.4	3,494	55.4
Mother cares for child at work*	618	2.9	134	6.4	365	2.8	119	1.9

*Includes women working at home or away from home.

†Includes a small number of children (7,000) who used school as their secondary arrangement.

Source: U.S. Department of Commerce, Current Population Reports, Series P-70, No. 36, *Who's Minding the Kids? Child Care Arrangements: Fall 1991* (Washington, DC: U.S. Government Printing Office, 1994), p. 29.

A goal of managers of early childhood programs is for children to become self-motivated, directing their own activity.
University of Hawaii Child Development Laboratory, Honolulu

been developed in resorts, shopping malls, airports, and other areas. These are licensed centers where parents generally reserve a place on a temporary basis for their child. This setup allows the child to nap, eat, and play with appropriate toys while the parent is involved elsewhere. A philosophy that builds up parents' strengths and abilities to respond to their child and that never expects or attempts to supplant or replace the parents in the child's eyes or the child's affections is very basic.

Family day care is another form of supplemental care that is popular with parents. Usually the family day care home is in the neighborhood where the family lives, making it a convenient option. Some parents also prefer family day care because it is provided in a smaller, more homelike setting and offers a closer match to the values and caregiving style experienced by the child at home.

Family day care providers as a group are working toward more professional status through affiliation with organizations such as the National Association for the Education of Young Children. Frequently, people who begin by providing child care in their homes move on to become managers of centers as their business grows. Some center managers and family day care providers work out cooperative arrangements for pooling resources to purchase supplies in bulk or referring families to each other when needed services are beyond the scope of the particular provider. For example, a center that is licensed to care for children ages 2½–5 might develop a pool of nearby family day care providers to care for younger siblings. Or the center might make an arrangement for certain family providers to accept mildly ill children whose parents are unable to keep them at home. Such cooperation is appropriate and desirable.

Type 4: Remedial

Certain centers may enroll children to remediate particular difficulties the child has, although the recent trend is toward inclusion of children with disabilities in programs for children who are developing typically. This trend is an outgrowth of several federal laws, beginning with PL 90-538 of 1968, which set the stage by establishing the Early Education Program for Children with Disabilities and provides funding for model programs from which we can learn more about serving young children with disabilities and their families.[12] Six years later, PL 93-644 (1974) reserved 10% of available spaces in Head Start programs for children with disabilities. In 1975, PL 94-142, the Education for All Handicapped Children Act, established the right to a free public education for children with disabilities from age 3 to 21 and mandated the use of an Individualized Education Program (IEP).

States were encouraged to make plans for extending the scope of services to include children from birth to age 5 when PL 98-199 of 1983 provided funding for this purpose. In 1986, PL 99-457 instituted the Individualized Family Service Plan (IFSP) for infants and toddlers with—or at risk for developing—disabilities, and it offered incentives for states to provide services for them. In 1990, PL 101-576, the Individuals with Disabilities Education Act (IDEA), reauthorized PL 94-142 and further extended services by adding autism and traumatic brain injury to the list of recognized disabilities.

Most recently, PL 101-336 (1990), the Americans with Disabilities Act, prohibits discrimination against individuals with disabilities and requires that public and private services (including child development facilities) make reasonable accommodations to provide equal access to children with disabilities.[13] As a result of this legislation, children with typical as well as atypical patterns of development are being served together in the same child development programs, with distinct advantages resulting for both. The child with a disability acquires a group of peers to emulate and the satisfactions of play and friendship as rewards for progress. The children without disabilities gain social skills and compassion.

---

[12] Mark Wolery and Jan S. Wilbers, *Including Children with Special Needs in Early Childhood Programs* (Washington, DC: National Association for the Education of Young Children, 1994), p. 18.

[13] Mark Wolery and Jan S. Wilbers, *Including Children with Special Needs in Early Childhood Programs* (Washington, DC: National Association for the Education of Young Children, 1994), pp. 18–19.

As the movement toward inclusion gains momentum, many centers formerly reserved for children with disabilities are now actively recruiting children without disabilities to be included in those settings. Problems with funding arise, however, since priorities in this country designate subsidies for early education only for children with specific disabilities or determined to be at risk for developing such disabilities.

Once again, this focus of resources on deficits is in contrast to France and Italy, where belief in the "universal need" for high-quality care and family support services prevails, with the result that "priority may be given to children or parents with special needs, but the programs are not designed for this purpose or limited to this population."[14]

Type 5: Substitution

Institutions such as orphanages provide round-the-clock substitute care for children whose parents are completely unavailable for a number of possible reasons. Today, foster care is being more widely used, with very limited use of orphanages. This change has occurred in part because studies showed tendencies toward serious retardation in many children brought up in institutions. However, a suggestion to reinstate orphanages as an alternative to welfare for families of poor children was widely debated in the popular press during 1994. Many argued that well-managed residential facilities could be better for children than inadequate or harmful home situations, while others countered that the cost of such well-managed facilities would be far greater than programs to support families and enable children to remain at home. It remains to be seen whether we will see a resurgence of this type of program.

Type 6: Research and Teacher Preparation

Some centers are specifically organized to provide a group or groups of children for research in child development, child psychology, and early childhood education. At times these centers are also combined with teacher preparation programs to give university students an opportunity to learn various skills of interacting with young children. Although these centers give services to the children and families involved, the primary objectives are research and teacher preparation. If funding ceases or objectives change, these centers for children may be phased out. These centers are usually exemplary and highly valued in the community.

INSTITUTIONAL COOPERATION

The foregoing discussion gives you a picture of the range of child development center services. However, a new era may be dawning for early childhood educa-

---

[14]S. B. Kamerman and A. J. Kahn, A Welcome for Every Child: Care, Education and Family Support for Infants and Toddlers in Europe (Arlington, VA: Zero to Three/National Center for Clinical Infant Programs, 1994) p. 76.

A goal of managers of early childhood programs is to encourage children to enjoy vigorous outdoor activity.
Kansas State University Child Development Laboratory, Manhattan

tion that you will want to follow closely. For many years, several institutions in the United States have worked independently to provide some early childhood education and child care to children in various sectors of the population. The picture of philosophical, service, and funding differences that parents confront is often confusing.

The National Association of State Boards of Education (NASBE) made an effort in 1988 to bring together the diverse groups involved in early childhood education. The NASBE appointed a task force of 27 prominent people involved with education and early childhood education across the country. The task force met together, held hearings across the country, and filed their report of recommendations. The report is well worth reading if you have ever wished that all the different groups involved in early childhood education would get together.[15]

The recommendations of the Task Force of the National Association of State Boards of Education are addressed to all state boards of education and to the

[15]National Association of State Boards of Education, *Right from the Start* (Alexandria, VA: Author, 1988).

other groups interested in early childhood education. The recommendations are outlined here:

A. Promoting the Early Childhood Unit
 1. Sponsor experiments to test different models of the early childhood unit.
 2. Review and improve state policies related to curriculum and teaching in the early school years.
 3. Review and improve state policies related to the assessment and testing of young children.
 4. Review and improve state policies related to parent involvement and family support services.
 5. Review and improve policies on the training and certification of staff for early childhood programs.
 6. Sponsor efforts to inform and educate parents and citizens on the characteristics and benefits of high-quality early education.
 7. Provide additional resources for implementation of the early childhood unit.
B. Promoting Collaboration in Early Childhood Services
 1. Create systems for state agency collaboration in planning, standard setting, and program development.
 2. Build systems to encourage early childhood programs and professionals to help each other.
 3. Provide funding and incentives to support local collaboration in early childhood services.
 4. Support recruitment efforts to increase the supply and stability of the early childhood work force.
C. Financing Early Childhood Services
 1. Promote early childhood funding as an investment opportunity.
 2. Understand the importance of quality in developing programs.
 3. Promote equity and access to early childhood services.
 4. Utilize a blend of federal, state, local, and parental support.[16]

Zigler and Lang also support collaboration. They propose a "School of the 21st Century" centering on the public school districts across the country. This arrangement is attractive, economic, and efficient. These schools already pay an installed administrative hierarchy and need only leadership from a qualified educator to set up high-quality early childhood education of the type needed for all families in the district. In addition, the districts often have space to be made available. The proposal suggests that tuition from parents could help finance the endeavor, at least at the beginning. With this coordinated effort, early education and care could be provided for all children who need it.[17]

[16] NASBE, *Right from the Start*, pp. 34–40.
[17] Edward F. Zigler and Mary E. Lang, *Child Care Choices: Balancing the Needs of Children, Families, and Society* (New York: Free Press, 1991), pp. 190–214.

Conclusion

The science of managing a child development center is dynamic. The child development center is in the midst of growth and change as families are defining and redefining what they need for their children. You, as manager, will be on the front line of decision making that can be supportive of families. You can exercise leadership among your staff, among parents, and within your community and create a high-quality service that serves children in appropriate ways and helps them grow toward strong, skilled, and healthy citizens of the future.

This chapter has discussed trends in the area of child development services and outlined several types, including (a) investment in human capital, (b) a consumer good, (c) supplemental care, (d) remedial, (e) substitution, and (f) research and teacher preparation. The ensuing chapters detail managerial processes and procedures to use in carrying out the type of service your school or center offers.

Applications

1. Start a personal looseleaf notebook. Label one divider for each chapter of this textbook. Throughout the term, place notes from your supplementary reading, clippings, and articles in appropriate sections of your notebook. Give the notebook a title (e.g., "management notebook"). By term's end, you will have developed a useful resource for a position as manager of a child development center.
2. Check the yellow pages and the school listings in your local area for services to young children that might be called child development centers. List them and discuss them with your classmates.
3. Write an essay on the current state of the economy and its effect on child development centers.
4. Find out what governmental agencies in your state are responsible for licensing and regulating child development center programs. Report to your class.
5. Prepare a list of characteristics of good managers. Discuss these with your classmates.

Study Questions

1. Define *management*. List the various aspects of management.
2. Define *child development center.*
3. All early childhood education programs need at least two dimensions. What are they? Discuss why these dimensions need emphasis.
4. Look at Figure 1–1. What information does a manager derive from this figure?
5. Look at Figure 1–2. What additional information does a manager gain from the figure?
6. Look at Table 1–1. What information does this table give you as a manager of an organized child care program? A nursery school? What additional information do you need in your work at a local center?

7. Name and describe various types of child development centers that you might manage.
8. Parents seek services for their children depending on a number of criteria. What are six types of centers? Show how each serves a different need for parents.
9. What are the trends for incorporating infants and toddlers in early childhood programs?
10. What is the Zigler-Lang proposal for the "School of the 21st Century"?

SUGGESTED READINGS

Aronson, Susan S. "Care of Ill Children in Child Care Programs." *Child Care Information Exchange* 56 (July 1987), pp. 34–38.

"Beginnings Workshop: Considering Ethnic Culture." *Child Care Information Exchange* 90 (March/April 1993), pp. 29–55.

Briggs, Beverly A., and Connor M. Walters. "Single-Father Families: Implications for Early Childhood Educators." *Young Children* 40:3 (March 1985), pp. 23–27.

Bronfenbrenner, U., P. Moen, and J. Garbarino. "Child, Family and Community." In R. D. Parke (ed.), *Review of Child Development Research. Vol. 7: The Family*. Chicago: University of Chicago Press, 1984.

Brown, Bernard. "Head Start: How Research Changed Public Policy." *Young Children* 40:5 (July 1985), pp. 9–13.

Caruso, J. J. "Supervisors in Early Childhood Programs: An Emerging Profile." *Young Children* 45:6 (September 1991), p. 20.

Chandler, Phyllis A. *A Place for Me: Including Children with Special Needs in Early Care and Education Settings*. Washington, DC: National Association for the Education of Young Children, 1993.

Child Welfare League of America. *Standards for Organization and Administration for All Child Welfare Services*. New York: Author, 1990.

Diamond, K. E., L. L. Hestenes, and C. E. O'Connor. "Research in Review. Integrating Young Children with Disabilities in Preschool: Problems and Promise." *Young Children* 49:2 (January 1994), pp. 68–75.

Doud, J. L. *A Ten Year Study: The K–8 Principal in 1988*. Alexandria, VA: National Association of Elementary School Principals, 1989.

Gunzenhauser, Nina, and Bettye M. Caldwell. *Group Care for Young Children*. Skillman, NJ: Johnson & Johnson, 1986.

Hildebrand, Verna. *Introduction to Early Childhood Education*, 6th ed. Upper Saddle River, NJ: Merrill/Prentice Hall, 1997.

Jalongo, Mary Renck. "When Young Children Move." *Young Children* 40:6 (September 1985), pp. 51–57.

Kagan, S. L., Douglas R. Powell, Bernice Weissbourd, and Edward F. Zigler (eds.). *America's Family Support Programs: Perspectives and Prospects*. New Haven, CT: Yale University Press, 1987.

Kamerman, S. B., and A. J. Kahn. *A Welcome for Every Child: Care, Education, and Family Support for Infants and Toddlers in Europe*. Washington, DC: Zero to Three/National Center for Clinical Infant Programs, 1994.

Kamerman. S. B., and C. D. Hayes. *Families That Work: Children in a Changing World*. Washington, DC: National Academy Press, 1982.

Klein, T., C. Bittel, and J. Molnar. "No Place to Call Home: Supporting the Needs of Homeless Children in the Early Childhood Classroom." *Young Children* 48:6 (September 1993), pp. 22–31.

Kontos, S. *Family Day Care: Out of the Shadows and into the Limelight*. Washington, DC: National Association for the Education of Young Children, 1992.

Kostelnik, M., L. Stein, A. Whiren, and A. Soderman. *Guiding Children's Social Development*, 2d ed. Albany, NY: Delmar, 1993.

Lindner, Eileen W. "Danger: Our National Policy of Child Carelessness." *Young Children* 41:3 (March 1986), pp. 3–9.

Lindner, Eileen W., Mary C. Mattis, and June R. Rogers. *When Churches Mind the Children: A Study of Day Care in Local Parishes*. Ypsilanti, MI: High-Scope Foundation, 1983.

Miller, Patricia S., and James O. McDowelle. *Administering Preschool Programs in Public Schools: A Practitioner's Handbook*. San Diego, CA: Singular, 1992.

Morado, Carolyn. "Prekindergarten Programs for 4-Year-Olds: State Involvement in Preschool Education." *Young Children* 41:6 (September 1986), pp. 69–71.

National Association for the Education of Young Children. "Educating Yourself about Diverse Cultural Groups in Our Country by Reading." *Young Children* 48:3 (March 1993), pp. 13–16.

National Association of State Boards of Education. *Caring Communities: Supporting Young Children and Families (The Report of the National Task Force on School Readiness)*. Alexandria, VA: Author, 1991.

Neugebauer, R. "Employer Child Care Growing and Consolidating." *Child Care Information Exchange* 103 (May/June 1995), pp. 67–73.

Neugebauer, R. "Pre-K in the Public Schools: Status Report #1." *Child Care Information Exchange* 82 (November/December 1991), pp. 5–13.

Neugebauer, R. "An Up-to-Date Look at the Supply of Child Care." *Child Care Information Exchange* 83 (January/February 1992), pp. 14–18.

Phillips, Deborah A. "Whither Churches That Mind the Children? Current Issues Facing Church-Housed Child Care." *Child Care Information Exchange* 55 (May 1987), pp. 35–38.

Powell, Douglas R. "After-School Child Care: Research in Review." *Young Children* 42:3 (March 1987), pp. 62–66.

Roupp, Richard R., J. Travers, F. Glantz, and L. Coelen. *Children at the Center, Final Report of the National Day Care Study*. Vol. I. Washington, DC: Department of Health, Education, and Welfare, 1978.

Ruggie, Mary. *The State and Working Women: A Comparative Study of Britain and Sweden*. Princeton, NJ: Princeton University Press, 1984.

Schweinhart, L., and D. Weikart. "Success by Empowerment: The High/Scope Perry Preschool Study through Age 27." *Young Children* 49:1 (November 1993), pp. 54–58.

Warger, Cynthia (ed.). *A Resource Guide to Public School Early Childhood Programs*. Alexandria, VA: Association for Curriculum and Supervision Development, 1988.

Willer, B., S. L. Hofferth, E. E. Kisker, P. Divine-Hawkins, E. Farquhar, F. B. Glantz. *The Demand and Supply of Child Care in 1990*. Washington, DC: National Association for the Education of Young Children, 1991.

Zigler, Edward F., and Mary E. Lang. *Child Care Choices: Balancing the Needs of Children, Families, and Society*. New York: Free Press, 1991.

CHAPTER 2

Applying Theories in Managing a Child Development Center

· ·

You may feel that theory is something for scholars and outside the practical concerns of the manager of children's programs. However, any time you make a decision based on what you think the consequences of your actions will be, you are operating on a theory, whether consciously or not. You will find that applying appropriate theory will aid your work in managing a child development center.

A **theory** is an organized set of related ideas, concepts, and principles that describes a particular area of knowledge. A good theory fulfills three criteria. First, it is carefully defined in writing. Second, it is published in the public domain so other scholars can evaluate it carefully. Third, it has been tested out by independent scholars and practitioners with the results published in the public domain. Theory is not a fact. Once it becomes a fact, it no longer is called a theory.

When you read about theories, you should realize that people are still working on them, testing them out, and polishing them. New theories are being proposed as information accumulates.

You can assist in the work of theory development by thinking about and testing out theories in your day-to-day work. Perhaps you can refine or develop a new theory. Feel free to question a theory or ask whether it applies to your situation. You can make suggestions for modifications in light of your experience. Then, you and other scholars and practitioners in the field can test out these ideas to bring the activity into the realm of a science, with useful predictable outcomes arising from given procedures.

Managers of child development centers need to coordinate information from several areas of knowledge. First, they must think about how children grow and develop and how environments and activities help or hinder that development. Then, they need to remember that children do not exist in a vacuum; each child comes to the

Painting on the sidewalk with water is fun as well as good practice for controlling muscles and making letter or number shapes later on.
Early Learning Center, Appalachian State University, Boone, NC

center with a complex history and set of relationships with his or her family and community. Center directors thus need to consider how families relate to the center and how both relate to other systems within the larger community. Finally, directors must think about the best ways of managing complex organizations like child development centers in order to achieve their goals for children and families.

Experts in each of these broad areas of knowledge have developed a number of theoretical frameworks to organize ideas and create a rational basis for predicting outcomes. This chapter begins with a brief discussion of **developmental theory** to help managers focus on the needs of children enrolled in their centers. Then, the **ecological system framework** is presented, which helps focus on families and the interaction of the child development center with the other systems that comprise the family's environment. Finally, a brief review of **management theories** used by management science is presented.

DEVELOPMENTAL THEORY

Managers of child development centers need a theoretical basis for understanding and planning for children. Information about children's growth and development has provided a general consensus that a developmental theory is a sound basis for decisions about children. In 1987 the National Association for the Education of Young Children (NAEYC) published *Developmentally Appropriate Practice in Early Childhood Programs Serving Children from Birth through Age 8.*[1] This booklet, written by a commission of professionals, spells out how developmental theory can be applied to the operation of early childhood programs. Based on research showing the step-by-step development of children, it describes in practical terms the state of the art of applied child development at the time it was published. It has been widely discussed and extremely influential in shaping programs for children in all types of child development centers as well as public school settings. Other researchers have applied the concept to early childhood special education[2] and to standards for school-age child care programs.[3] Some early childhood specialists have criticized the booklet, however, because it seems to present only one "right way" of doing things and appears to favor white, middle-class patterns of child rearing. They argue that the practices defined in the booklet do not apply as easily to children from minority cultures or children with disabilities. NAEYC leaders have listened to these concerns, and the revised edition of the booklet (which is in process at the time of this writing) will address them by presenting a range of options for the early childhood practitioner to consider when making decisions.

In applying developmental theory, you start with general knowledge about the way children grow and develop to plan environments and activities for them. If you know you have a 5-year-old group, you plan activities and organize the environment according to what research and experience with 5-year-olds says the children are like. Then you look at the particular individuals in your group and adjust your generic planning to fit the developmental needs of these children. That is, if Emma is reading, you find books for her to read. If Peter needs climbing practice that does not match the typical 5-year-old, you see that he is able to practice climbing skills. Thus, there are two dimensions to developmental planning: (a) the typical characteristics of the age group and (b) the particular or personal characteristics of the children you enroll.

Our ideas about developmentally appropriate practice incorporate the work of many scholars. Maria Montessori and Rudolf Steiner prescribed particular practices based on their beliefs about how children grow and develop. Jean Piaget, Lev Vygotsky, Robert Havighurst, Benjamin Bloom, Erik Erikson, and B. F. Skinner described or explained development, leaving the application of their theories to others. Today's programs for young children reflect the thinking of all these

---

[1] Sue Bredekamp, ed. (Washington, DC: National Association for the Education of Young Children, 1987).

[2] Lise Fox, Mary F. Hanline, Cynthia O. Vail, and Kim R. Gallant, "Developmentally Appropriate Practice: Applications for Young Children with Disabilities," *Journal of Early Intervention* 18:3 (Summer 1994), pp. 243–257.

[3] Kay M. Albrecht and Margaret C. Plantz (eds.), *Developmentally Appropriate Practice in School-Age Child Care Programs* (Alexandria, VA: Project Home Safe, American Home Economics Association, 1991).

and many other people, although some programs may operate without being aware of their theoretical bases. Because they are working with human beings and complex interactions, early childhood professionals cannot slavishly adhere to a single theory. They constantly refine their understanding and adjust their practice as they attempt to provide the best for each child in their care. Nevertheless, as the manager of a child development center, you will want to be familiar with the people and theories whose ideas have helped shape your profession.

Montessori schools, for example, follow practices established in the early twentieth century by Maria Montessori, an Italian physician. She based her schools on techniques she had used successfully to raise the IQ scores of children who were mentally retarded. Many of those techniques rest on the concept of the "prepared environment," in which furnishings are child sized and self-correcting materials such as cylinders or blocks in graduated sizes are carefully displayed on low shelves so that children can select their own "work" and return the items when they have finished. The use of the term *work* for these activities conveys the sense of respect for the child that is further exemplified by the soft voices and serious demeanor of the adults as they interact with the children.

These ideas have become an accepted part of a developmental approach to early childhood education and can be seen in many programs that do not identify themselves as "Montessori" schools. Other qualities that some associate with a traditional Montessori approach include an emphasis on individual work at the expense of interaction with peers, and a devaluing of imaginative play. Even among Montessori practitioners, however, there is variation in the extent to which these ideas are followed.

Rudolf Steiner was a contemporary of Montessori, born in Hungary, who had also had an early success with a child with a disability—an example of what he called "curative education." He began his first school for the children of workers in the Waldorf-Astoria cigarette factory in Germany, and the schools that follow his teachings are now called Waldorf schools.

Steiner wrote and lectured widely on the relationships among life, art, and spirituality, and his schools for young children were designed to help maintain these universal connections. Instead of manufactured toys, a Waldorf kindergarten is stocked with soft, handmade toys and natural materials such as wood and unspun wool. Imaginative play and imitation of adults' real-life activities are encouraged in the classroom as well as in the natural outdoor environment. There are probably far fewer Waldorf schools in existence today than there are Montessori schools; however, Steiner's ideas, like Montessori's, can be seen in many early childhood programs that do not bear his name.

Piaget's theory is often labeled "constructivist" because it holds that children must construct knowledge for themselves as they experience the environment. The idea is that children are not blank slates or empty containers to be filled with information. Instead, they are like scientists with their own hypotheses about the world, which they constantly test and refine as they move about in that world. According to Piaget, children are not born knowing, for example, that an amount of water stays the same when poured from a tall, narrow container into a short, wide one. Nor can adults teach them that this is so. Each child must discover this through countless experiences with pouring. Piaget's concepts help early childhood professionals understand children's thinking more clearly. Managers can use the theory to help teachers and parents appreciate the intelligence that goes into what seems like "wrong" ideas.

The work of Lev Vygotsky, a Russian psychologist, has recently come into prominence because of its application in the preschools of Reggio Emilia, Italy, which gained worldwide fame through the traveling exhibit "The Hundred Languages of Children." Vygotsky adds to Piaget's idea of the child constructing knowledge, by suggesting that when more advanced learners—adults and older children in the culture—communicate with a child who is learning, they aid the child's thinking and learning. This concept is called the **social construction of knowledge**. Also of interest to Vygotsky is **private speech**, in which a child may be observed audibly talking through a problem-solving situation, such as, "I'll put the big block here to keep this roof up." The private speech may be addressed to no one in particular. Vygotsky's theory is called **dialectical**, meaning that thinking and reasoning proceed through dialogues and social interaction.

Seymour Papert, the creator of Logo, a computer language for children, has added to Vygotsky's ideas about the social construction of knowledge by suggesting that children interact with the things they make or build and get feedback that helps them generate or modify their ideas in much the same way as feedback from adults or older children. Papert calls his version of this idea **constructionism** (to distinguish it from constructivism).[4]

Robert Havighurst describes the developmental tasks of each age throughout the life span. A developmental task must be accomplished satisfactorily by the child at each early age in order to be successful in the tasks of later ages. Failure to accomplish a developmental task leads to failure with later tasks.

Benjamin Bloom's early research led him to state quite strongly the importance of the early years for later development. He feels that very significant learning takes place in the first 5 years of life. Some disagree as to whether that period is this critical. However, most early childhood educators will act on that basis even as they attempt remedial processes to help correct a child's problem. Bloom also contributed to the concept of behavioral objectives, believing that tasks can be broken down into achievable parts, which help the child succeed.

Erik Erikson proposes the theory of the Eight Stages of Man and describes those stages in his work. When infants' caregivers learn about helping their charges gain a sense of trust, they are borrowing from Erikson. When we tell parents that the toddler is building a sense of autonomy, we are confirming observations that Erikson made years ago. Erikson's theory is still dynamic

---

[4] See Seymour Papert, *The Children's Machine: Rethinking School in the Age of the Computer* (New York: Basic Books, 1993).

because, at age 86, he added a ninth stage—conflict and resolution—that culminates in old age.

B. F. Skinner is known for his behaviorist theory and its emphasis on reinforcement. People who have never even heard of Skinner are following one of his premises when they believe that a reward helps a child learn the behavior that is rewarded. What has also been explained by the behaviorists is that to eliminate a behavior (i.e., extinguish it), the behavior must never be rewarded (e.g., intermittent rewards, even when far apart, are still reinforcing).

Although he was not cited in the original NAEYC position statement, Uri Bronfenbrenner provides a useful bridge between child development theory and family ecology theory. He developed an ecological model of human development, picturing the infant as nested within a widening series of environments beginning with the family and culminating with the society at large. He describes development as consisting of the child's increasing competence within, and understanding of, wider spheres and holds that this growth results from challenging and supportive interactions.

The theories of how children grow and develop must be integrated with how adults work with the children and provide materials and learning activities to foster their growth and development. The foregoing theories each offer ideas for an activity in the curriculum or for interaction with children. For example, Constance Kamii studied with Piaget and has written several books suggesting ways that his theory can be used to help children build their understanding of arithmetic in more appropriate and effective ways. The *High/Scope Curriculum* is also based on Piaget's theories and has been widely used by child development programs as well as public schools. As mentioned earlier, the preschools of Reggio Emilia, Italy, base their curriculum in part on Vygotsky's theory, using the children's evolving interests and connections with the real world to determine which projects and activities will be undertaken. As a future manager of child development programs you will, no doubt, be taking additional courses in early childhood curriculum, where you will learn more about these and other theorists. Some additional resources are listed at the end of this chapter, or you can consult your library to find others.

Theory is often difficult for beginning teachers and caregivers to apply to their work. One of your tasks, as manager, is to help your staff apply more advanced ideas as they gain experience and ask questions that show they are thinking about what and how children are learning. Teachers have teachable moments, just as children do. You can be prepared to help teachers and caregivers explore children's development in more depth when you recognize one of these teachable moments.

Some scholars classify theories of child development as belonging to one of four types. **Maturationist** theories emphasize that growth and development come largely from within the child and follow a predictable timetable. **Environmentalist** or **behaviorist** theories focus on the ways that growth and development can be influenced from the outside. **Interactionist** theories explore the ways that inside and outside forces interact to create change, suggesting that children with different backgrounds will experience the same environment in very different ways. **Ecological** theories consider the individual within the context of all the systems that make up his or her environment.[5]

Thus, a maturationist, for example, when confronted with a 4-year-old who cannot (or will not) repeat a simple rhyme might suggest simply waiting until the child has time to mature and develop greater language skills. An environmentalist might try using drill and practice sessions, with rewards such as stickers for successful performance. An interactionist might consider internal factors, such as the child's previous language experience and interest in the project, as well as external factors, such as the cultural relevance of the rhyme or the manner in which the activity was presented. An ecologist might look at family and social contexts for this particular ability.

Because they reflect the complex nature of the human beings involved, child development programs rarely embody these theories in their pure form, although one type or another has seemed to predominate at various periods in the history of early childhood programs.[6] NAEYC's *Developmentally Appropriate Practice*, as noted earlier, incorporates ideas from all four types of theorists, with a particular emphasis on **constructivism**, a specific form of interactionist theory.[7] And, as mentioned previously, some theorists are already at work modifying and extending the ideas of constructivism.

Further complicating matters, different professionals working with young children have been trained according to different theoretical frameworks, and these frameworks have evolved over time, just as they have in the field of early childhood education. Bruce Mallory, for example, describes the theoretical models that shape early childhood special education as **developmental-interactionist**, **functional** (or **behaviorist**), and **biogenetic**, and he argues that a "triangulated" approach, using ideas and methods based on all three, is necessary to serve children most effectively.[8] Now imagine the even greater challenge created by this variety of perspectives when a child with a disability is included in a program based on constructivist views of typical child development. All the professionals involved will need to work together to develop a common vocabulary and function effectively as a team.

Theory is always in a state of change until it becomes accepted as fact. Solid facts are seldom achieved in the arena of human development and behavior. You might be feeling that these continual changes make the study of child develop-

[5] See Marjorie J. Kostelnik, Anne K. Soderman, and Alice P. Whiren, *Developmentally Appropriate Programs in Early Childhood Education* (Upper Saddle River, NJ: Prentice Hall, 1993); and R. Murray Thomas, *Comparing Theories of Child Development* (Belmont, CA: Wadsworth, 1992).

[6] Thomas, *Comparing Theories of Child Development*, pp. 473–489.

[7] Sue Bredekamp, "Advanced Remarks: Lessons from Reggio," Annual NAEYC Conference, Atlanta, GA, November 30, 1994.

[8] Bruce Mallory, "Inclusive Policy, Practice, and Theory for Young Children with Developmental Differences," in Bruce L. Mallory and Rebecca S. New (eds.), *Diversity and Developmentally Appropriate Practices: Challenges for Early Childhood Education* (New York: Teachers College Press, 1994), pp. 44–61.

ment theory too confusing and time-consuming for a busy program manager. But the theory (or theories) that underlie your program will influence the ways you see children and families and all the decisions you make as you interact with those children and families. Theory is behind action even if it consists of only the informal theories we all learn in the process of growing up. If you talk with staff members or parents about their beliefs about behavior, you will see striking examples of this point. Ask, for example, "What makes a 2-year-old hit another child?" The answers you receive will reveal a wide range of theories.

Learning a few terms from those who have made the study of behavior and development their life's work will help you discuss these opinions more intelligently. Studying theory will make your work with children and families more exciting as you see examples of what the theorists mean in the behaviors before your eyes, or when you find possible explanations for things that have puzzled you.

DECISIONS, DECISIONS . . .

 Consider a child development program where you have worked or observed. List the theory or theories that seem to form the basis for its practices with children and families.

THE ECOLOGICAL SYSTEM FRAMEWORK

A manager of a child development center has three main goals: (a) to understand the families needing and desiring child development center services, (b) to understand the intricacies of a child development center operation, and (c) to integrate families' and children's needs, child development center operations, and societal standards. A useful approach to help achieve such goals is to find a framework for analysis, that is, a theory for examining the various parts and the whole. The **ecological system framework** helps meet this requirement. Ecology is a branch of science concerned with the interrelationships of organisms and their environments. The ecological system framework has proved useful for maintaining a holistic integrative perspective. It can help determine where specific inputs are needed or where resistance to change may be arising.

The biological sciences have long used an ecological system framework to explain interdependence among biological organisms and the encompassing environment. For example, scientists can show that the quality of a field of grass is dependent on many factors (e.g., the variety of grass present, photosynthesis, soil fertility, insect infestations, moisture, competition from other plants, length of the growing season, and the traffic or feeding in the field by animals). Scientists can measure the effect of a specific input—say, additional moisture—on the increased production of grass. You will note the solar **energy inputs** implied in this example and that an appropriate combination, balance, or equilibrium among the various inputs is required for the grass to grow well.

The ecological or ecosystem framework is useful in not only the biological sciences but also the social sciences for studying social organizations such as schools,

*A warm lap in a rocking chair
makes feeding time have some
of the conditions of a quality
home environment.*
Wichita High School, Wichita, KS

child development centers, and families. As in biological ecosystems, energy is needed to operate the system. Human energy is derived from food, and nonhuman energy is derived from fossil fuels. A balance or equilibrium is the goal toward which the ecological system moves. The term **human ecological system** is used to refer to the areas of human life and interaction.

Researchers Bubolz and Sontag have proposed a model of a human ecological system for analyzing interactions within human organizations.[9] They suggest a relationship among the following three environments that helps one keep a holistic, integrative view rather than a fragmented view of interactions taking place:

1. The **physical-biological environment** refers to the environment formed by nature, such as soil, climate, and natural resources.

---

[9] Margaret M. Bubolz and M. Suzanne Sontag, "Human Ecology Theory," in P. G. Boss, W. J. Doherty, R. LaRossa, W. R. Schumm, and S. K. Steinmetz (Eds.), *Sourcebook of Family Theories and Methods: A Contextual Approach* (New York: Plenum, 1993), pp. 419–448.

Figure 2–1

A family ecosystem

Source: Adapted with permission from Margaret M. Bubolz and M. Suzanne Sontag, "Human Ecology Theory," in P. Boss, W. Doherty, R. LaRossa, W. Schumm, and S. K. Steinmetz (eds.), *Sourcebook of Family Theories and Methods: A Contextual Approach* (New York: Plenum, 1993), p. 432.

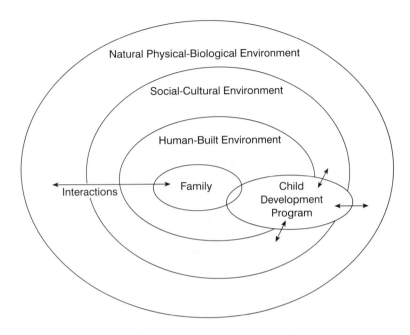

2. The **human-built environment** entails the environment that human beings have constructed or altered to fit their needs, such as factories, roads, farms, and pollution.

3. The **social-cultural environment** includes other people as well as the more abstract results of interactions among people, such as cultural values and institutions.

Figure 2–1 shows the way these environments are nested within each other. The child development program comprises part of the family's human-built environment (building, equipment, materials) as well as part of the family's social-cultural environment (including, e.g., the social institutions that fund and regulate child care and education, and the human interactions that take place among children, staff, and families at the center). The child development program interacts with other parts of the human-built and social-cultural environments, as well as the physical-biological environment.

The Physical-Biological Environment

The physical-biological environment affects the operation of a child development center in many ways, both obvious and subtle. For example, centers located in extremely hot or cold climates will spend more on heating and air conditioning; a Head Start program located in a rural area will need to budget for higher transportation costs because of the distances between children's homes; and all centers need to plan for coping with natural emergencies such as tornadoes. Natural resources also relate very directly to the wealth of the community and individuals within the community. The presence of many natural resources will provide productive jobs for the parents of children, increase the amount of income they receive, and stimulate their desire for early childhood education for their children. On the other hand, an absence of natural resources is likely to be correlated with unemployment or low-paying jobs for parents and an inability to pay for high-quality service.

The amount and quality of natural resources influence the funding available to pay for operating the child development center—salaries, facility, utilities, and supplies needed. Persons in oil-importing countries who are familiar with costs since the 1972 increase in the price of oil realize this fact all too well. Inflation and unemployment occurred in areas short of oil. Child care center costs also rose during this period; then enrollments dropped as out-of-work parents economized by withdrawing their children from child care centers. Tax collections also decreased, damaging publicly financed centers.

A country's economic base depends on two main factors: (a) the natural resources from the physical-biological environment, such as fossil fuels, arable land, and suitable climate, and (b) the citizen's ability to use these resources—an ability directly related to the country's willingness and capacity to invest in educational opportunities for its citizens. Japan, for example, is a country that has minimal natural resources but that has invested wisely in human capital—the education and skills of its citizens needed to develop high-technology products. This output, in turn, brings economic wealth to the inhabitants.

Natural resources become more valuable economic resources as they move through factories, businesses, farming enterprises, and into retail consumer markets. Jobs for citizens result from such enterprises. Some of the holders of these jobs are the parents of the children in our child development centers.

Historically, countries that have developed strong economic bases have evolved institutions that give more services to family members. For example, there are more medical, educational, and social services for families in economically developed countries than in the less developed countries.

DECISIONS, DECISIONS . . .

 Discuss the physical-biological environment of your locality, and explore its connection to jobs that parents of children in your center might hold. Estimate how parental employment in your community relates to the demand for child development center services.

The Human-Built Environment

The human-built environment depends on the physical-biological environment, but it also transforms that environment in many ways. Some transformations are purposeful, while others may be accidental by-products of human actions. The results of such transformations might be beneficial, apparently neutral, or at times harmful. The child care center itself is a part of the human-built environment: a physical structure created to serve specific human purposes. Good roads and efficient public transportation systems make it easier for parents to get their children to the center and themselves to work.

Some changes wrought by humans are less benevolent, as in the case of air or water pollution. These might seem like issues far removed from your role as manager of a child development center, but of course people in a child development program breathe the same air and drink the same water as people elsewhere in the community. High concentrations of automobile exhaust in a city can result in pollution levels that keep everyone indoors for several days. An emergency resulting from bacterial contamination of a city's water supply can mean that a center must purchase bottled water, spend extra energy boiling a supply of drinking water, or perhaps suspend services until the situation is brought under control.

Interactions flow within the center as well as between the center and other parts of the human-built environment. For example, public utilities provide needed water and energy supplies and remove waste. This flow of interaction requires a great deal of both human and nonhuman energy to operate.

The Social-Cultural Environment

The social-cultural environment is the product of people interacting with each other and with elements of their environments, forming relationships and creating cultural patterns and social and economic institutions. The extended family and neighborhood network of friends are two examples of social-cultural environments. Teachers, caregivers, cooks, and custodians of child development centers interact with children and parents to create another social-cultural environment. Just as in the human-built environment, interactions within the cultural environment require energy—emotional and intellectual energy, as well as physical energy.

Social expectations regarding people's roles are another aspect of the social-cultural environment. In the 1950s, for example, women were expected to stay home and take care of their families. Although attitudes today have changed to the extent that working mothers are considered commonplace, ambivalence persists about how much society should support families with low-cost, high-quality child care options. In addition to a cultural tradition of self-contained, independent nuclear families, the economic institution of a market economy is part of the social-cultural environment for families in the United States. Child care is viewed as a service to be purchased by the family rather than as a family support and an investment in human capital that will benefit society as a whole. This view is in contrast to that of countries such as Italy, where child care and family support services are considered a right of all families. Thus, although more working parents create a greater demand for child care services, a lack of funding means tight budgets for those centers.

Regardless of how they are funded, child development centers are established by human beings to provide physical care and to foster the individual development, growth, and education of children coming from the family systems. The child development center supplements the efforts of the children's parents and is obligated to help further develop the child's human resources—strengths, knowledge, skills, abilities, loyalty, and the like. Such attributes are often called **human**

capital. With a higher level of human capital development, each person can make a larger contribution to society. Without human capital development, a person may become a burden to society. Evidence suggests that an investment by a country in early childhood education yields a high return.

In the United States during World War II, when women were pressed into factory work to produce military goods, economic resources were allocated by the government to provide child care for the children of women workers. Today women workers with children from newborns to age 5 are demanding services for their children.

There has been a general trend for families to have fewer children, which has resulted in fewer children below school age in the population during the last decade. When families are small with one or two children, as is the current trend, child development centers can provide the companionship and associated learning that children need. Single parents who are solely responsible for young children particularly recognize the need for child development centers to supplement their parenting efforts.

Throughout this book, you will repeatedly recognize the social-cultural environment when topics such as parent-child relations, staff relations, teacher-child relations, professional relations, or public relations are discussed. Also, the interaction taking place with people, such as vendors, bankers, licensing officials, or fire safety officers, are examples of a manager's involvement with the social-cultural environment.

DECISIONS, DECISIONS . . .

 Which systems in your community are involved with building, regulating, and monitoring child development centers? Learn how the processes work, and discuss them in class. What will you need to know about these systems to manage an individual center effectively?

Equilibrium and Energy in the Ecosystem

A striving for **equilibrium** or balance within the ecological system is an important characteristic of the human ecological system. Families create an internal family ecosystem and also interact with environments outside the family; they attempt to maintain equilibrium between themselves and the other systems. A child development center interacts with numerous systems, and it too must seek to maintain an equilibrium. Disequilibrium or disharmony is a state to be corrected by changes leading to equilibrium and harmony. Rules may be devised to handle disharmony. Legal systems may also be used to help settle disputes that other procedures cannot resolve.

Feedback from one environment may make adjustments in others necessary. The manager of a center observes the feedback and makes adjustments to help maintain some balance, equilibrium, or stability. For example, if the number of

Playful interactions between adults and children are part of developmentally appropriate programs.
Early Learning Center, Appalachian State University, Boone, NC

children increases, the manager moves to increase the number of adults proportionately and likewise the amount of food and supplies. Licensing regulations from the political system set certain standards for child-adult ratios, which managers must follow. When a health problem arises, the manager seeks appropriate advice for corrective measures from the health system of the community.

Moving toward energy equilibrium is an important aspect or tendency of all ecological systems. In the example of the field of grass mentioned earlier, probably water, soil, and solar energy were the major inputs. In a child development center, nonhuman resources such as fossil fuel energy, natural raw materials, and solar energy are used in the structure and to heat and cool it. Nonhuman resources are organized and activated by human energy—the energy people derive from food. Human energy, represented by skill and know-how, is needed in every aspect of the child development center operation. Much of the knowledge and skill present in staff members results from energy that was expended in other systems such as their homes, schools, and colleges. This point illustrates how an investment in the human being (in human capital) at one time often pays off at another time.

Many printed resources are used in a child development center—books for children as well as professional books for staff members. Printed material requires human energy to prepare, produce, and distribute. In addition, some natural materials such as paper, glue, and ink are required for making the physical objects containing the printing.

A human service such as a child development center can be called energy intensive, requiring high energy inputs from many people. Rearing a child requires high energy inputs and resources purchased with dollars coming from parents and other sources.

The child development service supplements parental energy. The children's energy is channeled into exploring their own learning activity and helping with some of the work of the center. For example, children learn to pick up after themselves and take care of their own needs, reducing the demand on teachers for energy inputs. The quality of human energy inputs is represented in costs to the community and the family. Studies show that when a teacher with one assistant has no more than 18 children to know and plan for, the desired outcomes for individual children are higher.[10] One can readily hypothesize that the quality of programs for children is related to the available energy of teachers and caregivers for each child. Energy includes knowledge, skills, and stamina to carry on the work. Present studies suggest that if there are more than 18 children in a group, the children receive an inferior program owing to inadequate individual attention. Thus, the rationale for suggesting standards with respect to group size and staff requirements depending on the number and ages of the children in the groups is evident.

An Application of the Ecological Model

The human ecological systems model is useful in planning and coping with problems that arise. Simply checking to discover which environment is the major source of the problem is a first step toward a solution. For instance, if children are not eating the food being prepared for them, one could use the model in the following way. First, check the physical-biological environment to see whether the food is produced with adequate quality and flavor. Second, check the storage and handling of foods (the human-built environment), because improper storage and handling may result in a loss of quality. Finally, check the procedures of food service personnel (the social-cultural environment), because their lack of skill or knowledge may result in unappetizing or culturally inappropriate food combinations, excessively large servings, or inaccurate recipe calculations. Once the manager determines the source of the problem, corrective solutions can be selected. Note that none of these examples suggests doing anything with or to the children. The human ecological system framework serves as a useful tool for suggesting avenues to check for possible solutions. In general, solutions dealing with things rather than people are more easily implemented and should be tried first.

---

[10]Richard R. Ruopp, J. Travers, F. Glants, and C. Coelen, *Children at the Center (Final Report of the National Day Care Study)*, Vol. 1 (Washington, DC: Department of Health, Education, and Welfare, 1978; Cambridge, MA: Abt, 1979).

Consider another problem from the human ecological systems perspective: Suppose that nap time in the center where you work is chaotic, with children crying and fussing instead of resting peacefully. List the elements you might check in (a) the physical-biological environment, (b) the human-built environment, and (c) the social-cultural environment in order to make nap time more peaceful.

MANAGEMENT THEORY

As individuals, we all live and work within families, agencies, and groups. All these entities have goals for their existence, they use resources, and they serve the needs and desires of the individuals within the society. All groups need an activity or process that coordinates individual efforts toward achieving goals, allocates resources effectively, and serves needs. That activity is called **management**.

Management is needed in every effective group to attain the desired goals with the least expenditure of time, energy, and money. Whether the operation is an agency, school, business, or family, whether it is operated for profit or on a non-profit basis, management is needed.

A **manager** is the person who applies management theory and uses management techniques. A manager today may also be called the administrator, executive, chief executive officer (CEO), supervisor, director, or boss.

Management is a science with a number of theories and volumes of studies designed to test those theories. Different theories appear to describe management of one type of organization better than another. There is not total agreement on the proper management theory to use, which can also be said for child development theories; thus, this condition of inconclusiveness should not bother you.

A **management theory** is an organized set of related ideas, concepts, and principles that describe the process of managing an enterprise. Management has been growing in its recognition as a science. Studies that support the techniques and procedures are cited throughout the book.

A few people still consider managing an art because it encompasses creativity, where new approaches and new ways of looking at old procedures are required. Many even argue that individuals should stay as managers for only a short time because they use up their fresh ideas. However, even the most creative manager must use management science as a basis for actions. A trial-and-error or intuitive method alone will surely prove less effective.

Ten Theoretical Approaches

Fulmer outlines 10 approaches to management:

1. *Empirical or case approach*—based on studying experience; focuses on mistakes and successes

2. *Interpersonal behavior approach*—based on the idea that things get done through people; thus, managers should study interpersonal relations.
3. *Group behavior approach*—based on sociology and social psychology; concerned with the behavior of people in groups in the workplace
4. *Cooperative social systems approach*—based on the idea of giving emphasis to well-organized cooperation
5. *Sociotechnical systems approach*—based on understanding how the technical system (machines and methods) affects the social system of the workplace, especially industry
6. *Decision theory approach*—based on the decisions that managers make
7. *Management science approach*—based on mathematical processes, concepts, symbols, and models
8. *Contingency or situational approach*—based on the circumstances of the workplace
9. *Managerial roles approach*—based on observation of managers and broadening the concept of management beyond the fundamental functions of planning, organizing, leading, staffing, monitoring, and controlling
10. *Eclectic approach*—based on using fundamental functions of management—planning, organizing, leading, staffing, monitoring, and controlling—and parts of other approaches.[11]

Total Quality Management

One approach to management that has gained increasing popularity in the United States recently is total quality management. Ironically, this approach is based on the ideas of two Westerners, W. Edwards Deming and Joseph Juran, who developed it in Japan more than 40 years ago when U.S. industries were firmly entrenched in a "top-down" approach to management. Japan's achievements in gaining a large share of the world market for automobiles and electronic equipment prompted U.S. manufacturers to take a closer look at Deming's theories. The Ford Motor Company hired him as a consultant in 1980, and his ideas have caught on from there.

Total quality management contrasts with traditional management methods in several ways:

1. Power is shared. Ideas flow upward from the people actually doing the work as well as downward from the organization's leaders.
2. Responsibility is shared. Everyone is expected to understand and be committed to the organization's mission, spot problems, propose solutions, and take appropriate action to solve them.
3. Customer satisfaction is the central focus.

---

[11] Robert M. Fulmer, *The New Management* (Upper Saddle River, NJ: Prentice Hall, 1983), p. 98.

4. Quality is achieved by doing even the small things right the first time. When products or outcomes are faulty, the process is examined and altered as needed.

5. Successful businesses do not rest on their laurels but strive for continuous improvement.

According to Dorothy Hewes,[12] who has studied the history of educational management systems, total quality management may have seemed revolutionary to U.S. industry when it came into vogue in the 1980s, but it should sound very familiar to those of us in the field of early childhood education, where prominent leaders have been espousing self-government and bottom-up management for over a century. In fact, the accreditation process of the NAEYC begins with a detailed self-study by all the people involved in a child development center, followed by self-initiated movements toward greater quality. This process is discussed in greater detail in the next chapter.

MANAGING REQUIRES A SYSTEMS APPROACH

When an organization is designed, it must be considered in light of its relationship to the external system and, also, its internal system. A **system** is a set of interconnected things that are put together to make a coherent whole. Your house has an electrical system, a water system, a sewer system. In houses with a well, the water system depends on the electrical system to operate the pump. The sewer system carries away the household waste but cannot do so without water. In other words, these various systems are *inter*connected as well as connected to systems outside the house.

The **human ecological system framework** is useful in understanding the interconnectedness of various systems in a human service enterprise such as a child development center. Child development centers are part of a larger system of human services in a community, state, and nation. Child development centers are one of many services societies develop to meet their citizens' needs.

Open systems is a concept that describes the interaction and interchange that exists between and among systems. Openness is represented by the two-way arrows in Figure 2–1. Using the systems notion in planning and evaluating is helpful. If there is a perceived need, where does a change need to be made? For example, does a new agency need to be added to the social-cultural environment? Will this action require new legislation in the political system? Or can the private business sector serve the need? Resources usually are an early question. Resources are derived from the physical-biological environment, whereas their development depends on the human resource (skill and knowledge) development, the institutional structure, and the regulation by organizations in the social-cultural environment.

---

[12] Dorothy W. Hewes, "TQ What? Applying Total Quality Management in Child Care," *Child Care Information Exchange* 98 (July/August 1994), pp. 20–24.

Teachers confer frequently to develop programs that meet the many needs of children.
Michigan State University Child Development Laboratory, East Lansing, MI

CONCLUSION

Management of a child development center requires an integration of theories and principles—from child development, human ecology, and business. A theory is an organized set of related ideas, concepts, and principles that describe a particular area of knowledge. A theory must be stated as clearly as possible, published in the public domain, and tested by independent scholars who also publish their results in the public domain. Theory is dynamic and evolving. It is not fact.

APPLICATIONS

1. Make a list of the institutions and agencies in the human-built environment with which managers of child development centers can be expected to interact (a) frequently and (b) occasionally. Discuss these interactions.
2. Make a list of physical-biological environmental factors that influence the operation of a child development center in your present locality. Discuss how those factors might change if you moved to another locality, say, 2,000 miles away to a location of your choice.

3. Study the list of theoretical approaches to management, and select those that appear to relate best to human service organizations. Discuss what you value as an approach to management.
4. Study the ecological system of your family and the interactions your family members have within and between each environment.
5. Find an article in a journal about the work of one of the theorists mentioned, read it, and file it in your management notebook.

STUDY QUESTIONS

1. Define a theory, and state three requirements of a good theory.
2. List the theorists mentioned and look them up in an encyclopedia or a reference listed in Suggested Readings. List ideas each theorist advocates that relate to children in a child development center.
3. Define developmental theory. What are its two parts?
4. Define human ecological systems theory.
5. a. Name and describe each of the three environments of the ecological systems model.
   b. Give examples of how each environment contributes to operating a child development center.
6. Define management theory. List different management theories.
7. Define open system and show how a child development center is an open system.
8. List systems you will be interacting with as you manage a child development center.
9. Explain why a theory is not a fact.

SUGGESTED READINGS

Andrews, M., M. Bubolz, and B. Paolucci. "An Ecological Approach to Study of the Family." *Marriage and Family Review* 3 (Spring/Summer 1980), pp. 29–49.

Berk, Laura E., and Adam Winsler. *Scaffolding Children's Learning: Vygotsky and Early Childhood Education*. Washington, DC: National Association for the Education of Young Children, 1995.

Bloom, B. S. *Stability and Change in Human Characteristics*. New York: Wiley, 1964.

Bloom, B. S., M. D. Engelhart, W. H. Hill, and D. R. Krathwohl. (eds.). *Taxonomy of Educational Objectives: The Classification of Educational Goals*. Handbook I: *Cognitive Domain*. New York: Longmans Green, 1956.

Bronfenbrenner, U. *The Ecology of Human Development*. Cambridge, MA: Harvard University Press, 1979.

Bubolz, Margaret M., and M. Suzanne Sontag. "Human Ecology Theory." In P. G. Boss, W. J. Doherty, R. LaRossa, W. R. Schumm, and S. K. Steinmetz (eds.), *Sourcebook of Family Theories and Methods: A Contextual Approach*, pp. 419–448. New York: Plenum, 1993.

Childs, Gilbert. *Steiner Education in Theory and Practice*. Worcester, Great Britain: Floris, 1991.

Cleverley, John, and D. C. Phillips. *Visions of Childhood: Influential Models from Locke to Spock*. New York: Teachers College Press, 1986.

Dodge, Diane T., and Laura J. Colker. *The Creative Curriculum for Early Childhood*. Washington, DC: Teaching Strategies, 1992.

Doggett, Libby, and Jill George. *All Kids Count: Child Care and the Americans with Disabilities Act*. Arlington, TX: The Arc, 1993.

Edwards, Carolyn, Lella Gandini, and George Forman. *The Hundred Languages of Children: The Reggio Emilia Approach to Early Childhood Education*. Norwood, NJ: Ablex, 1993.

Erikson, Erik H. *Childhood and Society*. New York: Norton, 1963.

Flippo, Edwin. *Management: Concepts and Effective Practice*. New York: West, 1986.

Forman, George, and David S. Kuschner. *The Child's Construction of Knowledge: Piaget for Teaching Children*. Washington, DC: National Association for the Education of Young Children, 1984.

Fox, Lise, Mary F. Hanline, Cynthia O. Vail, and Kim R. Gallant. "Developmentally Appropriate Practice: Applications for Young Children with Disabilities." *Journal of Early Intervention* 18:3 (Summer 1994), pp. 243–257.

Gesell, Arnold. *The First Five Years of Life*. New York: Harper & Row, 1943.

Goffin, Stacie G. *Curriculum Models and Early Childhood Education: Appraising the Relationship*. Upper Saddle River, NJ: Prentice Hall, 1994.

Havighurst, Robert J. *Developmental Tasks and Education*. New York: McKay, 1952.

Hewes, Dorothy, and Barbara Hartman. *Early Childhood Education: A Workbook for Administrators*. Saratoga, CA: R & E, 1988.

Hildebrand, Verna, *Introduction to Early Childhood Education*, 6th ed. Upper Saddle River, NJ: Merrill/Prentice Hall, 1997.

Hohmann, Mary, and David P. Weikart. *Educating Young Children: Active Learning Practices for Preschool and Child Care Programs*. Ypsilanti, MI: High/Scope Press, 1995.

Kamii, Constance. *Numbers in Preschool and Kindergarten: Educational Implications of Piaget's Theory*. Washington, DC: National Association for the Education of Young Children, 1982.

Katz, D. *The Study of Organizations*. San Francisco: Jossey-Bass, 1980.

Kostelnik, M. "Myths Associated with Developmentally Appropriate Practice." *Young Children* 47(4) (1992), pp. 17–25.

Mallory, B. L., and R. S. New. *Diversity and Developmentally Appropriate Practices*. New York: Teachers College Press, 1994.

Maslow, Abraham H. *Motivation and Personality*. New York: Harper & Row, 1954.

Mitchell, Anne, and Judy David (eds.). *Explorations with Young Children: A Curriculum Guide from the Bank Street College of Education*. Mount Rainier, MD: Gryphon House, 1992.

Monighan-Nourot, Patricia, Barbara Scales, Judith Van Hoorn, and Millie Almy. *Looking at Children's Play: A Bridge between Theory and Practice*. New York: Teachers College Press, 1987.

Montessori, Maria. *The Montessori Method*. Cambridge, MA: Bentley, 1965.

Papert, Seymour. *The Children's Machine: Rethinking School in the Age of the Computer*. New York: Basic Books, 1993.

Pence, Alan R. (ed.). *Ecological Research with Children and Families: From Concepts to Methodology*. New York: Teachers College Press, 1988.

Peters, Donald L., John T. Neisworth, and Thomas D. Yawkey. *Early Childhood Education: From Theory to Practice*. Monterey, CA: Brooks/Cole, 1985.

Piaget, Jean, and B. Inhelder. *The Psychology of the Child*. New York: Basic Books, 1969.

Schiamberg, Lawrence. *Child and Adolescent Development*. Upper Saddle River, NJ: Prentice Hall, 1988.

Skinner, B. F. *Beyond Freedom and Dignity*. New York: Knopf, 1971.

Skinner, B. F. *Reflections on Behaviorism and Society*. Upper Saddle River, NJ: Prentice Hall, 1978.

Vygotsky, L. S. Thinking and Speech. In R. W. Rieber, A. S. Carton (eds.) and B. Minick (trans.), *The Collected Works of L. S. Vygotsky: Vol. 1. Problems of General Psychology*. New York: Plenum, 1987, pp. 37–285. (Original work published in 1934.)

CHAPTER 3

Management Processes and Approaches

• •

If you are going to be a manager of a child development center, what will you be doing? How will your job differ from the teacher's job that you may have been performing previously? How will your tasks relate to licensing regulations from your state and local governing bodies and to the accreditation standards established by your professional organization, the National Association for the Education of Young Children?

As you study the managerial processes and approaches, consciously reflect on all the managers you have known. How did they work? How did they relate to employees? How did they delegate assignments? How did they reward unusual performance? How did they correct inadequate performance? By watching other managers you can learn some things about managing. Wherever you are presently, begin thinking about service and organization from a manager's viewpoint.

THE MANAGERIAL PROCESSES

All managers use five basic processes regardless of what enterprise they manage:

1. Planning
2. Organizing
3. Staffing
4. Leading
5. Monitoring and controlling for quality

These processes are integral to every managerial task, and managers are evaluated both formally and informally on their ability to perform them. When evaluating the manager informally, parents or staff may refer to personality character-istics and the way the manager interacts with them. However, as important as interpersonal communication is, managers must successfully carry out many other tasks. When the sponsoring agency or industry evaluates the overall success of the child development center, the manager's handling of all managerial processes will be on the line.

These five basic managerial processes are topics for chapters later in the book. Let us look briefly at them here and relate each to characteristics of the manager of a child development center.

DECISIONS, DECISIONS . . .

 Think about a manager of any enterprise you have known who seemed either particularly effective or particularly ineffective. List and analyze the factors that enter into your judgment. Do they have to do with personality characteristics, such as cheerfulness and courtesy, or skills such as being well organized and "on top of things"? What connections do you see between the various aspects of management? Discuss.

Planning

Planning is defined as methods, formulated beforehand, for doing or making something. Plans usually specify goals as well as a course of action. A plan tells *what* should be done and *how* it is to be done.[1]

In the planning process, the manager must follow certain guidelines. First, he or she *develops, for planning purposes, a clear agreement and statement on the central concept of the center*. This statement describes the ultimate goal of the program in general terms. A center may have a central concept statement when the manager is hired, or one may need to be developed as the work proceeds. The wise man-ager will collaborate with all those who hold a stake in the center's operations when developing this statement: members of the policy board, parents, and staff. Involving parents will help the center understand and serve the needs of its cus-tomers; involving staff will help ensure that they are committed to the center's ultimate goals. The central concept may be a simple statement such as "The ABC Center will provide developmentally appropriate child care for 100 children ages 6 months to 6 years."

Often the central concept includes additional elements, however. An early childhood laboratory program on a college campus provides developmentally appropriate child care, but usually its major focus is to provide experience with children for the college students. An employer-sponsored child care center in a hospital also provides developmentally appropriate care, but its major focus is to provide a convenient service that will help the hospital attract and retain skilled

---

[1] Gary Dressler, *Management Fundamentals* (Reston, VA: Reston, 1985), p. 29.

Planning is needed at both the managerial and classroom levels so that the recommended activity can occur daily for a budding artist.
Michigan State University Child Development Laboratory, East Lansing

medical staff. Yet another child development center might be operated as a franchise of a large corporation with at least part of its purpose being to make a profit for stockholders.

DECISIONS, DECISIONS . . .

 Think about the three types of child development centers just described and list the decisions that a manager of each might make in regard to hours and days of operation, ages of children accepted, meals provided, equipment needed, and policies regarding mildly ill children. Discuss.

Next the manager *follows licensing and professional standards for the services proposed and ensures that staff members understand the standards and follow them.* Licensing standards vary from state to state, so it is important to have accurate information about the specific standards that apply in your state. For example, some states allow as many as twelve infants or toddlers or twenty 4-year-olds per caregiver. Regulations in other states come closer to the NAEYC recommendations of no more than four infants and toddlers, or ten 3-, 4-, and 5-year-olds per caregiver. Appendix A gives a comparison of key regulations in the 50 states; Appendix B provides the names and addresses of agencies responsible for licensing child care programs in each of the 50 states. Standards for high-quality programs that go beyond state minimums are described in the accreditation criteria booklet published by the NAEYC.

Third, the manager develops realistic and appropriate goals and objectives of the center. To many, goals and objectives are synonymous. To others, objectives depict the steps for arriving at the goal. For example, if one goal is to have a happy, well-adjusted child, then one objective to help attain that goal would be to provide developmentally appropriate activities. However you define the two, help your staff and others clarify the meaning of goals and the manner of evaluating when they have been achieved.

Fourth, the manager makes decisions based on overall goals and plans. A great deal of time goes into agreeing on goals and objectives. Thus, when decisions are made, those goals should be the basis of decisions. For example, given a goal of protecting the civil rights of children, parents, and staff, instances of denying those rights should not be allowed even in emergency decisions.

Fifth, the manager develops, evaluates, and revises programs and plans as needed. This responsibility is continuous from the first to the last day of a manager's tenure. As you enter the position, record a baseline of statistics, for example, on the number of classrooms, staff, and children; the amount of the budget; and the breadth of services offered. These data will provide a benchmark later for evaluating the program developments for which you have had some responsibility. In a sense, you are making an audit of the enterprise as you find it. Do not rely on your memory.

Finally, the manager consults regularly with governing board, staff, parents, and others on goals, programs, plans, and procedures. The manager is not an island making decisions alone. Among good managerial skills are those needed to gain the best thinking of many individuals.

DECISIONS, DECISIONS ...

 Suppose you are the manager of a child development center that is experiencing a budget crisis because of a large drop in enrollment. How might you "gain the best thinking of many individuals" in approaching this problem? What individuals would you want to involve? How should you approach them?

Organizing

Organizing is defined as arranging elements (people, supplies, and equipment) and coordinating joint activities so that all of the interdependent parts contribute effectively to the desired goal. This critical process begins after planning and requires assembling the people, physical space, equipment, and materials in an orderly process so as to accomplish the center's goals. Some people are very good at suggesting ideas or even at writing plans, but they fall short when time for implementation arrives. If you see this occurring, you may need to step in and guide them in this step. It is through organizing that the dreams begin to materialize as the hard work of the center gets done.

Organizing is needed to have appropriate manipulative toys available in a location where children can handle them without interruption from others.
University of Illinois Child Development Laboratory, Urbana

In the organizing process, the manager *delegates and organizes units to facilitate conducting the programs stipulated in the goals.* An internal logic and consistency should be applied to the delegation of duties. Also, the manager *assembles and uses space, facilities, materials, and equipment effectively to accomplish the work of the center.*

DECISIONS, DECISIONS . . .

 Your center is having an open house for parents to see what their children do that fosters learning. What elements and joint activities need to be organized in each classroom? How much preparation time is needed? In what way can the children be helpful?

DECISIONS, DECISIONS ...

 The family of a child who is blind has asked to enroll their child in your center, beginning next month. You know that the Americans with Disabilities Act requires that you make a reasonable effort to accommodate the child; besides, your center's stated philosophy is that all children are welcome. List the steps you will take to prepare for this child's arrival and the people you will involve. Discuss the resources (equipment, materials, knowledge) you will need.

Staffing

People make the major difference in any service institution. The importance of people is indicated by the statistic that salaries for the personnel of a center often consume over 70% of the operating budget. **Staffing** is a process of recruiting and dealing with the human resources (human capital) required to perform the functions of the center.

In the staffing process, the manager *carries out an objective assessment of qualifications, abilities, and achievements of potential staff members and recruits and assigns staff members to carry out the goals of the center efficiently.* High standards will begin with high-quality staff and continuous staff development. All teachers and caregivers have a big responsibility to children, families, and society to produce the best service possible for children.

Second, the manager *orients, advises, supports, develops, and evaluates staff members in a timely manner.* Staffing a center requires a great deal of time and is therefore expensive. Once the staff is in place, the manager must support its continuing development.

Third, he or she *maintains constructive relationships with staff and others.* Interpersonal communication skills will be essential for the manager and staff.

Fourth, the manager *carries out an objective evaluation of the performance of staff members and communicates concerning strengths and weaknesses.* Staff members will agree to their job description, which will serve as the basis for evaluation. Careful evaluations should be done during a staff member's probationary period to aid the individual to make corrections in practices. All staff members are evaluated regularly, at a minimum of once yearly.

Finally, the manager *plans and carries out a dynamic program of staff development.* In this vital field of service to children and families that deals with many vulnerable human beings, there is a great deal to learn. Staff members should be helped to realize the scope of their own human capital development and be encouraged and assisted to continue their personal development.

DECISIONS, DECISIONS . . .

Think back on your own work or school experience to a time when a supervisor or teacher gave you feedback on your performance. What did you like or dislike about the experience? What ways did the feedback cause you to change what you were doing?

Leading

Leading is a process of directing and influencing others through example, talent, information, and personal interaction skills. In the leading process, the manager *anticipates future developments in the services offered by the center.* From knowledge of the total profession and interaction at the national as well as the local level, the manager helps the staff, parents, and policy board look beyond the current situation and problems to possible future levels of service.

Second, the manager *maintains an attitude of looking forward to changes and improvements in services using up-to-date information and trends*. All individuals involved are helped to maintain a holistic and dynamic picture of their responsibilities. Planning for innovations keeps the problem of burnout or disinterest to a minimum among professionals who are deeply interested in the services they are performing.

Third, the manager *exercises leadership essential to his or her role*. A center without a manager who exercises leadership is like a ship without a rudder. It goes nowhere. Staff members will wait patiently for a time, hoping that the manager will exercise leadership. If leadership is not forthcoming, leadership will probably emerge from the staff, which will likely cause discomfort in the manager.

Finally, the manager *provides active leadership in professional activities in the community, state, and nation*. The strength of any profession lies in the strength of local units of service. Managers should realize that local associations contribute to their staff members' increasing professionalism and growing professional self-esteem.

DECISIONS, DECISIONS . . .

 What trends do you think the manager of a child development center should be thinking about today? Make a list of the three trends you consider most important. Compare your list with your classmates'.

Monitoring and Controlling for Quality

Monitoring and **controlling** are defined as the evaluative and action functions of maintaining high quality in the promised services. In other words, after a manager has developed a plan of action and put that plan into action, he or she must check regularly to see that the plan is actually being carried out and meeting its intended aims.

Standards are the measuring sticks used to determine how well the center is accomplishing its aims. A good manager will establish personal standards based on professional knowledge and individual experience, as well as observe the standards provided by one or more outside sources. All centers must adhere to licensing standards. These are minimum requirements established by the state for the protection of children when they are not in their parents' care.

Ideally, a state legislature mandates that such standards be created and delineates the broad areas that the standards will regulate. Then the legislature authorizes a particular agency, such as the health or social services department, to write the detailed standards with the help of experts in child development, fire safety, sanitation, and transportation, as well as input from parents and child care providers. During a lengthy process the resulting rules are reviewed many times and modified so that the end product represents the best thinking of the entire community about the basic safety and welfare needs of children.

Wise managers understand that the rules are minimum standards and that they are a collaborative effort of many people just like themselves. They ensure that their centers adhere to the rules and do not try to "get around" them. They also understand that they can have a voice in improving rules that need to be changed as new needs arise or new information develops. In other words, the manager of a child development center works in partnership with the licensing agency to establish a baseline of quality.

DECISIONS, DECISIONS . . .

 Get a copy of the licensing standards for your state and read them carefully. Find out when they were last revised. Are there any rules that you feel need changing? Find out what procedures are available for child advocates to make suggestions about rule changes in your state.

In addition to licensing standards, some centers are required to meet standards established by their funding bodies. Some states, for example, fund programs for 4-year-old children in public schools, and, in order to qualify for the grants, school districts must comply with specific guidelines. Federally funded Head Start programs have another set of detailed guidelines to follow. In each case, these regulations are above and beyond minimum licensing standards and must be followed consistently for the center to maintain its funding.

Any center, whether funded through a government agency or private tuition, can elect to meet a further set of standards designed to establish a benchmark of quality for centers beyond the minimum welfare and safety considerations of licensing regulations. These centers can work toward achieving accreditation from the National Association for the Education of Young Children (discussed later).

In the monitoring and controlling process, the manager *monitors compliance with standards and acts to maintain high standards of performance in every unit of the center*. Visiting units daily provides the manager with information on compliance with standards. Deviations from standards will be given immediate personal attention and action until corrections are made. Attention to both licensing standards (which are mandatory minimum standards) and accreditation standards (which are voluntary, high-quality standards) will be considered essential.

Second, the manager *listens to and understands others' views*. In leading staff members to high-quality performance, it is essential to practice good communication skills. Stress is reduced when individuals feel their view is respected. For example, some managers and policy boards found staff members worried and reluctant at first to agree to proceeding with the NAEYC accreditation process. However, when the staff realized they were all going to work together, they became strong proponents of the process. And when accreditation was finally awarded, they proudly waved the banner.

Finally, the manager *maintains objectivity in evaluating problems and issues*. A cool, calm manner of dealing with problems is essential. An attitude of seeking information before acting is part of careful management.

In Chapter 8, "Monitoring and Controlling for Quality," an evaluation form for managers is provided that encompasses the criteria under each heading listed in the chapter thus far. Managers, like all staff, can expect to be evaluated on their performance. Owners-managers should seriously consider the criteria for evaluating administrators.

A focus on high quality is a winning strategy in all human services. As parents become more informed consumers, child care centers will have to maintain high quality to succeed in business. Monitoring and controlling are essential to this strategy.

ACCREDITATION

Accreditation is a distinction awarded to early childhood schools and child care centers for having met the standards for high-quality programs and having completed the procedures for outside validation of that high quality in a process supervised by the National Academy of Early Childhood Programs, a division of the NAEYC.

The standards for accreditation of early childhood programs are published in the booklet *Accreditation Criteria & Procedures of the National Academy of Early Childhood Programs.*[2] These standards were agreed on by early childhood professionals and parents from across the nation before they were accepted by the NAEYC board. One section of criteria pertains to administration of centers. A **standard** is a measure of quality or quantity of a service or a product. To achieve high quality, you must be aware of the standards or criteria of quality.

When your center or school decides to work toward accreditation, as thousands of centers are now doing, administrative processes will be under scrutiny. If you have not yet investigated the accreditation process, decide today to look into it. The booklet stating the accreditation standards should be available to and used by each manager whether or not the center leadership has immediate intentions of entering into the accreditation process.

Sixteen Steps toward Accreditation
1. Purchase the Accreditation Criteria booklet from NAEYC by writing the NAEYC at 1509 16th St., N.W., Washington, DC 20036-1426, or calling 202-232-8777 or 800-424-2460.
2. Decide with your policy board and staff to enter into the accreditation process.
3. Tell the NAEYC you wish to start the accreditation process.
4. Complete the application forms and enclose your fee. The fee amount depends on the number of children served in your center.
5. The NAEYC sends you the record-keeping books. Study them and make a time line with your staff for accomplishing the self-study tasks.

---

[2] Sue Bredekamp (ed.), *Accreditation Criteria & Procedures of the National Academy of Early Childhood Programs* (Washington, DC: National Association for the Education of Young Children, 1991).

6. Teachers study and evaluate their classrooms. Improve shortcomings.
7. You complete the evaluation of the management system. Improve short-comings.
8. Ask parents to complete their evaluations after teachers and administrators have completed theirs. Correct any shortcomings.
9. Complete reports and send them to NAEYC and request a validation visit.
10. The NAEYC checks all your reports and, if everything is in order, sets up a visit for a validator. You pay your validator fee.
11. A **validator** is a regional professional familiar with the accreditation process and criteria who comes for a day (or two days in a large program) to check over your reports and to determine whether, in fact, the report you have submitted is an accurate portrayal of your program.
12. Following the visit, the validator files a report with the NAEYC.
13. If the NAEYC agrees that everything is accomplished, the report goes to the Accrediting Commission, which meets periodically to approve centers or schools presenting documents for accreditation.
14. The commission may request another review if they see something missing.
15. If the commission approves your center, the National Academy of Early Childhood Programs awards accreditation and forwards your certificate.
16. You inform your staff and the children's parents and frame the certificate. Send a press release to your local radio and television stations, newspaper, and NAEYC affiliate newsletter. You may now use the logo in your public relations materials.

Reaccreditation is applied for in 3 years or after a major shift in management of your center.

WHAT WILL BE YOUR STYLE OF MANAGING?

If you have some work experience, you have probably already analyzed a manager's approach to managing. Some managers use concepts of costs and increased efficiency. They analyze jobs and figure out the "best way" for the job to be done and expect that the job should be done that way. These are often called **classical managers**.

In another approach, the manager recognizes that the way workers feel about their jobs both individually and as a group has profound effects on job outcome. The people-oriented, or **behavioral**, approach gives employees more independence and helps them take more responsibility and develop maturity in their job. Flexibility is the rule. This approach generally fits educational institutions. Well-prepared professionals, especially in child development centers, approve of and expect adequate flexibility to meet individual needs of children and families.

Remember, well-prepared professionals vary widely, as all people do, in their modes of interacting and preferred learning styles. Some people are naturally more extroverted than others, enjoy dealing with the public, and feel comfort-

Management policies encourage parents to visit their child's school any time without invitation. Bringing a sibling along is accepted.
University of New Mexico Child Development Laboratory, Albuquerque

able speaking up about their ideas and feelings. Others are more reserved and prefer to watch from the sidelines, think things over, and interact with one or few people at a time. Some people find it easiest to gain new ideas and information by reading or listening to lectures. Others need to try things out for themselves and learn best by doing. Detailed rules for every operation will make some people feel secure, while they might be stifling for someone with a very playful disposition and high tolerance for risk taking. Some of these characteristics and preferences are related to cultural background; however, there is likely as much difference between individuals within a given culture as there is between cultures.

None of these differences mean that people cannot work together effectively. In fact, different personalities and approaches often complement each other. A wise manager will recognize that not everyone on the staff shares a similar interaction or learning style and will be careful not to make assumptions about people based on their cultural or ethnic backgrounds. Instead, a good manager should make an effort to learn more about people's individual differences and capitalize on the distinct contributions that each has to offer in meeting the center's ultimate goals.

DECISION MAKING

Decision making is the central activity of the manager of any organization. It is a mental activity that may require hours of sitting at your desk, reading relevant materials, making calculations or drawings, and developing draft copies of plans until the best possible plans have finally evolved. In some ways, decision making is a lonely activity. It certainly requires time. To some of your staff, who are busy getting things done, it may seem like loafing—after all, you are just sitting there at your desk with a pencil in your hand. When the right decision is made and the right direction is taken, things will look rosy. On the other hand, conditions may be gloomy if the wrong decision is made and the wrong direction taken. Dissonance frequently occurs as decisions are made. Your task is to reduce dissonance to a minimum and guide it toward constructive changes. Each of the basic functions of management just described—planning, organizing, staffing, leading, and monitoring and controlling—requires decision making.

Decision Types

Simon describes two types of decisions:[3] type 1, programmed-repetitive and routine decisions; and type 2, nonprogrammed decisions, that is, unstructured, novel, and consequential decisions. Fortunately for you there will be many type 1 decisions. As Dressler states, "Programmed decisions can be laid out in advance step by step. For example, an accounting department, computing each employee's withholding taxes, involves programmed decision making in that there is a clear step-by-step procedure to use to determine each one's withholding taxes."[4] However, numerous type 2 or nonprogrammed decisions will arise that may be difficult to plan for in advance.

DECISIONS, DECISIONS ...

 Mrs. Parker explained her shortage of funds for paying her daughter Jackie's weekly fees. As manager of the child development center, you explain that you can allow a 1-week grace period before Jackie would not be admitted. According to Simon, is this a type 1 or type 2 decision? Could it be classified as either? Would it be preferable to treat it as one type or the other?

Decisions are often interrelated in complex ways. One pattern of decision making is called a chain pattern, characterized by a straight line, each decision being dependent on the preceding choice.[5] The chain can stop and recommence at any point.

[3] H. A. Simon, *The New Science of Management Decision* (New York: Harper & Row, 1977), pp. 49–50.

[4] G. Dressler, *Management Fundamentals* (Reston, VA: Reston, 1985), p. 486.

[5] B. Paolucci, O. Hall, and N. Axinn, *Family Decision Making: An Ecosystem Approach* (New York: Wiley, 1977), pp. 108–109.

An example of chain-pattern decisions in a child development center might be as follows:

Decision 1: The policy board decides to organize a child care center.

Decision 2: The board members decide the first year to enroll only 3- and 4-year-old children.

Decision 3: They decide to establish a 4- and 5-year-old group the next year from last year's enrollees and continue the first classroom enrolling 2½- and 3-year-olds.

Decision 4: The following year they decide to add a new group for kindergarten children who need a place to go before or after their half-day of regular school.

Each decision is based on experience gained as a result of the preceding decision.

In the **central-satellite** type of decision making, a central decision is followed by several satellite decisions that are dependent on the central decision.[6] For example, in a child development center, a policy board decision to start an infant care unit would be a central decision. Then numerous satellite decisions follow, such as housing, equipping, staffing, and organizing the infant care center. If the central decision had been different, the other satellite decisions would not have followed.

One might conceptualize several central decisions as being strung together in a chain, with all decisions being related to overall goals of the center. The satellite decisions for each central decision may relate minimally to those of other central decisions. Here arise questions concerning cost in time and money for the manager to analyze. For example, is providing only one type of service more cost-effective or efficient than providing several services? Also, are the expanded services consistent with the central goal of the center?

DECISIONS, DECISIONS . . .

 Each Friday the laundry truck picks up the center's dirty linens. What type of decision has established this routine? In what ways does it save the manager's energy?

THE DECISION PROCESS

Four steps make up the decision process:

1. Identifying the problem
2. Developing alternatives
3. Analyzing alternatives
4. Making the final decision

---

[6] Paolucci et al., *Family Decision Making*, p. 106–108.

A brief discussion of these steps follows.

Identifying the Problem

Just as decisions can be categorized as to type, so too can problems be categorized as to where they arise. Type 1 problems—routine problems—arise because of a breakdown in something that should be regular or routine. Type 2 problems—nonroutine problems—arise where things are less structured and thus less predictable. When a problem arises, you can quickly determine whether it is a type 1 or type 2. In the routine type, such as having problems with deliveries, the problem could arise repeatedly, perhaps every day. Immediate attention to the sequence of events heads off trouble for many other days. At times stopgap measures must be taken, but routine is desired and is the goal.

DECISIONS, DECISIONS . . .

 Center XYZ has 240 children enrolled. At 10 A.M., just when foods requiring the oven were ready to bake, the power went off. A call to the power company indicated it would be off at least an hour. What type of decision is required? What would you do?

DECISIONS, DECISIONS . . .

 Your phone rings early one morning; one after another several staff members report having the flu. What do you do? What type of decision is required?

The nonprogrammed problems often have elements that can be programmed or routinized in advance. For example, the *problem* in the first example is 240 children who must have food at noon. The *problem* in the second example is to replace ill staff members with people capable of carrying out the work. Each of these problems can be foreseen to some extent, making the solutions somewhat routine, though stress producing nonetheless.

Developing Alternatives

The possible alternative solutions can be arrived at by stimulating the creative thinking of everyone involved. Staff members can be very helpful in generating alternatives if a climate of trust exists so that their creativity can emerge. One way is to brainstorm among the staff for alternatives—even seemingly impossible alternatives should be written on a board and valued as a contribution. Any idea may have usable elements or stimulate thinking leading to better ideas. Avoid premature evaluation. As manager, you can offer several alternatives showing your trust of the process.

Appropriate programs allow time for children to pause and reflect on what they are doing.
Early Learning Center, Appalachian State University, Boone, NC

Information is essential for developing alternatives. Your staff has information accumulated by years of experience. Various readily available publications will have relevant information. Sometimes you may wish to bring in consultants or contact a consultant for specific information. For example, information on children's diets could come from a dietitian. Information on employee insurance could be derived by getting bids from a number of companies and questioning other child development center managers regarding their solutions to the employee insurance problem. Information generally has a cost, in time or money, that the organization must bear if the best possible decision is to be made.

Analyzing Alternatives

In a group discussion among staff members, allow each person to state the pros and cons of the various alternatives. By consensus you can begin to erase some from the list that are not right for your situation at this time. Listen carefully to staff members and value each one's contribution.

Making the Final Decision

Soon only a few alternatives may remain, and these can be voted on or decided by consensus. Improved decisions result when staff members have had a voice, particularly in person-centered organizations such as child development centers. Normally a problem has many aspects, and talking things over helps the manager gain perspective on the problem. Obviously, there is very little substance to the decision-making process if at least two alternatives are not considered.

DECISIONS, DECISIONS . . .

 Pressure is mounting for your center to lower the age of admission from 2½ to 2. The often-heard pro argument is that parents who need or want care for their 2-year-olds will choose a competing center that accepts them. Then, when the child is 2½, parents will not bring their child to your center because the child is already happily adjusted to another center. What is the decision process?

RATIONALITY IN DECISION MAKING

Decision making in a human services organization such as a child development center will be rational in some respects and extrarational in other respects. **Rational decision making** is considered to be objective, logical, based on hard data, and useful for **technical decisions**. For example, regarding the center's physical plant maintenance, you decide on floor covering, quality of paint, or parking lot covering based on objective criteria such as cost of installing, cost of upkeep, and predicted longevity. These are all technical decisions. **Extrarational decisions** require judgment or wisdom in addition to available objective facts. Extrarational decisions are often **social decisions**. Paolucci et al. say that social decision making occurs when there is a conflict in values, goals, or roles.[7] Social decisions occur frequently in children's classrooms as values, goals, and roles of parents, teachers, and children become integrated into the human service that is child care. Teachers use social decision making repeatedly during each day as they mediate interaction among children.

The National Association for the Education of Young Children has developed a Code of Ethics to help guide managers and caregivers in their interactions with children and families. The code consists of a set of basic ideals and principles regarding responsibilities to children, families, colleagues, and society that members of the profession have agreed on. A copy of the code can be obtained by calling or writing the NAEYC.[8]

Sometimes a situation occurs that creates a conflict between two or more of these basic principles. This is called an **ethical dilemma**, and it can only be resolved through careful reflection and discussion among all parties. Ideally, they will find a way to sustain the spirit of both principles; if not, they will have to decide which principle takes precedence.

For example, a parent might demand that a caregiver use spanking to control a child's behavior. The center adheres to the basic principle of cooperating with parents and respecting their individual styles of child rearing. However, the center also follows a fundamental principle of using positive guidance techniques

---

[7] Paolucci et al., *Family Decision Making*, p. 104.
[8] NAEYC, 1509 16th St., N.W., Washington, DC 20036-1426; 202-232-8777 or 800-424-2460.

with children, which means that all forms of corporal punishment are prohibited. A state licensing regulation prohibits corporal punishment, so you might argue that the center could make this a routine decision, simply by citing that regulation when denying the parent's request. But that solution does not resolve another conflict between two ideals regarding ethical responsibilities toward families: to respect families' ideas about child rearing while at the same time sharing information that will enhance parenting skills.

Thus, the center finds itself in an ethical dilemma. The manager, teacher, and parents all need to talk openly and try to come to some understanding of the reasons behind each position. In this case, the parents might lack information about other, more effective methods of getting their child to "behave." They might view the center's positive guidance techniques as spoiling the child. If, after honest and open discussion, the parents and center cannot come to some agreement, it may be necessary for them to "agree to disagree," and perhaps the family will decide to withdraw the child.

Whatever the final outcome, the thoughtful manager realizes that ethical decisions like this one are complex, requiring consideration of several competing ideals and principles. Laws against corporal punishment may make this dilemma seem fairly simple to solve. Other situations may involve more "gray areas."[9]

DECISIONS, DECISIONS . . .

 Suppose that the family of a 3-year-old boy has asked their child development center to use a "time-out chair" to punish him when he wets his pants. The center's policy is to handle toilet accidents calmly and matter-of-factly, without punishing or drawing attention to the child. Role-play this situation with a classmate, with one of you taking the part of the parent and one taking the part of the center manager. Decide how you will resolve this dilemma. List the consequences you can anticipate from your decision.

TIME MANAGEMENT

Time is a valuable nonrenewable resource. Managing this resource carefully is essential if you are to achieve the goals set forth in your plans. If you are moving up in the ranks from a teaching position to managing one or more units, you may have difficulty in delegating some of the responsibility and may tend to take some of your time to do things that your teachers or other staff can do well for themselves. You must learn to let others do their share of the work and leave your time for the managerial and leadership functions that are now your responsibility.

---

[9] See, for example, "When Parents and Professionals Disagree . . . Using NAEYC's Code of Ethics," *Young Children* 50:3 (March 1995), pp. 64–65.

Management expert Stephen Covey says that the essence of time management is to "organize and execute around priorities." He suggests that managers determine those priorities using criteria of importance and urgency:

1. Activities that are both important *and* urgent
2. Activities that are important but not urgent
3. Activities that are urgent but not important
4. Activities that are neither urgent nor important[10]

As the manager of a child development center, you may find yourself constantly dealing with crises of more or less importance, unless you manage to allocate significant amounts of your time to activities that, in Covey's language, belong to the "second quadrant"—that is, they are important but not urgent. Planning your center's public relations strategy, for example, may seem insignificant next to a broken water pipe, but neglecting it may lead to larger problems, such as declining enrollment.

Using these criteria, you might decide to take the time to recruit and train a volunteer to do routine tasks like sorting mail, knowing that your investment will pay off in many hours saved later on. Even tasks that qualify as both important and urgent can be delegated if you have selected your staff wisely and explained the task carefully. A staff member, for example, can keep children's time records and generate invoices or send reminders to parents, freeing you to work on a feasibility study for a new infant-toddler component in your center. Activities that may seem unimportant, such as having lunch with key board members or individual staff members, can promote valuable relationships and help your organization develop a clear, unified vision, making them well worth your time. Knowing *your* priorities will help you decide which activities to tackle, which to delegate, and which to put off for another time, as you face your weekly or daily "to do" list.

DECISIONS, DECISIONS . . .

 You have set aside time each afternoon to work on your center's budget and some grant applications. However, for the last several days, you have been called away from this task to help one of your teachers settle a behavior problem in her room. While in the room, you have noticed that few activities seem available and children are wandering aimlessly. You suspect that a more interesting variety of activities would reduce the behavior problems and free you from your unwanted role as "enforcer." As the center director, how will you manage your time so that there is better planning for children and you still have time to do your own planning?

Meetings may be frequent on your list of activities. Plan ahead for meetings that are your responsibility. Give people an agenda several days ahead of time so

---

[10] Stephen R. Covey, *The Seven Habits of Highly Effective People* (New York: Simon & Schuster, 1989), p. 149.

they can be prepared with thoughtful information and opinions on the various items. Follow your agenda and keep it moving along. Occasionally, people take more time than an item seems to warrant, thus preventing the group from moving to other items on an agenda. It may help to put time limits on agenda items with an agreement to table any item if it is not completed when the time is up. Keep minutes of your meetings, and send copies to members as early as possible. Do all informal visiting before or after the meeting.

You may be invited to numerous meetings because of your role as manager. After each meeting, make a careful analysis to determine whether a meeting of that organization really warrants the time you gave to it. You may decide to pass it up another time and just read the minutes.

You will soon become aware of cyclical periods when certain reports are due, requiring a larger time input. Learn to anticipate those periods to even out the work over a period of time as much as possible.

Put a picture of your family or other reminder of your life after hours on your desk so that you will remember to get things accomplished efficiently on time in order to have time for them. To be fresh and inspirational as a manager requires that you spend some time in a pursuit that revitalizes your psychic energy. Time is a precious nonrenewable resource. Use it wisely and guard it appropriately.

KNOWING YOURSELF

Some people aspire to managerial positions because they enjoy being responsible for a large operation. They like a major role in making things happen and enjoy the give-and-take that is required. Some people like the thoughtful solitude that decision making requires. They can tolerate the dissonance that may arise at times when all the staff members are not completely satisfied. Some people are challenged when helping solve problems and conflicts. Others, oriented excessively toward love of power and higher managerial salaries, may not be most effective in providing the managerial services needed. People who are organized enough to become good managers are needed in many fields. The principles discussed here will be useful to you as a teacher, but particularly if your interests and abilities lead you to seek a managerial position. Success in one experience may lead to success in a larger operation. Consider seriously your own personality and preferences as you study how to manage a child development center.

DECISIONS, DECISIONS ...

 Your center has a policy of sending a brief note home when children get scrapes and bumps on the playground. You have noticed that these are occurring more frequently of late and worry that a more serious accident could occur. How can you monitor the quality of care children receive on your playground? List the factors you will want to consider.

CONCLUSION

The managerial process has been described as having five basic functions: planning, organizing, staffing, leading, and monitoring and controlling. The classical and behavioral approaches to management have been described. Decision making is discussed as a central activity of management. The managerial process and types of decision making apply whether a child development center is run for profit or as a nonprofit enterprise managed to render the service promised to the funding agencies. Funding agencies may be private corporations, governmental units (as is the case with a child development center in an elementary school), or a variety of philanthropic agencies, such as churches or foundations that operate child development centers. This management framework will be elaborated as the operation of a child development center is discussed in detail in following chapters.

APPLICATIONS

1. Diagram a central-satellite decision in which the center is initiating an after-kindergarten group.
2. Diagram a chain-pattern decision in which a church starts a child care center to utilize some existing resources.
3. Describe a manager you have worked for by listing the person's best and weakest qualities for managing the enterprise. Omit his or her real name.
   a. Evaluate the manager's effectiveness in accomplishing goals.
   b. Evaluate the manager's effectiveness in handling staff.
   c. In class discussion, compare with other students and make a list of do's and don'ts for managers.
   d. Was this manager a classical manager, or was the manager using a behavioral approach?
4. Discuss the questions in the "Decisions, Decisions" boxes throughout the chapter. Share with your classmates examples that you think of as you discuss the questions.
5. Check your library for publications such as *Child Care Information Exchange*, *Child Care Quarterly*, *Day Care and Early Education*, or *Young Children* (see Chapter 7 for addresses of these and other publications), and locate an article addressed specifically to managers. Make an abstract or a photocopy of the article, and discuss its contents with classmates, who also will be locating articles. Based on the articles, answer the question "What are the satisfactions and frustrations of managers?"
6. Continue to add to your management notebook. Watch the business pages for stories on successful managers. Clip the stories for your notebook. Compare the characteristics of these managers with those of child development centers. Are they similar or different?

STUDY QUESTIONS

1. Define the following terms:
   a. licensing
   b. standards
   c. accreditation
   d. classical manager
   e. behavioral manager
2. List and define the five managerial processes.
3. Give an example of each of the five managerial processes.
4. Distinguish and discuss the concepts of mandatory and voluntary standards.
5. Define and give examples of two types of decisions.
6. Define and give examples of two types of problems.
7. Show the interrelatedness of decisions by explaining:
   a. chain-pattern decisions and
   b. central-satellite decisions.
8. State the four steps in the decision process, *and* give an example using all four steps.
9. Define and give examples of:
   a. rational decisions,
   b. technical decisions,
   c. extrarational decisions, and
   d. social decisions.
10. State five ways for a manager to use time most effectively.

SUGGESTED READINGS

Belensky, Mary, Blythe Clinchy, Nancy Goldberger, and Jill Tarule. *Women's Ways of Knowing: The Development of Self, Voice, and Mind*. New York: Basic Books, 1986.

Bredekamp, Sue (ed.). *Developmentally Appropriate Practice in Early Childhood Programs Serving Children from Birth through Age 8*. Washington, DC: National Association for the Education of Young Children, 1987.

Bredekamp, Sue. *Regulating Child Care Quality: Evidence from NAEYC's Accreditation System*. Washington, DC: National Association for the Education of Young Children, 1990.

Cherry, Clare, Barbara Harkness, and Kay Kuzma. *Nursery School and Day Care Management Guide*. Belmont, CA: Lake, 1987.

The Children's Foundation. *1995 Child Day Care Center Licensing Study*. Washington, DC: Author, 1995.

Click, Phylis M., and Donald W. Click. *Administration of Schools for Young Children*, 3d ed. Albany, NY: Delmar, 1990.

Decker, Celia A., and John R. Decker. *Planning and Administering Early Childhood Programs*, 6th ed. Upper Saddle River, NJ: Merrill/Prentice Hall, 1997.

Feeney, Stephanie, and Kenneth Kipnis. *Code of Ethical Conduct and Statement of Commitment*. Washington, DC: National Association for the Education of Young Children, 1995.

Fritz, Roger. *Rate Your Executive Potential*. New York: Wiley, 1988.

Gardner, Howard. *Frames of Mind: The Theory of Multiple Intelligences*. New York: Basic Books, 1983.

Gonzalez-Mena, Janet. *Multicultural Issues in Child Care*. Mountain View, CA: Mayfield, 1993.

Hewes, Dorothy, and Barbara Hartman. *Early Childhood Education: A Workbook for Administrators*. Saratoga, CA: R & E, 1988.

Myers, Isabel Briggs, and Peter B. Myers. *Gifts Differing*. Palo Alto, CA: Consulting Psychologists Press, 1980.

National Association for the Education of Young Children. *Programs for 4-Year-Olds: NAEYC Resource Guide*. Washington, DC: Author, 1986.

Paolucci, B., O. Hall, and N. Axinn. *Family Decision Making: An Ecosystem Approach*. New York: Wiley, 1977.

Smith, Stanley. "When the Licensing Rep Comes." *Texas Child Care Quarterly* 9:1, Summer 1985, pp. 2–6.

Stine, Sharon. "Shipboard Reflections—When the Chosen Journey Is Rough." *Child Care Information Exchange* 59 (January 1988), pp. 39–42.

Storm, Sherry. *The Human Side of Child Care Administration: A How-To Manual*. Washington, DC: National Association for the Education of Young Children, 1985.

PART II

Management Principles and Tasks

CHAPTER 4

Planning

• •

Planning is a basic function of a manager. **Planning** is defined as methods, formulated beforehand, for doing or making something. Plans tell *what* should be done and *how* it is to be done, usually specifying goals as well as a course of action.[1]

As a teacher, you have made daily plans, monthly plans, yearly plans, lesson plans, and individual children's plans. If you have taught in a small center, you may also have experience doing some of the managerial tasks described in Chapter 3. If you become a manager, you can expect to move beyond planning for a single group to planning a center operation with a number of classrooms, greater numbers of children and families, larger staff, bigger budget, and perhaps more varied services.

Managers are frequently involved with such activities as planning an expansion of programs, planning to reorganize existing programs, and planning coordination of several centers throughout a city or region. In addition, managers must assist, monitor, and suggest improvements in the planning done by staff members for their units.

The accreditation procedures of the National Association for the Education of Young Children (NAEYC), discussed in earlier chapters, set standards for high-quality programs. Managers and staff members should use this booklet to aid in planning, with an eye toward eventually becoming accredited. Or, if the center is already accredited, staff members will need to know standards to maintain. If you are a manager of a Head Start center, you will also be required to meet per-

---

[1] Gary Dressler, *Management Fundamentals* (Reston, VA: Reston, 1985), p. 29.

formance standards as well as your state's licensing standards. Standards for school-age child care are becoming more clearly defined as the programs increase in number.[2]

THE POLICY BOARD

The policy board is usually the ultimate authority in an organization having legal authority to make plans for services, hire individuals to carry out the plans, and monitor the provision of the services. The board of education is elected to carry on these functions for the public schools. In child development centers, the board may derive its authority from private or public sources. Community people usually make up boards of this sort, and sometimes the funding agency mandates specific groups to be represented on the board.

When you are hired to manage an existing child development center, this board will likely be in place already and will have made the decision to hire you. If you are hired to direct one of many centers owned by a large corporation, you may have little or no dealings with the policy board. If, however, you are fortunate enough to participate in the establishment of a new policy board, you will want to be aware of the considerable political strategy to use when encouraging people to run for or be appointed to a board. The strategy of getting many groups involved, informed, and supportive of the child development services suggests that people from the community's groups should serve on the board. That is, persons from labor unions, businesses, or farm organizations help reflect the needs and views of these groups in the community. Having professionals from child development and health organizations as members will facilitate some of the technical planning of the board. Of course, parents, as consumers of the service, should be represented, including parents of children with disabilities and ethnic or cultural minorities. The board should reflect the diversity of the population served by the child development center so that there is a good fit between a center's policies and the needs of its clientele.

Whether you have a voice in creating a policy board or are hired by an existing board, your job as manager will be to carry out decisions made by that board. You will also need to help the board make the best decisions by providing your expertise in child development as well as information about the center's operations. You will be an intermediary between the policy board and the staff, children, and families of the center. This means that you will have to develop your communication skills to a high degree, cooperating where possible and

---

[2] Sue Bredekamp (ed.), *Accreditation Criteria & Procedures of the National Academy of Early Childhood Programs* (Washington, DC: National Association for the Education of Young Children, 1991). Also see *Head Start Program Performance Standards* (Washington, DC: U.S. Department of Health and Human Services, Head Start Bureau, November 1984); and Kay M. Albrecht and Margaret C. Plantz (eds.), *Developmentally Appropriate Practice in School-Age Child Care Programs* (Alexandria, VA: American Home Economics Association, 1991).

being assertive enough to stand up for what you believe to be right when necessary. It will be important for you and the board to have clearly stated expectations of each other from the beginning, so that you do not waste a lot of energy trying to do each other's jobs.

DECISIONS, DECISIONS . . .

 A member of your policy board has suggested that your child development center begin using a popular commercial phonics instruction program with the 3-year-olds. The issue has been placed on the agenda for your next board meeting. What will you do in preparation for the discussion? What will you say at that meeting?

The main agenda for the policy board is to write the bylaws and set broad policies for the child development center, leaving the managerial details in the province of the manager. **Bylaws** are rules adopted by the organization to give the details of how representation is established, how decisions are made, and how changes can be made through the organization. Figure 4–1 shows an example of policy board bylaws that may be adapted to fit the particular circumstances of each child development center. Amendment procedures for the bylaws should be somewhat complex to help maintain stability of the organization. Items that may change periodically, such as enrollment figures and tuition fees, should be kept out of the bylaws and left to the decision of the policy board.

ADVISORY BOARDS

If a policy board's function is to create policy, it follows that an advisory board exists to give advice. It may be formally or informally organized. You can simply select a few people to be your eyes and ears in your community, give you feedback on innovations you are considering, or provide insight on problems. This type of a group can be very useful to you in your somewhat lonely authority role of manager.

As a manager of any enterprise, you will need an avenue for keeping in touch with people in other organizations who have a connection both to providers of children's care and education and to families. You might identify persons in city government, the League of Women Voters, the school board, health or mental health providers, civic clubs, the media, labor unions, churches, or the cooperative extension service. Choices might include parents of formerly enrolled children. An advisory group that taps members of such groups gives you a different and larger perspective from that of the parents and teachers you see daily. It also widens your circle of influence in the community, with each member becoming a type of ambassador for your center within his or her own sphere.

Bylaws
XYZ Child Development Center

Article I. Name

The corporate name of the center is the XYZ Child Development Center located at 123 Rightway, Child City, Michigan 48823.

Article II. Purpose

The center aims to promote child development

2.1 Through the operation of group child care services.

Article III. Policy Board

3.1 The corporate powers of the center are vested in the Policy Board.

3.2 The Policy board shall consist of a minimum of five (5) and a maximum of nine (9) members.

3.3 One Policy Board member shall be selected from each of the following community groups: business, labor, parents, community services, and early childhood education. Four at-large board members may be appointed by the Policy Board.

3.4 The Policy Board shall meet a minimum of eight (8) times a year.

3.5 The Policy Board, by resolution adopted by a majority of the members, may delegate to the Executive Committee the management of the affairs of the XYZ Child Development Center.

3.6 A quorum of one over half of the duly constituted Policy Board shall be able to transact business.

Article IV. Officers

4.1 The Policy Board shall elect annually from their number a President, First Vice President, Second Vice President, Secretary, and Treasurer, who shall constitute the Executive Committee.

    4.1.1 The offices of President, Second Vice President, and Treasurer shall be filled by election in odd-numbered years. These officers shall serve for two years.

    4.1.2 The offices of First Vice President and Secretary shall be filled by election in even-numbered years. These officers shall serve for two years.

    4.1.3 Each officer may serve only two consecutive terms in an office.

4.2 The President shall preside at all meetings of the Policy Board and of the Executive Board.

4.3 The First Vice President shall preside and perform the duties of the President in the President's absence.

4.4 The Second Vice President shall preside and perform the duties of the President in the absence of both the President and First Vice-President.

4.5 The Secretary shall record and preserve the minutes of all meetings of the Policy Board and of the Executive Committee.

4.6 The Treasurer shall keep the Policy Board informed of the financial status of the center. The Treasurer shall countersign checks in excess of a designated amount as authorized by the Policy Board. The Treasurer shall be a member of the Finance Committee. Auditing shall be done yearly.

Figure 4–1
Sample bylaws

Article V. Staff

5.1 The Policy Board shall appoint the manager of the XYZ Child Development Center.

5.2 The manager shall employ such staff as are required to carry out the purposes and objectives of the XYZ Child Development Center in accordance with policies established by the Policy Board.

    5.2.1 The manager shall keep the Policy Board fully informed on all aspects of the XYZ Center's program.

    5.2.2 The manager shall keep a record of all information of value to the XYZ Center and shall be the medium of communication between all units of the XYZ Center and the Policy Board.

Article VI. Organization

6.1 The work of the XYZ Child Development Center shall be organized under the standing committees named in Article VII of these Bylaws and under such other committees as shall be authorized by the Policy Board.

6.2 The membership of all committees, excluding the Executive Committee, shall be appointed by the President.

Article VII. Standing Committees

7.1 *Committee on Personnel.* This committee shall be headed by the Second Vice President.

    7.1.1 This Committee shall recommend the appointment of the manager of the XYZ Child Development Center.

    7.1.2 This Committee shall serve as the screening group for center staff.

7.2 *Committee on House and Grounds.* This committee shall be headed by the First Vice President.

    7.2.1 This Committee shall handle problems related to equipping and maintaining the facility of the XYZ Child Development Center.

    7.2.2 This Committee shall make recommendations for any improvements, expansion, or renovation.

7.3 *Committee on Finance.* This Committee shall be headed by the Treasurer.

    7.3.1 This Committee shall prepare the budget with the manager.

    7.3.2 This Committee shall assist in obtaining funds necessary for the operation of the center.

7.4 *Committee on Program.* This Committee shall handle problems dealing with the child care services program.

7.5 *Committee on Nominations.* This Committee shall be headed by the President.

    7.5.1 This Committee shall prepare the slate of officers to fill any vacant positions or list those rotating up for election.

    7.5.2 New board members shall take office at the January board meeting.

Article VIII. Amendments

8.1 Amendments to these Bylaws may be proposed at any regular meeting of the Policy Board having a quorum of three present. The vote on the proposed amendment shall be taken at the next meeting of the Policy Board and requires a two-thirds majority to pass.

Figure 4–1, continued
Sample bylaws

Start with a small group that you can afford to invite to a simple dinner while you get acquainted. Keep meetings short with planned agendas so as not to infringe heavily on people's schedules. If you want to keep things informal, you may keep dated notes on your organization's activities, participants, and accomplishments rather than use a set of bylaws for your advisory committee. Once you become acquainted with these individuals, you will be able to call them for advice as particular situations arise.

DECISIONS, DECISIONS . . .

 Your center's policy board, in an effort to accommodate the needs of working parents, has decided to offer an additional service that would allow mildly ill children to continue coming to the center rather than exclude them, as has been the practice. How will you tap the expertise of your advisory board to help you carry out this plan?

WHY PLANNING IS IMPORTANT

The owner of a winning baseball team once said, "Luck is the residue of design." In other words, success does not occur by accident. It results from careful planning. Planning charts a course by which goals can be reached most effectively. You will meet with the responsible employees in each unit to plan their work and to delegate work to them. Some beginning-level employees may need very specific assistance as they learn to plan. One cannot assume that if given the time the worker will produce the written plans needed—lesson plans, activity plans, menus, maintenance plans, record-keeping plans, and the like.

When planning is undertaken by staff members and the course is outlined so that all understand clearly and reach agreement, then everyone can follow the directions required for success. Everyone will know what must be done to contribute to the goals of the organization. All units—classroom units, food service unit, service units, and so on—will know what they must do to help reach the goals. Plans for emergencies should be posted, for example, when inclement weather keeps children from using the play yard or when the head teacher is absent.

Planning helps develop an *esprit de corps* among staff members. Not only do they get better acquainted working together to formulate plans, but they also develop a common sense of purpose while making plans. Consequently, they feel a joint obligation to work toward the fulfillment of those plans.

Planning specifies in writing what is to be accomplished. For example, your center's plan to add a new classroom becomes a goal that can be measured during the process of controlling (discussed in Chapter 8). Planning requires many steps and numerous pads of paper for preliminary drafts of various types of plans. Forms for planning can be provided. (See Chapter 14 for forms for planning children's curricula.)

When planning for infant caregiving, each caregiver must have time to talk and nurture each infant, making the infant-adult ratio especially important.
University of South Carolina Child Care Center, Columbia

TIME FOR PLANNING

Planning is very time-consuming, and time set aside for planning is often eaten away by what seem like more pressing concerns. The wise manager, however, recognizes that planning is an investment that will save time and energy in the future. Therefore, do not allow your planning time to be interrupted by telephones or casual visitors if you hope to be most efficient. Effective planning is closely related to high-quality outcomes. When you, as manager, are allocating time for tasks for your staff, you should realize that they, too, need planning time if they are to accomplish the professional job you expect. You too should be paid for your planning function as manager. And teachers, food service personnel, and others also should be paid for their planning. Teachers' planning, menu planning, and health planning are covered in related chapters later in the book.

Paid planning time is required in the accreditation criteria.[3] Public schools expect teachers to use time after school each day for planning and organizing for the next day and beyond. In addition, public schools reserve inservice days when children do not attend school. Inservice days can be used for planning and other curricular issues. If teachers operate two classes of kindergartners each day, they have a great deal of planning to do. It is very difficult for kindergarten teachers with two groups to provide the individual attention they would like for each child.

---

[3] Bredekamp (ed.), *Accreditation Criteria & Procedures*, p. 37.

Good planning is needed to pro-vide the space, materials, and support that children need to play cooperatively.
Early Learning Center, Appalachian State University, Boone, NC

This is one reason that some schools are moving toward full-day kindergarten, with teachers having only one group for a longer period each day.

The new "full day" is equal to the elementary school day, not to a full 8-hour day that helps working parents by providing child care. Those before- and after-school services needed by many school-age children, if available, are offered by a different organization within the school and require careful planning to serve the children's needs for a change in pace.

Finding time for planning in a busy child development center requires careful management. However, since planning is so essential to the achievement of goals in high-quality programs, one of your first tasks is to designate time for planning. Both designation of planning time and respect for that planning time are required. This means that once scheduled, it is essential that the time actually gets used for planning. Such designations may mean an evening meeting or a weekend retreat at center expense for centerwide planning. It can mean simply 2 or 3 hours of designated time each week for teachers to make plans for their classrooms while someone else manages the children. Of course, such arrangements are costly in time and dollars, but unplanned programs are also costly because they are far less likely to deliver the quality of services promised to children and their families.

Managers often discover that staff members need assistance with planning. Managers should meet with small groups to generate curriculum ideas, discuss interaction processes, perform evaluations, and so forth. At other times, staff members need help with planning for individual children, understanding behavior, and discovering ways the curriculum can help alleviate part of a problem the teachers face in the classroom.

Pairing less experienced staffers with the more experienced and suggesting specifically that your purpose is for the latter to assist the former in planning and organizing the unit can facilitate cooperation. Without a verbal assignment in the presence of both parties, one may feel that it is not appropriate to advise the other.

Of course, once planning is done, materials must be assembled, rooms and play yard arranged, and other actions taken that will take time and are more efficiently done when children are not present. Time spent in having everything ready for children is one of the best ways of preventing behavior problems. Busy children are seldom bad! Some of the allotted paid time should be allowed for these organizational tasks, which will be discussed in more detail in Chapter 5.

Decisions, Decisions . . .

 Discuss what you as the manager might say when assigning Theresa, a new teacher's aide, to work with a head teacher. You would like for the teacher to "mentor" the new worker, training her to help plan and encouraging her to become effective with the children. If you have been the new person in a similar situation, reflect on how you were trained or mentored.

STEPS IN THE PLANNING PROCESS

Managers generally use an established series of steps when planning, according to Dressler. Attention to these steps ensures attention to important details and prepares the unit for measuring performance at a later date.[4]

Step 1. Define the Central Concept of Your Child Development Center

What are the services your center will provide to society? How will your center create those services? Will your center have some distinctive services or methods of creating services? The policy board and the manager will take this step together. For example, you can state, "The ABC Center shall provide for 10 hours a day developmentally appropriate care and education for children 18 months to 6 years of age."

Step 2. Establish Goals That Your Center Will Pursue

Your center's objectives or goals will be based on the statement of the central concept. For example, one objective might be to provide a full-day child development program for forty 3- and 4-year-olds.

---

[4] Dressler, *Management Fundamentals*, p. 29.

A **goal** is defined as a specific achievement to be attained at a future date. For example, "Within 2 years from [date], an infant care center will be in operation."

Goals must first state clearly what service the organization is chartered to perform. Organizations may have numerous goals or useful targets that are being pursued simultaneously. For example, a child development center may pursue two goals simultaneously: (a) to enroll 10% more minority children within 2 years and (b) to increase employee benefits within 1 year.

Step 3. Develop Planning Assumptions and Forecasts

Do you know how many young children there are in your community? Population and birthrate figures help you estimate or forecast the potential demand for your child development services.

Do you know how many centers there are in your community and the extent of their services, costs, locations, and other details? Are industries or labor unions becoming involved in children's care? How many centers have been established recently or have gone out of business? This information should be available through licensing officials and will help you make judgments regarding the need for a new service.

Considering the ecosystem framework presented in Chapter 2, what is the forecast of potential and present jobs for mothers of young children in your community? Is the region attracting new businesses? If so, where are they locating? Are opportunities available in shopping malls and supermarkets? Is there an educational institution where parents of young children may be enrolling and thus need child care? Do single fathers need child care services? What is the community knowledge base regarding early childhood programming? Would families prefer one program or philosophy over another? How much can parents afford to pay?

These questions are important in planning regardless of whether your center is a profit or nonprofit institution. Accurate forecasting based on reasonable assumptions must be done before other plans are made.

Forecasting the number of children needing child development services is often of concern to managers and boards of directors. The public schools generally carry out a school census each year to enable them to forecast needs for classrooms and teachers for each age. People considering other types of child development centers might have access to the public school data, or they may wish to take their own census to survey the needs. They may develop and carry out a **needs survey** or **needs assessment**. By using a form similar to Figure 4–2 and questioning residents door to door in a neighborhood, you would discover the number, ages, and present care and education arrangement of the children in that community.

Perhaps you are considering the purchase of a child development center advertised for sale. Or your local board president is suggesting embarking on a new service in your present center or moving to a new site. It would be to the manager's advantage to know a lot about the neighborhood and how it has changed over time. Perhaps you will conclude that the neighborhood has become a community

Note: We wish to find out if families are in need of services—schools or child care—for their young children.

Name _____ Date _____

Address _____ Phone _____

_____

1. Please write the number of children you have in each age living in your home.

   a. None _____ f. 4 years old _____
   b. Below 1 year _____ g. 5 years old _____
   c. 1 year old _____ h. 6 years old _____
   d. 2 years old _____ i. 7 years old _____
   e. 3 years old _____ j. 8 years old _____

2. Do you hire a person to provide child care in your home? Yes _____ No _____

3. Listed below are several services for children. If you are currently using any of these for your child or children, write the age of the child and hours per week in the blank spaces provided.

	Age of Child	No. of Hours/Week
a. Family day care (home)	_____	_____
b. Child care center	_____	_____
c. Nursery school	_____	_____
d. Kindergarten	_____	_____
e. After-school care	_____	_____
f. Special education	_____	_____
g. Drop-in center	_____	_____
h. Other _____	_____	_____
i. None _____	_____	_____

4. If you are not now using a service such as one of those above, would you like to have such a service? Yes _____ No _____

5. If yes, indicate the type of service you need _____

6. If yes, indicate the hours and days of the week and number and ages of your children who would use this service.

   Number of children _____ Ages _____ Hours _____ Days _____

   How much would you be willing to pay each week?_____

   Where would you like the service to be located?_____

*Survey group name _____ Phone _____

Survey group address _____

Thank you. _____

Figure 4–2
Child development services need survey

with few young children. Thus, you might decide not to add a new service or not to buy out other owners who may have forecast that their enrollment is expected to drop and are hoping to sell their center to some unsuspecting client.

A needs survey, such as the one shown in Figure 4–2, can be useful to any group such as religious congregations when they are considering opening a child care facility in their church buildings. The questionnaire is easily inserted in a weekly newsletter, to be returned the following week. Besides serving the needs of families of the congregation, services for others could be planned by surveying the needs of nonmembers in the surrounding neighborhood. Churches frequently consider a child care program to be a helpful community service and thus part of their ministry.[5]

Forecasting should be done as carefully as possible. Managers generally find that forecasts are more optimistic than the immediate resulting enrollments. Consequently, managers must be prepared to be underenrolled for perhaps a year. It takes time for the reputation of a center to become known and for parents to shift to patronizing it.

Step 4. Evaluate Your Center's Resources

Resource types are financial, managerial, personnel, building and yard space, and equipment. Based on your evaluation, some programs or expansions may be more or less feasible. For example, if you have someone who knows how to manage an infant nursery, if space is available, if you already have cribs and other equipment, and if you have adequate financial backing, then planning to add an infant care unit may be relatively simple. If one type of resource is absent, the project faces added difficulties.

Step 5. Develop Alternatives

Alternatives or options must be present for real choices to be made. Creative thinking develops alternatives. One of the most important managerial tasks is to develop and maintain a climate that encourages the creativity of individual board and staff members. Creative people require room to move and think. A variety of alternatives may be suggested by creative staff, management, or a combination of the two. The essence of effective decision making is ascertaining and testing promising options or alternatives.

A wise manager uses groups and committees to help develop alternatives. When staff members participate in generating alternatives, they tend to accept the resulting choice. Remember that parents have insight, expertise, and connections that make them a fertile source of ideas. Ask them to help, too.

---

[5] Eileen W. Lindner, Mary C. Mattis, and June R. Rogers, *When Churches Mind the Children: A Study of Day Care in Local Parishes* (Ypsilanti, MI: High/Scope Press, 1983). Also see National Council of Churches, *Congregations and Child Care: A Self-Study for Churches and Synagogues and Their Early Childhood Programs* (Washington, DC: National Association for the Education of Young Children, 1991).

Step 6. Test Alternatives Against the Resources, Goals, and Central Concepts of Your Center

During brainstorming for alternatives, some far-out ideas may be put forward; yet to be realistic in decision making, you must weigh alternatives in relation to your center's central concepts, resources, and goals. The timeliness of alternatives may be a consideration. For example, in times of economic prosperity expansion alternatives may be considered, whereas during an economic downturn alternatives related to cutting back may be called for.

Step 7. Decide on a Plan

After making sure you have the available facts, you are ready to make a decision on a plan. Talk over the issues with everyone in your unit to be sure you have heard all points of view. Sort out and clarify your own thoughts and feelings. Knowing that personal moods could adversely affect a decision, delay decisions to another time if you or others are tired or grouchy. Avoid overstressing that a decision is final. Overstatement may box you in to a path that you would like to get out of later. Recognize each individual's personal values, and be open-minded to what others say.

Step 8. Implement the Plan

Implementing the plan is the action stage—and the exciting one. Organizing material resources, staffing the project with qualified people, and giving leadership as action moves ahead are all required.

Step 9. Evaluate the Plan

Checking up on every step as the plan is being accomplished is the needed evaluative or controlling function of a manager. It is essential to see that the plan is carried out and to check for quality—whether it is the quality of a floor covering or a human relationship. Evaluations and corrective action following evaluations are essential in every enterprise.

The world changes, people change, needs change, and plans must therefore change through periodic reevaluations to be sure aspects of the plan fit today's conditions and can readily be changed to fit tomorrow's.

Managers must be in the forefront of changes and must be looking ahead to be ready for those changes.[6] Years ago, when public school buildings were overflowing with children, a plan for introducing a prekindergarten program for 3- and 4-year-olds would have fallen on deaf ears. Today, with classrooms empty in many districts, administrators are more open to the notion of allocating classrooms for prekindergartners. Therefore, plans that formerly included only kindergarten now are being updated to include the younger children. The ratio-

---

[6] See Bettye Caldwell, "Should Four-Year-Olds Go to School?" *Young Children* 38:4 (May 1983), pp. 48–50.

nale includes (a) better preparation of the children, (b) service essential to parents working outside the home, (c) jobs for teachers, (d) efficient use of existing physical plants, and (e) a significant service to the general community. Before- and after-school care programs in the public schools are finally becoming part of the educational system in many cities in response to a pressing need. School-age child care is being extended to summer and vacation periods to accommodate working parents of school-age children.

A manager of a private center who sees the public schools moving toward accepting 3- and 4-year-olds will realize that many of the children being served in the private center will move into the free or low-cost public school. Will some private centers, like some harness makers who lost out to automobiles, just give up and quit? Or will the centers shift with the times and capitalize on the fact that they are likely to offer more comprehensive services than the public school programs? The longer daily schedule of a private center, for example, is more convenient for working parents and does not leave them without child care during summers and holiday seasons. In addition, by providing care for younger children than those accepted by public schools, private centers offer families the convenience of one drop-off and pick-up point for all the children in a family. Some private centers have even been able to contract with public schools to set up before- and after-school programs in school buildings. Other centers have worked out agreements with corporations, using either a **vendor approach** or a **corporate group rate approach**. In the first instance, the corporation guarantees direct payment to one or more centers for a specific number of child care spaces; in the second, the corporation pays a fee in return for reduced rates for their employees.[7]

DECISIONS, DECISIONS . . .

 Many employers are adopting family-friendly policies such as providing on-site child care, resource and referral services, and flex time options. Discuss the impact these policies might have on existing child development programs.

TYPES OF PLANNING

You can expect planning for your center to have several phases. Circulate as many rough drafts of plans as are needed among the staff for feedback before final budgeting and funding take place. Planning in a child development center may be considered **directional planning**, that is, giving the staff the broad direction in which they are expected to move. Directional planning is a characteristic of human service organizations. Plans calling for expanding services or retrenching are examples of directional planning.

---

[7] Sandy Duncan and Donna Thornton, "Marketing Your Center's Services to Employers," *Child Care Information Exchange* 89 (January/February 1993), pp. 53–56.

With good planing, simple materials like plain water, paintbrushes, and a sidewalk on a sunny day can provide an enjoyable group experience for children.
Early Learning Center, Appalachian State University, Boone, NC

Management by objectives is contrasted with directional planning. Fulmer states:

> Management by Objectives (MBO) is a system of setting up organizational objectives which then become the beginning, the middle, and the end of the operation. The objectives tell everyone where they are going; departure from the optimum path to those objectives causes corrective action to be initiated. Comparison with those objectives becomes the ultimate criterion for success.[8]

Management by objectives "is a participative system of managing in which managers look ahead for improvements, think strategically, set performance objectives at the beginning of a time period, develop action and supporting plans, and ensure accountability for results at the end of the time period."[9]

Innovative planning may offer exciting possibilities for early childhood professionals and parents. Innovative planning is a technique for getting concerned people together for the purpose of brainstorming possibilities for a new service or a new direction. Techniques focusing on bringing out innovative ideas might be used when new programs are being developed at the state and national levels. Professionals in organizations and agencies seeing trends developing may anticipate needs requiring legislative attention. As interest develops,

---

[8] Robert M. Fulmer, *The New Management* (Upper Saddle River, NJ: Prentice Hall, 1983), p. 96.
[9] Paul Mali, *MBO Updated: A Handbook of Practices and Techniques for Managing by Objectives* (New York: Wiley, 1986), p. 35.

creative thinking may be needed to envision how the ideas could be put into practice in given communities.

Occasionally, planning grants have been available. Or groups have donated their planning time with the expectation of being involved and benefiting if and when the final plan is adopted. For example, in the 1980s a coalition of organizations mapped strategy for federal legislation to help with child care as the needs became apparent, with 60% of mothers with children under 5 in the labor force. The result of their combined efforts was the 1990 Child Care Bill. In another example, North Carolina's "Smart Start" program provides state money to selected counties where broad-based community coalitions have identified needs and developed plans for enhancing services to children and families. These plans might include the establishment of new programs. Or they might provide support for existing programs, by training providers to work with children with disabilities, for example. A percentage of the state grant must be matched by corporate contributions.

Innovative planning in a center could be used for retrenchment, as well as for expansion into new programs. The leadership—manager or board president—generally sets the stage for brainstorming, giving information about forthcoming possibilities. Getting small discussion groups involved in making extensive lists of creative ideas without regard for the reality of present restraints or structures will lead to ideas triggering other ideas, in a synergistic effect—meaning that the total effect is greater than the effects taken independently.

Following brainstorming sessions, a committee may group the ideas into categories. Additional discussion sessions may follow. Perhaps another committee has met to devise a sample needs survey, and yet another committee has met to explore costs, locations, services, human skills, and so on, needed for some of the major categories proposed. Openness is desirable at all stages. People who are involved will feel more committed to the final outcome. In planning child development services, professionals should be careful to involve parents who can represent the user-consumer perspective. Eventually tentative and specific proposals can be developed by representative committees or task forces. If funding does become available, the reports of work already accomplished provide a basis for a final proposal for developing a new program or revising an existing program. (For information on writing funding proposals, see Chapter 9.)

Unit planning is the regular planning specific to each unit's operation. Unit planning goes on in the food service unit, the classrooms, the transportation unit, and so on. Staffing patterns will determine authority in those units. As manager, you delegate responsibility for planning to staff members who are qualified to carry out the responsibility. As you determine systems for communicating about unit plans with staff members in various units, your role will be that of a coordinator of the several units, keeping each unit's plans attuned to the overall standards, policies, and procedures. The total ecological framework within your center will come into focus as units use space and resources and meet the needs of children and their parents.

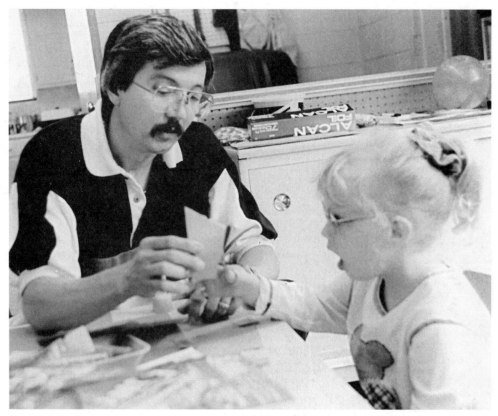

Supportive adults provide just the right amount of help for children to succeed at new experiences.
Lucy Brock Child Development Center, Appalachian State University, Boone, NC

POLICIES, PROCEDURES, AND RULES

Policies in your center, agency, or school will generally be established by the policy board after careful, thoughtful deliberation. Written policies, procedures, and rules aid consistent and timely decision making and discourage decisions being made without sufficient information. They are the blueprint for achieving the established goals of the center.

Policies should be stated in general terms to allow flexibility in dealing with specific situations. They should be put into writing and given to board members, staff, and parents. Once established, policies should be followed consistently. If they prove unworkable or if changing circumstances warrant it, changes should be made by formal board action. Finally, policies should be as complete as possible, covering all relevant categories: services to be provided, administration, and dealings with staff, children, and families. Some policies are required by state licensing regulations. Michigan, for example, requires that centers provide parents with policies for admission and withdrawal, food services, discipline, and schedule of operation.

Suppose, for example, that you are the manager of the ABC Center mentioned earlier, whose central concept is to "provide for 10 hours a day developmentally appropriate care and education for children 18 months to 6 years of age." Because your mission is to provide *appropriate* care and education, and research has established the link between staff training and quality of care,[10] you and your board have established the policy that the center will hire only teachers holding a valid early childhood credential or endorsement.

For each policy, your center will need procedures and rules for implementing that policy. **Procedures** specify how to handle certain tasks. **Rules** state particular detail regarding a procedure or how it is carried out. The procedure for implementing your staffing policy, for example, might be this:

> For each opening for a teacher, a job specification will be developed, stating the requirement that a candidate must hold a valid early childhood certificate or endorsement. Job specifications will be circulated in the state university placement centers where early childhood teacher preparation programs exist and in state associations where experienced teachers would likely see the notice. A nondiscriminatory hiring policy is in effect.

The following rule spells out in detail how the manager is to ensure compliance with the center's stated policy and procedure regarding teaching staff:

> The manager is expected to check the potential teacher's certificate personally to be sure that it is valid and of the type specified.

DECISIONS, DECISIONS . . .

 What procedures should the ABC Center develop to implement its policy that it "accepts all children, families, and employees on a nondiscriminatory basis without regard to race, color, creed, gender, or disability"?

TIME, SCOPE, AND CYCLING OF PLANS

Plans differ as to how much **time** they cover. In some centers a long-range plan covers only 1 year; in another it might be over 5 years. Some plans that are called short-range may cover a year or less.

The **scope** of plans differs, too. A comprehensive plan may cover the entire child care center or elementary school. Or plans can be narrower in scope, covering only one classroom or one service, such as the food service.

The level of the planning also influences the scope of plans. The classroom teachers develop plans that are implemented only in their classrooms. The

---

[10] Roger Neugebauer, "Cost and Quality Study Findings Unveiled," *Child Care Information Exchange* 102 (March/April 1995), pp. 80–81.

manager develops plans covering all the classrooms in a center. If several centers function within one organization, a superplan is probably made to cover them all.

Repetitiveness is also a feature of plans. A skeleton plan may cover the regular routine of a center, with teachers fitting in details on a weekly and monthly basis. Cycle menus and curriculum cycles are examples of planning for repetitive tasks. **Contingency plans** for emergencies can be repeated and should be made to aid decision making. For example, during inclement weather the playground may be unusable; a general plan for sharing an indoor space for large-motor activity of children avoids confusion for both adults and children, because needed changes in routines are known accurately in advance. A contingency plan for coping when illness strikes staff members is also essential. A plan for evacuating in case of fire or seeking protection in case of hurricane or tornado alerts is required, often by law.

PLANNING CATEGORIES

Plans are required at many levels in a child development center. The policy board sets the central concepts that encompass the broad objectives of the center. For example, the board might say, "We will provide 10 hours of child care for 60 children each working day throughout the year." The board then hires a manager to carry out the plans and allocates the funds. The manager, knowing that monitoring and controlling for quality are integral parts of management, will fit the control function into all plans to help ascertain when a plan has effectively been carried out. The manager will periodically report on progress to the policy board, when applicable.

On another level, the manager carries out the managerial functions—planning, organizing, staffing, leading, and monitoring and controlling—to maintain and improve the operation, delegating to qualified staff responsibility in appropriate areas for creating and delivering services.

The following categories of plans are usually required; each will be discussed in forthcoming chapters:

1. Children's programs
2. Physical plant and equipment
3. Staffing and staff relations
4. Food service
5. Children's health and safety
6. Budgetary matters
7. Parental relations
8. Public relations

Certain minimum standards are required by governmental licensing agencies in each state. Every manager must be fully aware of these standards and plan, organize, and give leadership to the staff in order that their services meet minimum standards. Forward-thinking managers will also want to be familiar with standards, such as NAEYC's accreditation guidelines, that go beyond minimum requirements and incorporate these in their planning.

CONCLUSION

Planning is a primary task of managers. Plans generally start with the policy board, which sets the central concepts of the center, allocates the money, and hires a manager. The manager has overall responsibility for planning, organizing, and delegating responsibilities to other staff members. Staff members participate in planning, especially where their units are involved. Nine steps in planning as well as policies, procedures, and rules have been discussed. Directional planning, management by objectives (MBO), innovative planning, and unit planning have been defined.

APPLICATIONS

1. Recall a place where you have worked or volunteered. Write a summary of the following (do not use names): What planning was done? Who did the planning? In your evaluation, was planning sufficient for meeting the objectives of the service? Did the place operate smoothly? Discuss with classmates.
2. Write three policies that pertain to the place where you have worked or volunteered. Following each policy, indicate who developed or articulated it.
3. Write three procedures that pertain to the place you have worked or volunteered. What is your evaluation of the procedures employed?
4. Imagine that your class has been commissioned to develop the first child care facility for a space station in outer space. Using each of the planning steps, explore this task with your classmates. Start by electing a manager. Use a chalkboard or large easel paper to list ideas and plans to enable everyone to become involved in the planning.
5. Each class member is to call or visit a different local center and secure a copy of the policy booklet or other printed matter containing policies, procedures, or rules. Discuss in class.
6. Add articles on planning to your Management Notebook.

STUDY QUESTIONS

1. Define planning.
2. List the categories of planning tasks in a child development center.
3. Explain the function of a policy board.
4. Describe the role of bylaws for the policy board. What are the avenues for changes in the bylaws?
5. Define an advisory board, telling how it differs from a policy board in function and composition.

6. List and define the steps in the planning process.
7. Explain what a needs survey is and describe its components.
8. Define and differentiate policies, procedures, and rules.
9. Define and differentiate directional, innovative, and unit planning.

SUGGESTED READINGS

Albrecht, Kay M., and Margaret C. Plantz (eds.). *Developmentally Appropriate Practice in School-Age Child Care Programs*. Alexandria, VA: Project Home Safe, American Home Economics Association, 1991.

Association for Childhood Education International. "Infants and Toddlers with Special Needs and Their Families." Wheaton, MD: Author, 1993.

Bredekamp, Sue (ed.). *Accreditation Criteria & Procedures of the National Academy of Early Childhood Programs*. Washington, DC: National Association for the Education of Young Children, 1991.

Bredekamp, Sue (ed.). *Developmentally Appropriate Practice in Early Childhood Programs Serving Children from Birth through Age 8*. Washington, DC: National Association for the Education of Young Children, 1987.

Cherry, Clare, Barbara Harkness, and Kay Kuzma. *Nursery School & Day Care Management Guide*. Belmont, CA: Lake, 1987.

Godwin, A., and I. Schrag. *Setting Up for Infant Care: Guidelines for Centers and Family Day Care Homes*. Washington, DC: National Association for the Education of Young Children, 1988.

Gonzalez-Mena, Janet, and Dianne W. Eyer. *Infants, Toddlers, and Caregivers*, 3d ed. Mountain View, CA: Mayfield, 1993.

Greenman, Jim. "Places for Babies: Infants and Toddlers in Groups. *Child Care Information Exchange* 92 (July/August 1993), pp. 46–49.

Hildebrand, Verna. *Guiding Young Children*, 5th ed. Upper Saddle River, NJ: Merrill/Prentice Hall, 1994.

Hildebrand, Verna. *Introduction to Early Childhood Education*, 6th ed. Upper Saddle River, NJ: Merrill/Prentice Hall, 1997.

Honig, Alice S. "High Quality Infant/Toddler Care Issues and Dilemmas," *Young Children* 41:1 (November 1985), pp. 40–52.

Moore, David. "Innovation and Entrepreneurship in Child Care." *Child Care Information Exchange* 55 (May 1987), pp. 22–26.

National Association for the Education of Young Children. *Facility Design for Early Childhood Programs: NAEYC Resource Guide*. Washington, DC: Author, 1987.

National Association for the Education of Young Children. *Infant Child Care: NAEYC Resource Guide*. Washington, DC: Author, 1987.

National Association for the Education of Young Children. *Kindergarten: NAEYC Resource Guide*. Washington, DC: Author, 1987.

National Association for the Education of Young Children. "NAEYC Position Statement on Licensing and Other Forms of Regulation of Early Childhood Programs in Centers and Family Day Care Homes." *Young Children* 42:5 (July 1987), pp. 64–68.

National Council of Churches. *Congregations and Child Care: A Self-Study for Churches and Synagogues and Their Early Childhood Programs*. Washington, DC: National Association for the Education of Young Children, 1991.

Neugebauer, Roger. "Status Report #8 on Early Childhood Education." *Child Care Information Exchange* 91 (May/June 1993), pp. 27–31.

Neugebauer, Roger. "20 Ideas for Improving Board/Staff Relations." *Child Care Information Exchange* 59 (January 1988), pp. 3–5.

O'Malley, Edward T. (ed.). *Visions for Infant/Toddler Care: Guidelines for Professional Caregiving.* Sacramento: California State Department of Education, 1988.

Rooney, Teresa. *Who Is Watching Our Children? The Latchkey Child Phenomenon.* Sacramento, CA: The Office, 1983.

Weiser, M. G. *Group Care and Education of Infants and Toddlers.* St. Louis, MO: Mosby, 1991.

Wolery, Mark, and Jan S. Wilbers (eds.). *Including Children with Special Needs in Early Childhood Programs.* Washington, DC: National Association for the Education of Young Children, 1994.

CHAPTER 5

Organizing

••

The goal is clear. Plans are made. Organizing begins. **Organizing** is defined as arranging elements (people, supplies, and equipment) and coordinating joint activities so that all of the interdependent parts contribute effectively to the desired goal. Organizing is the second component of the managerial process; that is, materials, equipment, space, and human energy must be assembled and integrated to get the program under way. An infinite number of details must be interrelated. The better you are at creating mental images of activities, their parts, and sequences, the better organizer you will be. Organizational arrangements are means to an end. The end is the goal of providing high-quality child care and educational services to families and children.

The experience of a child development specialist who was recently faced with the task of organizing services at a camp for orphans in war-ravaged Rwanda provides a good example of the value of organization. Jacqueline Hayden arrived at the camp with no supplies, no assistance, and no office space. Within 12 weeks, she managed to organize children into mixed-age, family-style groups, with an adult refugee assigned as "tent-mother"; found "foster families" for the youngest and most traumatized children; enlisted groups of children and adults to take care of cooking, laundry, foraging for supplies, making storybooks, and even making culottes to clothe the other children. Organization was certainly the key not only to the success of this child development program but to its very existence.[1]

---

[1] Jacqueline Hayden, "Applying Early Childhood Principles in Extraordinary Circumstances," *Child Care Information Exchange* 104 (July/August 1995), pp. 64–66.

A great deal of united effort and systematic interpretation is required to carry through the plans of the child development center. Such activity requires organizing. Your responsibility as manager is to assign or delegate to your staff the various tasks needed to accomplish goals previously outlined. They cannot read your mind; you must find some way to communicate. You are the coordinator—the orchestra director, if you will. As each accountant, cook, custodian, teacher, aide, or secretary does his or her tasks, the work of the center gets done, creating the services that you have promised to parents and the community.

Employees will have received job descriptions when hired. Thus, the tasks you delegate to them will not come as surprises. You will soon realize, if you do not already know, that some people can talk a good line when in a staff meeting but may have problems getting things organized to get the actual work done. You should be alert to this problem and work with these individuals to be sure they move their share of the work forward. You may have to help them break tasks into small bits so they may first accomplish one portion, then tackle the next bit, and so forth.

DECISIONS, DECISIONS . . .

 Think about a big job that you have tackled recently. How did you organize the task? Or did you? How would you break the job down into manageable steps if you were trying to teach someone else to do it?

TASK ANALYSIS

Looking at all the tasks required, how can you break them down into logical units? Who has talent appropriate for the tasks? How is coordination to be achieved, and how much coordination is needed? What services are provided for each classroom? Which type of control system will you establish to be sure the goals of your center are being achieved?

Once you know or have decided on how many staff members you have, the work of the center must be analyzed and delegated to these individuals. On receiving an assignment, the person makes an analysis of each of the many activities that come under the assignment. A form may be developed with the following questions to aid the employee with the analysis:

1. What activity must be done?
   What are the steps of the activity, listed in order?
2. Where is the activity to be performed?
3. When is the activity to be done?
4. What other staff member, if any, is involved?
   How is cooperation to be achieved?
5. What materials and equipment are needed?
6. What is the expected level of performance?

Materials for every activity must be assembled in an area suitable for the activity, a part of the teacher's organizing task.
Edgewood Cooperative Nursery School, East Lansing, MI

Some examples of task analysis will be presented later. The value of having the staff members do their own task analysis is that they concentrate more fully and get involved with making their own job description. A new employee may be able to make the task analysis while having the opportunity to work with someone who is already in the job.

The manager's task is to keep the broad picture in mind. Logical and excellent task decisions in child development centers generally result from a classroom organization where professionally trained teachers are in charge of each classroom. Regulations generally require a minimum of two teachers or caregivers per group of children—more adults if younger children are in the classroom. (See the accreditation criteria of the National Association for the Education of Young Children [NAEYC] for recommended staffing ratios.)[2]

To make decisions about group size and staffing ratios, you will need to become familiar with your state's minimum requirements. Appendix A

---

[2] Sue Bredekamp (ed.), *Accreditation Criteria & Procedures of the National Academy of Early Childhood Programs* (Washington, DC: National Association for the Education of Young Children, 1991). Also see Sue Bredekamp (ed.), *Developmentally Appropriate Practice in Early Childhood Programs Serving Children from Birth through Age 8* (Washington, DC: National Association for the Education of Young Children, 1987).

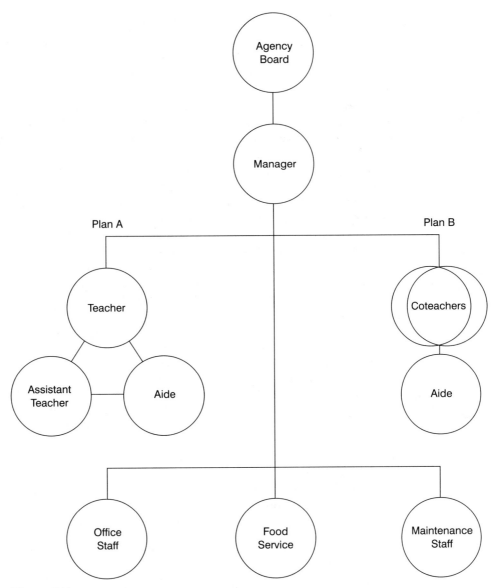

Figure 5–1
Organizational plan

provides a list of licensing agencies for each state. If you are a recently hired director, you can request a copy of your state's regulations from the appropriate agency. If you are a student, your instructor might be able to provide you with a copy to view.

Given an organization where major responsibility is delegated to the teachers in the classroom, the organizational chart would look similar to Figure 5–1.

AUTHORITY AND RESPONSIBILITY

In assigning certain authority to teachers or coteachers who manage their own class-rooms, a clear definition of responsibility is essential. For example, handling of business matters, such as the collection of fees, could remain the task of the manager's office. Each Monday morning a clerk meets parents as they arrive with their children. Fee payment and record keeping are routinely managed with most of the parents. Teachers do not concern themselves with fee collection. Teachers arrange space, storage, learning centers, and so on, according to the best professional recommendations, making adaptations for individuals and situations in their classrooms.

Giving teachers authority to manage their own classrooms is an example of **decentralizing authority**. This decentralization generally makes for a responsive, creative, and adaptive organization. This characteristic is highly desirable in child development centers because child development centers are people-centered operations. You will remember from the discussion in Chapter 2 that a central tenet of quality management is the empowerment of all staff members so that each one has the maximum feasible authority with which to carry out his or her responsibilities. Teachers who have the authority to manage their own classrooms will invest more creativity and energy than those who simply have the responsibility to carry out your plans.

Delegating these managerial functions to teachers requires an organizational system that allows paid time for these management functions. Adequate time set aside for planning and organization is sorely lacking in many centers today. Yet, in terms of improving services, it would be money well spent. As indicated in Chapter 4, paid planning time is stipulated in the accreditation criteria of NAEYC.[3]

Links among classrooms and the center's service units—maintenance, food service, and business—are essential. If families enroll siblings in more than one group, special attention may be needed for fostering sibling relationships. Here a need for openness in the organizational operation becomes evident. Also, in a decentralized plan a system for acquiring material, supplies, and equipment must be developed. Each teacher could be assigned a budget for use in the classroom. Teachers could make appropriate inventories and place requests for supplies, which can then be ordered collectively. In a centralized plan the manager would assume more responsibility for ordering, allocating, and distributing supplies.

DECISIONS, DECISIONS ...

A local club has just raised $1,000 for your center to purchase some new play equipment. Since your philosophy is to delegate as much authority as possible to your teachers, you ask them to decide how to spend the money. How can you accomplish this and yet have assurance that the money will be spent wisely, that is, on materials of high quality? How will you organize the task to accomplish both goals?

---

[3] Bredekamp (ed.), *Accreditation Criteria*, p. 37.

Task Analysis: Collecting Fees (Example for an Office Worker)

A. Activity: Collecting fees
    Receive cash or checks, write receipts, stamp checks, place in money box, thank parent.
B. Where: Front corridor table
C. When: 7 A.M. to 9 A.M. Monday, 11 A.M. to noon Monday, 1 P.M. to 2 P.M. Monday, 3 P.M. to 6 P.M. Monday; other times in the office
D. Other staff member: No
E. Equipment and materials:
    Adult table and chair
    Money box with lock
    Fee receipt book
    Account book
    Pencils and pens
    Calendar
F. Level of performance:
    Be accurate. Date and sign receipt. Write clearly.
    Be polite and friendly but quick.
    Record any deviation.
    Put money in a box with a lock.

Authority is granted to some employees to direct the work of other employees. The organizational chart shows this generally. In the B-type organizations (see Figure 5-1), the coteachers share authority. This type of organization is used when job specifications call for teachers of equal training and experience. It suggests a symbolic expectation of equal sharing of the work and responsibility.

Task Analysis: Serving Breakfast (Example for a Child Care Aide)

A. Activity: Serving breakfast
    Set tables with anticipated number of places.
    Welcome children.
    Bring food on menu for each child.
    Sit with children.
    See that each has what is needed.
    Encourage self-help and cleaning up after self.
    Replenish food as needed.
    Bring recording sheets if used.
B. Where: Breakfast room
C. When: 7 A.M. to 9 A.M. daily
D. Other staff members: Take directions from the cook
E. Equipment and materials:
    Tables, chairs, place mats, napkins, glasses, spoons, forks, cereal bowls, wastebasket, milk pitcher, juice pitcher
F. Level of performance:
    Be clean and sanitary with food.
    Encourage children to eat, but do not cajole.

Respond to child as an individual. (Some are more awake than others.)
Avoid leaving a child alone.
Talk to the children and not to adults.
Record what the children ate.

Some lines of authority are needed. Lines of authority help employees know where to turn for solutions to their problems. They also help parents and even children know who can make a final decision. Unless your center is very small, it is a good idea to put these lines of authority down on paper, in the form of a flow-chart or graph that clearly shows the chain of command. This visual representation can be supplemented with written policies informing parents and staff where to go with particular concerns. Clearly delegating responsibilities lets people know where you, as manager, will refer problems rather than attempting to make all decisions yourself. Avoid allowing yourself to be pushed into hasty decisions when your center's established procedure calls for cooperative decision making.

In a behavioral-style organization that is designed to be person centered, such as a child development center, communication skills should be practiced among all the staff in such a way as to facilitate the unit's goals. Techniques of conflict resolution and—better yet—techniques for minimizing conflicts will be essential skills for you, the manager.

SPAN OF CONTROL

Each classroom with a teacher or coteachers as manager (see Figure 5–1) is a departmental unit. Within this classroom the children and their parents are the consumers of the care and educational services planned and delivered. How many people can one or two teachers comfortably and effectively influence through their caring and teaching? The rhyme about the old woman who lived in the shoe is applicable here. What was the old woman's sphere of influence or span of control?

Span of control is a concept with implications for classrooms and centers. Generally, it refers to the number of subordinates reporting to the manager. In the case of child development centers, span of control may also refer to the number of children and their parents for and to whom the teacher or caregiver is responsible. Thus, span of control incorporates the factors of teacher-child ratio and group size. When close supervision is required—and individual attention and analysis are the hallmarks of high-quality service—span of control has particular significance.

Group Size

Support for smaller groups is clearly indicated in the National Day Care Study.[4] Concerning group size and activity subgroups, Ruopp et al. state:

---

[4] Richard R. Ruopp, J. Travers, F. Glantz, and C. Coelen, *Children at the Center: Final Report of the National Day Care Study*, Vol. 1 (Washington, DC: Department of Health, Education, and Welfare, 1978; Cambridge, MA: Abt, 1979), pp. xxvi–xxvii.

The most important finding for policy and practice is that traditionally regulated core characteristics—group size and caregiver/child ratio—do have a major impact on important outcomes for children and that specific combinations of these characteristics can achieve better quality care at lower costs.

An important dimension of this finding is that group size and staff/child ratio are, in the real world, inextricably linked. When center directors and regulators set a ratio, they must also set an associated group size *as a multiple of the selected ratio*. A ratio of one caregiver for every five children (1:5) is associated meaningfully with group sizes of 5, 10, 15, 20 and so forth, a ratio of 1:7 with group sizes of 7, 14, 21 and so on.

It is for this reason that the concept of *classroom composition*, which involves *both* group size *and* staff/child ratio, is so important. How classrooms are composed contributes greatly to differences in both quality and cost for each child.

The most powerful element of classroom composition for quality is absolute group size—the total number of children for whom one or more caregivers is responsible; moreover, differences in group size are only slightly related to differences in cost. Smaller groups are better; more desirable caregiver and child behavior and child test scores are predictably found in smaller groups even when staff/child ratio varies within the range of 1:5 to 1:10. In a group of 14 children with two caregivers the mathematical ratio is 1:7, just as the *mathematical* ratio for 28 children and four caregivers is 1:7. The *human* ratio is, for the caregivers involved, twice as much in the second case as the first. *Each* caregiver has 28, not 14, children's names and needs to know.

Just as group size is an important predictor of differences in quality, so is the staff/child ratio dimension of classroom composition the most powerful predictor of differences in the cost of core care (that is, care exclusive of additional important health and social services). Because day care is a labor-intensive service, even minor variations in ratio can account for large variations in the cost per child.

Hence, NDCS [National Day Care Study] *findings point toward ways of achieving higher quality at a slightly lower cost per child*. Decisions about classroom composition are decisions about group size which affect the quality of care each child potentially will receive; they are also decisions about ratio which ultimately can determine how many children are served or what wages can be paid for a fixed amount of money expended.

The findings of the National Day Care Study to keep group size under 20 were followed in the accreditation criteria of the NAEYC (p. 41 in that piece) cited earlier.

A review of more recent research on effects of group size and staff ratios supports and extends the findings of the National Day Care Study.[5] Children in smaller groups with better ratios experience more appropriate activities and fare better on several measures of development. This has been found especially true of infants and toddlers. Furthermore, although improving ratio and group size requirements does raise the cost of care somewhat, it does not seem to deter centers from becoming licensed or make care so expensive that parents no longer enroll their children. For example, Arizona saw a rise in the number of regulated centers, and Ohio saw an increase in the number of children enrolled when they took these steps to improve the quality of care and education available for their children.

---

[5] "Research into Action: The Effects of Group Size, Ratios, and Staff Training on Child Care Quality," *Young Children* 48:2 (January 1993), pp. 65–67.

Table 5–1
Adult-child ratios and maximum group sizes recommended by the National Association for the Education of Young Children, the American Public Health Association, and the American Academy of Pediatrics

Age of Child	Maximum Number of Children per Caregiver		Maximum Group Size	
	NAEYC	APHA/AAP	NAEYC	APHA/AAP
Under 12 months	4	3	8	6
13 – 24 months	5	3	12	6
25 – 30 months	6	4	12	8
31 – 36 months	7	5	14	10
3 years	10	7	20	14
4 and 5 years	10	8	20	16
6 – 8 years	12	10	24	20
9 – 12 years	14	12	28	24

Source: "Research into Action: The Effects of Group Size, Ratios, and Staff Training on Child Care Quality," *Young Children* 48:2 (January 1993), p. 65; and *Caring for Our Children: National Health and Safety Performance Standards: Guidelines for Out-of-Home Child Care Programs* (Washington, DC: American Public Health Association; Elk Grove Village, IL: American Academy of Pediatrics, 1992), p. 1.

ORGANIZING CLASSROOMS OR GROUPS

Managers who want to take group size as well as adult-child ratios into consideration when organizing classrooms will need to look beyond their state's licensing regulations. While the minimum standards for adult-child ratios are included in each state's licensing regulations, they vary widely from state to state, as we have seen. Furthermore, as the findings of the National Day Care Study suggest, even a one-to-one adult-child ratio will not ensure a high-quality experience for children, if the manager does not also consider the number of children to be cared for in one group or classroom. Imagine a room full of 20 crying babies! In spite of its importance, group size is addressed by licensing regulations in only 32 of the 50 states.[6]

At least two sets of standards do address this issue, however. NAEYC accreditation guidelines emphasize that small group sizes and fewer children per staff member are associated with higher-quality care. The recommendations of the American Public Health Association and the American Academy of Pediatrics support those of the NAEYC, and they are even more stringent since they do not make allowances for staff with higher levels of training to care for more children. Table 5–1 shows the adult-child ratios and maximum group sizes recommended by each organization for children of various ages.

---

[6] Children's Defense Fund, *The State of America's Children Yearbook 1995* (Washington, DC: Author, 1995), p. 121.

Teachers, who must dress children frequently, organize the space and equipment to relieve strain on their backs.
University of South Carolina Child Care Center, Columbia

People have been concerned about kindergarten sizes as related to outcomes for children. Teachers' unions have bargained for enrollments of 24 children with additional children up to 30 enrolled with the teacher's agreement and extra pay. When one teacher was asked to take more children for extra pay she replied, "I'm not a teacher because of the money. I'm teaching for children." They divided the group in half, and she ended up with 19 children in the morning and 19 in the afternoon. With 19 she had a real opportunity to do a special job of teaching each child and interacting with parents.

Although they are often introduced for other, less appropriate reasons, full-day kindergartens do offer one special advantage. Recall the concept of **human ratio** (as distinct from **mathematical ratio**) discussed earlier in the report of the National Day Care Study. A kindergarten teacher with 24 children in the morning and another 24 in the afternoon is dealing with a mathematical ratio of 1:24 but a human ratio of 1:48 because that is the number of names, personalities, and families to know. With one group of 24 and the extended time frame, a teacher can conceivably get to know each child and each family far better than with 48. Some of the same logic is offered in support of mixed-age groups of 5-, 6-, and 7-year-olds, in which a given child stays with the same teacher over a 3-year period. The teacher, child, and family are spared learning about each other anew every year and are able to develop deeper relationships.

Children learn to organize their belongings when storage spaces are clearly labeled and arranged by the entrance.
Michigan State University Child Development Laboratory, East Lansing

In Plan A, on the left in Figure 5–1, the teacher is clearly the top authority figure, with the assistant teacher responsible to the teacher and the aide responsible to both the teacher and the assistant teacher. Some child development center managers prefer Plan B, on the right in Figure 5–1, that is, to hire teachers of equal qualifications and give them coteaching responsibilities. In either case, the aide is responsible to both teachers. Especially in child care operations exceeding an 8-hour day, having coteachers with staggered times of arrival and departure makes considerable sense.

How classrooms are organized internally is part of organizing. The arguments for single-age groups and arguments for multiage groups are many. Strengths and weaknesses exist on each side. Some teachers are more effective with one age grouping than with another. Multiage groups are thought to be more "family-like," and older children learn to be helpful to younger ones. Some argue that activities in a single age group can be more challenging, whereas in multiage groups the hard or complex activities appropriate for older children may be avoided in planning because the younger children become frustrated by the older children's activities or are confused when they are excluded from some activity that is thought to be too hard or dangerous for them.

Experienced teachers working with 5-year-olds, who have been in child care for a number of years, know that most are ready for exposure to additional intellectual challenges. Thus, some time alone with their age-mates with planned language, literature, science, or field experiences would be helpful, even when the majority of their time is spent in multiage groupings. On the other hand, a mixed-age group allows opportunities for the 4-year-old who might be ready for some additional experiences to participate, while it avoids pressuring the 5-year-old who might not be ready to enjoy the same activities as his or her age-mates.

The decision about grouping should be determined by conferring with the staff and analyzing staff desires and capabilities as well as parental desires and the needs of individual children enrolled to determine the appropriate groupings for the current situation.

ORGANIZING SERVICES

Office Services

Child development centers are businesses and require a system for record keeping and interacting and communicating with parents and the public. Records must be kept for such matters as regulation compliance; financial matters such as fees, bills, rents, taxes, and so on; family names with home addresses and phone numbers, work addresses and phone numbers, and the like; vendors' addresses and phone numbers; services the center requires such as health, fire, and social services with names and addresses of contacts; and information on various professional organizations with which relationships might be developed.

A larger center usually hires an office person or secretary at least part-time. Smaller centers may attempt to get by with volunteer help, perhaps from a parent. It is shortsighted for qualified managers of child development centers to spend much of their time typing, sorting mail, filing, and answering the phone. A person to do these tasks can usually be hired at relatively small cost to the center, leaving the manager free to concentrate on major issues. If the manager has extra time, it could likely be spent more productively, for example, with teachers or parents.

The center's office is the "window to the world," so to speak. People receive their first impressions of your center through a phone call or visit to the center. Therefore, careful training of office staff is essential to be sure that information is given accurately and pleasantly. It is nice to hear a voice say amicably, "This is the XYZ Center. May I help you?"

A routine arrangement for collecting fees from parents, writing receipts, paying bills, banking money, and the like, must be instituted. An accounting system should be established with the aid of a qualified accountant. Payments of salaries, benefits, withholding and Social Security taxes, bills, rents, and the like should be made on time and in an approved manner. Accounting services may be contracted for by a center that does not hire a specially trained person.

Computer systems are useful in small businesses such as child development centers; therefore, managers should seek advice regarding computers and their continual new developments. With a little know-how of basic software, you might enjoy constructing your own spreadsheet to manage financial records or database of children's records. If you feel you are not ready yet for that step, parents with computer skills might be willing to help you set up such a program. Or, you can look into the wide array of software specifically designed for the management of child development programs. Professional journals and organizations regularly publish updated reviews of available software.[7] Sample tutorial disks or demonstrations are often available from software dealers on request. These enable the center managers to use the programs on their machines with an option to purchase. Software dealers provide hotline service to purchasers of their software. Instruction may come with the purchase as well.

Though using the computer is not difficult, an operator may need some time to learn to use the software and computer to their fullest extent. Training your bookkeeper to reap the full benefit of the computer system will increase your office budget item. Some older staffers may be fearful of attempting the conversion but become reassured once they start using computers.

Once you have the equipment, you will find it has many uses. Word processing, as opposed to typing, is such a delight, with errors being far more easily corrected. Centers will require time to convert all their paper forms to the computer. Even then printouts will be required. Desktop publishing techniques, using the computer, have made putting out newsletters remarkably easy. Some centers have parents sign in children at a computer. Inventory, payroll, and billing are handled by computer. Recording children's immunizations and generating reminders of needed boosters is made less tedious. Consult your public health department, which may be able to provide needed software for this task. Even lists with children's birthdays can be printed out.

Certain equipment is essential, such as a typewriter, calculator, file cabinet, storage cabinets, bookshelves, desk, chairs, and the like. Efficiently organizing and storing the center's various forms (admission, health, financial, and so on) and the needed office supplies should be accomplished early in order to facilitate handling routine matters.

Food Services

The food service standards of the U.S. Department of Agriculture are followed in both licensing regulations and accreditation. A qualified cook will be able to plan the meals and all the activities of the kitchen and dining room. As manager, you may have to plan the meals for a less qualified cook or contract for the services of a dietitian to plan the meals.

Regulations must also be met with regard to food services. The cook may just cook, with the manager doing purchasing or ordering of food; or the cook may provide the shopping lists of food and supplies needed to a purchasing division, if one exists. Purchasing, organization, and control must be carefully planned because of budget considerations and the risks of loss, waste, theft, and food spoilage. The U.S. Department of Agriculture food reimbursement program is discussed in Chapter 13, along with other details regarding food services.

Food service personnel organize the kitchen and dining area. All appliances and cupboards are to be put in spotless condition and kept that way through rou-

---

[7] See, for example, Roger Neugebauer, "Child Care Center Management Software Buying Guide (Ninth Annual Market Survey)," *Child Care Information Exchange* 104 (July/August 1995), pp. 87–100.

To teach children to do their share of the work, the teacher organizes a "jobs chart" with pictures and print that children "read" to discover their task for the day.
Michigan State University Child Development Laboratory, East Lansing

tine cleaning schedules. Routine storage must be organized and labeled for foods and supplies kept on hand. Inventory control is essential to prevent loss through improper storage or theft. Paper supplies present a fire hazard; therefore, storage should conform to fire regulations.

Adequate attention to kitchen and dining room sanitation is essential. A vacuum cleaner helps keep food bits cleaned up and will be helpful in discouraging food-eating insects and rodents. All staff must be firmly impressed with food-handling regulations, hand-washing requirements, and personal health and care regulations.

Keeping track of children who depart on irregular schedules has been organized by this center using a simple blackboard displayed where every adult can readily see it.
Sinclair Community College Early Childhood Center, Dayton, OH

Within the organization of food service, it is desirable, for economy and efficiency, to plan for links with the classroom. Thus, foods used as parts of various learning experiences can readily be purchased in large lots with other foods. These food items may be incorporated into regular menus. For example, having children squeeze their own orange juice for their snack requires an orange per child. A decrease in the usual snack-time beverage becomes appropriate.

A number of food items used in learning activities are not eaten. Play dough requires flour and salt, as an example. The cooks can be responsible for making fresh play dough periodically.

The organization chart does not show all the tasks that could be mentioned in the discussion of the cook's duties. Task analysis and a job description are needed. In the organizational plan it is important, for example, to stipulate who asks the cook to make play dough. Do teachers ask, or do they request play dough through the manager's office? If making it is specified in the job description for the cook or cook's assistant, then making play dough can become a simple routine activity like filling the napkin holders. If making play dough is not clearly specified, the cooks may feel burdened by the request.

As you organize the various functions and tasks associated with food service for your center, keep human factors clearly in mind. One of the hallmarks of excellence in the renowned early childhood centers of Italy—indeed, of many high-quality centers in this country—is the family atmosphere that is engendered when cooks and cleaning staff interact with the children regularly and become rich resources along with teachers. Even though your management techniques must be professional and business-like, your center will provide high-quality care to the extent that it resembles a home more than a business.

Maintenance and Cleaning Services

These services apply to the entire center, covering all the classrooms, service areas, and play yards. Cleanliness and safety are essential and very dependent on adequate attention to maintenance details on a daily, even hourly basis. A custodial-maintenance person may provide the most effective arrangement, with the center manager helping with overall goals and timetables. In small units, one individual may carry the total responsibility. The job specifications should be carefully drawn, because a person who can relate well to children is highly desirable. Women can be efficient in this position; limiting a search to men is shortsighted. In the organization's plan, procedures for acquiring maintenance tools, cleaning tools and supplies, and services are needed. A washer and dryer are considered a must by many managers for laundering clothing and bedding as well as dress-up clothes, aprons, and soft toys.

Maintenance and cleaning must be organized to ensure a sanitary, healthful, and safe environment. Duties include light and heavy cleaning, trash and garbage removal, storage and repair of equipment, painting and general upkeep, and disinfecting kitchen and food service areas and the toilet rooms. Carpeting presents special cleaning problems that must be considered before it is installed. Adequate cleaning (at least occasionally professionally done) is required to keep carpeting sanitary and odor-free.

Each unit's staff should be delegated some responsibility for preparing its unit for cleaning. The children enjoy helping in the classrooms. Food and waste paper should be removed from lockers. Objects that may appear unsightly should be picked up.

Maintenance personnel should regularly give attention to the outdoor space, being sure that it meets high standards of cleanliness and repair. Grass must be mowed when children are indoors or not at the center because of the danger that flying objects may be projected by lawn mowers. Children can be taught to be helpful in beautifying the yard. Parents may enjoy offering assistance or advice.

Transportation Services

Transportation services are important benefits to some customers of a children's center. Clearly, licensing standards for the qualification of drivers, seat belts for children, and extra adults are all essential. Having a bus or van does make trips somewhat easier compared to centers without a vehicle. Transportation is a costly item, and finances must be calculated carefully. It is also a safety item, and insurance must be adequately provided.

Emergency Services

Several emergency services must be organized in order for the staff to be prepared. For example, medical services, utility services, or repair services may be needed in a hurry. Prior arrangements help a center receive the right service at reasonable prices. A list of phone numbers of persons to call in emergencies should be posted near all phones. Be sure to include police and fire department numbers. Tornado and fire drills are required safety measures. Parents must be alerted as to the procedure for these drills and be assured that your center will follow procedures carefully in a major emergency.

CONCLUSION

Organizing the materials, equipment, space, and human energy to get the plans under way is the second step in the managerial process. Details flow from the type of service your center is designed to deliver. Specific decisions regarding the type of organization, organizational charts, authority, span of control, and task analysis all relate to managing a child development center.

APPLICATIONS

1. Choose four of the tasks given here, develop a task analysis, and list needed materials according to examples shown in text. Exchange analyses with your classmates. Discuss.
   a. Dishwashing
   b. Serving lunch
   c. Serving snack
   d. Mixing and baking cookies
   e. Mixing and setting Jell-O
   f. Preparing nap room
   g. Washing windows
   h. Dusting shelves and so forth
   i. Storing trash and garbage
   j. Cleaning toilet room
   k. Developing dramatic play–housekeeping area
   l. Creating literature area
2. Diagram the organizational chart for the place you worked. Evaluate the organization. (Omit names.)
3. Visit a child care center and make notes on organizational techniques observed. Discuss with your classmates what you saw.
4. Add task analysis (application 1) to your management notebook.

STUDY QUESTIONS

1. Define organizing. Give an example of an activity at the center you have been involved in helping to organize.
2. Define task analysis. List tasks that should be analyzed around a center with which you are acquainted.

3. Diagram the organizational plan for a center known best to you. List what you think are the pros and cons of this plan.
4. Define centralized and decentralized authority. Discuss the difference.
5. Define span of control. Tell how it relates to operating a child development center.
6. Make a chart showing group size, age, and staffing requirements under NAEYC accreditation, and beside them list the same requirements for your state's licensing. Discuss your experience regarding group size, age of children, and number of staff in relation to what you think was good for children.
7. Find out what your state allows and/or requires for kindergarten size. Discuss what this means to teachers. Do they teach two groups daily? Do they do any work with parents?
8. Inquire of your public school officials whether there is any movement toward full-day kindergartens or programs for children for before or after school hours. Discuss their reply in class.
9. List the areas of organization you feel needed in a center you know well. Visit a center you are unfamiliar with, and compare your perceptions of its organization with that of the center you know.
10. Write out a task analysis of one routine activity that one employee of a center typically does.

SUGGESTED READINGS

American Public Health Association and American Academy of Pediatrics. *Caring for Our Children: National Health and Safety Performance Standards: Guidelines for Out-of-Home Child Care Programs*. Washington, DC: Author, 1992.

The Children's Foundation. *1995 Child Day Care Center Licensing Study*. Washington, DC: Author, 1995.

Endres, J. B., and R. E. Rockwell. *Food, Nutrition and the Young Child*, 4th ed. Upper Saddle River, NJ: Merrill/Prentice Hall, 1994.

Goffin, Stacie G., and Claudia Q. Tull. "Problem Solving: Encouraging Active Learning." *Young Children* 40:3 (March 1985), pp. 28–32.

Harms, Thelma, and R. M. Clifford. *Early Childhood Environment Rating Scale*. New York: Teachers College Press, 1980.

Harms, Thelma, and R. M. Clifford. *The Infant-Toddler Environment Rating Scale*. New York: Teachers College Press, 1988.

Hildebrand, Verna. *Guiding Young Children*, 5th ed. Upper Saddle River, NJ: Merrill/Prentice Hall, 1994.

National Association for the Education of Young Children. "What Is Curriculum for Infants in Family Day Care (or Elsewhere)?" *Young Children* 42:5 (July 1987), pp. 58–62.

CHAPTER **6**

Staffing

··

People are the human resources that hold the key to meeting the goals of a service organization such as a child development center. Of course, many nonhuman resources—such as facilities, equipment, and supplies—are needed, but these resources stand idle or are ineffectively used without skilled people to put them into appropriate operation. Staffing is another major function of a manager. **Staffing** is the process of recruiting and dealing with the human resources required to perform the functions of the center.

A child development center is a labor-intensive operation. That is, lots of human energy or labor is essential for the center to reach its goals. No mechanical robots can perform the needed services. People's knowledge, skills, abilities, stamina, enthusiasm, and love are aspects of their human energy. Such attributes are called **human capital**. Close to 1 million people are employed in staffing child development centers in the United States. This is a rapidly expanding profession, with increases expected to continue well into the 21st century.

HUMAN CAPITAL IN THE CHILD DEVELOPMENT CENTER

To help understand the concept of human capital, you may recall that a capital investment is one for which you expect a later payoff. That is, if you invest your capital (dollars) in a factory by buying stock, you would expect dividends as the payoff for your investment and, hopefully, some capital gains if you sell your stock. Similarly, from human capital investments you expect a payoff when the new knowledge and abilities accumulated are put to work; they provide needed and improved services and products that yield a profitable return captured by individuals and also by society. Think of human capital as human assets.

Of course, children's human capital—knowledge, skills, and abilities—is expected to develop in the center. Research is now showing that an investment in children's preprimary education pays off later in less need for special education and fewer school failures.[1] Child development centers complement parents' contribution to the development of the human capital potential of children. Parents, for a variety of reasons, desire or need assistance with nurturing and educating their young children. At these ages, nurturing and educating go hand in hand whether programs are full-day or part-day, public or private.

Ideally every type of child development center should be considered a supplementary support system for the family, with goals for enhancing the human capital of the child and of the family members. Such centers would be warmly responsive to the needs, interests, and strengths of each child, parent, sibling, and even grandparent or guardian. A strong service orientation would prevail. Unfortunately, at this point many programs, in a misguided effort to offer "more than just child care," focus more on subject matter than on the total child and family and forget that much learning in the early years is incidental and naturally embedded in the day-to-day routines of caregiving. In their zeal to be "educational," these programs involve a lot of structured school-like activities, such as calendar, show-and-tell, or teacher-directed craft projects. At the other extreme, some centers focus so strongly on the caregiving that they fail to offer a stimulating program. They seem to assume that children are just marking time before school and, consequently, offer the same array of play materials day after day, with little or no effort to follow up on children's interests and ideas. Viewing all child development centers from the perspective of developing human capital, managers and staff can work together to steer a course between these two pitfalls and make the ideal a reality.

THE MANAGER'S ROLE IN STAFFING

In selecting and dealing with staff to implement the goals outlined for your center, you will want to make sure the following 10 tasks are accomplished. Remember, however, that although responsibility for the tasks rests with you, you will have help from a variety of sources, not the least of which will be your staff members themselves, if you are wise enough to tap that resource.

1. Locating the people who can best perform the required tasks
2. Encouraging creative performance and cooperative effort
3. Removing any roadblocks hindering success
4. Monitoring performance to assure the high-quality services that parents, children, and society deserve
5. Helping staff members remain motivated and energized to prevent burnout

---

[1] Lawrence J. Schweinhart, "Lasting Benefits of Preschool Programs," *ERIC Digest*, EDO-PS-94-2 (Urbana, IL: ERIC Clearinghouse on Elementary and Early Childhood Education, 1994).

Creative teachers are people to appreciate as they establish the environments that help children learn.
Family Life Center, Georgia Southern College, Statesboro

6. Developing a pleasant esprit de corps among the staff so they feel good about returning to work each day
7. Rewarding staff members for work well done with recognition and salaries that enable them to afford a similar service for their children
8. Preventing staff from exploiting the children or parents or harming their sense of self and sense of control in any way
9. Providing a pleasant and energy-saving physical environment where staff members can work comfortably, leaving them free to interact more with children rather than doing other work
10. Striving for a work environment that will help to keep a dependable and stable group of professional employees

Staff members, too, have a wealth of human capital that they bring to their positions. They have knowledge, skills, and abilities, which may already be developed to a high level through years of education and experience. Each has special qualities of love, warmth, and empathy. Each person should expect to continue developing these assets as the work of nurturing and educating children goes on. Increasing knowledge and skills should be anticipated and planned for. No staff member should stagnate but should continue developing. Regardless of a staff member's prior experience and education, much professional development is still to be accomplished, and it can go on in your center as work with children continues each day. There is research to analyze and apply. There are new situations to discuss that may suggest new and important researchable questions. Thoughtful responses to intellectual challenges continually occur when staff members feel the support of colleagues and managers in a child development center. When a career ladder is available within your particular center, staff members who show potential but lack education should be counseled to get more education so they can move ahead wherever appropriate.

The staff member who moves on to better opportunities outside your particular center would be a good example of professional development across a **career lattice**.[2] The lattice is the symbol used by the National Association for the Education of Young Children (NAEYC) to depict more accurately the interrelatedness of the many strands that make up the early childhood profession.

Imagine a lattice of woven wood slats in a rose garden. The vertical strands of the lattice represent the various settings in which early childhood professionals work: child development programs, family day care homes, resource and referral agencies, and so on. Horizontal strands represent increases in knowledge, responsibility, authority, and compensation within each of those settings. Professionals can move upward within the same setting (e.g., by being promoted at your child development program), they can move across settings (such as the caregiver who leaves your center to become a classroom aide in a Head Start center), or they can move diagonally (as a result of completing a community college training program, for example, which qualifies them to take a higher-level position in another setting). Furthermore, as professionals increase their core knowledge, they acquire a greater breadth of opportunities at increasingly higher levels on the career lattice.

Staff Members' Needs and Desires

Why will people care to work in your child development center? Why do people work at all? The research of psychologist Abraham H. Maslow has had a major impact on management education and practice.[3] To help explain people's motivation, Maslow proposed a "hierarchy of needs." He envisioned a ladder or pyramid representing the different levels of needs people have, as shown in Figure 6–1. However, it might be more appropriate, as some psychologists suggest, to envision a number of overlapping circles, each circle representing a need category, which would then portray each need as interacting and overlapping with all the other needs.

Maslow's hierarchy of needs places physiological needs, which include food, clothing, and shelter, at the foundation of the pyramid as the most basic. Maslow's idea is that once these basic needs are reasonably satisfied, the person becomes concerned about other needs at the next higher level. The second-level need is for safety and security. Once the first two levels of needs are met, the next higher needs come into prominence, and so on.

---

[2] Sue Bredekamp and Barbara Willer, "Of Ladders and Lattices, Cores and Cones: Conceptualizing an Early Childhood Professional Development System," *Young Children* 47:3 (March 1992), pp. 47–50.

[3] Abraham H. Maslow, *Motivation and Personality* (New York: Harper & Row, 1954).

Figure 6–1

Maslow's hierarchy of human needs

Source: Abraham H. Maslow, *Motivation and Personality* (New York: Harper & Row, 1954).

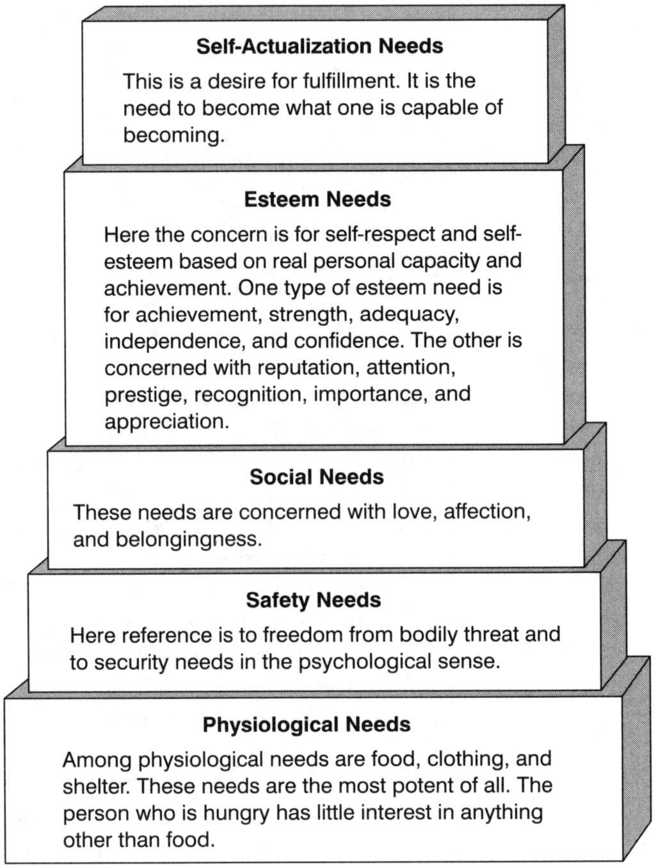

Self-Actualization Needs

This is a desire for fulfillment. It is the need to become what one is capable of becoming.

Esteem Needs

Here the concern is for self-respect and self-esteem based on real personal capacity and achievement. One type of esteem need is for achievement, strength, adequacy, independence, and confidence. The other is concerned with reputation, attention, prestige, recognition, importance, and appreciation.

Social Needs

These needs are concerned with love, affection, and belongingness.

Safety Needs

Here reference is to freedom from bodily threat and to security needs in the psychological sense.

Physiological Needs

Among physiological needs are food, clothing, and shelter. These needs are the most potent of all. The person who is hungry has little interest in anything other than food.

Maslow further suggests that in addition to the five basic categories of needs in Figure 6–1, people also have two basic desires: (1) the desire to know, that is, to be aware of reality, get the facts, and satisfy curiosity; and (2) the desire to understand, that is, to systematize and look for relations and meanings. Taken together, Maslow's concepts of basic needs and desires form a comprehensive look at the diversity of human motives present in work environments.

At the most basic level, the theory suggests that staff members whose salaries are too low to provide their own families with adequate food, clothing, and shelter will be unlikely to get much out of a staff training session. The same would be true of staff members who suffer from spousal abuse or live and work in violent neighborhoods. Unless their physiological and safety needs are met, staff members will be unlikely to benefit from efforts to address higher-level needs. Your function as a manager might, therefore, be to advocate for more adequate salaries, offer suggestions for counseling, or take part with your staff in neighborhood committees to combat violence.

Sections later in this chapter on employer-employee relations and staff communications provide suggestions for helping staff members feel a sense of belonging, which is the next stage of Maslow's hierarchy. You can help staff meet esteem needs by providing constructive feedback regarding their performance and calling attention to their successes when appropriate. Finally, you can encourage your staff to become all that they are capable of becoming by guiding them toward formal and informal training opportunities and challenging them with tasks that tap their new skills from time to time.

It is important to remember that progression through these stages is probably not a simple one-way process. Persons who are functioning at a very high level of self-actualization might revert to an earlier level in the face of a personal or family crisis. Recognizing which stage of personal development an individual staff member might be at in any given moment is one way that you can avoid "one-size-fits-all" motivation techniques and become a more effective manager.

Another important consideration for the manager concerned with staff members' needs and desires is the distinction between intrinsic and extrinsic motivation. **Intrinsic motivation** has to do with satisfaction in accomplishment or doing something for its own sake, while **extrinsic motivation** implies doing something simply for the sake of getting something else. Research has shown that "rewards cause people to lose interest in whatever they were rewarded for doing."[4] Other research suggests that teachers who enter the profession for extrinsic motives—using it as a stopgap, for example, until they can get into the job they really want—will be most likely to leave the profession.[5] These findings do not imply that extrinsic rewards such as adequate salaries are not important; rather, they suggest that rewards are necessary but not sufficient. Satisfying work and a living wage are both needed to keep our best professionals in the field.

As a manager of a child development center, therefore, your understanding of the complexity of human needs, desires, and motives will be essential. The following steps are helpful in locating, interviewing, and hiring the people whose human capital is essential to a child development center.

HIRING NEW STAFF

When a teacher resigns or retires, you have an opportunity to reanalyze that position, considering various alternative organizational structures. You can move the teacher of a group up to the next age group, keeping the children and teacher together another year. Perhaps you can reorganize your groups or promote a present staff member. Or you may want to hire an individual with more experience with the hope that hiring will not have to be done so often.

---

[4] Alfie Kohn, "The Risks of Rewards," *ERIC Digest,* December 1994, EDO-PS-94-14.
[5] See K. Fred Curtis, "On Entering and Staying in the Teaching Profession," *Childhood Education* 71:5 (1995), p. 288-F.

Depending on the size of your operation, you might hire a person to work as a part-time teacher and a part-time librarian or as a part-time parent educator. Or two people might be hired to share one position. In other words, the vacancy gives you an opportunity to think about new ways to structure the work assignments.

As you sort through these possibilities, you will probably consult with your policy and advisory boards. Your center may already have established policies concerning promotion from within or qualifications for specific jobs. If these options seem unworkable, you will need to work with your board to change them before proceeding.

Once a decision is made to hire, a committee should be formed to conduct the search. Unless your board is very small, it will be wise to include only selected representatives on the hiring committee. Other potential members of the hiring committee include parents of children enrolled in the center and staff members who will be working with the new teacher. Each of these groups can bring a valuable perspective to your deliberations. Parents will consider whether they feel comfortable leaving their child with a particular candidate or sharing their own concerns with that person. Staff members will be likely to wonder whether the candidate will pitch in and do a fair share of the work or be fun to work with.

Make it clear at the beginning who has authority for the final decision. Will it be a democratic process? Or will the committee provide recommendations, with the final authority resting with the manager? Each method has advantages, so you will want to weigh your decision carefully.

DECISIONS, DECISIONS . . .

 As the director of ABC Child Development Center, you are committed to a democratic style of leadership. You include two staff members along with two parents and two board members on the hiring committee for a teacher vacancy. You and the board members favor candidate A, whose experience in a center for children with disabilities will be an asset as your center moves toward full inclusion. The parents and teachers on the committee favor candidate B, whose personality seems friendlier to them. How will you decide? What are the potential outcomes of your decision in either case?

THE STAFFING SHORTAGE

Early childhood programs are widely reported to be facing a staffing crisis due to the large numbers of workers who either change jobs or leave the profession entirely every year.[6] In addition to this shrinking pool of qualified workers, the United States is entering an era in which potential employees may have many

---

[6] Ellen Galinsky, "The Staffing Crisis," *Young Children* 44:2 (January 1989), pp. 2–4.

more employment opportunities than previously. This means that centers may have fewer high-quality applicants and must do more recruiting. Of course, everyone involved with the center can become an ambassador, helping attract excellent employees. You should also consider the following five additional aspects of making your center or school an attractive place to work.

1. *Provide attractive salaries and benefits.*   One of the most obvious reasons people leave the early childhood profession is poor pay. Even those who love their work with young children must face the reality of supporting their own families. In a 1990 position statement, the NAEYC asserted that, because quality programs for young children benefit all of society, the financial burden of these programs should not be unfairly borne by parents and early childhood professionals. Instead, government, business, and all other segments of society should pitch in. The NAEYC established the following basic principles with regard to compensation for early childhood professionals:[7]

a. "Early childhood professionals with comparable qualifications, experience, and job responsibilities should receive comparable compensation regardless of the setting of their job." In other words, a teacher with a bachelor's degree in your center should be paid on a par with a teacher in a public school program.

b. "Compensation for early childhood professionals should be equivalent to that of other professionals with comparable preparation requirements, experience, and job responsibilities." Managers of child development programs, for example, can compare salaries for teaching assistants in their center with those of nurse's aides in their community's hospitals.

c. "Compensation should not be differentiated on the basis of the ages of the children served." The lead teacher in an infant room is doing work that is just as important as the high school biology teacher and should be compensated accordingly.

d. "Early childhood professionals should be encouraged to seek additional professional preparation and should be rewarded accordingly." Professional development does not end with the granting of a degree or certificate. New knowledge is accumulating all the time, and as ideas are discussed, new light is shed on what we thought we knew about children and families. Staying abreast of these changes is a lifelong process.

e. "The provision of an adequate benefits package is a crucial component of compensation for early childhood staff."

f. "A career ladder should be established, providing additional increments in salary based on performance and participation in professional developmental opportunities."

---

[7] In Barbara Willer (ed.), *Reaching the Full Cost of Quality* (Washington, DC: National Association for the Education of Young Children, 1990), pp. 51–54.

Women workers historically have been exploited, and it is time to call a halt to it. Men working in child development services also suffer because of the prevailing attitude that classifies child care as women's work. We expect professionalism in our employees; therefore, they should be paid what individuals with comparable education and responsibility are receiving. Center employees should earn far more than parking lot attendants.

Center managers who want to raise their voices and help the NAEYC with action that can bring about better compensation for our employees can begin by using the suggestions in *Reaching the Full Cost of Quality*. First they can estimate what that cost will be by comparing center salaries with salaries for comparable positions in their own community. Then they can build coalitions with parents, business and civic leaders, and child advocates to find ways to set and attain the goal of paying appropriate wages.

2. *Earn accreditation and increase your prestige.*   Another reason that child development professionals leave the field is low status that comes with a public perception that they are "just baby-sitting." Center accreditation is a nationally recognized hallmark of excellence, and staff members may have their own consciousness raised about the value of their work as they become deeply involved in the self-study process that it entails. Consequently, employees in accredited centers feel increased pride in their work, and this effect might spread to potential employees as well. One university student, searching for a center in which to complete her senior internship recently, limited her search specifically to accredited centers in her region. She reasoned that she wanted the best possible experience, and that strategy was one way to increase her chances of getting it. Of course, this approach means that the accredited centers have been given the first opportunity to recruit this enterprising and well-qualified young woman upon her graduation. In a tight labor market, the accredited center will have an advantage.

3. *Provide a supportive environment.*   "Friendly, caring, attractive" are ways you will want your center described. This goal means that both the physical and psychological environments of the center must be attractive to employees as well as children and families. Your center should offer a place where staff can relax or work on planning, in adult-size chairs, away from children. Child-size steps up to the diapering area can save employees' backs from the stress of lifting heavy toddlers. Your center will become known as a good place to work if you see to it that staff have the supplies they need to do their jobs, the power to exercise their creativity, and freedom from unnecessary pressures that get in the way of doing those jobs. Another NAEYC publication that will help managers with this goal is *A Great Place to Work: Improving Conditions for Staff in Young Children's Programs,* by Paula Jorde Bloom.

4. *Build a reputation of excellence.*   Satisfied parents, happy employees, and positive publicity within the community will encourage people to recommend

your center when a new person comes to town seeking employment or child care. Verbal recommendations from colleagues around the city or other managers who work with you in a manager's association may help you find employees and children who would like your center. News stories and attractive brochures describing your services available in the offices of the Chambers of Commerce and elsewhere can bring you employees as well as children.

5. *Work for stability in staff.* A hallmark of a good place to work is a center that seldom has a vacancy unless someone retires or has to move away because of a spouse's transfer. One way to help achieve this goal is by establishing a career ladder that gives new employees something to strive for and rewards competent staff members who obtain additional training and expertise. No one likes to stay in a dead-end job, and a lack of opportunity for advancement is what drives many from the early childhood profession. A stable staff is the dream of every manager. When the conditions mentioned in this section are met, staff stability is possible.

JOB ANALYSIS, DESCRIPTION, AND SPECIFICATION

The Job Analysis

When it comes to staffing the child development center, you will want to analyze the many tasks required to perform the services you expect to render. In the **job analysis** you determine exactly what each job requires of the individual. You can do a job analysis by observing the person or by having the person already in the job help analyze the job using a worksheet such as that shown in Figure 6–2, from the U.S. Civil Service. After careful analysis, you might decide to reallocate some tasks assigned to a given staff member. Using the Civil Service format, Figure 6–3 shows a sample job analysis of a cook in a child development center.

Because the items titled job analysis, job description, and job specification contain similar information, each example here, to be most helpful, is given for a different job in a child development center rather than giving all three items as applicable to a single position. To develop a complete set for one position, you can easily work from each example.

The Job Description

Following job analysis, you are ready to develop a **job description**. The job description lists the daily and occasional tasks the individual will be expected to perform. When hiring the individual, you should have the job description available. This document will serve as the basis for periodically monitoring or evaluating the staff member's work. Given the manager's responsibility for maintaining standards, you should write the job description so that adherence to standards

Step by step: the information to obtain when doing a job analysis.

Identifying Information
(such as)
Name of incumbent
Organization/unit
Title and series
Date
Interviewer

Brief Summary of Job
(This statement will include the primary duties of the job. It may be prepared in advance from class specifications, job descriptions, or other sources. However, it should be checked for accuracy using the task statements resulting from the analysis.)

Job Tasks
What does the worker do? How does he do it? Why? What output is produced? What tools, procedures, aids are involved? How much time does it take to do the task? How often does the worker perform the task in a day, week, month, or year?

Skills, Knowledge, and Abilities Required
What does it take to perform each task in terms of the following?
1. Knowledge required.
    a. What subject matter areas are covered by the task?
    b. What facts or principles must the worker have an acquaintance with or understand in these subject matter areas?
    c. Describe the level, degree, and breadth of knowledge required in these areas or subjects.

2. Skills required.
    a. What activities must the worker perform with ease and precision?
    b. What are the manual skills that are required to operate machines, vehicles, equipment, or to use tools?

3. Abilities required.
    a. What is the nature and level of language ability, written or oral, required of the worker on the job? Are there complex oral or written ideas involved in performing the task, or simple instructional materials?
    b. What mathematical ability must the worker have? Will he use simple arithmetic, complex algebra?
    c. What reasoning or problem-solving ability must the worker have?
    d. What instructions must the worker follow? Are they simple, detailed, involved, abstract?
    e. What interpersonal abilities are required? What supervisory or managing abilities are required?
    f. What physical abilities such as strength, coordination, visual acuity must the worker have?

Figure 6–2
Model Civil Service worksheet for obtaining job analysis data
Source: U.S. Civil Service Commission.

Physical Activities
Describe the frequency and degree to which the incumbent is engaged in such activities as: pulling, pushing, throwing, carrying, kneeling, sitting, running, crawling, reaching, climbing.

Environmental Conditions
Describe the frequency and degree to which the incumbent will encounter working under conditions such as these: cramped quarters, moving objects, vibration, inadequate ventilation.

Typical Work Incidents
1. Situations involving the interpretation of feelings, ideas, or facts in terms of personal viewpoint.
2. Influencing people in their opinions, attitudes, or judgments about ideas or things.
3. Working with people beyond giving and receiving instructions.
4. Performing repetitive work, or continuously performing the same work.
5. Performing under stress when confronted with emergency, critical, unusual, or dangerous situations; or in situations in which work speed and sustained attention are make-and-break aspects of the job.
6. Performing a variety of duties, often changing from one task to another of a different nature without loss of efficiency or composure.
7. Working under hazardous conditions that may result in: violence, loss of bodily members, burns, bruises, cuts, impairment of senses, collapse, fractures, electric shock.

Worker Interest Areas
Identify from the list below the preferences for work activities suggested by each task.

A preference for activities:
1. dealing with things and objects
2. concerning the communication of data
3. involving business contact with people
4. involving work of a scientific and technical nature
5. involving work of a routine, concrete, organized nature
6. involving work of an abstract and creative nature
7. involving work for the presumed good of people
8. relating to process, machine, and technique
9. resulting in prestige or the esteem of others
10. resulting in tangible, productive satisfaction

Figure 6–2, *continued*

Identifying Information
Name of Incumbent: Mary Jones
Organization: XYZ Child Development Center
Title: Food Service Employee: Cook
Date: [Today's date]
Interviewer: Janie Bolls

Brief Summary of Job
The cook prepares breakfast, lunch, and midmorning and midafternoon snacks for children and staff in the center; assists with serving breakfast and lunch, prepares market orders; and keeps kitchen, dining areas, and food storage areas clean and sanitary.

Job Tasks
Cook's Duties: Daily (8 hours, 5 days weekly; 6:30 A.M. to 3:00 P.M.)
1. Prepares breakfast and helps serve to center's young children and staff.
2. Prepares lunch and helps serve to center's young children and staff.
3. Prepares snacks for children and break beverages for staff.
4. Supervises assistant who sets up tables, chairs, etc., for meal.
5. Washes dishes and pans using dishwasher.
6. Cleans countertops, appliance tops, floors.
7. Directs assistant's work and gives training as needed.

Occasional Duties
1. Cares for kitchen appliances, keeping alert for problems.
2. Orders foods for classroom project as directed by manager.
3. Prepares play dough, fingerpaint, cookie dough as directed by manager.
4. Keeps food and paper inventory up-to-date.
5. Makes market orders from menus supplied.
6. Confers with manager regarding menus, food on hand, etc.
7. Attends inservice workshops or meetings.
8. Makes year-end inventory of food and supplies in June.
9. Recommends maintenance or replacement of appliances or painting of surfaces in the unit.
10. Attends staff meetings as designated applicable.
11. Helps with or attends inservice education events.
12. Prepares (with help) food for special occasions such as parents' meeting, director's meeting, staff meeting.

Knowledge, Skills, and Abilities Required
1. Knowledge required
   a. Knowledge of appropriate cooking techniques for typical foods served in the center
   b. Knowledge of nutritional requirements for children
   c. Knowledge of characteristic food habits of children
   d. Knowledge of sanitation principles related to food and food service

Figure 6–3
Job analysis, following the Civil Service outline

2. Skills required
    a. Skill to prepare foods
    b. Skill to organize materials for and prepare several foods to meet the serving schedules of the center
    c. Skill to operate and maintain appliances of the kitchen
3. Abilities required
    a. Ability to read recipes, regulations, written memos
    b. Ability to write shopping lists, memos, etc.
    c. Ability to calculate quantities for recipes and costs of food using simple arithmetic
    d. Ability to explain or demonstrate to an aide or assistant how to do an activity such as prepare a food or set up the dining room
    e. Ability and willingness to be friendly to children, parents, staff members, and vendors
    f. Ability and stamina to be on your feet, to lift or move 25–50 pounds of food or equipment

Physical Activities
Include walking around the kitchen, storeroom, and dining room for most of the 8 hours and lifting up to 50 pounds.

Environmental Conditions
Environment is kitchen, storerooms, and dining room. Generally pleasant, may be extra warm when ovens are used. A variety of interpersonal relationships with staff, children, and parents of the center. Generally a moderately quiet place except for happy sounds of children playing.

Typical Work Incidents
1. Conferring with manager regarding menus, inventories, purchase orders (generally Fridays)
2. Cooking is routine activity, yet not repetitive because different menus are used daily in 3-week cycles. Considerable challenge to get a large number of meals on the table at a set time.
3. Routine cleaning tasks are generally minimal because they are done daily.
4. Emergencies may arise if orders do not arrive or appliances do not work; thus, ingenuity is required to keep the service at a high-quality level.
5. Assistants in the kitchen, other staff, children, and parents are an unusually pleasant group to work with, generally caring about individuals and their interests.

Work Interest Areas
1. Involves work for the good of others
2. Involves work satisfaction when meals are served on time, taste good, are attractive and nutritious, and are enjoyed
3. Involves variety, yet some routine
4. Involves activity relating to home activity

Figure 6–3, *continued*

easily follows. Figure 6–4 is an example of a job description for a cleaning and maintenance supervisor. On the job description, please notice the space for both the manager and the employee to sign and date the job description. The staff member should read this document carefully and agree to the tasks. Later, the manager and staff members should confer before reassigning or adding tasks. This document serves as an agreement and acknowledgment that the job description will be used as the basis for periodic evaluations.

Job descriptions should be available to all employees and kept on file in their personnel folder. They will feel a commitment to the responsibilities specified there. Many managers find that the job description should contain some statement regarding employee participation in professional development activities, which keep a staff member alive and growing year by year. Child development centers are dynamic rather than static. They often grow and develop to meet changing community needs. Job descriptions must be current and reflect any changes that occur when staff are reassigned or given additional duties as a result of this growth.

The Job Specification

After preparing the job description, you are ready to devise a **job specification** to be used in advertising and listing your open position. This document specifies the type and level of education and previous experience required. It lists essential personal characteristics such as judgment, initiative, physical effort, physical skills, communication skills, emotional characteristics, and sensory demand such as seeing, hearing, and smelling. The responsibilities of the position are clearly stated. Figure 6–5 is an example of a job specification for a child development center teacher.

The job specification is the basis for an advertisement to run in your area newspapers. You can duplicate it and hand it out to possible candidates at a meeting or post it where potential employees might see it. Be sure all essential information is included. Some managers type the center's phone number all across the bottom of the page, cutting little slots between each number. A potential employee may thus tear off one number and take it along. They will then have the correct number and may be more likely to follow through and call. To be able to screen the telephone calls from applicants, you may wish to use an answering machine on your telephone. Your printed job specifications and ads should reflect this arrangement. State, for example, "Please leave your name, phone number, and previous experience on the following phone answering machine: 111-4444."

Job Classification

Classifying a job in your center relative to other jobs requires considering the level of difficulty, responsibility, and preparation required for that job, as well as the amount of supervision required. Salary can then be based on the level of the job in the classification. Classification shows the career ladder. Figure 6–6 shows one classification.

Job Title
Cleaning and Maintenance Supervisor

Tasks
Cleaning and maintaining the XYZ Child Development Center

Daily Responsibilities
(Generally 11:00 A.M. to 7:00 P.M.)

Daily Activity
1. Be friendly to children, parents, and staff.
2. Be responsive to teacher's needs (Discuss priorities with the manager.)
3. Keep public areas clean and tidy.
4. Floors—mop hard surface, vacuum carpets.
5. Bathrooms—disinfect and deodorize after cleaning. (Store cleaning solutions as recommended.)
6. Spot cleaning of children's fingerprints—lockers, walls, door frames, cupboards, and so on.
7. Set up cots for naptime; stack cots after naptime.
8. Run washer and dryer with children's washcloths, towels, sheets, and blankets. Fold and store items.
9. Assist at meals and snack time with any spills requiring mopping.
10. Dispose of trash properly.
11. Watch closely for signs of insects or rodents and report.
12. Lock doors and windows securely before leaving facility.

Occasional Activity
1. Wash children's lockers and furniture.
2. Check equipment and facility for indication of need for repairs or painting. Make list of needs for manager's attention. Change light bulbs as needed.
3. Oil and tighten bolts where needed.
4. Meet with staff as requested.
5. Scatter wood chips on mud after rain. Drain puddles, if possible, to enable children to use the yard.
6. Clean and reorder facility after parent meeting.
7. Wash windows and blinds. Vacuum draperies.
8. Check premises for compliance with fire and safety rules.

Signed _____   Signed _____
            Employee   Manager of XYZ
                                                                   Child Development Center

Date _____   Date _____

Figure 6–4
Job description

Job Title
Child Development Center Teacher

Qualifications
B.A. or B.S. degree in early childhood education or child development; must be certified to teach early childhood education in this state.

Experience
Minimal experience required is student teaching with children from 3 to 5 years of age.

Responsibility
Be in charge of program planning and implementing in a class of eighteen 4-year-old children.
Direct the work of an assistant teacher and aide. Plan parent education work for parents of children.
Make home visits once a year; hold evaluation conferences with parents twice yearly. Attend staff meetings and inservice professional days periodically. Write required reports.

Time
September 2, 1996, to June 6, 1997
School schedule is 8:30 A.M. to 3:30 P.M. daily with regular public school holidays.

Salary
Based on public school salaries for comparable preparation and experience.
Benefits: Health insurance, social security, unemployment compensation, paid holidays

Contact
Mary Right, Manager
Child's Life Child Development Center
Adam's Street 444
Baker, Texas 67777
213-555-4567

Procedure
Send vita and three letters of recommendation to address above.

Closing Date
July 1, 1996.

An Equal Opportunity Employer

Figure 6–5
Job specification

Level	Food Service	Teacher	Office	Maintenance
Level 7			Center manager	
Level 6				
Level 5	Dietitian	Experienced teacher	Accountant	
Level 4		Second-year teacher		
Level 3	Cook	First-year teacher	Bookkeeper	
Level 2				Maintenance supervisor
Level 1	Assistant cook	Teacher's aide	Clerk/typist	Housekeeper

Figure 6–6
Job classification scheme
Source: Adapted from *Day Care Personnel Management* (Atlanta: Atlanta Southern Education Board, 1979), p. 19.

FRINGE BENEFITS

Center employees will expect the same employment protection as they would receive in other employment. Public schools generally have a standard package of retirement, social security, worker's compensation, unemployment compensation, hospital, and medical plans. These benefits generally can be available to nonprofit community organizations. Be sure to check several companies to ensure that you have obtained the best fringe benefits possible for your employees. Keep abreast of the NAEYC's efforts and reports regarding fringe benefits by reading *Young Children* and calling their information line, (800) 424-2460. Employees have choices, and businesses without fringe benefits will find it difficult to locate good staff members or keep them from moving as they find employment having fringe benefits.

EDUCATIONAL PREPARATION OF TEACHERS

Numerous studies have demonstrated the connection between staff training and program quality.[8] As a manager committed to providing a high-quality program for young children, one of your major policy decisions will be the level of educa-

---

[8] "The Effects of Group Size, Ratios, and Staff Training on Child Care Quality," *Young Children* 48:3 (January 1993), p. 67.

Figure 6–7

Career ladder for early childhood teachers (job titles proposed by the NAEYC)

Source: Based on Sue Bredekamp (ed.),
*Accreditation Criteria & Procedures of the
National Academy of Early Childhood Programs* (Washington, DC: National Association for the Education of Young Children,
1984), p. 19.

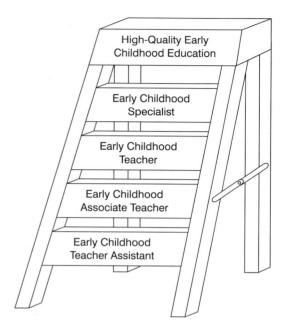

tion to require of your teaching and caregiving staff. The NAEYC has helped
managers and others focus on the educational preparation and experience of
teachers and caregivers, adopting the job titles and descriptions shown in Table
6–1. Clarifying the career ladder (see Figure 6–7) for teachers and assistants has
helped alleviate some confusion. As noted earlier, appropriate salary increases
should be built into this ladder.

The earlier discussion of Maslow's theory of basic needs and basic desires suggests that after meeting their basic needs, people increase their desire for more
information and knowledge. For early childhood professionals, this idea means
that individuals' satisfaction may come from increased information related to
their work with children. Figure 6–7 shows an increase in responsibility on the
part of individuals moving up the career ladder in early childhood education.

A wide range of formal and informal preparation is possible for working in a
child development center. Some employees may enter as aides with no training or
experience and develop skills for working with young children on the job. Others
may enter the center with experience from having reared children at home and
build on skills they have through on-the-job training, becoming excellent employees. Still others may come with formal training obtained in a variety of ways

Sources of Training

Secondary vocational schools and community colleges are offering many courses
and experiences that prepare caregivers and assistant teachers. Such programs
include child development courses and practicum courses that give the student
experience in working with children in a center. Some of the community college
programs, along with a few 4-year colleges, are cooperating with the Child Devel-

Table 6–1
Staff qualifications

Level of Professional Responsibility	Title	Training Requirements
Professionals who supervise and train staff, design curriculum and/or administer programs	Early childhood specialist	Baccalaureate degree in early childhood education/child development and at least 3 years of full-time teaching experience with young children and/or a graduate degree in ECE/CD
Professionals who are responsible for the care and education of a group of children	Early childhood teacher	Baccalaureate degree in early childhood education/child development
Professionals who independently implement program activities and who may be responsible for the care and education of a group of children	Early childhood associate teacher	CDA credentials or associate degree in early childhood education/child development
Preprofessionals who implement program activities under direct supervision of the professional staff	Early childhood teacher assistant	High school graduate or equivalent, participation in professional development programs

Source: Sue Bredekamp (ed.), *Accreditation Criteria & Procedures of the National Academy of Early Childhood Programs* (Washington, DC: National Association for the Education of Young Children, 1984), p. 19. Used with permission.

opment Associate (CDA) program. The CDA program was initiated by the U.S. Office of Child Development to provide a career ladder and credentialing system for workers in the child care centers. The CDA is led by a private nonprofit corporation, the Child Development Associate Consortium (CDAC), and is financed with federal funds. The consortium developed a system of assessing (measuring) the competence of individuals who work with young children. The competencies are spelled out in a booklet, *CDAC Competency Standards*, which is available from the Council for Early Childhood Professional Recognition (1341 G St. NW, Washington, DC 20005-3105; phone, [800] 424-4310). The child care worker may work individually or be in classes with other CDA candidates. The assessments are made in the center where the individual works. Project Head Start requires teachers to have a CDA or a teaching certificate.

Early childhood education programs in 4-year colleges are preparing individuals to work with young children. When completed, the graduate holds a bachelor's degree and a teaching certificate. In some states the certificate is in early childhood education; in others it is in elementary education with an endorsement in early childhood education. Programs have varied across the country as to the nature of the courses and experiences provided. Given the recent movement toward inclusion of children with disabilities in all programs for young children, some states, such as North Carolina and Kentucky, offer an early childhood certificate that combines course work and practical experience in child development, early childhood education, and early childhood special education.

Teacher certification may or may not be earned with a bachelor's degree; thus, as manager you will need to see evidence of certification. The NAEYC, after considerable discussion, published *Guidelines for Preparation of Early Childhood Professionals: Associate, Baccalaureate, and Advanced Levels* as a position statement in 1995. These guidelines were approved by the Division for Early Childhood, Council for Exceptional Children, and reflect requirements of the Individuals with Disabilities Education Act (IDEA) and the Americans with Disabilities Act (ADA) that *all* early childhood programs be willing and able to include children with disabilities and developmental delays or those at risk for such delays. The guidelines, available from the NAEYC, give institutions suggestions for the appropriate type of experiences to provide for qualified teachers of young children.

Preprimary programs within the public school systems typically require certification of all teaching personnel. Many centers expect to hire all certified teachers to lead each group of children and hire somewhat less educated persons to serve as aides or assistants. Other centers expect to hire one certified program director who works with all caregivers to plan the educational program for the center.

As you consider the education levels of staff members you wish to employ, you will also consider the work experiences the individual has had since completing his or her education. According to the National Day Care Study, "Education/training in child-related fields such as developmental psychology, day care, early childhood education or special education is associated with distinctive patterns of caregiver and child behavior and with higher gains in test scores for children."[9] Try to hire the staff with the highest qualifications your center can afford. Better yet, work toward the day when your center can afford to hire the staff with the high qualifications you want.

Early childhood specialists have a level of educational and practical experience that makes them sought after for many jobs. These positions may be in directing school and care programs, administering before- and after-school programs, teaching in teacher-training programs, serving as curriculum coordinators within a center or school, directing 4C (community-coordinated child care) programs, managing research grants, or serving as licensing specialists for government departments.

In a public school, the early childhood education specialist may be the coordinator under the school superintendent of all kindergartens, prekindergartens, and before- and after-school programs. If the Zigler-Lang model of the "School of the 21st Century" (see Chapter 1) were adopted, it would be essential that the early

---

9 Richard R. Ruopp, J. Travers, F. Glantz, and C. Coelen, *Children at the Center: Final Report of the National Day Care Study,* Vol. 1 (Washington, DC: Department of Health, Education, and Welfare, 1978; Cambridge, MA: Abt, 1979), p. 98.

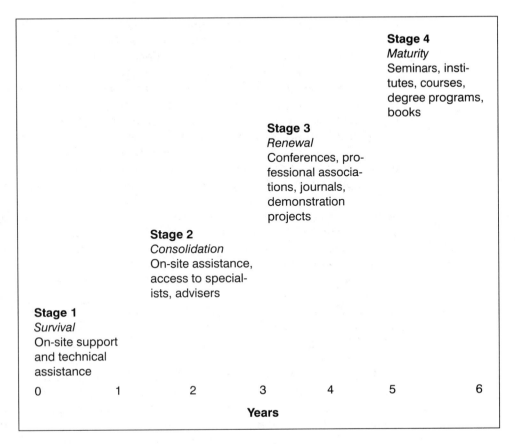

Figure 6–8
Teacher's developmental stages and inservice needs
Source: Based on Lilian G. Katz, "Developmental Stages of Preschool Teachers," in *Exploring Early Childhood* by M. Kaplan-Sanoff and R. Yablans-Magid (Upper Saddle River, NJ: Prentice Hall, 1984), pp. 478–482.

childhood program be led by someone qualified in early childhood education, rather than by a person trained in something entirely foreign to young children.

EXPERIENCED OR INEXPERIENCED?

As you plan to hire a person to fill a position, you will want to consider whether you can afford to hire an experienced person or whether you prefer or will accept an inexperienced person. Clearly, in nearly every job category an inexperienced person requires a period of adjustment before being able to contribute maximally. However, the experienced person generally will cost more in salary and benefits.

Lilian Katz, a prominent early childhood educator with experience in providing various types of preservice and inservice education for early childhood teachers, suggests that there are four developmental stages for early childhood teachers (see Figure 6–8).[10] Katz calls stage 1 "Survival," which lasts for about the first 2 years. These persons may at times feel overwhelmed at having the full responsibility for a group of immature but vigorous young children. These are the teachers you see at a conference eagerly harvesting ideas to take back to their classrooms for Monday morning. Katz says, "During this period the teacher needs support, understanding, encouragement, reassurance, comfort, and guidance."

Katz labels the second stage "Consolidation"; it usually covers from approximately 18 months to 3 years. By this stage the teacher has decided she or he can survive and is ready to consolidate gains. This teacher needs on-site assistance, access to specialists, colleague advice, consultants, and advisers, according to Katz.

"Renewal" is the third stage, which comes between the 3rd and 5th years. Now the teacher has become tired of the routine and wants to learn about new developments. The teacher finds it rewarding to meet colleagues from various programs at conferences and to compare notes with them. At this time teachers become objective about looking at their own classrooms, says Katz.

The fourth stage, "Maturity," is reached between the 4th and 5th years. The person has come to terms with being a teacher and is ready to look at deeper and more abstract questions. Conferences, institutes, or advanced-degree programs are needed to stimulate this person.

Considering the stages described by Katz, a manager, policy board, and staff can consider whether they hope to attract a person in an advanced stage of an early childhood career who seems stabilized in career choice and could offer leadership within the center and community, or whether hiring a fresh graduate and guiding his or her development fits in better with the center's plans or ability to pay. Finances may be a deciding factor; but if there is a choice, the various options should be weighed within the decision-making process. Since a nearly universal cry of child care managers is that they are continuously in the process of training staff, it follows that being able to hire experienced staff will eliminate some of these problems.

SUPERVISORY STAFF

An employee called a **curriculum coordinator** or assistant to the manager may be assigned to help plan children's programs and advise teachers regarding curriculum and children's behaviors. This position may be staffed when a manager has several building sites and cannot be available to oversee details of each classroom. Hiring curriculum coordinators sometimes substitutes for hiring more highly qualified teachers who could do their own planning. Put differently, a curriculum coordinator may be necessary when teachers are not well prepared for their jobs and need someone to help with planning daily programs, setting up training programs, and ordering appropriate equipment

---

[10]Lilian G. Katz, "Developmental Stages of Preschool Teachers," in *Exploring Early Childhood* by M. Kaplan-Sanoff and R. Yablans-Magid (Upper Saddle River, NJ: Prentice Hall, 1984), pp. 478–482.

and supplies. Special attention must be given in planning for the supervisory role to keep it from becoming "just one more layer of expensive administration," as many claim.

In centers where less than highly qualified teachers are hired to operate the classrooms, a qualified early childhood teacher or specialist is generally assigned to coordinate programming or planning of specific activities for children. This supervision may be required by licensing regulations. In this case, joint planning is required, which means that the supervisor and teachers need a time and place to go over plans and get their ideas coordinated so that the teachers can carry out the program plans. Plans must be understood, match each teacher's ability, and fit the characteristics of the children in the group. Details of the coordination should be spelled out in the job description of each teacher and the supervisor.

In centers with well-qualified teachers, placing a supervisor over teachers often leads to frustration for both supervisor and teachers. Generally it is more effective to have qualified teachers responsible directly to the manager and for these teachers to assume more managerial roles within their own units than teachers with less training or experience would be able to handle. The problems of supervisory management are pointed out by Hitt et al., who indicate that supervisory managers are pulled in two directions: toward higher management and toward subordinates who can withhold cooperation. The supervisor usually is upwardly oriented, thus alienating subordinates, who see the supervisor as too management oriented.[11]

Another way to look at this position has been developed in the early childhood programs of Reggio Emilia in Italy, where a *pedagogista* works collaboratively with teachers from several programs "to analyze and interpret the rights and needs of each child and family, and then use this knowledge in [their] work with children."[12] The *pedagogista* also facilitates parent-teacher relations and organizes meetings where they can discuss and extend children's curriculum projects. There is no exact translation for the job title in English, but some programs in the United States are finding it useful to have such a facilitator who can help teachers reflect on their observations and interactions with children and families as they plan where to go next in their curricula.

PROFESSIONAL SERVICES STAFF

A number of professionals in addition to the manager and teachers may be employed within a child development center, depending on the breadth and depth of services desired. The National Day Care Study reports, "Many day care

[11] M. A. Hitt, R. Dennis Middlemist, and Robert L. Mathis, *Management: Concepts and Effective Practice* (St. Paul, MN: West, 1986), pp. 25–26.

[12] Tiziana Filippini, "The Role of the *Pedagogista*," in Carolyn Edwards, Lella Gandini, and George Forman, *The Hundred Languages of Children: The Reggio Emilia Approach to Early Childhood Education* (Norwood, NJ: Ablex, 1994), p. 116.

Patiently supporting a child as he tackles a new piece of equipment is a frequently played role for early childhood teachers.
Michigan State University Child Development Laboratory, East Lansing

centers have professional specialists on their staff, but many others apparently obtain the services of such specialists from community agencies or on a consulting basis." The conclusion was drawn by comparing those centers that drew on community services and those employing professional staff. The researchers found that 8% of centers had hearing, speech, or vision specialists; 8% had psychologists; 21% had social workers; 33% had nurses; 35% had child development specialists; and 46% had none of these specialists.[13] Others may be employed as assistant manager, aide or assistant teacher, food service aide, recreation specialist, and so on. Each type of position requires a job analysis, job description, and job specification. Many positions have a probationary period, with an agreed-on means of evaluating the services at the end of a given period.

LISTING THE JOB

Experience will help you determine the best source of applicants to fill the jobs in the child development center. The U.S. Department of Labor maintains

---

[13] Ruopp et al., *Children at the Center,* p. 98.

employment offices in most cities, where your job can be listed. Of course, the daily newspaper is a place a candidate might see an advertisement. Placement services may be operated by unions, professional organizations, and colleges. Personal contacts in agencies can be excellent sources of referrals. Your goal is to give your job specifications as much visibility as possible so as to attract a number of qualified applicants, from whom you can select the best one for your specific job. In addition to meeting applicable affirmative action regulations, you will want to enrich the diversity of your applicant pool as much as possible by making sure that your advertising methods do not inadvertently exclude any particular group, especially groups that are underrepresented in your center's staff.

After your job specification is prepared, you must use a number of avenues to put it before the public so possible candidates will most likely see it. Some of the resource and referral services may also be helpful with employee needs in centers they serve. State, county, and 4C offices may also help find employees in the child care field.

THE JOB APPLICATION

You may wish to develop a job application form for candidates to fill out to provide the information your screening committee needs (see Figure 6–9). For professional jobs, a curriculum vita or résumé and a letter of application may be preferred. A note on the job specification announcement should state where applications are available and, if desired, where letters and résumés should be sent.

Some managers like a letter from applicants to help gauge the quality of the candidate's writing and language usage. When they arrive in the office, they can fill out the needed application forms. The content of an application form should include name, address, phone, educational background with credits or degrees, work experience, most recent work and a reference from that work, list of previous employers and references, and general character references.

Many states now require that all child care workers be screened for serious criminal convictions and/or histories of abuse or neglect of children or adults. The two types of screening should not be confused: screening for criminal convictions will not reveal a history of child abuse unless the person has gone to trial and been convicted in criminal court. Many or most instances of child abuse are handled in family or probate court and do not result in criminal convictions. Some states require this screening for the director only, while others require it for each employee. Some require it at initial licensure only, and some require it annually. Some states allow employees a provisional period during which they may work until clearances are obtained; others require clearances to be on file before an employee starts work. Ask your licensing consultant for correct procedure in your particular state.

Having completed the necessary screenings, however, does not mean that you have, in fact, eliminated all applicants with such histories. Police records are incom-

XYZ Child Development Center Employment Application Form
123 Children's Drive, Happyville, MD 45669, Phone: (345) 555-6666

Applicant's Name _____

Address _____ Phone _____

_____

Educational Record
Provide dates, schools, credits or degrees.

_____

_____

Work Experience
List the two most recent positions you have held.

Employer	Your title	Dates employed	Name of supervisor

_____

_____

References
Provide two professional references (include name, address, and phone numbers).

_____

_____

Provide two personal character references (include name, address, and phone numbers).

_____

_____

Your signature certifies that the above information is accurate.

Signed _____ Date _____

Figure 6–9
Sample application form

**Screening Procedures for Employees and Volunteers
XYZ Child Development Centers, Inc.**

All employees and volunteers having contact with children in care must have on file a signed copy of the Abuse, Neglect, and Criminal History Statement. Signed statements will be maintained on file at each center.

In the event that the statement reveals a conviction for a misdemeanor or felony, or substantiated involvement in abuse or neglect of children or adults, the following information will be reviewed to determine acceptability:

1. A criminal history file search
2. The nature and seriousness of the offense
3. The date of the offense
4. Relationship of the offense to the job assignment

If the candidate is determined to be satisfactory after these reviews, he or she will be referred to the Department of Social Services for final review and approval.

Figure 6–10
Sample screening procedures

plete in some instances, and perpetrators of abuse can assume false identities to elude their past records. Experts on child sexual abuse contacted during a federal study of child care employee screening practices concluded that the best safeguards were "(a) education and alertness of parents, staff, and children; (b) careful listening and observation by parents and staff; (c) child care participation and monitoring by parents; and (d) parent networks within programs.[14] Figures 6–10 and 6–11 provide an example of one organization's written procedures for screening applicants.

I hereby certify in good faith that a case of abuse or neglect has not been substantiated against me, nor have I been named the Respondent in any petition that is pending for abuse or neglect in either juvenile or criminal court. I also certify that I have not been convicted of any crime more serious than a traffic offense, nor are there felony charges pending against me. I understand that falsification of this or any part of my application will be grounds for discharge from employment.

_____   _____
Date   Signature

Figure 6–11
Sample employee statement

---

[14]Carl C. Staley, Edna Runnels Ranck, Joe Perrault, and Roger Neugebaur, "Guidelines for Effective Staff Selection," *Child Care Information Exchange*, January 1986, p. 23.

REFERENCES

Before the interview, you should check up on the references provided by the applicant. References can help guide the ranking of applicants in order of preference. Contact each reference by telephone rather than relying on written statements an applicant might submit. In addition to verifying the authenticity of the written statements, you will be able to follow up on areas where you have questions and listen for subtle cues or hesitations that suggest the person's recommendation for a particular candidate is less than wholehearted. Of course, these are names provided by the applicant, and they probably can be expected to give a positive view, but when telephoning, you can ask whether the reference can give you the name of another person or two who would be acquainted with the applicant's job performance. By calling those persons, you may be able to get a more balanced picture than if you call only the applicant's references.

LEGAL ASPECTS OF STAFFING

Most managers of child development centers gradually become familiar with the numerous laws concerned with operating their centers. Many of these laws relate directly to hiring staff and procedures for paying and promoting staff members. Small paperback books published by the American Civil Liberties Union detail the provisions of laws that protect employees.[15] Employees have the legal right to receive fair wages, work in healthy environments, receive unemployment compensation if unemployed, receive compensation if injured on the job, and have an equal opportunity to be hired and promoted regardless of their race, sex, religion, age, or national origin. To keep up-to-date on provisions of the law, write to the following sources for current information on various laws.

Federal Laws[16]

Write to: U.S. Equal Employment Opportunity Commission
2401 E St. NW
Washington, DC 20706
1. Civil Rights Act of 1964—Title VII (amended in 1972)
Prohibits discrimination because of race, color, religion, sex, or national origin.
2. Equal Pay Act of 1963
Requires equal pay for men and women performing similar work.
Write to: Employment Standards Administration
Office of Federal Contract Compliance Program
Third and Constitution Avenues NW
Washington, DC 20210

---

[15] See, for example, David Rubin, *The Rights of Teachers* (New York: Avon Books, 1972); and Susan D. Ross and Ann Barche, *The Rights of Women* (New York: American Civil Liberties Union, 1983).

[16] Much of the following discussion is based on information contained in N. Travis and J. Perreault, *Day Care Personnel Management* (Atlanta, GA: Southern Regional Education Board, 1979), pp. 7–12.

3. The Fair Labor Standards Act of 1938 (1972 amendments)
Establishes a minimum wage, equal pay, and record-keeping requirements.
4. Vietnam Era Veterans' Readjustment Assistance Act of 1974
Prohibits job discrimination and requires affirmative action to employ and advance in employment qualified Vietnam veterans.
5. Executive Orders 11246 and 11375
Require an affirmative action program by all federal contractors and sub-contractors with a contract of $10,000 or more.
6. Rehabilitation Act of 1973
Prohibits job discrimination because of disability and requires affirmative action to employ and advance in employment qualified workers with disabilities.
7. Americans with Disabilities Act of 1990
Title I prohibits discrimination against individuals with disabilities by requiring equal employment opportunities. (Title III does not pertain to staffing but does concern the manager of a child development program because it prohibits discrimination in public accommodations, including child care facilities. See Chapter 12.)[17]
8. The Federal Wage Garnishment Law
Sets restriction on the amount of an employee's earnings that may be deducted in any one week through garnishment proceedings and on discharge from employment by reason of garnishment.
Write to: U.S. Social Security Administration
6401 Security Blvd.
Baltimore, MD 21235
9. Social Security (Social Security Act of 1935 and Federal Insurance Contributions Act)
Provides retirement, disability, burial, and survivor benefits to eligible employees and self-employed individuals.
Write to: U.S. Treasury
Washington, DC 20224
10. Federal Income Tax Withholding
The employer is required to serve as a collector of employees' income tax and deposit same in a federal depository. Failure to comply is a criminal offense.
Write to: U.S. Department of Labor
Occupational Safety and Health Administration
Room S-2315
200 Constitution Ave. NW
Washington, DC 20216
11. Occupational Safety and Health Act of 1970
Requires that employers shall furnish employees a safe place to work.
Write to: U.S. Department of Labor
Employment Standards Administration

---

[17] *Guide to American Law,* 1994 Supplement, p. 455.

Wage and Hour Division
Washington, DC 20210

12. The Age Discrimination in Employment Act of 1967 (amended in 1978)
Prohibits discrimination against persons 40–70 years old in any area of
employment.

In addition to specific federal laws affecting hiring and promoting staff members, managers are reminded of the basic rights that are enshrined in the Bill of Rights of the U.S. Constitution. The rights of staff members, parents, and children are all protected. Freedom of speech, assembly, and religion, and the right to due process and equal protection apply very directly to managing a child development center.[18]

State and Local Laws

Laws vary considerably among the various states and localities. Managers should seek information through their legal advisers, accountants, and licensing agency to be sure that they are aware of and in compliance with laws that relate to their center. Discussions with other child development center managers will help clarify the applications being made of certain laws and the appeal procedures available.

THE INTERVIEW

After the closing date for receiving applications is passed, the applications are organized in individual folders with all relevant attachments, such as letters of reference, transcripts, personal letters from the candidate, and any notes you may have made during contacts. A selection committee may be assigned or elected to assist with interviewing. Balancing the committee with board members, teachers, and parents is often helpful, particularly when hiring professional staff. The committee meets and places the applicants in order of apparent desirability based on information contained in the folder.

Appointments are made with the most promising candidates—those meeting all the requirements listed in the job specification. The committee meets to interview candidates. The main objective is to get the applicant to talk about previous experiences, knowledge of the job at hand, and, for teachers, a knowledge of the philosophy of disciplining children and organizing classrooms. Of course, knowledge is one thing and attitudes are quite another. Some people believe that they can teach appropriate methods to a person who has an open and caring attitude toward children and a genuine enthusiasm for learning much more easily than they can change a negative attitude in a person who knows all the theories and "right answers." You can gauge a candidate's initiative and leadership potential by asking questions about new ideas they have introduced or helped implement in their previous jobs.[19] Keep in mind that all the parts must fit together: your job

---

[18] See Verna Hildebrand, Lillian A. Phenice, Mary M. Gray, and Rebecca P. Hines, *Knowing and Serving Diverse Families* (Upper Saddle River, NJ: Merrill/Prentice Hall, 1996).

[19] Margie Carter, "Developing Strong Self-Images—It's Important for Teachers, Too!" *Child Care Information Exchange* 104 (July/August 1995), pp. 60–62.

Position Open _____

Applicant Name _____

Education	Meets minimal specification?	Comment

Experience:

References:

Interview:

Recommendation:

Signed _____

Title _____ Date _____

(Retain in applicant's folder for affirmative action reports.)

Figure 6–12
Applicant interviewing form

description will reflect your center's basic philosophy; performance evaluations will be based on the job description. Therefore, your interview questions need to try to tap the qualities that you will be evaluating later.

If your program has a clearly stated philosophy, and if you and the committee have done the homework of writing a complete job description, you should be able to use that description to help formulate the kinds of questions you want to ask. The interviewing committee may use a structured form for reporting impressions, such as Figure 6–12. Using a system like this helps you make sure you are treating each candidate equally and fairly. Retain these forms for your affirmative action records, where you may be asked to report the objective basis for your decision.

As part of the interview, you may wish to pose hypothetical situations appropriate to the job the person is seeking. For example, to a candidate for a teaching position you could ask the following questions:

1. "Four-year-old Johnny comes to school with a holster holding a toy gun attached to his belt. What would you do?" (Comment: Since the typical center does not equip itself with weapons, it does not allow children to bring and use them. Thus, gun and holster would be stored in the teacher's desk and sent home at the end of the day. The teacher would acknowledge Johnny's pride in his toy.)
2. "Three-old Jennie picks a dandelion in the yard and shows it to you. What would you do?" (Comment: A perceptive teacher probably would talk to Jennie about the color, smell, and name of the flower, then help extend her knowledge regarding concepts such as plants, growing, spring, and so on.)
3. "A business donates to your center a thousand multicolored handbills printed on one side that were unusable for them because they contained wrong information. Because your center is short of funds for supplies, you appreciate the donation. What would you do with the handbills?" (Comment: Note the creativity expressed by the candidate in this situation.)

Using this technique for interviewing requires prior planning of situations and avoiding "leading"—giving applicants your answers. Of course, you will want to avoid unlawful or unfair questions that serve only to discriminate against certain groups and do not have direct relevance to the person's ability to do the job. For example, you may ask what languages an applicant speaks fluently, which would have a direct bearing on the job of a teacher in a center where children come from several different ethnic backgrounds. However, you may not ask about an applicant's ancestry or nationality. Since most states regulate the minimum age at which a staff member can be counted in the adult-child ratio, you may ask a question such as, "Are you 18 years old or older?" To avoid discrimination against older people, you should not ask, "How old are you?" or "What is your date of birth?"[20] Contact your state's Department of Civil Rights for further guidance.

From the Candidate's View

The applicants must be allowed ample time to ask questions. Wise candidates do their homework and know a lot about your child development center before arriving for the interview. They will want to check out information they have heard or read. Giving applicants a tour of the facility and an opportunity to meet the staff will help them get a feel for working conditions in your center. A firm sense of where he or she would be working helps encourage the applicant to be ready to respond when you are ready to make an offer.

---

[20]Michigan Department of Civil Rights, *Pre-Employment Inquiry Guide* (Detroit: Author, 1985).

You may be in a recruiting mode more than in a screening mode; that is, you are trying to get the best person in as much as keeping the unqualified out. Certain positions should be advertised widely—even nationwide. You may overtly encourage professionals to become candidates for certain positions, rather than just taking your chances on high-quality people just applying in response to a published job specification. You may solicit suggestions for candidates from your professional colleagues across the country, especially for your highest-level positions. Many programs are using the Internet to publicize openings to the widest possible audience. Chapter 7 contains information on how to access this resource.

People who are highly qualified may have many choices of positions when seriously considering moving from their present job. They may interview for several positions simultaneously. Thus, your screening process must be short enough to encourage candidates to stay with you throughout. Continued communication with them and prompt action will be essential. If you are too slow, they may select another position while you are still in the process of considering their application. While you want to be very careful and hire just the right individual, you must also realize that the applicant also has criteria for selecting a position. If another organization fulfills most of those criteria, they may decide in that direction, leaving you back where you started.

Committee Deliberations

Following the series of interviews, the committee members sort out the facts they have learned. They take their job of decision making seriously. Hiring staff is a lengthy, costly process that you and the committee do not want to repeat frequently. The center's goal would be to hire excellent people to stabilize the staff, making openings infrequent.

THE OFFER

Following ample discussion, each committee person ranks the applicants. Finally, the most desired one is selected to receive an offer. The manager may seek an agreement within the committee to proceed down the prioritized listing should the first-choice candidate drop out of the running. Generally, an offer can be made by phone, with a follow-up letter sent immediately after. The salary, working hours, and assignment should be stated on the phone and in the letter. The fringe benefits that the job carries should also be stated. Presumably the applicant has received a job description; this should be attached to the letter with any modifications that may have been negotiated. For example, if the applicant's child received admission to the child development center as part of the offer, then that agreement should be put in writing. You and the candidate should come to an agreement on the starting dates for the position. Generally there is a probationary period for new employees, and this point should be stated clearly both orally and in writing to the person being hired.

In some instances, a physical examination is required. Therefore, the job offer may be tentative until that technicality has been taken care of. If the applicant is to bear the expense of this exam, this requirement should be clearly stated from the beginning. Routine tuberculosis tests are generally available at a public health center if these are required.

Some centers prefer a contract that is signed by the candidate, manager, and head of the policy board. Whether a contract or letter is used, copies of all hiring documents should be carefully sent to all parties and filed. They are legal documents. Once you have signed documents from a candidate, you should communicate that information to your staff.

INFORMING UNSUCCESSFUL CANDIDATES

Common courtesy requires that as soon as possible after you have made an offer of employment and the papers are finalized, you inform the other applicants that the decision has been reached. A pleasant letter such as this one might be sent to help maintain each person's self-esteem even when a candidate was not selected:

Dear Mr. Allen,

Thank you for applying for a teaching position at the XYZ Child Development Center. Due to the number of high-quality applicants, the selection process was a lengthy one. We have finally made the decision and are sorry to have to let you know that you were not selected. With your qualifications, I'm sure you will soon find a position to your liking. I hope so.

Sincerely,

Mary T. Jones
Manager, XYZ Child Development Center

ON-THE-JOB ORIENTATION

Finally the new employee arrives. There are payroll, social security, and income tax withholding cards to sign. Keys are issued at this time, and any printed information prepared for new employees is given out (see Figure 6–13).

You, as manager, or your designee should be responsible for orienting the new employee. If she or he can work alongside another employee, early anxiety can be alleviated. For example, teachers should be encouraged to take new teachers under their wing and help them feel at home. Managers should expect this and specifically ask for help. If a new employee has to rely on the manager for orientation, then competition between new and old staff may develop unnecessarily as the new employee begins turning to the manager for advice.

An experienced staff member who becomes a mentor for a new employee helps assure a smooth transition within the unit—the acceptance, comfort, and enjoyment of the new person are thereby facilitated. The mentoring process also benefits the more experienced employee, who will probably welcome the recognition of his or her abilities and may be challenged to think a little more deeply

Employee Name _____

Position _____

Date of Hire _____

Note: The purpose of this checklist is to be sure that you have been adequately oriented to the XYZ Child Development Center and to the policies for which you will be responsible. Please initial and date the items listed below as they are accomplished. When all are completed, please sign the form and return it to the office for the manager's signature and date.

_____ 1. Explanation of orientation process

_____ 2. Hiring conference

    _____ Discussed and signed job description

    _____ Signed contract

    _____ Provided center policy handbook and state licensing rules

    _____ Provided timetable for introductory phase

    _____ Discussed probationary period

    _____ Set date for first day of work

_____ 3. Routine procedures and policies

    _____ Set daily schedule

    _____ Completed paperwork (payroll_____, W-4_____, health certificate_____, child abuse form_____)

    _____ Clarified call-in procedures

    _____ Discussed pay dates

_____ 4. Professional responsibilities (see handbook)

    _____ Dress and appearance

_____ Code of conduct

_____ Discipline policies

_____ Supplies for your work

_____ 5. Orientation to the school

    _____ Received tour of facilities and designated personal space

    _____ Issued keys and supplies

    _____ Introduced to staff members

    _____ Introduced to children and parents

    _____ Explained coworker relationship

    _____ Explained emergency procedures

_____ 6. Probationary conference

    _____ Discussed center policy handbook and licensing rules

    _____ Results of initial observation of skills shared

    _____ Clarified inservice expectation

    _____ Had opportunity for your questions

Comments:

Signature _____ Date _____
           Employee

Signature _____ Date _____
           Manager or Designee

Figure 6–13
Orientation checklist for XYZ Child Development Center

about the reasons behind procedures being demonstrated or explained to the new employee.

When a new employee is somewhat different from previous employees, this warm reception is especially helpful. "Different" may mean a male in an all-female staff, a black in an all-white staff, a younger person in an older staff, and so on. The skills and talents the person brings to the job, rather than any differences, should become the focus.

ON-THE-JOB PERFORMANCE

In your orientation with a new employee, you should clearly state how you go about evaluating on-the-job performance and other activities. You should state how often you monitor the performance—monthly, quarterly, yearly—with the proviso that you will make efforts to become familiar with their work by dropping in frequently and getting acquainted.

You and your staff should remember that during the candidate's probationary period, the candidate is not the only one being evaluated—the center is also being evaluated by the candidate. After spending so much time in hiring, you should want to make every effort to make your new employee comfortable and successful.

You can make an evaluation sheet by using the job description and placing categories before or after the items, such as these:

1. Poorly done or not at all
2. Partially done, improvement needed
3. Adequately done
4. Very well done—congratulations!

Be sure to let your staff know that you will be evaluating them from time to time. Also, remember to date your observation.

If your monitoring procedures are working, you will have early indications when an employee has some trouble doing the work or meeting the standards. Frequent visits, frank discussions, and specific efforts are needed to get the individual's work on track. Using the checklist made from the job description will help you and the employee focus on what needs to be done. The standards of performance may need clarification. Keep copies of each dated evaluation sheet, because if you need to dismiss the employee, these sheets are your evidence. Also, memos of your conferences with dates and actions will help you make the record that gives you sufficient evidence to dismiss the individual. This process should not be done lightly, but in full regard for the individual's due process rights. An outside observer might be requested, if you wonder whether a personality conflict is more the basis of problems than the quality of work. However, within the probationary period, the manager is obligated to monitor new employees' work to see that they are performing up to standard.

Hiring and orienting new employees are expensive tasks; therefore, the orientation should be planned carefully to help the employee succeed. A chance to talk over progress should be provided every week or two at first, then less frequently as the employee adjusts. Support and positive feedback are essential during the early weeks as well as later on as full responsibility is assumed.

DISMISSING STAFF MEMBERS

Sometimes an employee simply does not work out satisfactorily. After helping sessions designed to get the performance on track and other individual and group sessions, you, as manager, may have to say to the person, "We have a problem. Somehow this job is not right for you. I want to help you find a job more suitable for you, where you can feel adequate and happy." Then you can discuss ways you can help the person relocate. Your humane attitude lets the person know that you care about him or her as an individual, but you must act when performance is not up to par because many people depend on a staff member's performance. Generally an employee is surprised to find warmth and grateful for the opportunity to depart gracefully and will leave in a short time. In the meantime, you have an obligation to limit the person's duties to those where children would not be harmed in any way. Such a humanistic procedure will do less harm to the total morale of the remaining staff members than outright firing would.

Obviously, such an approach cannot be used in cases of suspected physical abuse of children, where your obligation to protect the children will take precedence over other concerns. In these cases, licensing and law enforcement authorities become involved, and, if the abuse is substantiated, immediate dismissal is warranted.

EMPLOYEE-EMPLOYER RELATIONS

The manager of a child development center has an obligation to assist employees—especially those in similar jobs—to have time together and become friends who care about each other. To facilitate cooperation, communication, and friendship, some center managers have parties and potluck suppers periodically. Nurturing and educating children require warm, sensitive people who also are interested in and care about their coworkers. Without special effort, employees may become isolated in their own domains and have little time for getting to know each other.

Certainly teachers see many children and parents each day, but they need a break when they can share their own lives and concerns with colleagues. How can some of this caring and sharing be arranged? If it is not planned, you may find staff talking about personal concerns when they should be listening to and talking to children. Certainly in some centers teachers have a difficult time getting away from children even to go to the bathroom. Through thoughtful scheduling, volunteers or part-time staff can give relief while teachers take a 10-minute break.

Nutritious beverages and cold water should be available from the kitchen for teachers on breaks. Coffee and colas with caffeine can increase, rather than decrease, tensions; fruit juice or milk can provide needed energy for the work at hand. Smoking is now generally illegal in public buildings and certainly should be illegal in child development centers. Nonsmoking in the center can be a condition of employment, because of the need to maintain healthful air and a safe environment for all. Parents, too, should be requested to leave smoking materials outside the center.

Dollars invested in planning will pay off in higher-quality programs. Relief teachers could be employed as needed to take over a classroom while the coteachers share ideas and do planning. Another helpful approach would be to pay teachers for a few hours some evening or on a Saturday each month to do planning. Joint planning aids the esprit de corps that center managers should be pleased to see developing among staff in various divisions. The issue of setting aside time for planning is particularly acute in child care centers operating 5 days weekly for 10 or so hours a day. Here the teaching staff and others must be scheduled to arrive at staggered early or late hours to cover the entire time children are present and to avoid working more than 8 hours a day. Staggered hours work against staff socializing, which is needed to aid rapport building. Paid planning times outside the center's usual hours of operation can help overcome this difficulty.

At times staff members need individual conferences with the manager; at other times the issues raised require the attention of several staff members. If asked for an appointment, the manager can ask the person whether the issue is personal or of concern to others. Some people may attempt to get the manager to side with them, when, from the point of view of group harmony, discussing the issue with the entire staff and coming to a group consensus would be a better long-range solution.

Managers must develop some means for keeping in touch with the people in each of the units being managed. Finding time for sharing views and information and solving problems may be difficult. Public schools, with their shorter hours and time for professional days, find staff meetings less difficult to manage than child care centers, with their longer operating days. Efforts must be made to overcome these handicaps. Some centers are able to use paid substitutes to relieve staff for these meetings; others have developed a pool of volunteers or made arrangements with parents who are able to take days from their own jobs to fill in for teachers during staff meetings. Even full-day centers find their attendance dwindling as 5 P.M. approaches, and many follow a practice of combining classrooms and dismissing teachers in order to reduce payroll. Instead of sending staff home early, it might be possible to keep them on the clock and allocate these hours to planning meetings.

Managing by walking around is a recently discussed management style. Applied in a child development center, this approach involves the manager walking around, dropping into classrooms, playgrounds, and lounges and mingling with staff and children as they are involved in their activities. Thus, the manager becomes a familiar person, seen as relaxed and approachable, giving staff members a feeling that their work is known and appreciated. Using this style, a manager personally and quietly can give a word of praise here and a suggestion there or may make a notation on a shortage of material or a needed repair job that had not yet been noticed or reported.

DECISIONS, DECISIONS . . .

 You have noticed that the bulletin boards in your center's classrooms are becoming yellow and frayed with age. Someone suggests that you offer coupons for free pizzas to teachers as an incentive for changing the displays more often. Is this an intrinsic or extrinsic reward? What are the likely results? What will happen when you run out of coupons? What alternatives can you imagine?

STAFF COMMUNICATION

A child development center is a person-centered organization. Knowing and responding to human needs is surely a major objective. Some communication between staff members and you, the manager, occurs incidentally or perhaps routinely every day. Can you be open and encourage this communication? Some managers are so aloof and unapproachable that employees quake at the thought of entering their offices. Other managers try the pal approach and one hardly realizes who the manager is. Which style works best for a child development center? Probably some midpoint position is best. Managers, like all other people, have unique qualities to be used advantageously. They must be approachable; yet they must also be leaders.

Communication among staff members is also an important part of a person-centered operation. Ironically, in organizations such as early education and care, where advocates profess belief in person-to-person communication, often little time is set aside for personal communication among staff members. Planning time, as discussed in Chapter 4 and also earlier in this chapter, focuses on the curriculum and the children. However, your staff are people with personal concerns; it should be legitimate for teachers to have time to converse about personal matters.

DECISIONS, DECISIONS . . .

 When do teachers and aides working with children typically have time to talk over personal matters? What purposes, if any, do conversations serve? Discuss how a manager can provide such opportunities.

Clearly, when teachers are managing their group of children, they need to pay close attention to the children and not be visiting about personal matters. Even when everything is peaceful in the playroom, the teachers need to be observing the children to know what each child is doing and thinking. Usually teachers are also responsible for children at lunch. If at break time one teacher takes charge of the children with the support of an aide while the other teacher is out of the room, the teachers have no time together to learn about each other. These are the typical situations interfering with personal communications. What can you, as manager, do?

You and an aide could run the class from time to time while the teachers socialize together. You may actually hire a qualified teacher whose job it is to substitute for teachers, taking over teaching and managing each class for a half-hour or so once a week to give the teachers time together. One school has a librarian who periodically plans a special story-music period for the children, thus giving teachers a break together. You can plan evening or weekend events that bring teachers together to socialize freely. Arranging visiting time will help ensure that caregivers are focused on the children when they are on duty.

What is evidence that staff members need personal time together? First, a common sight is to see adults in a corner of the playroom or yard conversing and largely ignoring the children. Second, a staff member has an emergency at home with a family member (child, spouse, or aged parent), and other staff members do not even know. Third, misunderstandings arise over little things that might have been worked out in a friendly fashion if people had been talking together. Fourth, staff have differences that are interfering with their working together for the children's benefit. Fifth, individuals show evidence of feeling unappreciated. Finally, absenteeism increases.

Active Listening

Many early childhood professionals and parents are acquainted with the concept of **active listening** as defined by Thomas Gordon.[21] Gordon has adapted the method for teachers and managers as well.[22] He writes, "Active listening is certainly not complex. Listeners need only restate, in their own language, their impression of the expression of the sender." In Gordon's example, the sender says, "I don't know how I'm going to untangle this messy problem." The listener responds, using active listening, "You're really stumped on how to solve this one."[23] Thus, active listening focuses on the feeling expressed rather than on the content of a person's complaint. The reflected response is nonjudgmental. If it is in error, the sender can correct the impression immediately. The sender with a complaint thus can take responsibility for the feeling expressed and find a solution to the problem.

I-Messages

Managers will also find Gordon's concept of **I-messages** useful. I-messages are better than "you-messages" and are for informing staff members of behavior that

---

[21] Thomas Gordon, *P.E.T.: Parent Effectiveness Training* (New York: Wyden, 1970), pp. 41–94.

[22] Thomas Gordon, *T.E.T.: Teacher Effectiveness Training* (New York: Wyden, 1974) and *Leadership Effectiveness Training: L.E.T.* (New York: Bantam, 1978).

[23] Gordon, *L.E.T.*, p. 57.

At times providing a comfortable lap is essential for meeting a child's emotional needs.
Wichita High School Child Care Center, Wichita, KS

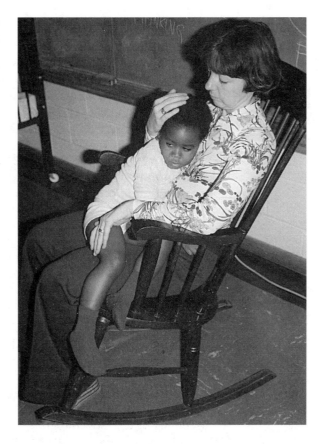

is not suitable. Using an I-message such as "I waste a lot of time looking for the painting aprons" is more effective than charging the child care aide with "You should have left the painting aprons where I could find them." The aide would feel more willing to modify the behavior when not accused or put down.[24]

One manager reported feeling really frustrated by a series of complaints from several staff members. Rumors seemed to be going around the center, yet the source could not be located. Finally, the manager announced, "Thursday night we'll have a pizza supper at my house for the entire staff. Please bring your complaints and rumors. I'm feeling very frustrated by all the rumors and complaints I hear, and I want to get them out so we can settle them." On Thursday night when the people arrived, the manager discovered that many of the complaints had already been settled informally among the people affected. The staff had a pleasant evening together discussing some of the problems that had been rumored. The weather had been terrible for weeks, which, acknowledged the manager, often tires people out and makes them more difficult to get along with.

---

[24] Ibid, pp. 98–99.

EVALUATION CONFERENCES

Deliberately scheduling evaluation conferences with each staff member at least once each year is desirable. Here evaluation of the past and projections for the future can be made. Both praise and problems should be on the agenda. Each member should be invited to bring a list of accomplishments since the last conference. Regularizing the process helps keep individual staffers from feeling they are being favored or picked on. A summary letter should follow the meeting. (This topic is discussed further in Chapter 8.)

Remember that the job description (Figure 6–4) is designed to serve as an evaluation tool. It is your agreement with each employee as to what he or she is expected to do on the job. Thus, in planning for evaluation conferences you will think about each item listed on the job description and organize information to discuss with the employee. If you are considering changes in the job description, this would be a time to discuss those proposed changes. The new job description would then apply for the coming year.

STAFF MEETINGS

Staff meetings can serve as one avenue of communication. Staff meetings should be held during paid staff time. Managers should be sure that staff meetings serve communication goals, not just from manager to staff but also from staff to manager and among staff members.

Goals should be developed for meetings. Meeting for the fun of it is fine, but individuals should know the purpose of the meeting in advance, even then. Meetings of task-specific groups are often more productive than total staff meetings. Dealing with some staff individually may be more effective than having people attend meetings with items on the agenda that do not affect everyone.

Be sure to give staff members an agenda when the meeting is announced. Meetings should be announced at least a week in advance, except in dire emergencies. Encourage members to come prepared to discuss agenda items. Start the meeting with a few moments of individual announcements and concerns of members who wish to speak. Such items of special interest can become agenda items for future meetings, if desired. Keep the meeting moving along by sticking to the agenda topics. Avoid wearing out a topic just because time allowed for the meeting has not elapsed. Dismissing a staff meeting a few minutes early is refreshing, and staff members can do needed individual work. Record minutes or agreements reached at the meeting, and circulate them within the next few days. Minutes give you a record for future reference.

PROFESSIONAL DEVELOPMENT

The idea that each staff member is expected to participate in ongoing professional development is suggested in the job analysis, job specification, and job description documents. Stipulating this expectation at the point of hiring helps avoid the complaint that it is an "extra" or that a person is being picked on. The assumption is that every staff member, including you as manager, must keep up-to-date in your profession. Recall the expanding "cone of knowledge" discussed earlier. An even more positive view holds that professional development is a "right of each individual teacher *and* of all teachers within the school" (emphasis in original).[25]

Professional development can be viewed as an ongoing process that is fostered whenever staff observe children closely, reflect on those observations, and share their ideas with parents or other staff. Margie Carter, who has worked extensively in the area of professional development in early childhood programs, finds that by focusing on observations of children's play, staff members are able to gain insights and develop new knowledge without the stress and defensive feelings usually incurred by focusing on staff behaviors.[26]

Professional development can be stimulated through interactions with individuals, small groups from the same job category, or the entire staff. Such interactions can occur at the center or in conferences elsewhere. Depending on the topic and your knowledge of your staff members' individual learning styles, you might distribute a handout for all staff to read and discuss; you might, with permission, visit a classroom to observe, reflect, or model some technique; you might suggest that teachers visit each other's classrooms; or you might bring in an outside consultant. Whatever mode or location is selected, professional development activities cost money and must become a budget item.

Hines has suggested 10 guides for professional development activities:[27]

1. *Focus on the positive traits and behaviors of the staff member rather than dwelling on the negatives.* For example, say, "I like your soft, firm voice when you guide children" or "It was really effective when you stooped down to Pete's level and looked him in the eye when you wanted him to stop hitting Jacob."

2. *Offer the person a variety of choices for action whenever possible when critiquing any behavior or action.* For example, you might say, "You could place fewer chairs at the art table, or you could ask for help from the aide, or you could plan a less complicated project. Which one do you think would help solve the problem of children pushing each other out of the way at the art table?"

3. *Avoid using judgmental comparisons to motivate individuals to improve.* For example, say, "I like the way you are working on using positive forms of guidance," rather than "Why can't you quit saying 'don't' and begin using positive guidance like Doris does?" Such comparisons may create a dislike of Doris.

---

[25] Carlina Rinaldi, "Staff Development in Reggio Emilia," in Lilian Katz and Bernard Cesarone, *Reflections on the Reggio Emilia Approach* (Urbana, IL: ERIC Clearinghouse on Elementary and Early Childhood Education, 1994), p. 55.

[26] Margie Carter, "Catching Teachers 'Being Good': Using Observation to Communicate," in Elizabeth Jones (ed.), *Growing Teachers: Partnerships in Professional Development* (Washington, DC: National Association for the Education of Young Children, 1993), pp. 38–53.

[27] Rebecca Peña Hines, "Techniques for Preparing People to Work with Young Children," *Illinois Teacher* 26:5 (May/June 1983), pp. 186–187.

4. *Take time to be sure the individual is fully aware of what can be expected of your style of inservice education.*   If you are going to observe, take notes, and report, let the staffer know. If you are going into the classroom to demonstrate and then observe while the staffer practices, let him or her know that. Telling staff members that they will get feedback right away is very important. They will generally cooperate more that way than if feedback is delayed.

5. *Avoid setting yourself up as "the expert" or as knowing "the one way" things are done.*   Acknowledging personality differences and a variety of ways in which tasks can be carried out helps people feel they can find their own style as they experiment to discover what works best for them.

6. *Use a variety of teaching techniques to help meet individual learning styles of staff members.*   One person may learn well from demonstrations, another may learn best from reading a book or article, and another might like a discussion. Try to perceive which is the best technique for the person and for the information you wish to impart.

7. *Help staff members appreciate how improving their skills helps children.*   Many staff members will do almost anything if they observe that children are happier, friendlier, or the like. Therefore, help the staffer recognize the evidence of children's growth.

8. *Make your interpersonal relationships consistent with your own advice.*   If you expect staff members to see the positives in children, then you must try to see the positives in the staff members. If you want staffers to be consistent with children, then you should model consistent behavior with them.

9. *Act on staff members' suggestions for inservice education in areas where they feel the need.*   Simply asking staff members where they feel the need for help often brings surprising suggestions. These choices should be given high priority. Motivation can be expected to be high.

10. *Remind staff members that you, as manager, have grown and expect to continue to grow in knowledge and will share with them new things you learn from people with whom you confer.*   Take time to give individual staff members clippings or mention a topic of interest to them. As a way of sharing, bring innovative ideas back to the staff.

Variety of Professional Development Activities

Professional development for your staff is much like curriculum planning for children; that is, start where individuals are and use their interests as guides. This procedure assumes the individuals have some interest in their work and in improving themselves. You might let small groups take turns making suggestions. Some possibilities are described here:

1. Videotape a teacher-child interaction in each classroom, then use the clips for a discussion of guidance, using accreditation criteria.
2. Observe in classrooms, then select topics that would broaden or give more depth to interaction or curriculum you observed.
3. When an especially significant project takes place in one group, be sure other teachers, and sometimes the children, get a chance to visit that classroom and see the evidence (e.g., children's block structures, dramatic play

props, paintings, etc.). Encourage them to share with others the fun they and the children had.

4. Use documentation panels (an idea developed in Reggio Emilia and adopted by many programs in this country) to capture the excitement and insights that characterize each stage of a project undertaken with the children. Documentation panels are visual displays that include photographs, drawings and diagrams by children and teachers, and printed transcripts from recorded conversations that reveal children's thought processes.

5. Take a hot news story from newspapers or TV and use it as a basis for additional information.

6. Exchange workshops with another center—for example, a couple of teachers coming over to show art activities, and two of your teachers going there to show science.

7. Get teachers to volunteer for a local, state, or national conference and practice on center staff.

8. Invite a local college faculty member to bring students to do a hands-on workshop of science or art ideas for your teachers.

9. Use a parent's complaint or statement as a discussion topic and a springboard toward improving parent-teacher communication.

10. Bring back the current interesting news from your managers' meetings and share details with your staff.

11. Tap into expertise that may exist within your pool of parents and ask them to share it—with an individual staff member, a small group, or a meeting of the entire staff. A nurse, doctor, or emergency medical technician may be able to offer first aid or CPR training. An artist or craftsperson might provide new ideas for the possibilities inherent in fibers or clay. Members of various cultural groups can share information, stories, songs, and customs that can become part of the curriculum as well as sensitize everyone to individual differences.

12. Do not stop with parents. Grandparents, aunts, uncles, even older brothers or sisters may have skills to share. Staff members who feel timid about using computers with children in their classrooms, for example, might be made more comfortable through a mini-workshop with a 10- or 11-year-old "expert."

13. Have staffers share insights from a conference presentation they have seen and new ideas they are going to implement in their work.

14. Buy new books related to teachers' work, annotate them, and send out information in a memo encouraging reading and discussion of the books.

15. Post clippings and cartoons to stimulate conversation among staff and parents.

You might advance the idea of cooperation among schools and centers in your locality for inservice events. Often you, or your experienced teachers, will be leaders in the local affiliate of the NAEYC, helping to set up such events. In some communities, several child development organizations (e.g., a Head Start agency, the local school district, and corporate child care chains) have pooled their resources to establish a consortium for professional development. This approach enables them to bring in several outside speakers throughout the year, and they all benefit from a wider array of activities than any one would have been able to afford. Always give these events your extra support by sending staff members— paying their way or giving released paid time. One way to stretch the stimulation staff members gain from a conference is to duplicate the handouts they receive and let them give a report to appropriate staff members.

DECISIONS, DECISIONS . . .

 Dottie and Debbie are two teachers who went to their state's AEYC meeting. They were constantly together in each workshop they attended. What does their behavior tell you about them? How would attendance at different sessions facilitate more new ideas for your school? How can attending together strengthen their resolve to do something new when they are back at your school?

Centers often pay for one conference a year for regular staff members, give them paid time to go, and pay a substitute in their absence, especially for local or state conferences. A few pay hotel and transportation for national and regional conferences, too. Although expensive, this is an excellent means of fostering professional development. The money is well spent if the staff member makes full use of the conference. Some guidance may be needed. Encourage various staff to plan their conference agendas ahead of time and attend different workshops rather than all from your center going to the same one. Encourage them to speak to conferees in order to make new friends and learn about innovations from them, and discourage them from using the time primarily for shopping and eating out. A stipulation to report back to the staff who missed the event helps the conference goers feel their responsibility to others.

VOLUNTEERS

Volunteers are valuable assets, giving considerable amounts of their human capital to child development centers each year. Their presence is in addition to the required minimum for child-staff ratios. To make the best use of this valuable resource, you should attend to the same types of tasks with volunteers as you do with paid staff. That is, you will have to locate people whose skills and attitudes make them suitable for work in a child development center; acquaint them with your center's organization and policies; provide necessary training; assign them worthwhile tasks; monitor and guide them in the performance of those tasks; let them know how they are doing; and give appropriate recognition for a job well done.

Volunteers can be very well educated and experienced, or they may lack much of both traits. Some volunteer for an hour or two a month; others volunteer

Volunteers receive satisfaction from the positive and pleasurable relationships they build with children.
Early Learning Center, Appalachian State University, Boone, NC

many hours each week. As manager, you can make contacts with groups that encourage volunteering, such as churches, civic clubs, high schools, colleges, and the like. Many parents enjoy volunteering to help in their child's classroom—as in parent cooperative early childhood schools. Some willingly take time from their job to help in their child's class. Ruling out people who are employed is shortsighted when considering volunteers. Fathers, who are often more able than women to take time off work with minimal explanation and are frequently assuming a more caregiving role, may be available to volunteer or visit—if invited positively. Some fathers complain that when they have volunteered, they were treated in a sexist manner, as though men could not do the tasks properly. Of course, such treatment should never occur.

Senior citizens are often available to volunteer regularly in schools and centers. Some funding has occasionally been available for transportation. Many warm laps and wonderful storytellers are available among the senior citizens for giving one-to-one attention to children. You may be more successful in recruiting among older people you know rather than among senior citizen groups. After a few older men and women start and enjoy helping, others are likely to want to help the children, too.

The more you treat your volunteers like professionals, the more professionally they will behave. All your hard work at establishing a pleasant esprit de corps among your regular staff will pay off in keeping the volunteers you recruit. Remember to include volunteers in the professional development opportunities you make available for staff, and guard against always giving them the dirty work or the cold side of the play yard while paid staff take the more pleasant tasks or stay indoors where it is warm.

Volunteers give from their storehouse of human capital. They also receive satisfaction from the positive and pleasurable relationships they build with children and staff. They might receive more tangible benefits in terms of work experience to add to their résumés, and they should be encouraged to keep records of their volunteer time. Perhaps most important, volunteers usually become stronger people, more knowledgeable and more committed to serving children and their families. They are marvelous allies to have in a community. Having connections with many groups, they can rally political support should that become necessary.

CONCLUSION

People possess the human capital—that is, the assets of knowledge, skills, and abilities—that can be put to work with nonhuman resources to produce the services of the child development center. Many steps are required for hiring staff, orienting them to their new job, facilitating communication, and evaluating their performance. The need for ongoing professional development for all staff is crucial, and suggestions have been provided for accomplishing this. Volunteers can play a helpful role. The manager's relationships with staff members are most vital. With good relationships, a stable staff and a pleasant, healthful working environment can develop, which will contribute enormously to the children and families for whom the service is planned.

APPLICATIONS

1. Write a job description for a cook in a child development center.
2. Write a job specification for a cook in a child development center.
3. Write a job analysis for a teacher following the Civil Service job analysis outlined in the chapter.
4. Write a job description for a teacher.
5. Divide the class into interviewing teams, and role-play an interview session with a job applicant. Discuss the major points stressed in the example. Suggest improvements.
6. Discuss experiences each class member has had seeking a job and interviewing for a job. What have you learned?
7. Write a letter of application for a manager's position. Exchange letters in class and critique them constructively.

8. To your management notebook, add forms on job analysis, job description, job specification, and job classification.

STUDY QUESTIONS

1. Define human capital. Explain how human capital applies in a child development center.
2. Make a chart showing the 10 tasks of managers. List actions of the manager that relate to each task, as discussed within the chapter.
3. Describe Maslow's hierarchy of needs and explain how his theory applies to management, staffing, and employee relations in a child development center.
4. State five steps needed to make a center an attractive workplace for a staff member.
5. Describe and differentiate among job analysis, job description, and job specification.
6. List job titles for early childhood education workers, indicating years of education and experience needed for persons with each job title.
7. Differentiate among the following three levels of teachers:
   a. CDA (what do the letters stand for?)
   b. Certified teacher
   c. Associate degree teacher
8. Describe each developmental stage of a teacher as identified by Katz. Tell how knowing these steps can be useful to a manager.
9. Describe the way a manager can manage the hiring process for teachers to determine their ability to work with children.
10. Describe the use of the job description in hiring and evaluating an employee.
11. Describe the means of communication with staff members using the following:
    a. Management by walking around
    b. I–messages
    c. Feedback
    d. Evaluation conferences
12. List Hines's 10 guidelines for planning professional development activities. Give either a negative or positive example of each from your own experience.
13. List the types of professional development opportunities available in your community.
14. Develop a list of guidelines for involving volunteers in your center.

SUGGESTED READINGS

Albrecht, Kay. "Helping Teachers Grow: Strategies for Diversifying Performance Evaluation and Feedback." *Child Care Information Exchange* 74 (August 1990), pp. 34–36.

Benham, Nancy, Thomas Miller, and Susan Kontos. "Pinpointing Staff Training Needs in Child Care Centers." *Young Children* 43:4 (May 1988), pp. 9–16.

Carter, Margie, and Deb Curtis. *Training Teachers: A Harvest of Theory and Practice.* St. Paul, MN: Redleaf, 1994.

Cherry, Clare, Barbara Harkness, and Kay Kuzma. *Nursery School & Day Care Management Guide*. Belmont, CA: Lake, 1987.

Clewett, Ann S. "Guidance and Discipline: Teaching Young Children Appropriate Behavior." *Young Children* 43:4 (May 1988), pp. 26–31.

Galinsky, Ellen. "Parents and Teacher-Caregivers: Sources of Tension, Sources of Support." *Young Children* 43:3 (March 1988), pp. 4–12.

Granucci, P. L. "Kindergarten Teachers: Working through Our Identity Crisis." *Young Children* 45:3 (March 1990), pp. 6–11.

Green, M., and E. Widoff. "Special Needs Child Care: Training Is a Key Issue." *Young Children* 45:3 (March 1990), pp. 60–61.

Hendrick, Joanne. *Why Teach?* Washington, DC: National Association for the Education of Young Children, 1987.

Hill, Lynn T. "Helping Teachers Love Their Work." *Child Care Information Exchange* 104 (July/August 1995), pp. 30–34.

Johnson, Julienne, and Janet B. McCracken (eds.). *The Early Childhood Career Lattice: Perspectives on Professional Development*. Washington, DC: National Association for the Education of Young Children, 1994.

Jones, Elizabeth (ed.). *Growing Teachers: Partnerships in Staff Development*. Washington, DC: National Association for the Education of Young Children, 1993.

Jorde-Bloom, Paula. *A Great Place to Work: Improving Conditions for Staff in Young Children's Programs*. Washington, DC: National Association for the Education of Young Children, 1991.

Jorde-Bloom, Paula. "Teachers Need 'TLC' Too." *Young Children* 43:6 (September 1988), pp. 4–8.

Klass, Carol S. "Childrearing Interactions within Developmental Home- or Center-Based Early Education." *Young Children* 42:3 (March 1987), pp. 9–13, 67–70.

Logue, Mary Ellin, Brenda K. Eheart, and Robin L. Leavitt. "Staff Training: What Difference Does It Make?" *Young Children* 41:5 (July 1986), pp. 8–9.

Miller, Patricia, and V. Stayton. "Combining Early Childhood and Early Childhood Special Education Standards in Personnel Preparation Programs: Experiences from Two States." *Topics in Early Childhood Special Education* 13:3, pp. 372–387.

Modigiliani, Kathy. "Twelve Reasons for the Low Wages in Child Care." *Young Children* 43:3 (March 1988), pp. 14–15.

Morgan, Gwen, S. Azer, J. Costley, A. Genser, I. Goodman, J. Lombardi, and B. McGimsey. *Making a Career of It: The State of the States Report on Career Development and Early Education*. Boston: Center for Career Development in Early Care and Education, 1993.

Neugebauer, Bonnie. *The Anti-Ordinary Thinkbook*. Redmond, WA: Exchange, 1991.

Neugebauer, Bonnie. "Substitutes—We're the Real Thing!" *Child Care Information Exchange* 82 (November/December 1991), pp. 19–20.

Perreault, Joe, and Roger Neugebauer. "An Ounce of Prevention: How to Write an Employee Handbook." *Child Care Information Exchange* 59 (January 1988), pp. 21–24.

Phillips, C. B. "The Child Development Associate Program: Entering a New Era." *Young Children* 45:3 (March 1990), pp. 24–27.

Phillips, Deborah, and Marcy Whitebook. "Who Are Child Care Workers?" *Young Children* 41:4 (May 1986), pp. 14–20.

Rinaldi, Carlina. "Staff Development in Reggio Emilia." In Lilian Katz and Bernard Cesarone (eds.), *Reflections on the Reggio Emilia Approach*. Urbana, IL: ERIC Clearinghouse on Elementary and Early Childhood Education, 1994.

Scallan, Patricia. "How to Implement a Coaching Program in Your Center." *Child Care Information Exchange* 59 (January 1988), pp. 35–37.

Scallan, Patricia. "Teachers Coaching Teachers: Development from Within." *Child Care Information Exchange* 58 (November 1987), pp. 3–6.

Stephens, Karen. "The Art of Building (and Re-Building) Staff Unity." *Child Care Information Exchange* 102 (March/April 1995), pp. 63–68.

U.S. Department of Labor. "The Fair Labor Standards Act: Are Your Employees Paid Legally under Federal Law?" *Texas Child Care* 19:1 (Summer 1995), pp. 18–20.

Venditti, Phillip N., and Brook Zemel. "Selecting the Best Staff." *Texas Child Care* 12:2 (Fall 1988), pp. 25–28.

Weber-Schwartz, Nancy. "Patience or Understanding?" *Young Children* 42:3 (March 1987), pp. 52–54.

White, Barbara P., and Michael A. Phair. "'It'll Be a Challenge!': Managing Emotional Stress in Teaching Disabled Children." *Young Children* 41:2 (January 1986), pp. 44–48.

Whitebook, Marcy, and R. C. Granger. "Assessing Teacher Turnover." *Young Children* 44:4 (May 1989), p. 11.

Whitebook, Marcy, Deborah Phillips, and Carollee Howes. *The National Child Care Staffing Study Revisited: Four Years in the Life of Center-Based Child Care*. Oakland, CA: Child Care Employee Project, 1993.

CHAPTER 7

Leading

•••

Who are the leaders you have followed as a child, as a student, and as an adult? What characteristics did they possess? Why was it important for those leaders to be there?

Now look at yourself as a potential leader. What talents do you have that would make you consider becoming a manager of a child development center and therefore a leader of a staff? Certainly as a teacher you have had considerable opportunity to plan, organize, and deal with employees. Your classroom represents a microcosm of the larger unit you will now manage. Therefore, you already have at least some leadership experience if you have managed a classroom for a few years. You may now wish to begin thinking about preparing yourself to be a leader. You can consider being a principal of a school, the manager of a child development center, or a manager of some other human services unit such as a United Fund agency, a senior citizen center, or a family planning agency. Leadership in various human service organizations requires many similar skills.

Leading is defined as the process of directing and influencing others through example, talent, information, and personal interaction skills. It is a basic function of managers.

MANAGING AND LEADING DIFFER

Management consultant Stephen Covey argues that leaders have the necessary vision to focus on the larger picture, anticipate trends, and set new goals, while managers concentrate on finding the most efficient ways of accomplishing established goals.[1] In Covey's example, the workers are clearing a path through a jungle; the managers are surveying the site and procuring better tools to clear the path; and the leader is the person who climbs a tree to discover that they are in the wrong jungle!

One might argue that, for too long, we in the early childhood profession have been good workers and managers, trying to clear better and faster paths through the jungle, making do with fewer and fewer resources, with church basements and cast-off materials. A leader, on the other hand, is someone like Loris Malaguzzi, the Italian thinker and prominent early childhood educator, whose fundamental premise was that children are competent and powerful and deserve the finest equipment and materials, most beautiful spaces, and best thinking of the best minds. As a result of his leadership, the early childhood programs of Reggio Emilia have flourished for 30 years and are providing models of excellence for the world. In a similar way, leaders in the United States and other countries are challenging our old ideas about curriculum, professional development, and ways of serving all children, regardless of race, ethnicity, gender, income, or ability.

Managing and leading differ in at least four respects, according to Robert Albanese:[2] (a) the context in which each occurs, (b) the legitimacy of authority, (c) the nature of accountability, and (d) the motivation of followers. He notes that in managing, relationships are required in an organizational context between the manager and those people being managed. Leadership, on the other hand, can occur anywhere and does not have to have an organizational context. A manager's authority is vested in a job position in a formal organization; a leader owes legitimacy to voluntary followers and not to authority vested in a formal job position. Managers are accountable for the job behavior of themselves and those they manage; leaders are accountable only for themselves. People follow managers because their job description requires it, but they follow leaders voluntarily and for reasons of their own.

Though managing and leading are different and difficult to distinguish at times, Katz and Kahn argue that effective managing requires leadership that elicits voluntary follower behavior beyond that associated with required performance on a job.[3] These points seem particularly appropriate when considering managing and leading in a child development center, because you, as manager, will be vested with some leadership authority yet will value the voluntary, spontaneous, and creative differences among your staff. How will you motivate your staff to produce a really model program for young children? How much responsibility is yours and how much is your staff's?

When considering organizational leadership, it is worthwhile to review a classic research study on the effects of leadership styles in formal organizations. White and

---

[1] Stephen Covey, *The Seven Habits of Highly Effective People* (New York: Simon & Schuster, 1989), p. 101.
[2] Robert Albanese, *Managing toward Accountability for Performance* (Homewood, IL: Irwin, 1978), p. 370.
[3] Daniel Katz and Robert L. Kahn, *The Social Psychology of Organizations* (New York: Wiley, 1966), p. 302.

Lippitt investigated the effects of three different styles of leadership on worker productivity and morale.[4] The three styles of leadership ranged from **laissez-faire** to **democratic** to **autocratic**. The results of the study are summarized in Figure 7–1.

DECISIONS, DECISIONS . . .

In your infant-toddler program, children are moved "up" to the next room as they begin crawling, then walking, and so on. This approach makes room for new infants entering the center and allows your staff members to become "experts" on a particular developmental level. You have noticed that this change is stressful for the children, who must become accustomed to new caregivers, and some parents have expressed disappointment at ending a relationship with someone they had grown to know and trust. You have been reading about the importance of continuous relationships for infants and toddlers and about programs in other countries where children stay with the same group of children and the same teachers for as long as 3 years. You wonder about adopting this practice in your center, but the present system seems so efficient. List the advantages and disadvantages of each. Discuss how a leader would approach this problem differently from a manager.

LEADERSHIP AND ACCREDITATION

Leadership is related to many aspects of the center accreditation project. The National Association for the Education of Young Children (NAEYC) initiated the accreditation project that voluntarily involved leaders in the profession from all types of children's programs throughout the entire country. The criteria were developed, read, and analyzed by hundreds of early childhood professional and lay leaders several times until the criteria were approved by the association and were ready for publication and use in accrediting programs across the country. The decision to work for accreditation requires leadership within a center or school staff. Accreditation is voluntary, not compulsory.

Managers of centers and schools, usually with the concurrence of (though sometimes as a result of pressure from) their staff and advisory board, begin the process of self-study, which is the first stage of becoming accredited. Large numbers of centers and schools in each state are now accredited, and others are beginning the process. In each case, leadership has been required to encourage individuals and centers to understand and work for accreditation.

People are beginning to know the meaning of high quality in early childhood care and education programs. Professionals are convinced that with accreditation of schools and centers, decision makers have grown increasingly interested in

---

[4] Ralph White and Ronald Lippitt, "Leadership Behavior and Member Reaction in Three 'Social Climates,'" in C. Cartwright and A. Zander (eds.), *Group Dynamics* (New York: Row, Peterson, 1953), pp. 585–611.

Laissez-Faire Leaders (LF)	Democratic Leaders (DE)	Autocratic Leaders (AU)
Directions Given		
Gave no suggestions unless specifically requested to do so; performed a minimum of leader functions; neither praised nor punished group members	Generally tended to encourage members to participate in the decision making; did not give rigid rules; gave suggestions, information, and praise to groups as a whole rather than to individuals	Made final decisions for the groups; told them how to do things; supervised closely; praised and punished individual members
Productivity		
Less productivity than DE or AU	Greater productivity than LF	Greater productivity than DE or LF in short run
Worker Involvement When Leader Absent		
No change	Only slight drop when leaders were out	Groups collapsed
Quality of Work		
Lower than DE	Higher than LF and AU	Lower than DE
Worker Contentment		
More discontentment than DE	Less discontentment expressed than AU or LF	More direct and indirect discontentment expressed than LF or DE
Social Cohesiveness		
Less cohesiveness and satisfaction than in DE	Expressed greater cohesiveness and satisfaction than either LF or AU	Greatest amount of hostility, aggressiveness, and scapegoating; greatest apathy
Absenteeism		
Less than AU	Less than LF or AU	Most absenteeism and dropouts
Independent Behavior		
More than AU or DE	More than AU	More submissive and dependent than DE or LF

Figure 7–1

Leadership styles and their results

Source: Based on White and Lippitt, "Leadership Behavior," pp. 585–611.

Leading children to learn about and try new things is an essential responsibility of teachers.
Oakwood College, Huntsville, AL

government and industry to assist with the important task of improving the services of caring for and educating young children in this country. Information is being dispensed to the citizens at large through radio, television, and print media regarding high-quality early childhood programs and what they mean to children, parents, and society. The association has helped citizens become informed regarding reliable sources of information on child care.

An important role in the accreditation process exists for you, as manager, and your staff who are working hard to uphold the standards for high-quality early education. You should know and implement the standards, become accredited, assist others to become accredited, and help others learn about the criteria or standards of high-quality early childhood education.

The NAEYC has been a dynamic professional organization for many years. Its membership has doubled several times since the early 1970s. Its local affiliate groups serve the needs in communities and relate directly to the state, regional, and national associations. Communication flows from the grassroots to the national level, and vice versa. Dynamic action on behalf of young children has been the result. The NAEYC is the largest professional association focusing on the development, nurturance, and education of young children. A welcome mat is out for you at every level of this dynamic professional association. Similarly, your leadership can be expressed through many avenues in your organization.

LEADERSHIP IN A CHILD DEVELOPMENT CENTER

The manager in a child development center has certain required relationships with people in the organization. The manager's authority is derived from the job's relative position. The manager is accountable for his or her job behavior and that of the staff as well. The staff are required by the terms of their job descriptions to follow the manager. Looking at Figure 7–1, we can note that the democratic leadership style includes many of the desired outcomes of child development center management. That is, it is desirable to have independent workers who feel some cohesiveness in their work, who can work when the leader is absent, and who turn out high-quality performances.

Leading means being out in front of a working unit. Leading can be contrasted to driving, which is done from behind the energy source. For example, you drive a horse from behind and lead it from the front. Leading tends to be democratic and cooperative, whereas driving tends to be autocratic. Leadership in a child development center requires a person who can plan, organize, and delegate work appropriately to people working in the center. Leading in a child development center is a person-centered function requiring skills in interpersonal relationships in order to develop rapport and motivation among all employees to provide high-quality services.

Important characteristics for leaders are intelligence, vision, initiative, supervisory ability, maturity, decisiveness, and self-assurance. As a leader you must also develop credibility with your employees through your performance. Your training, publications, and experience as a teacher can help you build this credibility as you work in a child development center. Professional courses, internships, reading, and experience can help prepare you for management in many human service organizations.

Your professional preparation and experience undoubtedly have helped you understand that people like to be treated as human beings rather than as inanimate cogs on a wheel. As a successful manager you will develop attitudes that show interest, friendliness, and support for members of your staff. People are certainly more effective as workers if they sense these positive attitudes toward them than if they feel you are uninterested, hostile, or unfriendly.

To be an effective leader, you must be good at decision-making techniques that involve and gain the support of your staff through democratic decision-making processes. Decision making requires an intelligent gathering of facts and initiative on the part of the leader. It also demands the self-assurance that comes from thorough comprehension as you move to put plans into action.

VALUES

Values are those philosophical ends in life that each person holds dearly. They are involved when you say that something "ought" to exist or "ought" to be done. They influence all you do. You have been acquiring your values throughout your life. Very early in a leadership position you may confront values that differ from

Children catch a love of books from adults who care about books and take time to "read, read, read," as one child begged.
Family Life Center, Georgia Southern College, Statesboro

your own. Your values may differ from those held by board members, for instance, who control your operation. Parents who are the consumers of your service may adhere to still other values. Some general understanding on values must be arrived at for your center to function effectively. Without some consensus about basic values, dealing with conflicts constructively will be difficult.

The values expressed in the U.S. Constitution will surely be recognized in your leadership. The freedoms of speech, assembly, and religion, as well as due process, come quickly to mind. Such values matter in a child development center.

DECISIONS, DECISIONS . . .

 A student teacher assigned to a child development laboratory in a state university noticed that the center had a practice of saying a nondenominational "grace" before snack. She asked whether this policy were appropriate in a state-sponsored facility. What do you think? What would you think if the prayer were addressed to "Allah" or "Krishna" instead of "Lord"?

What are your values regarding family life and parental rights? A child care center generally is designed as a support system for families. A public school may focus its objectives on children's education and not include the family in its objectives. Is this as it "ought" to be? How much right has a parent to make decisions about the early education the child receives?

How would you, a child development center manager, react to the following illustration of a value conflict and resolution? The event, concerning a white child whose two best friends were black children, occurred in an integrated kindergarten and was cited in an article by Bettye M. Caldwell, a distinguished early childhood educator at the University of Arkansas. The parents of the white kindergartner, disturbed by these friendships and thinking of withdrawing their child from the integrated kindergarten, held a conference with the teacher and, with the teacher's encouragement, decided to leave the child in the school. The following day the lively little girl entered the classroom and

> in her customary didactic style, pointed individually to each child in turn and announced, "I can play with you, and you, and I can't play with you, or you, or you. . . . " It took no great categorizing skill to perceive that skin color was the basis of the classification. With the honesty of a child she freely verbalized the agreement that had allowed her to remain in school: "If I do, my momma's going to whip me and my brother's going to beat me up." The earlier favorite friends of the child were crushed and the child herself had obvious difficulty remembering the new rules as she fell into her school routine. Fortunately, with the help of a sensitive teacher who gently interpreted that homes had rules and school had rules and that they were not always identical, the admonition was quickly forgotten and old friendships were restored.[5]

Americans must be the first to recognize that in an earlier era—when other values prevailed—these children would have been schooled in separate buildings with separate teachers, never having the opportunity to play together. Should a child development center staff value the breadth of vision needed to help achieve the equality ideals embodied in the U.S. Constitution? Do these ideals of equality help our pluralistic society become a happier home for all families? Is equality a significant part of the American dream?

Recently, leaders in the NAEYC and elsewhere have taken a more proactive stance toward the issue of discrimination and young children. Recognizing that, as illustrated in the quoted example, children begin at a very early age to develop awareness of and ideas about differences regarding race, gender, and disabilities, Louise Derman-Sparks and others formed the Anti-Bias Curriculum Task Force to examine ways that early childhood professionals impact that process.

---

[5] Bettye M. Caldwell, "Can Children Have Quality Life in Day Care?" *Young Children* 28:4 (April 1973), p. 206.

The task force wanted to move beyond pretending that differences do not exist or that children do not notice them. They also wanted to move beyond a "tourist curriculum" that acknowledges differences but teaches about them in a trivial way. They recommended that early childhood professionals examine their own feelings about race, gender, and disability and form support groups to help each other do this. The next step is to cast a critical eye on classrooms and curriculum materials to eliminate distorted images and make sure that all people are fairly represented. The following four basic goals of an antibias curriculum reflect the principles of NAEYC's developmentally appropriate practice:

1. To foster each child's construction of a knowledgeable, confident self-identity
2. To foster each child's comfortable, empathetic interaction with diversity among people
3. To foster each child's critical thinking about bias
4. To foster each child's ability to stand up for herself or himself and for others in the face of bias[6]

What are your values regarding children's early years? That is, are children expected to have full lives in all areas of human development during these years, or are these years only cognitive stepping stones to more important years in "real" school and beyond? Curriculum planning differs depending on your values. Interaction with children and parents also varies depending on your values.

What are your values regarding children's learning of right and wrong? Do you believe children are testing you when they do wrong? Do you believe that reward and punishment are the best means of developing "right" behavior in children? What is "right" behavior, anyway? What happens when your definitions of "right" and "good" differ from those of the parents?

What are your values regarding a teacher's right to choose the philosophical approach to be implemented in a classroom that is part of the center you manage? What would you do if the governing board were to demand a philosophical approach that you strongly disagree with?

What are your values regarding honesty and loyalty? What are your values regarding equality for males and females, all races, old and young, or persons with disabilities? Your administration may well be tested on these values in one way or another—especially as society enacts and enforces rules concerning affirmative action and integration.

Parental involvement was one of the innovations of Project Head Start. Parents participated at numerous levels to help bring about changes benefiting the whole family, but especially the children in the Head Start group. What are your values regarding parental involvement? What if your teachers or the children's parents have another view?

---

[6] Louise Derman-Sparks, "Reaching Potentials through Antibias, Multicultural Curriculum," in Sue Bredekamp and Teresa Rosegrant (eds.), *Reaching Potentials: Appropriate Curriculum and Assessment for Young Children,* Vol. I (Washington, DC: National Association for the Education of Young Children, 1992), pp. 114–127.

DECISIONS, DECISIONS ...

The parent advisory group in a Head Start program decided to ask each parent to contribute $2 to purchase small gifts for each child in the program. They knew that this would be a hardship for some parents but reasoned that the advisory group could raise a little extra money to pay for children whose parents could not contribute. One somewhat affluent parent, whose child had been included in the program for reasons other than economic status, approached the teacher and donated a sum of money to cover gifts for the entire class, with the condition that her identity remain anonymous. When the teacher told the leaders of the parent group about the donation, she was surprised that their reaction was one of anger, and they insisted on going through with their original plan. What values are in conflict? Discuss how a program manager could help negotiate this conflict.

Our society emphasizes the individual, that is, developing each person for a self-fulfilling career to meet personal desires and self-esteem needs. In some other societies, such as in China, more emphasis may be placed on what the individual can do for the group or the country. Personal sacrifices tend to be expected in China to help the country change and prosper, with society's goal generally being ranked higher than the an individual's goal. These values are changing as China makes the transition to a market economy, and many Chinese citizens, reared under the old ideals, are lamenting that "money seems to be all everyone thinks of these days." Will China be better off if more people adopt Western values? Would the United States or the world be a better place if we taught children to be more concerned about the good of society as a whole—in both a national and a global sense?

Values Questionnaire

This section has contained numerous questions to which there are only very individual answers. Value clarification goes on at several levels. As a manager, you will be in the midst of many discussions and decisions involving values and will need to be able to explain clearly the value issues at stake.

The questionnaire in Figure 7–2 helps people focus on and better understand some value orientations in early childhood programs. The questionnaire has been used as a research tool and device to start people thinking and talking about values. The nine stories draw attention to some of the philosophical differences that may exist in child development centers as different teachers apply their preferred goals or values concerning early childhood education.

DECISIONS, DECISIONS . . .

Stop here and read each of the nine stories. Feel free to use "he or she" when reading them. The feminine pronouns are used throughout to avoid bias based on gender of the teacher. After reading all the stories, select the one that illustrates a value that you would rank at the top of your list and one that you would rank at the bottom. Be prepared to explain the reason for your selection.

1. Teacher A thinks it important for children to learn to get along with others. She feels children should learn to get along, help each other, and share by having freedom to interact. Her classroom is usually a beehive of activity. She willingly puts off a science lesson if there is a spontaneous group activity in progress at the moment. Teacher A makes friends with children and parents and arranges situations so that each child will know and make friends with all the others. When difficulties arise, she prefers to let children work out the problem, intervening only as a last resort. She sometimes helps parents arrange their children's play groups during weekends or vacations.

2. Teacher B believes that children should be well prepared for "real school." Her classroom schedule is arranged so that she gets lots of basic learning material covered each day. She avoids getting sidetracked during a class project; therefore, she is able to carry out lesson plans completely. She believes she must teach children a good deal of information, including ABCs, colors, shapes, and numbers. Her children frequently achieve above average on standardized tests, which indicates to her that they are learning the material. Her talks with parents focus on children's preparation for first grade. She participates in lectures and seminars to enlarge her own learning whenever available.

3. Teacher C is concerned that children develop a sense of morality and good judgment. She often discusses with them how they ought to behave. She tells them her own views and introduces religious stories and ideas to the children. The children are taught what is right and wrong and are expected to behave accordingly. Manners and saying "please" and "thank you" are stressed. Teacher C discusses any topic that is of interest to children, especially if she feels it will aid their character development. She encourages them to correct each other if they feel someone is doing something wrong.

4. Teacher D keeps her classroom looking attractive at all times. She takes special care that the colors are harmonious and that various artifacts are displayed in the room. Children's art objects and paintings are carefully mounted and labeled. Creative movement and music, including works of the great composers, are a part of the program. Well-written children's literature is used regularly. Teacher D wears colorful and fashionable clothing. She helps children arrange their hair and clothing to look their best.

5. Teacher E's schedule and activities are outlined by the school's director, and she carefully follows these guidelines. She is grateful for the leadership of her school's director and values the opinions of fellow teachers and parents. At the beginning

Figure 7–2
Value orientations
Source: Verna Hildebrand, *Guiding Young Children* (Upper Saddle River, NJ: Prentice Hall, 1980), pp. 394–397. See also Verna Hildebrand, "Value Orientations for Nursery School Programs," *Reading Improvement* 12:3 (Fall 1975), pp. 168–173.

of each year the director distributes a list of policies and regulations that give Teacher E a guide for administration in her classroom. She believes that the director is a competent administrator and knows a lot about running the class. She is pleased when the director brings in new learning programs for her to use.

6. Teacher F likes for children to have lots of fresh air and sunshine. She carefully checks to see that the children have sufficient light, correct temperature, and chairs and tables of suitable height. Each morning she checks up on their habits of good breakfast, daily bath, toothbrushing, and proper rest. She checks throats and chests for signs of contagious disease and has children taken home when they seem ill. Routines of toileting and hand washing are frequent in her schedule. Nutritious foods are always available for snacks.

7. Teacher G feels that children should really plan their own program. She avoids thinking ahead about what children will be doing each day but brings toys out as children arrive and indicate their interests. She may choose an activity because she particularly wants to do it that day. She tries to respond to children's needs of the moment and avoids pushing them into organized learning tasks. She emphasizes spontaneous learning, picking up on some project that the child seems interested in. Her schedule is completely flexible, and rarely do the children follow the same schedule for 2 days in a row.

8. Teacher H believes that each child learns in a different way. She considers the child a person first and a student second. Her program is arranged so that each child can express his or her individuality. A supportive atmosphere prevails that allows the child to feel free to venture into new experiences, but at the same time it is not one of indulgence. Teacher H strives to plan a rich variety of experiences with fresh views of familiar scenes, excursions to new places, or walks in parks. She uses many methods of motivation and novel ways of sparking children's imaginations.

9. Teacher I stresses protecting the school property and conserving materials. She teaches the children to use supplies such as paint, paper, and glue sparingly. She searches for "found" materials to supplement her supplies and utilizes all volunteer services available. She shows children how to use all their paper for a picture even if they paint a small spot and start to leave. Teacher I is also concerned with saving time, works at being efficient, and expects to teach children these traits. She thinks education is a way of improving one's station in life and a way of making a good living.

Figure 7–2, *continued*

In these nine situations, the primary value orientation in each story is as follows:

1. Socialization
2. Intellect
3. Morality
4. Aesthetics
5. Authority
6. Health
7. Freedom
8. Individuality
9. Economics

The findings of the research indicate that both the parents involved and the experienced professional teachers chose as the most desired focus story 8 stressing individuality, with story 1 stressing socialization as second choice.

DEVELOPMENTALLY APPROPRIATE PRACTICE

Using up-to-date child development research, an NAEYC commission has published a helpful guide for managers and their staff members who want to be sure their programs are on a firm developmental base.[7] The foundation for planning and interaction in a child development program is children's development. The report is age graded, so if one is dealing with infants and toddlers, 3-year-olds, 4- and 5-year-olds, or 5- to 8-year-olds, easily located information is available. "Developmentally appropriate" in the NAEYC context refers to both age appropriateness and individual appropriateness of processes. As noted in Chapter 2, the NAEYC is in the process of revising these guidelines to incorporate a wider diversity of viewpoints.

Developmental Task Framework

The developmental task framework is another avenue that is useful for encouraging discussion of how children's total developmental needs are met by a philosophical approach under consideration. Lilienthal and Tryon, using work of Robert Havighurst, propose 10 developmental tasks that a young child must be working on simultaneously though seldom consciously.[8] When each task has been achieved at one age, the child moves comfortably to tasks at a higher level. This developmental task framework is useful because it integrates aspects of genetic

---

[7] Sue Bredekamp (ed.), *Developmentally Appropriate Practice in Early Childhood Programs Serving Children from Birth through Age 8* (Washington, DC: National Association for the Education of Young Children, 1987).

[8] J. W. Lilienthal and Carolyn Tryon, "Guideposts in Child Growth and Development," *National Education Association Journal*, March 1950, pp. 188–189. Also see a discussion of these tasks related to curriculum for the early childhood center in Verna Hildebrand, *Introduction to Early Childhood Education* (Upper Saddle River, NJ: Prentice Hall, 1991), pp. 42–46.

inheritance, individual psychological and physical development, and sociological or cultural expectations. The 10 developmental tasks are as follows:

1. Achieving an appropriate dependence-independence pattern
2. Achieving an appropriate giving-receiving pattern of affection
3. Relating to changing social groups
4. Developing a conscience
5. Learning one's psycho-social-biological gender role
6. Accepting and adjusting to a changing body
7. Managing a changing body and learning new motor patterns
8. Learning to understand and control the physical world
9. Developing an appropriate symbol system and conceptual abilities
10. Relating one's self to the cosmos

When using the task framework for philosophical clarification, it helps to define each task and itemize the tasks on a board; then parents and others can discuss which, if any, task(s) might be left out or not given emphasis in the early childhood experience. Given the choice of leaving one or more tasks out, most people agree that all the tasks are important. The teacher's job becomes one of incorporating aspects of all tasks into the child's experience in the school.

Whatever techniques you use to develop consensus among board members, staff, and parents regarding the philosophical approaches or value positions that are to be the foundation of your center, confront the value issues directly rather than respond defensively to a challenge. A center's publications, for example, can carry a straightforward position statement regarding the values or philosophical positions held by the center leadership. This way, all who choose to enroll children will know the center's position. Parents who disagree with your position may have other alternatives to choose from to obtain child development services. Managers may offer assistance in helping families locate a service that more closely fits their values. However, if your service is operated with public funds and parents have a right to the service, then, following discussions with parents, perhaps some accommodations will have to be made if widely differing viewpoints still prevail. Conversations in a one-to-one setting where real listening by both parties can take place may help reduce any dissonance or disharmony that has arisen.

Fisher and Ury have published an applicable method for negotiating personal and professional disputes. It is especially designed for leaders in management. It shows how to separate the people from the problem and how to focus on interests rather than on positions. Their techniques could be helpful in sorting out philosophical differences in approaches to early childhood education.[9]

Research is inconclusive regarding the superiority of one curriculum model of an early childhood education program over another. David Weikart's study in

---

[9] R. Fisher and W. Ury, *Getting to YES: Negotiating Agreement without Giving In* (Boston: Houghton Mifflin, 1981; New York: Penguin, 1983).

Children are leaders too, as they organize their dramatic play in a well-equipped center.
Texas Women's University Children's Center, Denton

Michigan tested curricular models in groups of economically disadvantaged children and found:

> that three diverse curricula could be equally effective in improving children's academic aptitude and achievement. The Curriculum Demonstration Project also provides information about program operations, and in particular about what actually happens in the classroom. Observations during this project demonstrated clear distinctions between curricula on such variables as cooperative play among children, fantasy and imaginative play, individualized teacher-child interactions, competition, extensive opportunities to use materials, and praise for mastering new challenges. Clearly the choice of curriculum will be influenced by adults' valuation of experiences such as these.[10]

Numerous discussions of various philosophical approaches in early childhood education in publications are listed at the close of this chapter. Only a few may be pure in the sense of following one model exclusively. Most blend many

---

[10] D. Weikart, "Reopening the Case for Public Preschool Education," *High Scope Report* 4, 1979, p. 3.

approaches, using what makes sense for their group or groups of children at given times. The managerial principles required to coordinate and operate the total organization, as set forth in this book, are generally applicable regardless of the philosophical approach employed.

In fact, some would argue that a slavish adoption of a particular curriculum model is incompatible with the movement toward greater professionalism in the early childhood field. If we expect teachers to draw on a broad knowledge base, responding with flexibility, creativity, and sensitivity to the needs of individual children, can we also expect rigorous compliance with preconceived models?[11]

COMMUNICATING

Communicating with people will be an important part of your leadership task. You will communicate with people in the governmental regulatory agencies—social services, fire department, health—and businesses and schools. Recall that all these interactions are part of the social-cultural environment. You will communicate with staff and parents. And you will communicate with children. Ten rules for good communication are listed here:

1. Stop talking so you can really hear the other person.
2. Make the other person feel at ease and feel free to talk.
3. Show an interest in what the other person has to say.
4. Keep your eyes on the person who is talking.
5. Reflect the feelings the other person is expressing.
6. Put yourself in the other person's position.
7. Avoid expressing anger or arguing.
8. Allow plenty of time without hurrying.
9. Avoid all distractions.
10. Stop talking and listen to learn and understand.

A common trait of managers when dissonance arises is to talk and talk—hence rules 1 and 10. You will not know the other person's view if you do all the talking. Many times a person will talk him- or herself out of the complaint if you listen attentively and reflect the feelings expressed. Thomas Gordon's book *Leadership Effectiveness Training: L.E.T.,* as suggested in Chapter 6, is recommended to help learn active listening. Gordon's techniques make a useful focus for educational meetings for staff or parents.

Innovation and futuristic thinking are needed in every business, agency, and profession. How are you dealing with new conditions coming down the pike? Are you encouraging your board to make suggestions? Your staff? Your children's parents? Are you reading widely and listening to trend predictors to be aware of

---

[11] Stacie G. Goffin, *Curriculum Models and Early Childhood Education* (Upper Saddle River, NJ: Prentice Hall, 1994), pp. 213–214.

future trends that might affect your service? New ways of doing things can be stimulating to staff members. They can also be scary. How will you change as the times change? A creative use of communication measures will be essential. Taking a chance, being creative, trying new things—these will all be essential. How will your leadership hold up to it all?

PROFESSIONAL SUPPORT

Taking leadership in local, state, and national professional organizations will be important for you, as manager, and for your teachers and the other professionals in your center. It may seem contradictory with so many children around, but teachers working with young children often feel alone, just as parents who stay home with young children all day feel alone.

Local organizations are useful to give teachers professional stimulation periodically throughout the year. Teachers may easily get "burned out" or lose motivation unless they can meet with other teachers to share common problems and learn new ideas that can be used in their classrooms. Your center can aid such refreshing activities by inviting the community branch or affiliate of such groups as your local Association for the Education of Young Children, the Association for Childhood Education International, or your local managers' group to meet in your facility. A list of organizations and their journals is given at the end of this chapter.

Your teachers should be encouraged to join and participate in organizations through incentives such as paid registration or days off to attend state, regional, or national professional meetings. You can encourage teachers to offer to be on programs and to volunteer for leadership roles in local professional organizations. Professional participation helps keep your teachers up-to-date and also contributes a service to your community. Visibility on programs for you and your staff serves to advertise your center, letting people know that high-quality people work there. Such visibility is valuable to you and the center.

Of course, to release staff for meetings requires funds for substitute teachers. A reasonable policy is to release staff members to attend one meeting of their choice each year. Some centers allot an equal dollar amount to each staff member for his or her attendance. All teachers need refreshing activities. Some equitable policies for released time and funding must be planned. Meetings often are on Saturday; therefore, incentives such as travel and registration for teachers to attend should be built into your center's planning budget.

After you or your staff members return from attending such a meeting, present an opportunity to share new ideas with the stay-at-home staff members as soon as possible, while important details are fresh in one's memory.

Your teachers can give as well as receive new ideas through workshops. An indication of readiness for this new role is when you hear your teachers complain that they already knew the ideas presented in a speech or workshop. Professional leadership need not go in one direction only. Many professional organizations need good programs on innovative measures that teachers find successful. Thus, you might encourage your teachers to organize in groups of two or three to specialize in some aspect of children's programming and develop workshops to present to other teachers. Your own staff and parents can serve as trial runs for their efforts. Usually by being on the program the participants receive complimentary admission to the conference—an additional incentive for making these extra efforts. Also, becoming contributors may bring victims of burnout back into the professional fold where they can help other teachers do their job better.

Another avenue of professional networking is developing on the "information superhighway." Managers equipped with a modem for their computers and Internet access, through a university, public school or library, or one of the commercial on-line services, can obtain information from the ERIC Clearinghouse on Elementary and Early Childhood Education and several other databases. They can also join discussion groups on topics of interest to early childhood professionals, such as parenting, or the Reggio Emilia approach to early education, where people express opinions, request information, and share ideas and resources. Internet addresses for some of these discussion groups are included with the list of organizations at the end of this chapter. A new publication from the ERIC Clearinghouse will help newcomers find their way around in the new technology: *A to Z: The Early Childhood Educator's Guide to the Internet.*[12]

THE PROFESSIONAL LIBRARY

Professional organizations publish numerous journals and other worthwhile publications. Circulating new materials among staff members is a way to help keep staff up-to-date. These materials and others can become the core of a center's library. Besides being useful for teachers, materials can be checked out to parents, who will appreciate the help that they offer concerning their parenting role. Sometimes articles can be circulated to staff members with the notation that the topic is on the agenda for a future staff meeting. This way you can encourage people to prepare to give their own input to a discussion.

PROFESSIONAL RESEARCH AND WRITING

Many leaders in the profession gain prominence through their research and writing. They keep in touch with the issues faced by their professions and make various kinds of analyses. People read their work as they make an effort to become informed on a subject. One should read reports critically. When you are writing such an item, you must be as careful as possible regarding your conclusions.

As a manager, you may start research studies to which your various groups can make contributions, and you and your teachers may share in authorship of

---

[12] Available from ERIC Clearinghouse on Elementary and Early Childhood Education, 805 W. Pennsylvania Ave., Urbana, IL 61801-4897. See also Diane Rothenberg, "The Internet and Early Childhood Educators: Some Frequently Asked Questions," *ERIC Digest*, May 1995, and "Internet Starting Points for Early Childhood Educators," *ERIC Resource List*, May 1995.

the publication of results. You may offer your center to be the site of a research study by a university faculty researcher. Such activities often stimulate staffers to work hard, learn together, and maintain professional interest and enjoyment. Such involvement may inspire a staff member to go back to college for more work or to finish a degree. (Professional writing is discussed in more detail in Chapter 15.)

Even without university participation, you can encourage your staff to develop investigations and become part of a growing trend in teacher education.[13] Recall from the discussion in the previous chapter that careful observation and reflection are primary avenues for professional development of staff members. In the experience of Margie Carter, a respected teacher educator, "As teachers get more intrigued with children's play, they become more intentional and appropriate in their actions in the classroom."[14]

Conclusion

Your manager's role is by its nature a leadership role. Leadership requires initiative, creativity, and forward-looking attitudes. Leadership is *vested* in your position. Your employees are obligated to a certain extent to follow your leadership. You can also exercise *voluntary* leadership among your staff, with parents, and professionally within your community, state, and nation to create a high-quality service that serves children appropriately and helps them grow to become strong, skilled, healthy citizens of the future. There is room for individual differences in style. However, research indicates that democratic leadership is more likely to lead the organization to the person-centered services desired in a child development center.

Value orientations have been identified, and suggestions made for clarification of values. Communication and leadership in professional organizations have been discussed. Leadership has been involved in many respects in the NAEYC's accreditation project. Managers will find that accreditation assures parents of a center's high quality and stimulates interest in child development centers by government policy makers and industrial leaders.

Professional Organizations and Their Journals

Adult Education Association
1225 19th St. NW
Washington, DC 20036
Publishes *Adult Leadership*.

American Association for Gifted Children
(AAGC)
15 Grammercy Park
New York, NY 10003

---

[13] See, for example, Carolyn Black and Rebecca Huss, "Teacher as Researcher Projects: A Constructive Process," *Journal of Early Childhood Teacher Education* 16:2 (Spring 1995), pp. 3–7.

[14] "Catching Teachers 'Being Good': Using Observation to Communicate," in Elizabeth Jones (ed.), *Growing Teachers: Partnerships in Staff Development* (Washington, DC: National Association for the Education of Young Children, 1993).

American Association of Psychiatric
Services for Children
1133 15th St. NW, Suite 1000
Washington, DC 20005

American Child Care Services
P.O. Box 548
532 Settlers Landing Rd.
Hampton, VA 23669

American Educational Research
Association (AERA)
1230 17th St. NW
Washington, DC 20036
Publishes *Educational Research*.

American Foundation for the Blind
15 W. 16th St.
New York, NY 10011

American Home Economics Association
(AHEA)
1555 King St.
Alexandria, VA 22314
Publishes *Journal of Home Economics* and
Home Economics Research Journal.

American Montessori Society (AMS)
150 Fifth Ave.
New York, NY 10011
Publishes *The American Montessori Society
Bulletin*.

American Orthopsychiatric Association (AOA)
1790 Broadway
New York, NY 10019
Publishes *American Journal of
Orthopsychiatry*.

American Public Health Association
(APHA)
1790 Broadway
New York, NY 10019
Publishes *American Journal of Public Health*
and *The Nation's Health*.

American Speech, Language, and Hearing
Association
10801 Rockville Pike
Rockville, MD 20852

Association for Childhood Education
International (ACEI)
11141 Georgia Ave., Suite 200
Wheaton, MD 20902
Publishes *Childhood Education*.

Association for Supervision and
Curriculum Development (ASCD)
125 N. West St.
Alexandria, VA 22314
Publishes *Education Leadership*.

Child Welfare League of America, Inc.
440 First St. NW
Washington, DC 20001
Publishes *Child Welfare*.

Children's Defense Fund
122 C St. NW
Washington, DC 20001

The Children's Foundation
725 Fifteenth St. NW, Suite 505
Washington, DC 20005
Publishes annual survey of licensing
requirements in all states.

Council for Early Childhood Professional
Recognition
1341 G St., Suite 400
Washington, DC 20005
Publishes *Competence*.

Council for Exceptional Children
1920 Association Drive
Reston, VA 22091
Publishes *Exceptional Children*.

Council on Interracial Books for Children
1841 Broadway, Room 500
New York, NY 10023

ERIC Clearinghouse in Elementary and
Early Childhood Education
University of Illinois
805 W. Pennsylvania Ave.
Urbana, IL 61801

Families and Work Institute
330 Seventh Ave., 14th Floor
New York, NY 10001
Publishes frequent resources regarding
employer-sponsored child care.

International Reading Association
800 Barksdale Rd.
P.O. Box 8139
Newark, DE 19714
Publishes *The Reading Teacher*.

National Association for Gifted Children
4175 Lovell Rd., Suite 140
Circle Pines, MN 55014
Publishes *Gifted Child Quarterly*.

National Association for the Education of
Young Children (NAEYC)
1834 Connecticut Ave. NW
Washington, DC 20009
Publishes *Young Children* and *Early
Childhood Research Quarterly*.

National Coalition for Campus Child
Care, Inc.
P.O. Box 258
Cascade, WA 53011

National Council on Family Relations
1219 University Ave. SE
Minneapolis, MN 55432
Publishes *Family Relationships* and *Journal of
Marriage and the Family*.

National Education Association (NEA)
1201 16th St. NW
Washington, DC 20036
Publishes *NEA Reporter*.

National Science Teachers Association
1742 Connecticut Ave. NW
Washington, DC 20009
Publishes *Science and Children*.

Organisation Mondiale pour l'Education
Prescolaire (OMEP) (World Organization
for Early Childhood Education)
U.S. Representative
P.O. Box 66
Garrett Park, MD 20896
Publishes *International Journal of Early
Childhood*.

Society for Research in Child Development
5801 Ellis Ave.
Chicago, IL 60637
Publishes *Child Development* and *Child
Development Abstracts and Bibliography*.

Southern Association for Children under
Six
5403 Brady Station
Little Rock, AR 72215
Publishes *Dimensions*.

Worthy Wage Campaign
c/o National Center for the Early
Childhood Work Force
733 15th St. NW, Suite 800
Washington, DC 20005

Zero to Three
National Center for Clinical Infant
Programs
2000 14th St. North, Suite 380
Arlington, VA 22201-2500
Publishes *Zero to Three*

Additional Early Childhood Periodicals

Child Care Information Exchange
17916 NE 103 Ct.
Redmond, WA 98052

Child and Youth Care Quarterly
Human Sciences Press
72 Fifth Ave.
New York, NY 10011

Children's Environments
Chapman and Hall Journals
115 Fifth Ave.
New York, NY 10003

Day Care and Early Education
Human Sciences Press
72 Fifth Ave.
New York, NY 10011

Early Child Development and Care
Gordon and Breach Science Publishers
1 Park Ave.
New York, NY 10016

*Exceptional Parent, Parenting Your Child with
a Disability*
PO Box 3000 Dept. EP
Denville, NJ 07834

Innovations in Early Education: The
International Reggio Exchange
The Merrill-Palmer Institute
71-A E. Ferry Ave.
Detroit, MI 48202

Instructor
P.O. Box 6099
Duluth, MN 55800

Parents' Magazine
Bergenfield, NJ 07621

Teaching Pre K–8
40 Richards Ave.
Norwalk, CT 06854

Texas Child Care
P.O. Box 162881
Austin, TX 78716-2881

EARLY CHILDHOOD DISCUSSION GROUPS ON THE INTERNET

CYE-L   (Children, Youth and Environments)
Mail to: cye-l-Request@cunyvms1.gc.cuny.edu

ECEOL-L   (Early Childhood Education on Line)
Mail to: Listserv@Maine.Edu (via Internet); Listserv@Maine (via Bitnet)

ECENET-L   (Early Childhood Education Net)
Mail to: Listserv@VMD.CSO.UIUC.EDU (via Internet);
             Listserv@UIUCVMD.BITNET (via Bitnet)

REGGIO-L   (Reggio Emilia Approach to Early Education)
Mail to: Listserv@VMD.CSO.UIUC.EDU (via Internet);
             Listserv@UIUCVMD.BITNET (via Bitnet)

Send a message via E-mail to the group you want to join. Put the address listed above in the "To:" section and your own E-mail address in the "From:" section. In the body of the message, write the following: Subscribe ECENET-L (or whatever list you are joining). Then put your full name. You will get a message back confirming the fact that you have joined the list, as well as instructions for posting messages and signing off the list, should you want to do so.

APPLICATIONS

1. Choose one child development center manager whom you have observed at work. Call him or her "X."
   a. List the behaviors you have observed that indicate that person's leadership style.
   b. Using the White and Lippitt study reported in Figure 7–1, classify the child development center manager's behaviors listed in item a.
   c. Discuss the classification with your classmates.
2. Plan a 1-minute advertising statement for one of the value stories in Figure 7–2. Other students will select or be assigned a different story. Assume your audience is a group of parents; orally present a statement telling them why they would want their child to attend your center with its emphasis as found

in the value story. After the presentations, discuss how you felt about the various values depicted.

3. From your instructor get the names of centers that have become accredited. Assign one student to call each manager to discuss the outcomes—for staff, parents, and children. Report back to the class.

4. Investigate three organizations on the list of professional organizations to which a manager might give leadership. List and define the purposes of each organization.

5. If you have access to the Internet, sign on to one of the discussion lists given later in the chapter, and read all the postings for a week or two. Prepare a report for your classmates that summarizes the current main topics of discussion and any points of disagreement that have become apparent.

6. Collect news stories or articles for your management notebook regarding leadership by child development center managers and professionals.

Study Questions

1. Define leading. Give examples of how leading applies to the manager's role in a child development center.

2. Explain how managing and leading differ.

3. Name the three leadership styles identified by Katz and Kahn, and tell how each might be associated with a child development center.

4. Discuss how leadership and NAEYC accreditation are related.

5. If you, as manager, or your board members wish for your center or school to become accredited, how will your leadership be needed?

6. Define values. State 10 values, and describe in a sentence for each how they apply to a child development center.

7. Define developmental tasks as used by Havighurst. Give an example of each task as applied to children in a child development center.

8. List 10 rules for communication with staff and others. Give an example of each rule from the perspective of the manager in a child development center.

9. Write the name, location, publications, and purpose of two early childhood professional organizations.

10. List five ways a manager can encourage staff members to participate in professional organizations and meetings.

Suggested Readings

Alexander, Nancy P. "ATLIS: Early Childhood Development and the Electronic Age." *Young Children* 49:5 (July 1994), pp. 26–27.

Boje, David M., and Dave Ulrich. "The Qualitative Side of Leadership." In Robert Tannenbaum, Newton Margulies, and Fred Massarik (eds.), *Human Systems Development*, pp. 302–314. San Francisco: Jossey-Bass, 1985.

Brett, Arlene. "Online for New Learning Opportunities." *Dimensions of Early Childhood* 22:3 (Spring 1994), pp. 10–13.

Briggs, Patty. "The Early Childhood Network—We Work Together for Young Children." *Young Children* 40:5 (July 1985), pp. 54–55.

Covey, Stephen. *Principle-Centered Leadership*. New York: Simon & Schuster, 1992.

Derman-Sparks, Louise, and the A.B.C. Task Force. *Anti-Bias Curriculum: Tools for Empowering Young Children*. Washington, DC: National Association for the Education of Young Children, 1989.

Dinkmeyer, Don. *The Parent's Handbook: Systematic Training for Effective Parenting (STEP)*. New York: Random House, 1982.

Eheart, Brenda K., and Robin Lynn Leavitt. "Supporting Toddler Play." *Young Children* 40:3 (March 1985), pp. 18–22.

Epeneter, Susan. "Our Most Memorable Staff Meeting." *Child Care Information Exchange* 55 (May 1987), pp. 17–20.

Fisher, R., and W. Ury. *Getting to YES: Negotiating Agreement without Giving In*. Boston: Houghton Mifflin, 1981; Penguin, 1983.

Gartrell, Dan. "Punishment or Guidance?" *Young Children* 42:3 (March 1987), pp. 55–61.

Gordon, T. *Leadership Effectiveness Training: L.E.T.* New York: Bantam, 1978.

Greenman, Jim. "Some Things to Keep in Mind While Trying to Change the World, General Motors, or Your Child Care Program." *Child Care Information Exchange* 55 (May 1987).

Jones, Elizabeth, and John Nimmo. *Emergent Curriculum*. Washington, DC: National Association for the Education of Young Children, 1994.

Jorde-Bloom, Paula. *A Great Place to Work: Improving Conditions for Staff in Young Children's Programs*, Washington, DC: National Association for the Education of Young Children, 1991.

Kagan, Sharon L. "Leadership: Rethinking It—Making It Happen." *Young Children* 49:5 (July 1994), pp. 50–54.

Kamii, Constance. "Leading Primary Education toward Excellence: Beyond Worksheets and Drill." *Young Children* 40:6 (September 1985), pp. 3–9.

Katz, Lilian G., and Sylvia C. Chard. *Engaging Children's Minds: The Project Approach*. Norwood, NJ: Ablex, 1989.

Katz, Lillian, and E. Ward. *Ethical Behavior in Early Childhood Education*. Washington, DC: National Association for the Education of Young Children, 1978.

Kipnis, Kenneth. "How to Discuss Professional Ethics." *Young Children* 42:4 (May 1987), pp. 26–30.

Moore, David. "Innovation and Entrepreneurship in Child Care." *Child Care Information Exchange* 55 (May 1987), pp. 22–26.

National Association for the Education of Young Children. "Child Care Information Service: Begins Operation." *Young Children* 40:6 (September 1985), p. 50.

Paley, Vivian. *White Teacher*. Cambridge, MA: Harvard University Press, 1979, 1989.

Spodek, Bernard, Olivia Saracho, and Donald Peters (eds.). *Professionalism and the Early Childhood Practitioner*. New York: Teachers College Press, 1988.

Tobin, Joseph J., David Y. H. Wu, and Dana H. Davidson. *Preschool in Three Cultures: Japan, China, and the United States*. New Haven, CT: Yale University Press, 1989.

Uphoff, James K., and June Gilmore. "Pupil Age at School Entrance—How Many Are Ready for Success?" *Young Children* 41:2 (January 1986), pp. 11–16.

York, Stacey. *Developing Roots and Wings: A Trainer's Guide to Affirming Culture in Early Childhood Programs*. St. Paul, MN: Redleaf, 1992.

CHAPTER 8

Monitoring and Controlling for Quality

A manager's fifth major function is to monitor and control for quality in the child development center. **Monitoring and controlling** are defined as the evaluative and action functions of maintaining high quality in the promised services. The manager is charged with knowing the standards, establishing systems to meet those standards, constantly comparing performance to standards, and, when performance falls short, moving into action to correct the problem.

In 1995, the Cost, Quality and Child Outcomes in Child Care Centers Study captured national attention with its finding that "child care at most centers in the United States is poor to mediocre, with almost half of the infants and toddlers in rooms having less than minimal quality." The study also found that states with more stringent licensing regulations had fewer poor-quality centers and that centers that were able to provide better than average care had access to outside resources through donations, employer sponsorship, or public funds.[1]

As discussed in Chapter 2, child development programs are part of the social-cultural environment, and this study clearly demonstrates how a governmental system, as part of that environment, impacts the quality of those centers. Other elements of the social-cultural environment that either establish or impact standards for child development centers include professional organizations, market forces, and public opinion. All of these elements interact to raise or lower the level of quality deemed acceptable for out-of-home child care.

For example, child development professionals might advocate for more stringent standards regarding educational qualifications of child care workers, but if

---

[1] Cost, Quality, and Child Outcomes Study Team, *Cost, Quality, and Child Outcomes in Child Care Centers, Executive Summary* (Denver: Economics Department, University of Colorado, 1995), pp. 2–5.

the public does not understand or concur with the importance of such qualifications, parents are unlikely to be willing to pay the higher rates charged by a center that tries to attract and retain highly qualified staff with adequate salaries. Nor will governmental bodies see the need to subsidize such centers. And, finally, when centers violate the higher standards, regulatory agencies will be unable to secure the needed support for enforcement actions from the judicial system, if rules are perceived as unfair or too stringent.

Thus, when quality is viewed from the perspective of the ecological systems framework, it becomes clear that monitoring within the child development center must go hand in hand with establishing good relations with parents and public, and with professional advocacy on behalf of children and families. Those areas are discussed in detail in Chapters 15 and 16, respectively.

STANDARDS

Standards are defined as the definite level or degree of quality that is proper and adequate for a specific purpose. As the manager of a child development center, you will be obliged to comply with your state's licensing regulations that establish minimal standards for children's safety and welfare. These rules govern the amount of space and equipment you must provide, the number of staff and their qualifications, health practices, fire safety, and many other areas. Adhering to your state's rules is a necessary, but certainly not sufficient, condition for providing a high-quality program for children.

In addition to meeting licensing regulations, if you direct a state-sponsored program in a public school setting, you will probably have an additional set of standards set by your state Department of Education. If you direct a Head Start program, you will need to follow the *Head Start Program Performance Standards,* and, because one of those standards requires that your staff possess the Child Development Associate credential, you will need to be familiar with the *CDAC Competency Standards.*[2]

The American Public Health Association and the American Academy of Pediatrics have collaborated to produce national standards for health and safety in child care programs.[3] The American Consumer Product Safety Commission has established guidelines for playground equipment and surfacing. The National Life Safety Fire Code provides standards for safe storage and use of hazardous materials and protection from "conditions hazardous to life or property in the occupancy of buildings or premises."[4]

---

[2] *Head Start Program Performance Standards* (Washington, DC: U.S. Department of Health and Human Services, Head Start Bureau, November 1984). For CDA competencies, see *CDAC Competency Standards* (Washington, DC: Council for Early Childhood Professional Recognition, 1992).

[3] See *Caring for Our Children: National Health and Safety Performance Standards: Guidelines for Out-of-Home Child Care Programs* (Washington, DC: American Public Health Association, 1992).

[4] The Children's Foundation, *1995 Child Day Care Center Licensing Study* (Washington, DC: Children's Foundation, 1995).

The NAEYC's (National Association for the Education of Young Children) *Developmentally Appropriate Practice in Early Childhood Programs Serving Children from Birth through Age Eight* provides a comprehensive set of high standards for any child development center. These standards have been revised and expanded for school-age child care programs.[5]

Child development program managers who accept "developmentally appropriate" as the degree of quality that is proper and adequate for their purpose can use the NAEYC's guidelines to establish levels of quality in all areas of their program. They can also use the guidelines to assess the appropriateness of their efforts to respect and affirm cultural differences and to include children of all abilities.[6]

ACCREDITATION

Accreditation for the school or center provides another level of standards, typically higher than licensing standards. **Accreditation** is defined as a distinction awarded to early childhood schools and child care centers for having met the standards for high-quality programs and completed the procedure for outside validation of that high quality in a voluntary process supervised by the National Academy of Early Childhood Programs, a division of the NAEYC. The standards are spelled out in a booklet titled *Accreditation Criteria & Procedures of the National Academy of Early Childhood Programs.*[7] Steps toward becoming accredited have been described in Chapter 3.

Accreditation is a voluntary system that was developed in 1984 by the NAEYC to give policy boards, managers, and staff members involved in programs for young children an incentive to work toward a high level of program development and recognition for reaching that high-quality standard. In addition, the designation of accreditation gives parents and the general public the information that early childhood programs have various levels of quality and that when choosing an accredited center they can be assured that qualified people have investigated the center and have found it of high quality. Large numbers of schools and centers have now been accredited through this voluntary accrediting system. Centers that are providing developmentally appropriate programs will want to strive for the public recognition of their efforts that comes with accreditation.

---

[5] Kay Albrecht and Margaret C. Plantz (eds.), *Developmentally Appropriate Practice in School-Age Child Care Programs* (Alexandria, VA: Project Home Safe, American Home Economics Association, 1991).

[6] See Louise Derman-Sparks, "Reaching Potentials through Antibias, Multicultural Curriculum," in Sue Bredekamp and Teresa Rosegrant, *Reaching Potentials: Appropriate Curriculum and Assessment for Young Children,* Vol. I (Washington, DC: National Association for the Education of Young Children, 1992,) pp. 114–127; and Lise Fox, Mary Frances Hanline, Cynthia O. Vail, and Kim R. Galant, "Developmentally Appropriate Practice: Applications for Young Children with Disabilities," *Journal of Early Intervention* 18:3 (Summer 1994), pp. 243–257.

[7] Sue Bredekamp (ed.), *Accreditation Criteria & Procedures of the National Academy of Early Childhood Programs* (Washington, DC: National Association for the Education of Young Children, 1991).

DECISIONS, DECISIONS . . .

 Compare your state's licensing rules with the NAEYC's accreditation criteria for each of the following areas: adult-child ratios, staff qualifications, and discipline. Make a chart showing what differences you notice.

MONITORING AND CONTROLLING DEFINED

Monitoring means being alert to and continuously observing for compliance with standards. **Controlling** means that you (a) state the standards you expect each service in your center to achieve, (b) measure the performance against the standards, and (c) correct deviations from established standards and plans. Monitoring and controlling for quality are functions that each staff member must be concerned about daily, hourly, and moment to moment.

Monitoring and controlling are already a part of your life. Consider this illustration: If you are going somewhere in your car, you monitor your speed, road conditions, the time, and dozens of other factors continually. You have standards to meet in the form of traffic regulations, common courtesy, perhaps an appointment to keep, and personal ideas about efficiency or beauty of the route you select. As you drive, you measure your performance against those standards and correct deviations: adjusting your speed, moving the steering wheel when the road curves, perhaps deciding to take another route if there is too much traffic congestion. A child care center manager makes similar observations and adjustments to maintain efficiency and quality in the workplace.

Once you decide which standards apply to your center, every staff member should become familiar with them and know why specific procedures are followed. Your ability to maintain high quality depends, in part, on encouraging each staff member to take responsibility for his or her performance and to make adjustments whenever inadequacies occur.

You will go a long way toward encouraging this type of responsibility if you select your staff carefully, orient and train them thoroughly, and provide feedback on their performance as necessary. But you will need to go further and make it easy for them to do the right thing by structuring the environment, providing needed supplies, and making sure that other supports are in place.

A staff member left alone with too many crying infants, for example, may be tempted to take shortcuts when it comes to sanitizing a diapering table in between changes. Similarly, if there is no running water nearby or no hand lotion to soothe chapped hands, busy caregivers are less likely to be conscientious about hand washing.

PROGRAM EVALUATION

The quality of the children's program is one area of major concern for monitoring and controlling. At least five different groups of people may provide helpful information or viewpoints regarding the quality of programs in the center.

Children Evaluate

As you move about the building, it will be obvious when children are constructively occupied in the play yard or various classrooms. Children's happy responding behavior will be a positive clue that children are receiving the program well and that it is meeting many of their needs.

Of course, a "snapshot" of a few children here or there does not give you a picture of what the program is like for all the children, nor what it is like for one particular child over a longer span of time. You will want to augment this informal checkup with some more systematic data collection. You might, for example, choose one or more children to shadow throughout a day or week, noting things such as the child's activity, mood, and partners in play or conversation at regular, predetermined intervals.

This approach will put you in the child's shoes, so to speak, and help you see the program through his or her eyes. Are you greeted pleasantly when you arrive? Or are you left to find your own way of entering the play of other children? How much of your day is spent hurrying to keep up with others or waiting for others to catch up with you? How much is spent wandering, and how much constructively engaged? How much time is devoted to teacher-directed crafts or games, and how much to projects that you and the other children instigate?

Another way the children can give you a broad picture of how your center is doing is through their own development. You may record baseline information on the child to have a standard for comparing later growth and development. Tests may at times be used in a formal way to measure the outcomes of your program on children. However, you and your staff must be fully aware of the shortcomings of tests. Tests must be administered correctly and interpreted accurately. Avoid placing too much confidence in a single test score. Giving specific scores to parents generally is considered unwise, as is comparing any child to the group. You can provide parents with much more meaningful information about their child's development if you keep dated notes of your observations and samples of the child's drawings and other work. This way parents can readily see how much their child has changed over the months at the center. Children's programs are discussed further in Chapter 14.

DECISIONS, DECISIONS . . .

? Looking over the notes of your day's observation of 4-year-old Tanya, you see that at least four times during the day, she cried for several minutes (when another child took something she was using, when she could not get her boots on, when she fell on the playground, and when she was told to lie on her cot at nap time). No adult approached her during any of these incidents, and each time she gradually stopped crying and went on to some other activity. What does this behavior suggest to you? As center manager, what should you do? Discuss your ideas with your classmates.

Children thrive when there are enough adults to provide them with individual support and attention.
Early Learning Center, Appalachian State University, Boone, NC

Teachers Evaluate

The teachers, too, will be evaluating their planning, organizing, and interacting with children, measuring their actions against professional standards such as those shown in Figure 8–1. Teachers will make adjustments to correct shortcomings. Teachers are wise to monitor, evaluate, and control from moment to moment. For example, if they present a learning task to children and notice that children are unable to perform the task, they may conclude that the task is too difficult. That is evaluation. The standard of performance is in the teacher's mind, based on prior knowledge and experience with children of this age. Using instant evaluation, the teacher has at least two alternatives. The activity can be postponed until a later date when children are more mature and able to do the activity; or the rules can be modified, enabling the children to accomplish some minimum success with the activity. Children deserve to be in small enough groups that teachers have time to observe closely and interact, as was needed in this example. A teacher's participation and encouragement make a positive difference in the children's reception of a new activity.

Program Guidelines	Fair	Good	Excellent
The Program I Observed			
1. Was planned from the point of view of the whole child in the immediate environment.	_____	_____	_____
2. Valued the child's healthy, happy, responding, secure approach to living.	_____	_____	_____
3. Provided for the emotional growth of the child.	_____	_____	_____
4. Balanced active and quiet activities.	_____	_____	_____
5. Provided appropriate opportunities for children to grow in self-direction and independence.	_____	_____	_____
6. Established and maintained limits on behavior for protection of individuals, groups, and the learning environment.	_____	_____	_____
7. Challenged children's intellectual powers.	_____	_____	_____
8. Provided media of self-expression.	_____	_____	_____
9. Encouraged children's verbal expressions.	_____	_____	_____
10. Provided opportunities for social development.	_____	_____	_____
11. Helped children learn to understand their bodies.	_____	_____	_____
12. Provided opportunities for each child to play outdoors each day.	_____	_____	_____
13. Provided opportunities for vigorous action.	_____	_____	_____
14. Was fun for the children.	_____	_____	_____
15. Considered the interests and needs of parents as well as children.	_____	_____	_____

Remarks:

_____

_____

_____

Figure 8–1
Program evaluation
Source: Verna Hildebrand, *A Laboratory Workbook for Introduction to Early Childhood Education* (Upper Saddle River, NJ: Prentice Hall, 1991), p. 125.

If teachers keep a daily diary, they can review the problem areas from time to time and search for solutions. For example, if they note that undressing children requires excessive amounts of time, they could make efforts to correct the situation by exploring a number of available alternatives for facilitating self-help.

Teachers can make a summary of their daily lesson plans and analyze them for a month or so to discover the variety of curricular offerings that the group of children received over a given period—that is, how many different days for each art medium, science activity, song, and so on. Of course, knowing what the group of children was offered does not show what an individual child chose to do just as knowing the cafeteria menu does not tell what a child selected for lunch. Thus, the teachers must make efforts to record information on individual children from time to time.

Teachers should routinely go through their list of children and think about what they have observed each child doing. Making notes on a few children each day helps a teacher keep from forgetting to observe certain children. These observations can be added to each child's portfolio along with dated samples of drawings, writing, and photographs of block or clay creations. Like the portfolio of an artist or model, a child's portfolio contains representative samples of his or her work. Young children are constantly developing, so when representative samples of their work are saved at regular intervals, they can dramatically capture the process of that development. Writing samples collected over a year's time, for example, may well progress from marks that look like "scribbling" to the uneducated eye to work that begins to resemble conventional script more closely.

Teachers can collect these samples in legal-size file folders, large resealable plastic bags, manila envelopes, or many other receptacles. Once they have mastered the technique of routinely collecting observations and work samples, teachers can move on to organizing portfolios, perhaps with sections for physical, social, emotional, and cognitive development, so that they can be sure that they are truly observing and documenting the growth of the whole child. When time for a conference with a parent arrives, the teacher will have a cumulative record of observations that can be discussed. Parents feel trust and confidence when the teacher can cite specific examples. A brief conversation with a parent when he or she picks up a child could let the parent know what the child has done of interest during the day. This information often helps parents engage their child in conversation, and the child will tell the parents more than "We just played" when asked about school.

How can a manager help teachers appreciate the value of watching a child closely? How can managers be sure there is enough time for teachers to do the observations needed? Keeping records on children helps teachers show parents and others that children are achieving developmental milestones. Teachers' observations are also an important part of the assessment process for children with disabilities or developmental delays. And observations form the basis of planning for the individual needs of all children.

Students, through reading books and listening to children's comments and questions, can determine when children are learning new concepts.
Michigan State University Spartan Village Child Care Center, East Lansing

---

DECISIONS, DECISIONS . . .

 Michael, a 3-year-old with Down's syndrome, has been coming to the XYZ Child Development Center for 2 months. The lead teacher in his classroom has observed that Michael has never joined in during large-group songs and games. Instead he sits somewhat listlessly a little behind the others, his gaze wandering toward the ceiling. Discuss what the teacher should do. What should the manager do?

The teachers in charge of each group need to meet to discuss goals, evaluate programs, and settle on the best plans for the future. Discussion of individual children's needs and strategies for meeting those needs requires planning opportunities. This coordination of effort is difficult in child care centers where the staff members have staggered hours, but time must be found if a high-quality program is to be achieved. Thus, the teachers of each group can contribute much to the evaluation effort.

In high-quality programs, teachers have time to share quiet moments with individual children.
Early Learning Center, Appalachian State University, Boone, NC

Parents Evaluate

Parents' evaluation of satisfaction will be apparent when your center gets requests for admission from families who are friends and acquaintances of families with children already enrolled. On the other hand, if parents take their child out of your center because of dissatisfaction, this decision too is evaluation and may hurt your image in the community. Checking admissions, dropouts, and reasons for both can help you gain clues regarding parents' evaluation of your center's program and service.

DECISIONS, DECISIONS . . .

Two families abruptly withdrew their children from your center last week. They did not say anything to you, but another parent with whom you have a long-standing relationship has suggested that they were unhappy because it seemed a different teacher was in the room every week. Your center *has* undergone several staff changes recently: one teacher had a baby and decided to stay at home, another found a better-paying job in the public school system, and one of the new teachers you hired just did not work out. What should you do as manager of the center?

Parents' viewpoints and suggestions can be solicited periodically to learn how the program is meeting the needs of the parents and their children. Many questions can be answered in a private conference, where it is easier to get more elab-

Dear Parents:

Please rate your child's child development center experience on each of the items listed below. Use the following numeric scale.

4—very satisfied   2—somewhat dissatisfied
3—somewhat satisfied   1—very dissatisfied

Your rating, keeping your own child in mind:

( ) 1.   Amount and quality of warmth and understanding received?

( ) 2.   Amount of individual attention given?

( ) 3.   Amount of planning and effort teachers invest in the program?

( ) 4.   Amount and diversity of experiences and materials available?

( ) 5.   Amount of activities fostering creativity?

( ) 6.   Amount of activities enriching intellectual ability?

( ) 7.   Amount of activities enriching language development?

( ) 8.   Amount of activities encouraging your child's social development—making friends, being with children, etc.?

( ) 9.   Amount of activities enhancing motor skills such as running, climbing, throwing, catching, and the like?

( ) 10.   Amount of activities helping your child feel good about himself or herself?

( ) 11.   The amount of encouragement given for your child to take care of himself or herself and become more independent?

( ) 12.   Number of children in the class?

( ) 13.   Number of adults helping in the class?

( ) 14.   Amount of space available in the classroom and play yard?

( ) 15.   Amount, type, and quality of equipment in the yard?

( ) 16.   Communication network for keeping parents informed?

( ) 17.   Opportunity you have had to visit the classroom or teacher?

( ) 18.   Your child's overall progress this year?

( ) 19.   Write below or on the back of this page your concerns that do not seem to be covered in the questions above.

Figure 8–2
Parents' program rating sheet

oration on a point than if only written questionnaires are used. You can ask such questions as "Do the hours fit your family's needs?" "Are your needs for consulting with the teacher being met?" "What changes would you suggest?" A questionnaire such as that in Figure 8–2 may be developed to get some helpful feedback. A questionnaire may also draw parents' attention to features of your service that make it high-quality.

DECISIONS, DECISIONS . . .

On checking teachers' lesson plans and observing the classroom at the same time each day for a week, you, the manager, note that easel painting, collage making, and play dough manipulating, which were listed on the lesson plans for each of 3 days, were not being carried out in the classroom. Crayons and paper were the only materials available. Should you care about the discrepancy? Why? Discuss the standard that applies. What questions would you ask the teachers?

The Community and Professionals Evaluate

Some outside evaluations occur because they are required by law or a center's funding source, including licensing personnel or representatives of the state Department of Education. Others are solicited voluntarily, such as the final evaluation of a center's application by the accrediting commission of the National Academy of Early Childhood Programs (which is the accreditation arm of the NAEYC). The people of the community also form evaluative opinions about the center from what they see and hear around the community.

DECISIONS, DECISIONS . . .

Manager X stepped out of the office to watch children playing on the playground. No teacher or adult could be seen among the children. Checking more closely, the manager found the adults conversing indoors near the coat rack. Children not being supervised is a violation of state regulations and the center's standards. What should the manager do?

Some managers have found it valuable to exchange evaluation services with other centers. They often gain some helpful perspectives when they see how others handle similar functions. For example, in a visit to a center, Rachel, a manager, observed a smoothly operating session of adults helping children get dressed in their outdoor winter clothing. Five or six children took their boots and snowsuits to the middle of the playroom where a teacher or an aide sat on a small chair. Sitting on the floor near an adult, the children dressed themselves, with the adult offering a few verbal suggestions and a tug on a boot here or there. Rachel recorded the smooth operation and vowed to make some changes in the system she operated. She had gained a new perspective during the exchange visit with another center. She commended the center when discussing her observation with them.

The Manager Evaluates

As manager, you will monitor the children's program for the purpose of comparing performance with the goals of the center and with current professional standards. Informal spot checks can be done daily. Periodically, more formalized procedures are needed, such as checking lesson plans, taking detailed notes in each group, or using checklists.

The evaluations, standards, and feedback systems need to be planned with the teachers and carried out in an agreeable, supportive way so as to increase the confidence, motivation, and ability of the teachers and the center to perform better. The evaluation checklist in Figure 8–1 is coordinated with the planning guidelines suggested in Chapter 13, indicating an important relationship among planning, monitoring, and controlling. Remember that when you are expecting to monitor or evaluate teachers or others on aspects of quality in the program, you need to communicate this information early to allow planning and development time. It is unfair to staff members to have new items for judging them brought out at evaluation time.

Ideally, the elements of quality to be evaluated will be established in collaboration with your teachers and other stakeholders in the center. Recall from the discussion of management techniques that staff are more likely to follow through on goals for which they feel some ownership. When they do, the manager can evaluate by serving more as a mirror than as a judge.

Instead of saying that a staff member has failed to offer an adequate variety of art experiences for children, the manager can reflect that he or she has observed the same watercolors and manila paper on the art table for the last week. This remark could give staff members an opportunity to explain that they were trying to make sure every child had an opportunity to waterpaint or that they wanted the children to explore additional possibilities with the same media.

Of course, the possibility remains that a teacher's performance simply is not acceptable, in which case it will be the manager's job to make this clear and state expectations for improvement as well as consequences for failure to do so. Ongoing professional development activities, as suggested in Chapters 6 and 7, will help teachers become more effective partners in this aspect of their evaluation.

DECISIONS, DECISIONS . . .

 Manager X gave the teachers the day off with pay to attend a conference and later learned that one teacher had not attended the conference at all but had gone shopping. What should the manager do? What standard applies?

The manager and teachers can develop habits of giving teachers with innovative ideas positive feedback as evidence of their creative work becomes apparent. It is as simple as saying, "That bulletin board really captures the children's ideas about the eggs and the baby chicks!" Sometimes harmful competition develops, and people fail to be supportive of each other. Sharing is a much better type of relationship than competition. If you find competition developing, you might say, "When I feel competition rather than sharing developing, I fear we may have feelings that might interfere with our work with the children." Managers should not compare two staff members to get one of them to work harder. Such a technique is apt to backfire, causing hard feelings instead of improvement.

DECISIONS, DECISIONS . . .

 Manager X receives a report from a teacher's aide that the teacher with whom she works has hit certain children with a ruler to make them behave. What standard applies? What should the manager do?

MONITORING OTHER UNITS

All units of the child development center must be the focus of the manager's monitoring and controlling function. That is, you will set a minimum standard and make corrections when deviations are observed. For example, in relation to the policy board, it is appropriate to evaluate the manner of decision making, presenting items to the board, increasing professionalism, serving more children and families, and increasing the effectiveness of the board members. If any item does not measure up to standards, you will initiate corrective action.

Any deviations from standards should be brought to a staff member's attention immediately, especially matters having an effect on children. Hiring new staff is very expensive; therefore, attention to improving the performance of those who have been hired is desirable. It is reasonable to expect people to be punctual and to carry out the job as described in the job description. Following the standards set by the profession or service is also to be assumed. Teachers are expected to have certain professional standards. Food service personnel have other standards. Staff members can be helpful in setting the criteria or standards on which they will be judged. To be fair, criteria for pay raises, promotions, or dismissal should be set early and communicated to the staff, rather than established only when it is time to make the judgment, say, at the end of a year.

All employees should be hired with the agreement that they will participate in professional development. The assumption here is that growth and change are necessary for all staff members in a human services organization. Help may be given individually, in job-alike groups, and during total staff meetings. Outside consultants may be brought in. Activities may be planned by the staff members themselves as a response to some felt need or frustration in their work. If an observer is going to visit a teacher's class, take notes, and make recommendations, the teacher should understand that process in advance.

DECISIONS, DECISIONS . . .

 The fire inspector refused to pass the PDQ Center until the hot water heater closet was properly lined with fire-retardant material. What should the manager do? What standard applies?

Sometimes a consultant, educator, or manager may wish to model or give demonstrations to show individuals how to do something new, or old, more effectively. Credibility and a better understanding of problems are maintained by managers who demonstrate areas of competence by periodically performing staff members' tasks.[8] With respect for the domains of staff members, the staff improvement function should be carried on regularly. (Ten guides for professional development activities have been suggested in Chapter 6.)

The Monetary Area

Money management must continuously be evaluated. You will be responsible for careful, accurate, and honest accounting in both collecting fees and paying expenses. Budgets should be adhered to in both profit and nonprofit organizations. In profit-making centers, figuring a reasonable additional percentage for profit is necessary. Establishing an accounting system with the assistance of a competent accountant will be essential. More details regarding monetary control are discussed in Chapter 9, which is devoted entirely to money management in the child development center.

The Physical Plant

The safety, sanitation, security, and aesthetics of the entire physical plant of your child development center may be your responsibility, or you may have only a portion of a building as your concern. Certain maintenance tasks will be high on your agenda. For example, daily cleaning, mopping, vacuuming, trash removal, and cleaning of the classrooms, kitchen, and toilet rooms must be done. The playground must be scrutinized periodically for dangerous equipment and objects. Outdoor equipment must be painted regularly to keep it attractive. General tidiness should be encouraged among the staff. When children's needs have priority, as they should in centers, then it becomes easy to lay items down here or there instead of putting them in appropriate storage. When items are routinely left around, one might evaluate the situation to see whether a change of storage arrangements or additional storage space would help. Attractive bulletin boards and displays stimulate children's thinking. Some bulletin boards may contain items of interest to parents. Bulletin boards should be neatly organized and outdated materials removed.

Safety, especially fire safety, must always be high on your agenda. Staff members should understand that exits must be kept accessible. Smoke detectors and alarms must be available. Fire and tornado drills should be practiced regularly so that each staff member knows his or her responsibility during an alarm. Parents also need clear information regarding where you plan to take the children for safety during actual emergency situations. Depending on the location of your center and

---

[8] See V. L. Lombardi and V. Hildebrand, "Modernizing Administration," *Education* 101:3 (Spring 1981), pp. 270–272.

specific features of your community, you may also need clearly formulated plans for other types of emergencies, such as earthquakes or chemical spills.[9]

Security of your facility during nights, weekends, and vacations must be planned and controlled. Many centers have difficulty keeping nonenrolled children out of their yards, a fact that may dictate choosing heavier equipment than the size and age of the center's enrollees would require. That is, older and larger children may swing or slide, necessitating more substantial equipment; otherwise, the visitors are likely to damage the equipment. Security locks are also essential. Some of these "visitors" might be of the four-legged variety, so you will need to cover outdoor sandboxes when they are not in use to prevent them from becoming unsanitary litter boxes.

Parking space must be adequate and safe. Extreme caution is essential in moving children to cars. Most preprimary children are so small that they may not be seen in rearview mirrors. If you are providing transportation, adhering to the state's guidelines will help ensure seat belt compliance and safe traveling for children. Those guidelines must be followed when taking children on field trips, too.

Food Service

Items for evaluating the food service area (also discussed in Chapter 13) include the following:

1. Do meals offer sufficient quantity, variety, and nutritive content to meet recommended daily allowances?
2. Are children's attitudes toward meals, manners, and nutrition education positive?
3. Are foods adequate for staff?
4. Are kitchen and dining areas arranged efficiently?
5. Are noise levels low?
6. Is space adequate to attend to individual children's needs?
7. Are good sanitation procedures strictly adhered to?
8. Are all food workers healthy, clean, and dressed to deliver clean, healthful food?
9. Is the interaction between teachers and food service staff facilitating the use of food in learning activities in the classroom?
10. Is information on children's food intake and nutrition being disseminated to parents?
11. Are snacks for midmorning and midafternoon nutritious, adequate, and attractive?
12. Are teachers receiving a nutrition break, too?
13. Have you monitored the food shopping with regard to costs, waste, and leftovers?

---

[9] See, for example, Delaine Certo, "Helping Children and Staff Cope with Earthquakes," *Child Care Information Exchange* 102 (March/April 1995), pp. 71–74; and Elizabeth Smith, "Toxic Fumes: Knowing What to Do," *Texas Child Care Quarterly* 13:1 (Summer 1989), pp. 13–16.

DECISIONS, DECISIONS . . .

For 2 days in a row, the cook served apples and grapefruit juice for the children's midmorning snack instead of food from two food groups as stated on the menu and as required by state nutrition guidelines. What should be done? Discuss the standard that applies.

Children's Health and Safety

Items requiring evaluation in this category (discussed at length in Chapter 12) include the following:

1. Have all children filed immunization records?
2. Are your records clear as to who is available to pick up each child if he or she becomes ill during the day?
3. Do all staff members know where these records are filed?
4. Have you arranged a place to keep a sick child comfortable, quiet, and away from the others until he or she can be taken home?
5. Have you made arrangements for continually monitoring children's health to be alert for signs of illness?
6. Do you require medical clearance for a child to return following an absence?
7. Is your nap room space adequate, free from drafts, and accessible to exits in case of fire?
8. Are sufficient staff available during nap time to evacuate the building in case of fire or tornado?
9. Does each staff member know his or her role in an emergency evacuation—for example, taking children's emergency information and an attendance list; calling for help and giving directions for reaching the center?
10. Are evacuation plans known and practiced?
11. Is the length of nap time communicated to parents?
12. Are provisions adequate for children who will not sleep?
13. Do you have sources of medical advice that can guide you or your staff on a moment's notice in case of emergency?
14. Are those medical advisers' phone numbers posted by each phone?
15. Is the temperature of your building correct for active children?
16. Have all appropriate precautions been taken to prevent child abuse of any kind?

Parental and Public Relations

There is some overlap in evaluating actions that affect parents and evaluating those affecting the general public. Careful attention is needed in the following areas (additional information appears in Chapter 15):

1. Are people's calls answered politely?
2. Are letters answered politely and promptly?
3. Are parents' needs being met?
4. Are advertisements, brochures, and newsletters adequate and up-to-date?
5. Are you making and carrying out plans to communicate with parents?
6. Are publications available to lend to parents to help them with their parenting questions?
7. Are parents clear on your procedures for dealing with a sick child and their responsibility for picking up the child and returning the child after the illness is over?
8. Do all staff have a clear understanding of who should speak with parents, the public, or media representatives when complaints or criticisms arise?
9. Are staff members who fill leadership roles in the community well prepared to represent the center?
10. Are parents well-informed about your food service and health policies?
11. Do parents know your routine during emergencies such as storm warnings?

DECISIONS, DECISIONS . . .

 The manager noticed that the adults' bathroom was not spotless when she arrived in the morning. She proceeded to check the children's bathrooms and recognized unpleasant odors and dirty conditions. She concluded that the rooms had not been cleaned the night before. What should the manager do? What standard applies?

EVALUATION OF MANAGEMENT

As manager you must also regularly seek evaluation of your own performance by the policy board and staff to improve both your management and the operation of the total enterprise. You can work with the board and staff in setting up the evaluation process and be able to learn much from it in a friendly, cooperative, and harmonious fashion, just as you expect your staff to learn from evaluations in a climate of goodwill in the interest of serving children better. Figure 8–3 is a suggested form for a manager's evaluation. Note the relationship between Figure 8–3 and the manager's duties discussed in Chapter 3.

CONCLUSION

Monitoring and controlling for quality are major concerns of a manager. By setting standards, measuring performance, and leading staff members to correct deviations from the standards, the manager performs essential monitoring and controlling functions. Local and state rules form the basis for minimum standards, but most managers want their center to have higher-than-minimum stan-

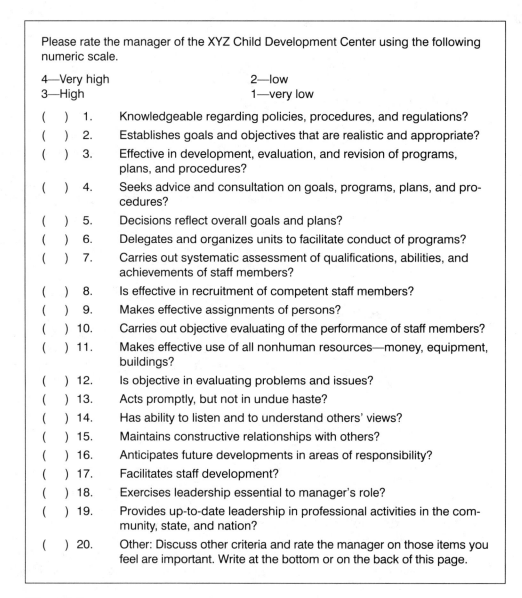

Please rate the manager of the XYZ Child Development Center using the following numeric scale.

4—Very high   2—low
3—High   1—very low

( ) 1.   Knowledgeable regarding policies, procedures, and regulations?

( ) 2.   Establishes goals and objectives that are realistic and appropriate?

( ) 3.   Effective in development, evaluation, and revision of programs, plans, and procedures?

( ) 4.   Seeks advice and consultation on goals, programs, plans, and procedures?

( ) 5.   Decisions reflect overall goals and plans?

( ) 6.   Delegates and organizes units to facilitate conduct of programs?

( ) 7.   Carries out systematic assessment of qualifications, abilities, and achievements of staff members?

( ) 8.   Is effective in recruitment of competent staff members?

( ) 9.   Makes effective assignments of persons?

( ) 10. Carries out objective evaluating of the performance of staff members?

( ) 11. Makes effective use of all nonhuman resources—money, equipment, buildings?

( ) 12. Is objective in evaluating problems and issues?

( ) 13. Acts promptly, but not in undue haste?

( ) 14. Has ability to listen and to understand others' views?

( ) 15. Maintains constructive relationships with others?

( ) 16. Anticipates future developments in areas of responsibility?

( ) 17. Facilitates staff development?

( ) 18. Exercises leadership essential to manager's role?

( ) 19. Provides up-to-date leadership in professional activities in the community, state, and nation?

( ) 20. Other: Discuss other criteria and rate the manager on those items you feel are important. Write at the bottom or on the back of this page.

Figure 8–3
Evaluation of the manager

dards. NAEYC accreditation is a distinction centers and schools can earn for producing high-quality programs.

Every aspect of the center must come under scrutiny from time to time and the resulting information put to use in improving program quality. The various publics share in the monitoring or evaluating function: the board, the teachers, the manager, other staff members, the parents, the community, and, most of all, the children, who reveal by their enjoyment of the activities and willingness to attend the center every day that they are happy with the nurturing and educating that they are receiving.

DECISIONS, DECISIONS . . .

 The yard cleaning crew arrived to clean up and mow the play yard. The manager had contracted for their services starting at 5 P.M,. and it was only 3 P.M.—just the time children were rushing out to play after their naps. The workers unloaded the lawn mower. Should the manager allow the workers to go ahead and mow the yard with the children there? Discuss the standard that applies.

APPLICATIONS

1. Refer to a manager you have known and check the evaluation form given in Figure 8–3 regarding his or her performance. Assuming you were the president of the policy board that was considering this manager, what recommendations would you make? Discuss with your classmates the desirable characteristics of managers.
2. Select four of the "Decisions, Decisions" features found throughout the chapter. Write your answer to the questions posed at the end of each. Use examples from actual centers where possible. Be sure to look up the source of the standards. Discuss with your classmates.
3. Add information related to monitoring and controlling to your management notebook.

STUDY QUESTIONS

1. Define the monitoring and controlling process. Explain the relationship of this process to the child development center operation.
2. Explain the relationship of monitoring and controlling to standards, licensing, and accreditation.
3. Write an essay describing how the following people evaluate a child development center:
   a. the children enrolled
   b. the parents of children enrolled
   c. the professionals and others in a community
   d. the manager
4. Go over the manager's evaluation form (Figure 8–3) and relate each item to a manager's responsibilities and behaviors discussed throughout this book. Is the form fair? How would you change it? Would any item be a surprise to a manager?

SUGGESTED READINGS

Albrecht, Kay M. *Quality Criteria for School-Age Child Care Programs*. Alexandria, VA: American Home Economics Association, Project Home Safe, 1991.

Bloom, Paula Jorde. "Shared Decisionmaking: The Centerpiece of Participatory Management." *Young Children* 50:4 (May 1995), pp. 55–60.

Bredekamp, Sue (ed.). *Accreditation Criteria & Procedures of the National Academy of Early Childhood Programs*. Washington, DC: National Association for the Education of Young Children, 1991.

Bredekamp, Sue (ed.). *Developmentally Appropriate Practice in Early Childhood Programs Serving Children from Birth through Age 8*. Washington, DC: National Association for the Education of Young Children, 1987.

Bredekamp, Sue. *Regulating Child Care Quality: Evidence from NAEYC's Accreditation System*. Washington, DC: National Association for the Education of Young Children, 1989.

Broussard, A. M. "Are You a Codependent Director?" *Child Care Information Exchange* 83 (January/February 1992), pp. 7–11.

Caruso, J. J. "Supervisors in Early Childhood Programs: An Emerging Profile." *Young Children* 46:6 (September 1991), pp. 20–24.

Cost, Quality, and Child Outcomes Study Team. *Cost, Quality, and Child Outcomes in Child Care Centers, Executive Summary*, 2nd ed. Denver: Economics Department, University of Colorado, 1995.

Dittman, Laura L. "Finding the Best Care for Your Infant or Toddler." *Young Children* 41:3 (March 1986), pp. 43–46.

Duff, R. Eleanor, Mac H. Brown, and Irma J. VanScoy. "Reflection and Self-Evaluation: Keys to Professional Development." *Young Children* 50:4 (May 1995), pp. 81–88.

Elkind, David. *Miseducation: Preschoolers at Risk*. New York: Knopf, 1987.

Elkind, David. "Readiness for Kindergarten." *Young Children* 42:3 (March 1987), p. 2.

Frost, Joe L. "Playground Equipment Catalogs: Can They Be Trusted? *Texas Child Care* 14:1 (Summer 1990), pp. 3–12.

Grace, Cathy, and Elizabeth F. Shores. *The Portfolio and Its Use: Developmentally Appropriate Assessment of Young Children*. Little Rock, AR: Southern Association on Children under Six, 1992.

Harms, Thelma, and R. M. Clifford. *Early Childhood Environment Rating Scale*. New York: Teachers College Press, 1980.

Harms, Thelma, and R. M. Clifford. *The Infant-Toddler Environment Rating Scale*. New York: Teachers College Press, 1988.

Hildebrand, Verna. *Introduction to Early Childhood Education*, 6th ed. Upper Saddle River, NJ: Merrill/Prentice Hall, 1997.

Kamii, Constance (ed.). *Achievement Testing in the Early Grades: The Games Grown-Ups Play*. Washington, DC: National Association for the Education of Young Children, 1990.

Katz, Lilian. "Early Childhood Programs: Multiple Perspectives on Quality." *Childhood Education* 69:2 (Winter 1992), pp. 66–71.

Koralek, Derry G., Laura J. Colker, and Diane Trister Dodge. *The What, Why, and How of High-Quality Early Childhood Education: A Guide for On-Site Supervision*. Washington, DC: National Association for the Education of Young Children, 1993.

Kostelnik, M., L. Stein, A. Whiren, and A. Soderman, *Guiding Children's Social Development*. Albany, NY: Delmar, 1993.

Leavitt, Robin L., and Brenda K. Eheart. "Assessment in Early Childhood Programs." *Young Children* 46:5 (July 1991), pp. 4–9.

National Association for the Education of Young Children. *Facility Design for Early Child-hood Programs: NAEYC Resource Guide*. Washington, DC: Author, 1987.

National Association for the Education of Young Children. "Good Discipline Is, in Large Part, the Result of a Fantastic Curriculum!" *Young Children* 42:3 (March 1987), pp. 49–51.

National Association for the Education of Young Children. *Kindergarten: NAEYC Resource Guide*. Washington DC: Author, 1987.

National Association for the Education of Young Children. "NAEYC Position Statement on Standardized Testing of Young Children 3 through 8 Years of Age." *Young Children* 43:3 (March 1988), pp. 42–45.

Puckett, Margaret B., and Janet K. Black. *Authentic Assessment of the Young Child: Celebrating Development and Learning*. Upper Saddle River, NJ: Merrill/Prentice Hall, 1994.

Rogers, Dwight L., Cathleen B. Waller, and Marilyn S. Perrin. "Learning More about What Makes a Good Teacher Good through Collaborative Research in the Classroom." *Young Children* 42:4 (May 1987), pp. 34–39.

Stanley, Sarah J., and W. James Popham. *Teacher Evaluation: Six Prescriptions for Success*. Alexandria, VA: Association for Supervision and Curriculum Development, 1988.

Zeece, Pauline Davey. "Quality Begins with Us." *Child Care Information Exchange* 102 (March/April 1995), pp. 75–79.

PART III

Managing Resources

CHAPTER 9

Managing Monetary Resources

• •

Managing monetary resources requires you, as manager, to perform objectively all the managerial functions of planning, organizing, staffing, leading, and monitoring and controlling. Your goal will be to keep your child development center on firm financial ground. You must believe that you can have a tough head for understanding, monitoring, and controlling the balance sheet and still have a tender heart for giving children loving care and education.

Accreditation criteria of the National Association for the Education of Young Children (NAEYC), which have been discussed throughout this book, require a child development center to be fiscally sound in order to serve the needs of children and families effectively and efficiently. Episodes should never happen such as that which occurred at one center where parents paid tuition on Friday for the following week's child care, only to find a "Closed" sign posted on the center door on Monday morning, because the center had filed for bankruptcy. The management informed neither parents nor staff members of the impending closing, so you can readily imagine the resulting frustration of parents, staff members, and the community.

FUNDING CHILD DEVELOPMENT CENTERS

Child development centers are funded in a variety of ways. Children's families may pay the total cost through tuition fees. Philanthropic donors may make contributions, or an organization such as a business or church may give in-kind support such as space, utilities, and custodial services. Taxes from local, state, and national levels may partially or completely fund a center. The picture is complex, however, for there are differences between a center's **expended costs** (cash outlays) and the **full cost** of providing child development programs. A 1995 study of centers in four states found that parents who paid full tuition provided about 90% of the amount centers expend in providing care. When parents whose care is subsidized are included, parent payments comprise about 70%. Cash payments from governmental sources and philanthropic donations by businesses or churches, for example, provide the remainder.[1]

Although they do not cover the full cost of child care, parents are having to devote increasingly greater portions of their paychecks for that care. The average weekly cost for child care rose from $64 in 1986 to $79 in 1993, with families devoting over 7.5% of their monthly income to child care in 1993. For families living below the federal poverty line, that percentage is much greater (10%). For the poorest of those families (those earning less than $1,200 per month), a full quarter of their income is eaten up by child care bills.[2]

Many advocates believe that families are already paying as much as they can for child care. They argue that, because a good beginning is in society's best interest, government has a responsibility to help families shoulder the burden. Government subsidies, however, whether direct or indirect, are subject to shifts in the political mood of the country, and many hard-fought gains for children stand to be lost in the currently popular move toward welfare reform.[3]

In the United States today, unfortunately yet another source of funding support exists for child development programs. According to the 1995 study of child development programs in four states, the average *full cost* of providing even mediocre child care services is $127 per week, while the average *expended cost* is $95 per week per child. Donated goods and volunteer time make up a small part of the difference between the two amounts. The *foregone wages* of the teachers and assistant teachers, who earn even less in child care than they would in other female-dominated professions, comprise the remainder, or 19% of the full cost of programs.[4]

Church-Supported Centers

Churches as a group are the largest sponsor of child care in the United States, housing more than 20,000 early childhood programs. These church-housed centers are largely full-time child care. Most are licensed and managers express the view that licensing protects the safety and welfare of the children. Only 13% sur-

---

[1] Cost, Quality and Child Outcomes Study Team, *Cost, Quality, and Child Outcomes in Child Care Centers, Executive Summary* (Denver: Economics Department, University of Colorado, 1995), pp. 5–7.

[2] Lynn M. Casper, "What Does It Cost to Mind Our Preschoolers?" *Current Population Reports,* P70-52 (Washington, DC: U.S. Department of Commerce, Bureau of the Census, 1994).

[3] See "Washington Update: Action of Child Care/Welfare Imminent," *Young Children* 50:5 (July 1995), p. 43.

[4] *Cost, Quality, and Child Outcomes in Child Care Centers, Executive Summary*, pp. 5–6.

veyed teach religious education. The Southern Baptist Convention and the Roman Catholic Church are the two largest providers of child care.[5]

Churches make their largest financial contribution to child care programs through providing classrooms and play yards. Most of the churches supply these without cost or at a reduced rent. A majority of those studied also subsidize utilities, building maintenance, and janitorial services. In some cases, the child care staff receives health and other benefits through the church organization's benefit package for other employees. Salaries in these church-related programs are low, as in most other child care programs.

Private Schools and Centers

The smaller, private for-profit schools operate, as they have traditionally in this country, to serve small groups of the more affluent clientele. Historically, these schools were usually short-day until recently, when many have been pressed to open full-day groups to accommodate the working mothers of children in their groups. Private schools and franchises are for sale just as are other types of businesses.

Parent Cooperative Centers

Parent cooperative child development centers are funded by parents through paying tuition, fund-raising projects, and contributions of parents' own labor to the operation of the school. Parents organize the center and hire the teachers. Some coops receive in-kind contributions of facilities from churches, schools, and community centers. Janitorial, secretarial, maintenance, or utilities may be other in-kind services donated by a sponsoring organization.

Franchise Child Care Centers

A steady growth industry in the United States is the franchise or chain of child care centers. Today 19% of all for-profit child care centers are operated by chains or franchises, up from 15% in 1969.[6] These centers have had the advantage of high-level management procedures. They have employed professional leadership to ensure uniform standards for curriculum, health, nutrition, and the like. Because of their size and multiple levels of management, franchise centers offer a manager more opportunities for career advancement than would be possible in smaller, individual centers.

Employer-Assisted Child Care

Employer-assisted child care centers have had a tremendous growth since 1978 when there were 100 programs, according to the U.S. Department of Labor. In a 1987 study, the Bureau of Labor Statistics found that employer-supported child

---

[5] R. Neugebauer, "Churches That Care: Status Report #2 on Church-Housed Child Care," *Child Care Information Exchange* 81 (September/October 1991), pp. 41–46.

[6] Roger Neugebauer, "How's Business? Status Report #9 on For-Profit Child Care," *Child Care Information Exchange* 108 (March/April 1996), pp. 60–64."

Investing in a supply of appropriate books for children helps cultivate a lifelong love of reading.
Early Learning Center, Appalachian State University, Boone, NC

care centers had become available in 25,000 of the nation's public- and private-sector workplaces having 10 or more employees. In addition, 61% of all establishments have one or more work practices that facilitate parents' caring for their children, such as flexible work schedules, voluntary part-time arrangements, and flexible leave policies.[7] More information on employer-operated programs is given in Chapter 10.

Tax Support

Many groups have long advocated that the federal government assist young children's care and education. Federal tax support would help assure that children are not deprived of care and education services simply because they are poor. A comprehensive child care bill was passed in 1971 only to suffer a presidential veto by Richard Nixon. Thus, for nearly 20 years, persons concerned with children, families, and female employees have worked for the legislation that was finally passed in the closing days of the 101st Congress.

The 1990 Child Care and Development Block Grant authorized $750 million in fiscal year (FY) 1991, $825 million in FY 1992, $925 million in FY 1993, and such sums as necessary in FY 1994 and 1995. State allocations were to be determined by a formula that included the number of children younger than age 5 in

---

[7] U.S. Department of Labor, Bureau of Labor Statistics, *Child Care: A Workforce Issue* (Washington, DC: U.S. Government Printing Office, 1988), p. 4.

the state, the number of children receiving free or reduced-price school lunch, and the state per capita income. No requirement was set for state matching funds.

Child care activities focusing on improving quality were allocated 5% of the monies from the 1990 Child Care and Development Block Grant legislation. In addition, Head Start was reauthorized and increased to $2.386 billion for FY 1991. The Head Start legislation indicated a minimum of one teacher with a child development associate (CDA) credential or other appropriate early childhood credential by 1994.[8] The states are required to make a plan for using federal monies. Thus, as a manager, you should contact your state authorities to learn your state's procedures.

The U.S. Department of Labor prepared the following information on tax support of child care as discussions proceeded on additional federal support.[9]

Federal Funding of Child Care

The Federal government already plays a major role in funding child care. Federal child care assistance programs and the Head Start program total $6.9 billion in FY '88.

The Federal child care effort is designed and targeted for various purposes, from helping the middle class (tax subsidies) to breaking the welfare cycle (jobs programs) to child development (food and education programs). A wide variety of laws provide the authority for these efforts.

Still, much of the Federal spending related to child care cannot be precisely stated. For instance, the dollar value of the employers' tax subsidy for providing child care is not ordinarily compiled by the Internal Revenue Service. Grants to states and communities under several programs authorize use of the funds for child care, but do not always require reports on how the funds are spent.

Child care–related spending began in 1943, when the first significant Federal funding for child day care was provided as a wartime emergency measure under the authority of the Lanham Act to care for children of mothers working in wartime industries.

Increases in costs of the tax subsidy seem to have kept pace with the 1980s growth of jobs and entry of women into the workforce. One of the most significant is a 225% jump in the cost of the income exclusion for employer-provided child or dependent care services. This tax rule means that parents may not pay income taxes on up to $5,000 in cash or services provided for child care assistance from their employers. Federal taxes that would have otherwise been collected amounted to $20 million in fiscal year 1986 and $65 million in fiscal year 1988, the most recent reporting date.

Federal tax funds are used for Head Start programs for low-income children throughout the United States, Puerto Rico, and Guam. Tax monies are also provided for training child care workers, especially those from the disadvantaged population. Title XX monies have been returned to states from the federal gov-

---

[8] Public Policy Report, "101st Congress: The Children's Congress," *Young Children* 46:2 (January 1991), pp. 78–81.

[9] U.S. Department of Labor, *Child Care*, pp. 2–3.

ernment. These may be allocated to child care, depending on the states' decision. Federal grants given for various child care–related research projects were very common in the 1970s. Federal funds have also played a significant part in improving the early childhood experiences for young children with disabilities from birth on through PL 94–142, PL 92–424, PL 99–371, and PL 99–457.

Many centers are eligible for food service programs under the U.S. Department of Agriculture. At times these programs give money, and at other times they allocate surplus foods; they are, of course, tax supported.

States play a role in child care funding as well, either through subsidies for care, tax breaks given to working parents, or various programs aimed at upgrading the salaries and training levels of caregivers. Arkansas, for example, doubles the tax deduction for child care when that care is provided in state-accredited homes. California's Child Care Initiative is a coalition of business and state agencies collaborating on a variety of strategies to fund new programs and improve those already in existence. Colorado, Connecticut, Maryland, and Wisconsin fund resource and referral systems, which not only help parents find care but also provide training programs and incentives to encourage the professional development of providers. Minnesota passed legislation in 1994 to raise $2 million for renovating child care facilities, while Washington's child care budget reached more than $200 million for a 2-year period. Michigan operates a Child Care Clearinghouse as part of its Jobs Commission to help employers structure child care benefits. In its third annual survey of states' child care records, *Working Mother* magazine called North Carolina the "most exciting state" because of its achievements in increasing funding, raising standards, underwriting education for caregivers, and extending tax credits.[10]

State and local tax support is the source of funding for many kindergarten programs. The first public school kindergarten in the United States was founded in St. Louis in 1873. Only recently have all states begun funding kindergartens. Thirty-two states provide publicly funded programs for 4-year-old children, usually limited to those identified as at risk for school failure. These programs do not have the stringent income criteria for admission that Head Start programs have, but like Head Start, they are unable to serve all, or even most, of the eligible children. In addition, because they are usually half-day programs, they do not offer a solution to the child care problems of needy families.[11]

School taxes also pay for laboratory child development centers in high schools and colleges, giving students practice working with children. Children's tuition may supplement the funds provided to high schools and colleges for such centers.

In many states, tax monies are also allocated to colleges and used to fund a child care center for children of students and staff. Tax money may be used for just the building or for custodial service or maintenance, with tuition covering operating expenses. Some colleges initiate child care services to facilitate the

---

[10]Vivian Cadden, "How Does Your State Rate?" *Working Mother,* March 1995, pp. 21–32.

[11]Children's Defense Fund, *The State of America's Children Yearbook 1995* (Washington, DC: Children's Defense Fund, 1995), pp. 39–40.

enrollment of students—both men and women. Low-income parent-students may receive financial assistance for child care through funds from taxes.

Philanthropic organizations that support child development centers directly or indirectly are in a sense tax supported, in that individuals who donate funds are able to subtract their gifts from their taxable income. The United Way, for example, often operates child care centers. People's donations to the United Way may be deductible from taxable income.

Churches are involved in child development centers in a significant way in some communities. Their facilities are not taxed, and, as long as the centers remain nonprofit, their income is not taxed. Therefore, the church-related centers have some indirect tax support. Churches often consider their center part of their outreach program.

Health and social services provided by the community are generally tax supported. Immunizations for children are tax supported. Licensing and monitoring of child development centers—both profit and nonprofit—are carried on by a state agency supported by tax dollars.

With this brief discussion, managers and boards can be aware that a number of tax-supported programs may be available to fund or supplement the funding of a child development center. Such funding is usually in a state of flux, subject to political winds. You can stay abreast of these changes by becoming involved in professional organizations, such as the NAEYC, whose bimonthly publication *Young Children* contains regular public policy updates. The licensing agency of your state government or your state's Department of Education may be able to provide information on potential sources of revenue. The wise manager will not neglect to investigate tax-supported avenues when searching for funds.

Fund-Raising

Locating and maintaining funding for a child development center will require a good deal of a manager's attention. A finance committee of the policy board may assume the responsibility. Occasionally members are selected for the board owing to their connections with a funding source. Fund-raising efforts will range from capital investment funding to funding operating expenses or special items such as a new play yard climber. The sources discussed earlier can suggest leads for funding certain types of programs. Some can help stretch the limited dollars you can raise locally. Writing proposals for these funds may require a considerable amount of your time. **Proposals** are documented requests showing your expertise and ability to fulfill the proposed project and your timetable, budget, and procedures. It is essential to follow directions and meet the deadlines set by the funding agency.

Smaller amounts of money may be raised with the support of parents and the community. Possibilities include sponsoring bake sales, rummage sales, rock concerts, or coffeehouse combos. In addition to raising needed funds, such events are often good for rallying the support of parents and the community.

During fund-raising, your center can receive valuable publicity in the media and among parents. Publicity should be thoughtfully planned. Businesses may publicize a center as part of their social action. A civic club or church may provide space or a number of hours of its members' labor if the center becomes its cause to support.

In the quest for funds, directors should not overlook the possibility of in-kind donations. Local businesses may be willing to donate used computer hardware or office furniture when they upgrade or redecorate. Others may have regularly discarded materials (such as wood scraps from a lumber yard) that can be used in a variety of ways at your center. This would be a good place to use the combined imaginations of your board members and staff to generate creative possibilities for new resources as well as uses. The suggested readings at the end of this chapter will give you other ideas to get started.

Proposals for Grants

Some centers can qualify for grants under a number of funding programs. Making proposals for funding various activities of your child development center can be simple or complex depending on the dollar size of the request, the funding agency, and the accounting requirements. Seeking funds may be as simple as writing a letter to a civic club requesting scholarship funds for a child or two. Such a request could be an unsolicited proposal—just a shot in the dark.

The Head Start program teaches children in Puerto Rico where, like stateside children, they like dressing up and playing with dolls.
Head Start, San Juan, Puerto Rico

On the other hand, you might develop a more systematic approach by actively searching out **requests for proposals**, called RFPs in the jargon of the trade. These are announcements put out by government agencies, philanthropic foundations, or other organizations, offering funds for programs to meet specific goals of the agency or foundation. You can make inquiries regarding currently available RFPs at public agencies, such as the Department of Education. Or you can visit your local library and consult a directory of foundations in your state. Such directories will often give information about the foundation's particular interest areas. When you locate one or more whose interests seem to match your own, you can write and ask for details about any pending requests for proposals: current interest areas, deadline, and process for applying. You may or may not be eligible for funding; therefore, you should carefully check out eligibility before proceeding. You and your board will decide whether you have the time and talents to develop a proposal and, if it is funded, whether you have the appropriate staff to carry out the proposal.

Writing your first proposal or two will be the hardest, because you will be getting materials together that will help with later proposals. Thus, you should be careful to file the various components properly, so as to have the information readily available to use in future proposal writing. You will discover that many funding applications require similar information. You will need familiarity with the typical parts of a proposal (Figure 9–1). If the funding agency has a specific proposal format, as many do, be sure to follow it as exactly as possible. Your ability to adhere to form is one measure of your ability to execute your plan successfully.

Preparation should be carefully done. A close friend whom you can depend on to be knowledgeable and frank should check over the proposal to eliminate any errors or unsound information or ideas. Once completed, the proposal should be professionally typed. Usually a specified number of copies is required. These should be delivered or mailed to arrive before the listed closing date.

The procedure of applying for grants of funds is exhausting, and the wait for an answer may be long, but the securing of funding of a proposal can extend the resources of your center, can stimulate your staff members to work harder or in new directions, and may bring recognition of your center and staff in the local, state, or national child development center arena.

Starting a New Business

Professionals working in a large child development center often dream of opening their own smaller center, being their own boss, and developing the type of program that fits their particular philosophy. Students in teacher education programs often cite running their own center as a career goal.

New child development centers need good management for success. Writing about the prospects for new businesses, Sylvia Porter, a noted business analyst, states that the odds of surviving in a new business for 2 years are less than 50–50. In "9 out of 10 cases the reasons underlying the failure will be the manager's incompetence, inexperience, ineptitude, or a combination of all three," she

1. **Title Page.** Title of project, name of organization, name of applicant, related addresses, agency to which it is submitted, total budget, appropriate signatures, and date submitted.

2. **Abstract.** In 200 to 500 words make a summary of the proposal. Refer to major points of the proposal. Stress need, objectives, procedures, and expected outcomes.

3. **Problem Statement.** Write a clear statement of the problem to be addressed by your center and why the problem should be solved. Help the funding agency understand why the problem is significant and relevant to society and to it. The innovativeness of your approach should be documented. Cite statistical data supporting your need.

4. **Objectives.** List the proposed outcomes that flow logically from the previously stated needs or problems.

5. **Procedures.** Describe how you and your group will meet the stated objectives, then give details including participants and time schedules.

6. **Evaluation.** Tell the funding agency how you will let it know that you have accomplished each objective.

7. **Dissemination.** Tell how and in what form your results will be shared with others. In making your budget, be sure to estimate this expense.

8. **Facilities and Equipment.** Your center may uniquely qualify you for certain projects; be sure to state those qualifications. For example, you may serve a group of single-parent families, or a particular ethnic or racial mix.

9. **Staff Required.** State clearly who the people are who will work on the project. Give their qualifications. Include their résumés in more complex proposals. If new staff will be needed, explain who they will be, their qualifications, and how they will be selected.

10. **Budget.** Show the total cost of the project in terms of major categories such as staff members, supplies, equipment, travel, dissemination, data collecting or processing, and so on.

Figure 9–1
Proposal format

says.[12] Porter presents a quiz for persons contemplating a new business. Her questions have been adapted in Figure 9–2 for those contemplating opening a new child development center. The questions are relevant, many managers would agree. If a potential manager must answer no to any of the questions, he or she is probably wise to spend more time studying the possibilities.

You may find it helpful in your deliberations about starting a new business to get relevant publications from the U.S. government's Small Business Administra-

---

[12] Sylvia Porter, "Hard Questions for Neophytes" (Universal Press Syndicate), *Lansing State Journal*, March 8, 1982, p. 8B.

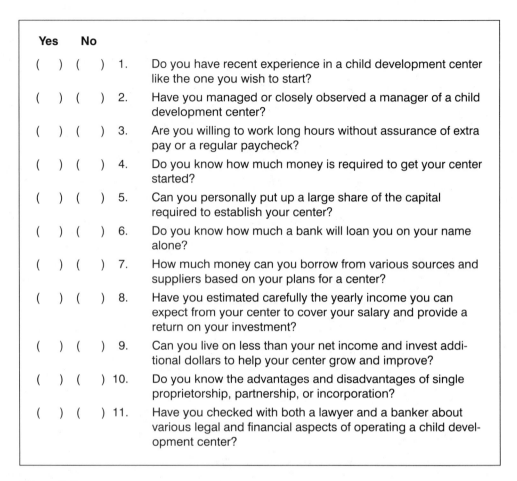

Yes	No		
( )	( )	1.	Do you have recent experience in a child development center like the one you wish to start?
( )	( )	2.	Have you managed or closely observed a manager of a child development center?
( )	( )	3.	Are you willing to work long hours without assurance of extra pay or a regular paycheck?
( )	( )	4.	Do you know how much money is required to get your center started?
( )	( )	5.	Can you personally put up a large share of the capital required to establish your center?
( )	( )	6.	Do you know how much a bank will loan you on your name alone?
( )	( )	7.	How much money can you borrow from various sources and suppliers based on your plans for a center?
( )	( )	8.	Have you estimated carefully the yearly income you can expect from your center to cover your salary and provide a return on your investment?
( )	( )	9.	Can you live on less than your net income and invest additional dollars to help your center grow and improve?
( )	( )	10.	Do you know the advantages and disadvantages of single proprietorship, partnership, or incorporation?
( )	( )	11.	Have you checked with both a lawyer and a banker about various legal and financial aspects of operating a child development center?

Figure 9–2
Test for a potential owner-operator of a new child development center

tion (SBA) in Washington, DC, on various aspects of operating a business. Also, you may find it convenient to visit one of the regional SBA offices located in many large cities to get current information on available assistance—loans, management and technical assistance, business classes, publications, procurement assistance, and so on. Finally, check your libraries for literature by and about the SBA.

TYPES OF RESOURCES

A **resource** is defined as a means—a person or thing—through or by which an end or goal is attained. Money is, of course, the medium of exchange for purchasing the resources needed to provide child development center services—the end or goal desired. To transform ideas into actions that will eventually become

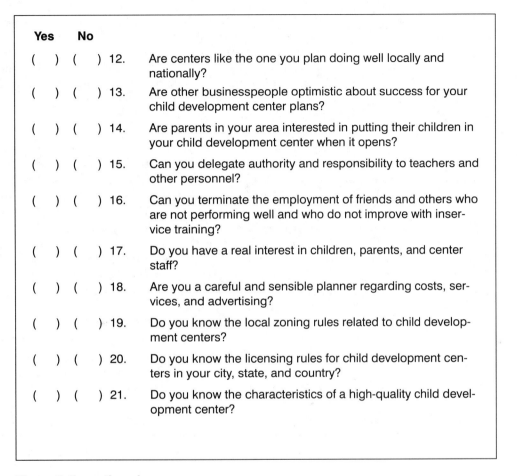

Yes	No		
( )	( )	12.	Are centers like the one you plan doing well locally and nationally?
( )	( )	13.	Are other businesspeople optimistic about success for your child development center plans?
( )	( )	14.	Are parents in your area interested in putting their children in your child development center when it opens?
( )	( )	15.	Can you delegate authority and responsibility to teachers and other personnel?
( )	( )	16.	Can you terminate the employment of friends and others who are not performing well and who do not improve with inservice training?
( )	( )	17.	Do you have a real interest in children, parents, and center staff?
( )	( )	18.	Are you a careful and sensible planner regarding costs, services, and advertising?
( )	( )	19.	Do you know the local zoning rules related to child development centers?
( )	( )	20.	Do you know the licensing rules for child development centers in your city, state, and country?
( )	( )	21.	Do you know the characteristics of a high-quality child development center?

Figure 9–2, *continued*

child development services, several different resources must be brought together in just the right combination. Resources are dormant until human ideas and human energy organize and use them to achieve goals.

Four groups or categories of resources are required for a child development center: materials, equipment, space, and human energy. Taking the first letter of each resource you have the acronym MESH; you can call this your **MESH formula**. Your task as manager is to mesh or synchronize these resources. The MESH categories may be expanded as follows:

1. *M for materials.*   Materials are all physical items and information materials used in the center.
2. *E for equipment.*   Equipment includes all toys—large and small—kitchen and office equipment, furnishings, and transportation.

3. *S for space.*   Space includes buildings, playgrounds, and interior arrangements; and organization, decoration, and utilization of space. Insurance expenses also fit in this category.
4. *H for human energy.*   Human energy or human capital includes the knowledge, skill, and abilities of all adults involved in developing and delivering the service. Children's energy is also a resource. Parents' and volunteers' energy may also contribute in some instances.

Money is required to obtain most resources—the materials, equipment, space, and human capital of teachers, cooks, custodians, and others. Children's energy is also valuable for getting the center's work done. When children's energy can be directed toward hanging up wraps, tidying up rooms, and serving and feeding themselves, less adult energy needs to be expended on those tasks; and of even greater importance, children are learning significant skills. One reason that infant care is so expensive is that proportionately more adults are needed to care for them; unlike somewhat older children, infants cannot yet serve themselves. Of course, one of the obvious objectives of early childhood education is the channeling and directing of children's energy into developing skills, talents, and independent behavior, including self-care.

Parents' energy, too, must be activated. Parents can bring their child to the center already dressed for outdoor play—using their energy to dress their child and saving that of teachers. Parents can study and observe to learn child-rearing skills that help prepare the child psychologically for adjusting to the school situation. In cooperative nursery schools, parents contribute organizational and leadership skills. They also give a number of hours of labor each month to the center operation. Most parents at times are asked to call on their child's energy, for example, by asking the child to carry extra clothes to the teacher, transmit a note or message, or carry an item such as a rock collection to school for a learning experience.

RESOURCES REQUIRED

Using the MESH categories, we provide a list of possible resources required for establishing and maintaining a child development center.

Materials

Most of the following materials are consumable and must be frequently restocked:

- Teaching and child care supplies
- Food and food service supplies
- Maintenance supplies
- Clerical supplies
- Postage
- Materials for newsletters and other reports

Equipment

- Classroom furnishings: tables, chairs, shelves, and lockers
- Play equipment for indoors and outdoors
- Furniture and equipment for kitchen, office, staff lounge, and workroom
- Maintenance equipment and tools
- Vehicles
  Rental and purchase
  Licenses and insurance—both liability and accident
  Maintenance and servicing
  Depreciation
  Chauffeurs' licenses

Space

Start-up Costs

- Capital costs for land, building the facility, developing the playground, or renovating existing space
- Connection fees and deposits for electricity, sewer, gas, water, and telephone
- Incorporation fees related to establishing the center
- Special tax assessments related to the building process
- Parking spaces

Operating Costs

- Rent or mortgage payments
- Property taxes
- Repairs and maintenance
- Decoration—art and artifacts
- Insurance—fire, liability, and vandalism

Human Energy

Start-up Costs

- Planning services before opening: a needs survey, location study, and so on
- Legal services: setting up structures for operation, taxes, liability insurance, building and land contracts, employee contracts, and so on
- Accounting services: setting up regular accounting and auditing systems
- Public relations: preparing copy, giving talks, and printing brochures
- Advertising: recruiting employees and children

Operating Costs

- Staff salaries
  Administrator
  Bus driver(s)
  Caregivers and teachers
  Clerical staff
  Cook

> Custodian
> Consultants: health, parent educator, and social services
> Substitutes for absent employees
- Benefits
> Social Security
> Worker's compensation
> Child care
> Maternity
> Health insurance
> Unemployment insurance
> Holidays or vacations
> Retirement
> Bonding
- Staff development
> Inservice training (consultant)
> Professional publications and resource books
> Fees and support for staff to attend conferences
> Dues for professional associations
- Public relations
- Recruitment of children
- Publicity, publications, and appearances

Insurance

One operational expense that has created the biggest shock among managers of child development centers in recent years has been the escalating expense of property and liability insurance, and even the dropping of policies that a company had held for a long time. The child care industry is not the only service organization hit by higher insurance rates.

Operators who are part of a larger organization such as a church or school seem to have fared the best, because their coverage is part of the parent organization's coverage. Other centers have had to raise large sums of money to stay insured. Very few operators can afford to be self-insured.

The NAEYC took the initiative and surveyed its members, finding out that 90% of the programs had never filed on their liability insurance policy. Of the 10% with claims, 80% were for less than $500, with the highest being $15,000. No claims were associated with child abuse. According to the NAEYC, the insurance companies have failed to produce evidence of large child care claims, to the NAEYC, Congress, or the U.S. General Accounting Office.[13]

To help the situation, the NAEYC initiated an insurance program through MarketDyne, a division of CIGNA Corporation, to provide property and center liability coverage and optional automobile, worker's compensation, and student

---

[13] National Association for the Education of Young Children, "NAEYC Position Statement on Liability Insurance Crisis," *Young Children* 41:5 (July 1986), pp. 45–46. See also background information in "Public Policy Report: Liability Insurance Update," *Young Children* 41:1 (November 1985), pp. 53–55.

accident medical coverage. Information regarding these policies and other insurance matters is available from the NAEYC at (800) 424-2460.

Managers can do their part to keep insurance costs down by making sure that they follow recommended safety precautions in all areas of their operation. The National Fire Protection Association and the Consumer Product Safety Commission's guidelines for playground surfaces and equipment set standards that may exceed licensing requirements in your state.[14] One multisite child care organization was denied coverage because its adult-child ratios did not meet the requirements of the National Fire Protection Association, it did not conduct criminal clearances on new employees, and some of its sites were operating over licensed capacity. Only in the last instance was it violating licensing regulations. One can conclude, therefore, that it is not only in the best interests of children to exceed minimum regulatory standards; it is in the best financial interest of the center as well.

MONETARY DECISIONS

Monetary decisions can be either **programmed** or **nonprogrammed**, as discussed in Chapter 3. A programmed decision is one that is routine and the same from time to time. For example, the formula for calculating an employee's withholding tax is the same and does not require new procedures each time it is done. On the other hand, when a parent cannot pay the tuition and asks for an extension, this is a nonprogrammed decision that necessitates procedures for weighing various considerations and arriving at the best decision for that individual and your center.

DECISIONS, DECISIONS . . .

The Smith family asks to be allowed to pay their tuition on the following Friday—5 days later than usual, after the child had been in the center all week. List criteria that would be useful in your policy to permit or not permit such a request.

Loans

Most businesses will operate with some borrowed money. Loans may be available from various sources, including the Small Business Administration. You may have money or have a benefactor with money. In any case, the rate of interest charged on loans merits careful consideration. And, even if you have the money, you will want to keep in mind how much interest or other earnings your funds could receive elsewhere.

A quick way to understand and calculate the cost of borrowing money is to use the **Rule of 72**. The Rule of 72 easily tells you how many years it will take for

[14]The National Fire Protection Association is located at Battery March Park, Quincy, MA 02269.

interest costs (or interest earned if you lend the money) to equal the principal, that is, the doubling time—the time required for the accumulated compound interest to equal the principal. To do the arithmetic, divide the number 72 by the interest rate to learn the number of years required to double. For example, if you borrow $1,000 and pay 10% interest, it will take 7.2 years (72 ÷ 10 = 7.2) for the compounded accumulated interest to equal the loan principal.

Written Policies and Procedures

Plans, policies, and procedures for monetary decisions need to be worked out and written down in your policy manual to keep consistency and fairness within your operation. Following your written policies as established by your board, procedures will be developed. For example, procedures can become programmed for determining full- and part-time or sliding-scale tuition fees, refunds, fees for families with more than one child enrolled, employee benefits, sick leave, holidays, and many other calculations. Once the policy is determined, the procedures can be established to facilitate speedy and consistent decision making, which you or a trusted employee can handle.

Budgeting

Establishing a realistic budget is difficult for a novice manager. Few budgets are published, partly because times change and inflation makes them unrealistic. In the Cost, Quality, and Child Outcomes Study completed in 1995, the average costs for the 400 randomly selected child development programs in four states were distributed in the following way:[15]

70% for labor

15% for facilities

15% for all other cash expenses

The same study found that the average fee charged by centers for full-time monthly care for infants was about $450 (or about $2.50 per hour); for preschool children, the fee was about $370 (or about $2 per hour). Using the accepted standards for group size relative to the age of children, you can calculate the probable income for a group of infants or young children. See Chapter 5 for recommended group sizes for various age groups.

The study showed that the average hourly wage for teachers was $7.22; for assistant teachers, $5.70, for directors, $11.33. Again, using accepted standards for adult-child ratios, and adding 25% to these salary figures for staff benefits, you can calculate probable labor costs for your hypothetical group of infants and young children. This calculation may become a little more complicated as you decide how many teachers and assistant teachers are needed and whether you

---

[15]Cost, Quality and Child Outcomes Study Team, *Cost, Quality, and Child Outcomes in Child Care Centers, Executive Summary*, p. 5.

(the director or manager) will be figured into the adult-child ratio. Your state licensing standards will help you make these decisions.

DECISIONS, DECISIONS . . .

 Find out how the average rates determined by the Cost, Quality, and Child Outcomes Study compare with child care costs and salaries in your community. Will you be able to charge competitive rates and still pay salaries that are at least equal to the averages found in the Cost, Quality, and Child Outcomes Study?

The National Day Care Study indicates that 69% of the budget went for personnel in the late 1970s, and this figure has not changed substantially in 20 years. Given the present effort by the NAEYC to bring salaries of child development services personnel up to a living wage with adequate benefits like other employees, the appropriate percentage is probably more like 90% of larger budgets.

Salaries of teachers and caregivers must be raised to a level in line with the level of education and experience required for the high-quality performance standards parents and society expect. Projections, based on low 1970 birthrates showing fewer workers for the 1990s, will dictate that child development services personnel be paid competitively. Employers in the other sectors are expected to provide child development services to entice employees, and families expected to leave the welfare rolls will need child care to do so; thus, the demand for services will increase. Unless salaries do improve, child service workers will move to other jobs where the pay and benefits are enticing.

Parents who can afford to must pay their share, and others must be assisted with public and philanthropic resources. It is outlandish that a professional couple who both are making large salaries and living an affluent lifestyle should receive subsidized child care services—subsidized at the expense of staff members who cannot even live securely and comfortably on their meager salary. In most cases, if child care services did not exist, one partner would have to quit work and face the reality of the opportunity costs of having a child. Obviously, the availability of high-quality child development services makes it possible for both parents to work.

Managers should take the lead in improving the salary, benefits, and working conditions of their staff members. The NAEYC publication *Reaching the Full Cost of Quality in Early Childhood Programs* offers a useful starting point for managers and policy boards interested in working toward this goal.[16] It suggests that centers estimate the full cost of quality by comparing staff wages with those for other

---

[16] Barbara Willer (ed.), *Reaching the Full Cost of Quality in Early Childhood Programs* (Washington, DC: National Association for the Education of Young Children, 1990).

occupations in the community with similar responsibilities and educational requirements. Using this information to establish target salaries, a manager can formulate a plan for reaching those goals and develop a coalition of parents and community advocates to create strategies for doing so. The resulting stability in staffing will be one result as employees remain on the job, rather than constantly looking for better-paying jobs.

THE EFFICIENCY RULE

The **efficiency rule** simply requires that the greatest possible good be achieved for a given resource expenditure. There are always competing demands for your limited supply of resources. In both profit and nonprofit child development centers, the manager needs to ask, "Have our resources been efficiently utilized?" Obviously, the financial backers of for-profit centers expect to make a reasonable return on an investment. In nonprofit centers, a break-even equilibrium is expected. In the real world, the group deciding allocation of funds must consider the many competing projects desiring funding, and, if efficiency is not maintained, other projects will get the funds.

A policy board may occasionally continue to fund a high-cost or inefficient operation because of other considerations. For example, a small town maintains a high-cost kindergarten for a few children. The taxpayers do not want to transport young kindergartners to a neighboring town many miles away, as may have already been done with the older elementary school children. Parents argue that to do so would add more to their personal costs and worries than the tax subsidy now costs. However, if there are fewer than five kindergartners for a teacher, would a high-quality kindergarten result even though the district is willing to fund such a high-cost operation? Perhaps in this case the board would want to consider expanding the class to include the 4-year-olds of the community. Given the fixed amount of available space, equipment, and teacher energy, in this way the community could be getting more services for the money; that is, fixed costs could be spread over more children, thus generating lower average total costs per child. Using the MESH formula, the board would expect some increase in requirements of material resources such as paper, paints, and crayons if the 4-year-olds are added to the class.

Efficiency is often related to specialization. In the case of child development centers, specializing might mean providing only one type of service (e.g., one for 3- and 4-year-olds only rather than including infants and toddlers). There are obvious savings in resources when specializing. However, some argue that to diversify or provide several services helps an organization meet the needs of the economy and the whims of the consuming public.

CONTROL OF FUNDS AND EXPENSES

Monitoring and controlling require comparing performance with agreed-on standards. Your written budget will set the standard for allocating and evaluating expenses. Each budget item in your MESH formula should be scrutinized. Financial data should be related to data on services rendered—enrollment and the like. You will be expected to report to the board periodically—quarterly or yearly.

Basically, you will develop a new budget as realistically as you can. You will use your previous year's budget and actual expenses as the basis for the new budget. Newly planned items, salary increases, and inflation should be incorporated into a new budget. You will need funds for expenditures related to the categories of materials, equipment, space, and human energy.

Setting the amount to charge for fees or tuition or making a proposal for funding from other sources, such as Head Start or United Way, also will be required. Some managers plan the new budget based on about 80%–90% of their licensed capacity, giving a 10%–20% leeway in case a few children drop out and cannot be replaced. For example, if you are licensed for 90 children, you might plan your budget based on tuition from an enrollment of 80 children.

An adequate supply of open-ended construction materials provides children with opportunities to develop fine-motor and representational skills.
Early Learning Center, Appalachian State University, Boone, NC

Once the amount per child is decided, you must decide when periodic tuition payments are to be collected. These collections may be weekly, monthly, or quarterly. It will probably depend on whether many of the parents are paid weekly, biweekly, or monthly.

As you and your policy board formulate policies regarding fees, you will need to consider the following questions as well:

1. *Will payment be required in advance or after services are rendered?*   Payment in advance, obviously, lessens the chance that the center will be "stuck" with a large outstanding balance if a family withdraws their child. However, for many families, this is not a realistic expectation. Furthermore, government agencies do not usually allow centers to bill for services until after they are rendered.

2. *Will parents be required to pay only for the actual days their child is in the center's care? Or will they be expected to pay for an agreed-on number of hours per week, whether or not the child actually attends those hours?*   On the one hand, parents usually balk at paying for a service they feel they have not been given; but on the other hand, centers must schedule and pay staff regardless of whether a particular child is out ill or a family goes on vacation one week. Some centers handle these fluctuations in attendance by sending employees home when few children are present, but this approach hardly seems fair to employees who must be able to count on at least their minimum salaries each week. On the other hand, government agencies will not pay for care while a child is actually home sick. Is it fair to charge the paying parent in this circumstance, and not the parent whose care is subsidized?

3. *Will families be required to pay additional fees if they arrive late to pick up their child?*   Certainly, this occurrence is an annoyance to staff members who are anxious to get home to their own children, but sometimes the costs in public relations exceeds the gain to be had by charging the extra few dollars. Is there a way to offer a "grace period" or to consider the number of times a parent has imposed upon the center this way?

Record Keeping

Carefully prepared budgets are essential and facilitate sound fiscal policy. Well-developed, clear procedures for record keeping are essential. These tasks are part of your organization function. Keeping business records, like teaching, is a professional skill. You or an employee will need special training to do an adequate job of keeping the books of your center, whether you are a for-profit or nonprofit center. Consulting an accountant or tax adviser is essential. Many centers contract with a regular accounting service.

When tuition is paid, a receipt is written in duplicate with one copy going to the parent. The second copy is used to post the ledger or account of each child. Parents' checks should be deposited promptly when received. Cash should also be promptly deposited. Be sure to develop a tight security system for cash receipts. All other receipts should likewise be posted and deposited in the bank. Business supply stores carry a variety of appropriate forms for record keeping.

Expenditures must be carefully recorded. You will develop salary and bill payments systems. Salaries are based on your prior agreement with each employee, less deductions for benefits and taxes. These benefit and tax withholdings must be properly paid and reported. For hourly employees, you will have a sign-in system, in which their hours worked can be easily calculated. Your accountant will prepare checks and deliver them to employees on a regular schedule.

Fixed expenses are routinely paid on receipt of bills by the authorized person. Other expenses may be discussed with the manager before payment. The accountant will carefully keep records of each payment so as to know very quickly how much money has been spent for budgeted items.

Some centers keep a petty cash fund for small items. Staff members should be given quite specific guidelines as to what can be covered by petty cash. There is danger that one person may purchase items impulsively that should be planned in advance and purchased in bulk. A specific record must be kept when petty cash payments are made. Petty cash can be an invitation to dishonesty and break-ins, so caution is required.

The goal for the accountant is to prepare records that are clear and accurate each month. These will be used to prepare quarterly and annual reports for the policy board. They will be essential for reporting income taxes. Sound accounting procedures are essential in both private and public child development centers and should never be considered lightly.

A personal computer can facilitate your financial record keeping, just as it will aid your word-processing needs of writing and printing letters, proposals, and newsletters. Personal computers have become relatively inexpensive to own and operate. Now specially designed software programs are available for child care center record keeping, with the software companies maintaining training programs and hotlines for advising people on how to use the software effectively.

Depending on your operation's size, you may want to invest in a computer and software. Learning to use the computer is not hard, but overcoming a staff member's anxiety toward the machine may be more difficult. It will be essential to secure the appropriate training, consisting of a few hours of instruction and supervised use, to reap the full benefit of the investment in the computer and software. According to Roger Neugebauer, who publishes an annual review of child care center management software, you will need to consider nine key questions in making your selection:

1. Does the software meet your center's particular needs, allowing you to generate the specific reports you want or to bill in the unit that you have established, whether hourly or weekly?
2. Is it sufficiently user-friendly that you can install and run the program with minimal outside help—but allowing you to skip time-consuming beginner steps as you become more familiar with the program?
3. Is it flexible enough to accommodate the new uses you will devise for it as you become more and more computer-literate?
4. Does the company back up its product with service?
5. Does it offer a warranty or a no-risk trial period?

6. Do you know other directors who are using the software and can tell you about how satisfied they are with it?
7. Have you tried the program yourself?
8. Is it within your budget *and* a good value for the money?
9. Do you have, or can you afford, the needed hardware?[17]

Internal Control of Supplies

New purchases must be added to inventory. Boxes should be checked to be sure they are full. You will need to develop or purchase a system for adding and deleting items from inventory. Having such procedures helps protect the inventory and keeps you from running out of needed supplies. The computer is an excellent tool for keeping track of inventory. Several flexible and efficient inventory control software programs are available for all brands of computers.

Pursuing your control function, you will help your staff avoid waste of food, supplies, and time. To help staff focus on the issue, get them to discuss ways to control waste or extravagant use of materials. For example, monitoring leftover foods can help you realize that some recipes are too big for your needs. Recipes can be adjusted to eliminate leftovers and avoid contamination, waste, or improper use by employees.

Competitive Bidding

Competition generally improves the performance of American businesses. To be sure you are getting a fair price for the resources you must purchase, you will want to compare prices. On large items, ask several companies to make bids. On smaller items, you can call for prices and make comparisons. Quantity buying will often give you a substantial discount. Paper goods, for example, can be purchased in quantity at considerable savings. Of course, you will need secure, fireproof storage places for items purchased in quantity. Centers in some communities purchase materials cooperatively to generate additional savings. You could investigate one of these cooperatives or organize one yourself.

Insurance and other employee benefits may be available at different prices from different carriers. The NAEYC has an arrangement for various kinds of insurance through a group plan for members. Interested managers of child development centers may wish to contact the NAEYC for information about these insurance programs. Always double-check the prices and benefits before coming to an agreement. Sometimes savings accrue if one carrier handles all of a center's insurance, rather than the center having several policies with separate carriers.

Tax-supported organizations usually do not pay sales tax. Be sure to arrange for such tax exemptions if you qualify. Avoid over-the-counter purchases where you must pay tax. (In some states, you can avoid paying sales tax for over-the-counter purchases by giving your tax-exempt number to the vendor.)

---

[17] Roger Neugebauer, "Child Care Center Management Software Buying Guide," *Child Care Information Exchange* 104 (July/August 1995), pp. 87–100.

Credit is expensive. Most purchases must be paid for within the billing month to avoid credit expense. Careful monitoring of such payments will save money. Income received will draw interest if invested properly and safely until needed. Idle money is expensive; therefore, it is worthwhile to seek out the best place to invest income.

Purchasing

Purchasing done consistently by one skilled person helps maintain control. Unit pricing in large supermarkets is very useful in cost calculations. Buying in quantity when the supermarkets have specials also saves money—if you have a place to store purchases. Large cans of vegetables are not always the best buys and may lead the cook to open too much to be used up on a given day. Therefore, purchasing small cans may be least expensive in the long run. Cycle menus using a 3-week repeat cycle aid the purchasing procedures and cut down foods stored for too long. Cycle menus also aid in managing the labor input for meals by suggesting menus that are manageable with a minimum of employees. (Sample cycle menus are offered in Chapter 13.) High standards for the nutritional quality of foods must be maintained. Some cooking procedures are better than others for maintaining a high quality of nutrition. Guiding the cook's use of appropriate cooking methods is essential; otherwise, the loss is costly.

Homemade play dough, fingerpaint, and paint extenders are cheaper than purchased items. Allocating an employee's (often the kitchen employees') time for mixing these items can save money. Having the items readily available ensures their frequent use by teachers and caregivers, thus enhancing the program.

Teachers and caregivers may think of waste prevention techniques, such as putting only small amounts of tempera paint out at a time (say, half a cup) to keep children from muddying large quantities, which will only be thrown out at the end of the day. Clearly, the savings in tempera alone by the end of a month could be significant.

"Found" or recycled materials are very useful in children's activities. For example, several old cardboard boxes, available at no cost, will be used creatively by children. Smaller boxes and toilet tissue cores can be used in art projects to make delightful three-dimensional sculptures. Such materials cost only the time of the adults—parents, teachers, and custodians—for collecting and storing them. Orderly fireproof storage is a must for any combustible found materials. Children's creative energies respond as effectively to found items as to expensive materials. Items such as expensive breakfast cereals should seldom be used in art projects but eaten instead.

Allocating a given quantity of supplies to each classroom teacher—even when supplies are ordered in bulk—can help motivate the classroom teachers to avoid waste yet not interfere with a high-quality program for children. Teachers can be allowed to use the savings to buy extras, such as a special story record, for their class. Teachers may neglect to request adequate supplies. If so, sufficient supplies may not be budgeted. Managers should help teachers make careful estimates of the needed supplies.

Teachers often complain that they use their own money to buy supplies. Managers should see to it that all nondurable supplies are purchased by center funds. If teachers have money of their own they wish to spend, it should go into something that lasts, such as books—especially music and poetry books—that they can take with them if they leave or use at home with their own children. A center that is so short-funded that teachers must purchase paper must be in bad shape financially; it may not be a good place for children and perhaps should be closed.

Heat and lights can be monitored carefully, and some savings can result by reducing bulb size, using energy-efficient fixtures, turning off lights, and turning down heat. Paper products, such as napkins, towels, and tissues, can be made to go further if dispensers are not overfilled and children are enlisted in an effort to conserve resources and protect the environment. Centers that use disposable tableware should make a cost comparison between continual purchasing of these supplies with a one-time investment in multiuse tableware and a commercial dishwasher. Remember to include any costs incurred for trash disposal with the former alternative and the cost of staff time to load and operate the dishwasher in the latter.

Saving Time

Time is an expensive resource. It is the only resource we all have in equal amounts. A professional's time and energy can be extended through the participation of aides, volunteers, and parents. By carefully marshaling human resources, extra hands and hearts can be made available to raise the quality of human interaction in centers. For example, every community has high school and elementary students who could participate for a period each day. Managers need to explore this resource with school boards, principals, and teachers. Many people believe that older children who participate with young children are learning responsible parenting attitudes in a natural way. Contacting the schools and youth clubs is a way for managers to begin. In addition, there are organized courses in child development or early childhood education for which the child development centers can serve as laboratories for both high school and college students. If your center is a high-quality center, it might qualify for this important teaching function. Naturally, such centers are screened by the educators to be sure that students would learn appropriate techniques. Such students bring fresh ideas, excellent energy, and stamina, and they are often enthusiastic and appealing to staff members who may be nearly burned out from day-in, day-out commitment. In exchange for serving as a laboratory for students, your staff could be invited to seminars and special programs that would help encourage professional growth.

A number of programs have demonstrated the effectiveness of having senior citizen volunteers participating in the child development center.[18] Volunteers of

---

[18] See Carol Seefeldt and Barbara Warman, *Young and Old Together* (Washington, DC: National Association for the Education of Young Children, 1990). See also Lillian Phenice, *Children's Perceptions of the Elderly* (Saratoga, CA: Century Twenty-One, 1981), a report on children who had senior volunteers in their child care center.

other ages frequently are available through colleges, church groups, and organizations such as the Junior League. Parents frequently enjoy helping out at school and will occasionally even take a day off from work to do it. Extending opportunities to parents should be specifically planned.

All of these untrained volunteers must be trained, supported, and rewarded if they are really to be of help and to stay on over a period of time. Guiding volunteers takes time—both the manager's time and the classroom teachers' time—but the efforts may have many payoffs. Children really value these new friends to know, talk to, and sit with or on. They give children increased personal attention, which children in child care frequently need.

Those who volunteer are growing in their knowledge and abilities to serve children. Many individuals learn to feel important and loved. Volunteers can become excellent defenders of your center when the political powers-that-be want to reduce funds during economic crises.

CONCLUSION

It takes a tough head to understand, monitor, and control the balance sheet of the child development center and still retain a tender heart for giving children the loving care and education a high-quality program requires. Your assertive leadership and vision will be essential to marshal the funds needed to operate such a high-quality early childhood program. You will spend a lot of your time securing funding, and, once received, in actively monitoring and controlling so that the best program for children that the available money can buy is possible.

NAEYC accreditation standards require that centers maintain a sound fiscal policy to meet their obligations to children and their families. Written policies and procedures are required to keep decision making consistent and fair. A formula for expenditures for materials, equipment, space, and human energy (MESH) must be developed. Funding sources are private, community, state, and national, including many businesses that are entering the child care arena to attract top employees.

Managers must develop a careful procedure for budgeting, purchasing, record keeping, and controlling expenditures. Each employee can be included in the monitoring process within his or her unit of responsibility.

APPLICATIONS

1. Check with your placement or employment agencies to learn the going salary rate for aides, teachers, cooks, managers, and custodians for a child development center. With these figures, calculate the personnel budget for three groups of children—one group of ten infants, one group of twelve toddlers, and one group of eighteen 3- and 4-year-olds. See Chapter 5 for the recommended number of adults for each age if you do not recall it.

2. Check with a child development center manager and ask the following questions:
   a. What is your biggest monetary problem as manager of your center?
   b. What have you done about solving your monetary problems?
   c. What type of assistance do you have with monetary matters? An accountant? A bookkeeper? A clerk?
   d. Do you plan on a monthly budget?
   e. Do you keep a petty cash fund?
   f. What happens if your spending goes over the budget?
   g. Report to and discuss in your class. Compare with classmates.
3. Call your licensing agency and inquire about the possible sources of funding assistance in the community. Make a list and discuss with your classmates.
4. Study equipment catalogs or visit an equipment store to compare tables and chairs you would need for a center. Discuss the pros and cons of various types. This approach can be repeated with many types of toys and furnishings for a center.
5. Check the current tuition or fee being charged by various centers for short- and full-day preprimary education.
6. Add material on managing monetary resources to your management notebook.

STUDY QUESTIONS

1. List and differentiate the funding sources for various types of early childhood programs.
2. List the numerous ways that child development centers receive direct and indirect support through the tax structure.
3. List the sources of tax support for child development centers from local and state sources.
4. Define an RFP and tell what information is generally required.
5. Photocopy Figure 9–2. Complete the form, making accompanying notes regarding yourself. Would you be a good candidate to own a child development center?
6. Give the definitions for each part of the MESH formula.
7. In budgeting, what are the percentages of total expenses typically used for personnel, space, equipment, and materials needed for operating a center?
8. Discuss programmed and nonprogrammed decisions in relation to monetary decisions.
9. Explain the Rule of 72. Give an example labeling all the parts.
10. Define the efficiency rule, explaining how it applies to a child development center.
11. List at least five ways of controlling waste, expenses, and funds.
12. List at least five ways to keep control of finances.

Suggested Readings

Ard, Linda. "How Can We Pay Staff Fairly?" *Texas Child Care* 14:1 (Summer 1990), pp. 16–20.

Boswell, Craig. "Developing a Proposal: When Opportunity Knocks, Will You Be Prepared?" *Child Care Information Exchange* 103 (May/June 1995), pp. 17–20.

Cherry, Clare, Barbara Harkness, and Kay Kuzma. *Nursery School & Day Care Management Guide*. Belmont, CA: Lake, 1987.

Eckstein, Richard M. *Directory of Building and Equipment Grants*. Loxahatchee, FL: Research Grant Guides, 1992.

Greenman, Jim. "Living in the Real World: 'Jean's Pretty Good, Kind of Affordable, Child Development Center' versus the Child Care Trilemma." *Child Care Information Exchange* 74 (August 1990), pp. 29–31.

Hewes, Dorothy, and Barbara Hartman. *Early Childhood Education: A Workbook for Administrators*. Saratoga, CA: R & E, 1988.

Hoffman, Carol M. *Public Education and Day Care: One District's Story*. Lancaster, PA: Technomic, 1985.

Howes, Carollee, Willa Pettygrove, and Marcy Whitebook. "Cost and Quality in Child Care: Reality and Myth." *Child Care Information Exchange* 58 (November 1987), pp. 40–42.

Lombardi, J. "New Federal Dollars: How Are They Being Used?" *Child Care Information Exchange* 82 (November/December 1991), pp. 56–57.

Lukaszewski, T. "Frequently Asked Questions Regarding Unemployment Compensation." *Child Care Information Exchange* 82 (November/December 1991), pp. 19–20.

Marx, E., and R. Granger. "Analysis of Salary Enhancement Efforts in New York." *Young Children* 45:3 (March 1990), pp. 53–59.

National Association for the Education of Young Children. "Liability Insurance Update." *Young Children* 41:1 (November 1985), pp. 53–54.

National Association for the Education of Young Children. *Infant Child Care: NAEYC Resource Guide*. Washington, DC: Author, 1987.

National Association for the Education of Young Children. "NAEYC Position Statement on the Liability Insurance Crisis." *Young Children* 41:5 (July 1986), pp. 45–46.

Neugebauer, Roger. "Is Your Salary Schedule Up to Speed?" *Child Care Information Exchange* 96 (March/April 1994), pp. 6–17.

Scallan, Patricia. "Ask and Ye Shall Receive: A Primer for Large-Scale Fundraising." *Child Care Information Exchange* 64 (December 1988), pp. 19–21.

Schrag, Lorraine, Ellen Khokha, and Ellena Weeks. "Sample Budget for an Infant Care Center," in Annabelle Godwin and Lorraine Schrag (eds.), *Setting Up for Infant Care: Guidelines for Centers and Family Day Care Homes* (pp. 51–52). Washington, DC: National Association for the Education of Young Children, 1988.

Stanton, Susan. "What Computer Companies Can Do for You, Charitably." *The Grantsmanship Center Whole Nonprofit Catalog*, Summer 1991, pp. 9–11, 27–30.

Stephens, Keith. *Confronting Your Bottom Line: Financial Guide for Child Care Centers*. Redmond, WA: Exchange, 1991.

Workman, Sherry. "Ideas for Collecting Fees." *Texas Child Care* 12:4 (Spring 1989), pp. 12–17.

CHAPTER 10

Child Care in the Corporate World

Managers of child development centers and those interested in moving into management will wisely become fully informed of the most recent growth phenomenon in the child development centers arena. That is, there is significant growth in the number of employer-assisted child care centers, increasing support by labor and management for providing child care for workers through labor contracts, and a sizable rise in for-profit child care corporations, according to the U.S. Department of Labor.[1]

Data from the Bureau of Labor Statistics show that in the 1990s, there will be a shortage of labor due to the decrease in the birthrates in the 1970s. Large numbers of the new employees will be women in their childbearing years. Even today, employers are beginning to feel the pinch of recruiting and retaining competent employees. They are also responding to pressure among employees for management to show more concern for family life by providing child care and maternity and paternity leaves.

CHILD CARE PROVISIONS

A range of child care provisions are offered by employers and through labor-management contracts, with variations based on selecting those best fitting particular employees' situations. Considering the ecological system discussed in Chapter 2, it is interesting to see these new developments in the social-cultural

---

[1] U.S. Department of Labor, Bureau of Labor Statistics, *Child Care: A Workforce Issue* (Washington, DC: U.S. Government Printing Office, 1988), pp. 125–142.

environment. That is, new institutions are being formed and links between institutions are being forged.

The early venture into industry-connected child care occurred during World War II when a federal law, the Lanham Act, financed centers to provide child care for children of women needed in the war industries. These were known by many as the "Lanham Act Nursery Schools." Advisers to the government for these schools were persons prominent in the field at that time. Many centers had state-of-the-art facilities, equipment, and programs. Following the war, most of these centers were abandoned. California, however, purchased the centers and maintained a momentum of concern for early education and child care that is still evident today.

In 1978, Kathryn Seen Perry published for the Women's Bureau in the U.S. Department of Labor a landmark report showing that there were 105 employer-supported programs, virtually all consisting of on-site child care.[2]

A Department of Labor study in 1987 states that, among workplaces with 10 or more employees, employers were giving direct child care help in 11% of the nation's workplaces. The kinds of direct help included operating day care centers (either on-site or nearby, 2%), giving financial assistance for child care (3%), child care referral (5%), counseling or other child care benefits (5%), and policies that facilitate child care (61%) (see Figure 10–1). Policies that help parents care for their children include flexible work schedules (called "flextime"), voluntary part-time and job-sharing arrangements, and flexible leave policies. The study shows that larger establishments with 250 or more employees were more likely to provide direct child care benefits such as sponsoring a child care center.[3]

More recent reports have found a slight dip in the proportion of employees having subsidized child care as an available benefit, but closer examination reveals that declines in one sector are offset by increased interest in another. As hospitals struggle more with budget problems than with recruiting nurses, they become less interested in providing child care. On the other hand, more mid-size companies (with 500–1,500 employees) are becoming involved.[4]

MOTIVATION FOR SUPPORTING CHILD CARE

Employers receive seven benefits from providing help with child care, according to the Department of Labor:[5]

- *Recruitment.*   In the information age, as the present period is being called, the workplace of modern America has become a white-collar situation in many

---

[2] *Child Centers Sponsored by Employers and Labor Unions in the United States* (Washington, DC: U.S. Department of Labor, 1978).

[3] U.S. Department of Labor, *Child Care*, p. 126.

[4] Roger Neugebauer, "Employer Child Care Growing and Consolidating," *Child Care Information Exchange* 103 (May/June 1995), pp. 67–73.

[5] U.S. Department of Labor, *Child Care*, pp. 128–130.

respects. Jobs require a high degree of education and training. Not just anyone can do the jobs. Recruitment takes time and money. Employers are finding that benefit packages help attract well-qualified employees. A considerable amount of corporate interest in child care comes from women in management and advanced technology fields who have special skills.

- *Retention.*   Keeping key employees, especially high-level administrators, scientists, women, and minorities, is a goal of many employers. In studies, employees state that they would not move anywhere else because of the child care center for their child.

- *Public relations.*   Companies are finding that their concern for employees' families is good for their public image. Their positive high-profile image helps in recruitment. It helps in business. Child care provisions of certain industries have attracted national media attention.

- *Productivity.*   Studies, such as a 1986 survey by AT&T, showed that employees reported spending unproductive time at work due to child care concerns. Of course, as any parent would state, admitting these concerns has often been taken as a personal weakness, so surveys may be underestimating the true effect of reduced productivity due to family concerns, such as child and dependent care. Employers are beginning to believe that their interest in and support of child care helps improve productivity.

- *Turnover.*   Once employees are recruited and specifically trained for the company's work, these employees have received a considerable investment of the company's time and money. Retention of such employees makes sense to dollar-conscious employers.

- *Absenteeism.*   Absenteeism and tardiness have been reduced by the child care assistance programs. On-site child care, sick-child care, and other provisions are very helpful to working parents. When before- and after-school services are unavailable, parents have to arrange for their children to be cared for by an older sibling or a neighbor, or they may be forced to allow the children to stay home alone. The period from 3 P.M. to 6 P.M. has been recognized as the most worrisome to parents, that is, when the latchkey children are at home alone. Suitable child care programs have considerably reduced workers' absence from the job.

- *Morale.*   Employers and employees alike report improved morale as the workplace becomes more friendly to parents and their children. Studies show that when child care arrangements break down, workers become stressed in ways that affect their health and work. Both men and women feel this stress; however, men ranked a nonsupportive supervisor more seriously than they ranked child care worries.

Ways Companies Are Involved

Roughly 11% of companies help with their employees' child care needs. This help falls into a number of modes.

On-site child care programs make it easier for parents to be on hand when their children need them.
Early Learning Center, Appalachian State University, Boone, NC

Child Care Center

Some companies decide that an on-site child care center is the best option for them. They either run the center themselves or rent space to a professional child care organization. For example, Stride Rite Corporation began its first on-site program in 1971 and opened a second center in 1982. The company used a sliding-fee scale. This gives the lowest-paid employees and parents with more than one child a break on fees. They serve the children of 40% of their employees.

According Neugebauer, fewer than 1% of U.S. companies select this option, although among those that do, the 10 largest providers more than doubled the number of centers they operated during the 15 months before a February 1995 survey. The five largest management organizations providing employer child care were Children's Discovery Centers/Prodigy Consulting with 90 centers, Bright Horizons Children's Centers with 86, Corporate Child Care Management Services with 48, LaPetite Academy, Inc., with 46, and KinderCare at Work with 41.[5]

---

[5] "The Exchange Top 30: The Nation's Largest Employer Child Care Management Organizations," *Child Care Information Exchange* 103 (May/June 1995), p. 73.

Many businesses are collaborating with school districts and community agencies to use school premises to provide before- and after-school care for elementary-age children.

Care for a sick child is becoming part of the service of some hospital-related programs and is available to others in the community. The 3M Company in Minnesota pays over 70% of the in-home nursing services offered by Children's Hospital in St. Paul.

Consortium Center

This type of center is shared and sponsored by a group of companies for the benefit of their employees. Employers provide funds for the initial expenditures for space and starting up. The companies may underwrite operating and partial tuition costs. The Downtown Day Care Center in St. Louis, Missouri, and the Horace Mann Center in Burbank, California, are examples of consortium centers.

Financial Assistance

Financial assistance or vouchers give parents subsidies for child care. Discounted tuition may be arranged at certain licensed centers. In this case, employers reserve, guarantee, or purchase enrollment spaces in centers for the benefit of their employees. Subsidies for child care may fit in with a company's overall benefit plan by giving employees a set dollar amount for benefits. Parents needing child care choose child care, and older employees select another benefit, thus helping avoid the charge of preferential treatment for families with young children.

One advantageous arrangement is for parents to receive the child care subsidy as a tax-free benefit. Thus, they do not have to pay taxes on those funds expended for child care.

Resource and Referral

One of the least expensive and quickest ways to implement child care options is to provide information and referral to child care resources in the community. The referral agency helps parents find suitable child care arrangements. Consulting organizations have been developed to do this type of referral for companies, or occasionally companies do it themselves. Some resource and referral groups also provide seminars on child rearing for parents. The computer retrieval systems used by many resource and referral services can help parents quickly with up-to-date information. As a manager, be sure the referral system has current information on your center.

Other

The Department of Labor reports that some companies are funding training grants to help prepare child care personnel. Some of these programs help recruit, train, and license family day care providers.

Other companies provide funds for telephone services to latchkey children. Societal concern is rising regarding the loneliness felt by these children, as is alarm over the growing evidence of danger from fire for children left alone.

LABOR-MANAGEMENT AND CHILD CARE

Dual-career families, single mothers, and single fathers are all benefiting from labor union attention and emphasis on child care as a benefit to be worked out in labor contract negotiations. These groups are becoming increasingly vocal in expressing their concern for affordable child care. The U.S. Department of Labor illustrates some of the concrete actions being taken in different parts of the country. This information shows the potential for labor-management relations as a strategy for addressing child care as a common concern of management and labor. The Department of Labor report shows:[6]

Private Sector

Automobile Industry

In their 1984 negotiations the UAW [United Auto Workers] and Ford agreed that the company would establish two pilot projects providing resource and referral services to assist employees in locating and selecting quality child care. On the basis of this first experience the parties agreed in 1987 to extend these services to all local units requesting them, with the necessary funds drawn from the joint Employee Development and Training Program. The UAW and General Motors followed a parallel course, extending a 1984 pilot program to a corporate-wide one in 1987, also providing resource and referral services upon the request of any plant.[7]

Steel Industry

At its 1986 constitutional convention the United Steel Workers expressed the intention to "make child care for working parents a priority issue in its collective bargaining." In what the USW describes as "breakthrough agreements" with Inland Steel, Bethlehem Steel and USX, the parties agreed to establish joint Union-Management Child Care Committees to undertake needs assessment and feasibility studies with the explicit understanding that "recommendations by the Committee shall be seriously considered."

Food Industry

In 1987 a local of the United Food and Commercial Workers purchased an existing day care center in Grand Junction, Colorado, to meet the needs of grocery store workers whose early and late hours did not match those followed by most day care centers. Open from 6 A.M. to 11 P.M., the new center provides reading readiness and computer training for children between the ages of two and ten.

Publishing Industry

The Bureau of National Affairs and the Newspaper Guild negotiated a contract provision requiring the establishment of a joint committee to study alternative methods of providing child care assistance. This led to the formation of the Metropolitan Child Care Network, a multi-employer supported resource and referral system available to all workers in the metropolitan D.C. area.

---

[6] U.S. Department of Labor, *Child Care*, pp. 138–142.

[7] Since this report was published, the UAW has established a child development center in Flint, Michigan, that is widely recognized as a model site because of its attractive facility, well-qualified staff, and high-quality care. See Cassandra Spratling, Michigan Day Care Sets National Standard," *News and Record*, Greensboro, NC, January 5, 1995, p. D6.

Communications Industry

In 1986 the Communication Workers of America and US West established a joint Child Care Feasibility Task Force to study child care options in the Phoenix area. A major outgrowth of the study was an agreement by US West to join in the partnership with America West Airlines in sponsoring a near-site child care center open on a 24-hour basis to meet the needs of shift workers. A number of slots are reserved for CWA members, with the company subsidizing a portion of the weekly costs.

Garment Industry

In 1981 the International Ladies Garment Workers Union petitioned garment manufacturers in New York City to provide assistance to care for the children of low-earning Chinese employees in the heart of Chinatown. Under the auspices of the ILGWU and the city's child development agency, a day care center was established by combining employer funds with those secured from federal, state and city child care programs. As a consequence, the enrollment fee was reduced to only $10 per week for each child.

Clothing Industry

The Amalgamated Clothing and Textile Workers Union has been among the most active and successful proponents of child care centers. By 1981 there were six ACTWU centers, funded primarily by the union's health and welfare fund to which management contributed as a requirement of the collective bargaining agreement. One site, in Baltimore, is supported by a special child care fund jointly administered by management and labor. Operating costs are heavily subsidized to hold down enrollment fees.

Health Care Industry

As a provision of their 1980 contract, the Service Employees International Union (SEIU) and the Kaiser Permanente Medical Group of Los Angeles established a child care committee to examine the needs of Kaiser employees. As an outgrowth of the study, Kaiser agreed to engage a Child Care Coordinator to operate a resource and referral service under the guidance of the union's Child Care Advisory Committee.

In Rhode Island the SEIU and the Lakeview Nursing Home jointly established an on-site child care center at no cost to employees. In addition to enrolling preschool children, the center also serves school-age children during vacations and holidays.

Public Sector

California

Through an agreement with the SEIU, the State of California created in 1983 a $1 million Child Care Fund, administered by a joint labor-management committee, to provide start-up grants to employee groups wishing to establish child care centers. Space is donated by the state. Currently, 11 centers, serving more than 500 children, are operational, with five new centers in the development stage.

In concert with two other unions, the SEIU and the City of Los Angeles Department of Water and Power agreed to a joint project outside of the formal bargaining structure. After surveying employee needs, the Department began phasing in a child care program by paying two local medical facilities to reserve spaces in their child care program. The Department subsequently agreed to extend the program by permitting employees to establish flexible spending accounts to pay for child care. The employer estimates that the $200,000 cost of this pilot effort will be easily balanced out by a savings of more than $1 million through improved productivity.

Massachusetts

Boston City Hospital and the SEIU established a joint labor-management committee on child care through negotiations in the late 1970s. As an outgrowth of it, an on-site child care center opened in 1982 to care for infants and pre-school children up to 2½ years old. With the hospital providing rent-free space, maintenance and utilities, the center is otherwise self-supporting and now planning an expansion.

In its 1986 negotiations with two SEIU locals, the Commonwealth of Massachusetts agreed to create a $150,000 child care fund to support an existing day care center for state employees, provide start-up costs for a near-site center, and publish a guidebook on child care options.

New York

By far the most ambitious and successful statewide program exists in New York, where in 1979 the Civil Service Employees Association (now an AFSCME Affiliate) and the Governor's Office of Industrial Relations negotiated an agreement to establish a day care center pilot program for state employees. This first center opened in Albany in 1979 with seed money provided by the Department of Health and Human Services. Since then, with the involvement of other state employee unions, 30 centers have been established, serving more than 2,000 children, with the expectation that Empire Day Care Services will in time have a network of 55 centers. Proposals from local labor-management committees for the establishment of new centers are reviewed by a state Labor-Management Child Care Advisory Committee. If approved, they are awarded start-up grants provided through collective bargaining agreements plus space, utilities and maintenance donated by the state. After receiving their initial grants, the centers are expected to be self-supporting. According to the Governor's Industrial Relations Office, "since most New York programs have been jointly conceived and implemented by management and labor, they present a compelling case for creative collaborative problem-solving in the workplace."

Also notable are the state employment policies providing assistance to working parents, including flexible work schedules, part-time employment opportunities, job sharing and voluntary reduced working hours.

Ohio

In Toledo an AFSCME local successfully negotiated for the establishment of an on-site center for the employees of the Medical College of Ohio. Licensed by the State, the center receives a substantial subsidy from the hospital, which picks up most of the costs for salaries, utilities, equipment and supplies.

Federal Government

The collective bargaining agreement between the Department of Labor and the American Federation of Government Employees stipulates that the Department must provide and maintain a child care center to be managed by a non-profit corporation with each party represented on its board of directors. The DOL on-site center opened in 1977, with start-up costs provided by the government and sufficient space to accommodate 100 children between the ages of 18 months and six years.

In the most ambitious federal sector effort to date, the Internal Revenue Service recently announced plans to establish 10 new on-site centers nationwide during FY 1988 to add to one already operative and three others about to open. The program emerged from cooperative talks between the IRS and the National Treasury Employees Union, at which time the IRS agreed to open one center on a trial basis. However, the facility was judged so successful that plans for further pilot tests were abandoned in favor of the full-scale national program. Operated by non-profit corporations with unions and management representation on boards of directors, the centers receive start-up costs from the IRS, with the expectation that they will thereafter be self-supporting.

Taken collectively, and as suggestive of what is beginning to take place on a much larger scale around the country, these accomplishments signal an emerging and, in all likelihood, irreversible trend toward (1) the acknowledgment of child care as a core rather than a peripheral concern of both parties; (2) the acceptance of child care as a legitimate matter for negotiation at the bargaining table and for cooperative problem-solving outside of formal collective bargaining; and (3) the realization that the invention of constructive solutions can be beneficial to management as well as labor, assisting employers to recruit and retain a stable and productive workforce while aiding unions to be responsive to their needs.

DECISIONS, DECISIONS . . .

Form a team with two or three classmates and prepare a proposal to convince a large employer in your community to provide one or more services that will help employees with child care needs. Be sure to consider the benefits to employer as well as employee, and any costs to employer. Present your arguments to your classmates

---

CHURCH-SPONSORED CHILD CARE

A number of national religious organizations oversee more child care centers than any other corporate group mentioned. Neugebauer summarizes several reports and shows that in 1991 there were probably more than 20,000 church-housed early childhood programs. Most are organized and sponsored directly by a local church group that generally makes its largest contribution through the provision of space, either free or at low rents. The church also usually provides building upkeep, janitorial services, and utilities. Some provide health and other benefits to child care staff through the church's benefit package for other employees. The motivation is generally to provide a community service. Only 13% indicate that they give religious instruction. The Southern Baptist Convention and The Roman Catholic Church are the two largest national church organizations providing child care.[8]

COLLEGE- AND UNIVERSITY-SPONSORED CHILD CARE

Community and 4-year colleges, technical schools, and universities are in the child care business to varying degrees. Most serve both students' and employees' children and have a sliding-fee scale to adjust for income differences. Some of

---

[8] R. Neugebauer, "Churches That Care: Status Report #2 on Church-Housed Child Care," *Child Care Information Exchange* 81 (September/October 1991), pp. 41–46.

the programs are especially designed to help maintain student enrollments. Some are used by state social service programs to provide care for children of parents who are receiving state assistance to participate in training programs that will help the parents become financially independent. The programs range from full-day child care to drop-in care during the daytime or evening while the student parents attend a class. Many of the programs operate with grants from the college for the building and its maintenance. Other grants help with subsidies for low-income students.

Hospital-Sponsored Child Care

Hospital and medical school complexes typically have a child care center for their staff and students. Hospital centers in some localities have responded to the flextime options for employees by extending the permitted hours a child can remain in child care. Some have instituted the sick-child care that taps their medical and nursing expertise. Another type of program is a playroom maintained by some medical facilities to serve children or their siblings while they await treatment or the results of tests.

Military Child Care

The United States Military has become a major component of the employer-sponsored child care field, with on-site care at bases around the world, serving nearly 200,000 children in 250 centers, 5,000 family child care homes, and other family services.[9] The centers are financed with a combination of government support and parent fees, and an effort was begun in 1989 to increase the quality of the centers. The "Caregiver Personnel Pay Plan" offers employees salary increases as they obtain additional training and demonstrate competence. Child care workers are thus treated more like other military workers and are less dependent on what parents can afford to pay for their compensation. Not surprisingly, these efforts have greatly reduced staff turnover at the centers.[10]

Conclusion

As managers and potential managers of child development centers, you should certainly feel encouraged to see the momentum of support for child care as it is developing in this country. The United States tends to be far behind most of the developed world, having ignored the needs of families for far too long. You can

---

[9] M.-A. Lucas, "Candidates for Vice-President," *Young Children* 49:3, March 1994, p. 55.

[10] Dan Bellm, Terry Gnezda, Marcy Whitebook, and Gretchen Stahr Breunig, "Policy Initiatives to Enhance Child Care Staff Compensation," in Julienne Johnson and Janet B. McCracken (eds.), *The Early Childhood Career Lattice: Perspectives on Professional Development* (Washington, DC: National Association for the Education of Young Children, 1994), pp. 161–169.

investigate where you can serve children in these new centers and new programs, or you can explore ways your existing centers could serve children of your local businesses, perhaps through contracts for services. Small businesses are an unknown entity as far as how they may respond to the lead exhibited by bigger firms and labor-management contracts.

As you recall the human ecological system (Chapter 2), it will seem logical to reason that with radical changes in the business sector, coupled with changes in the social-cultural environment in the form of more people working outside the home and a relatively smaller pool of workers, society is on the verge of moving toward higher status for child development services.

As these programs are developed, current professional leaders must take an interest in and support these new efforts. Our criteria for high-quality programs should provide a firm basis for these programs to become outstanding. American children deserve the best.

APPLICATIONS

1. Find out from your local NAEYC affiliate what employer-assisted child care centers are available in your area. Call the manager or employer's information office and learn as much as you can about the center's history and present operation. (Coordinate with your classmates so only one member will request information from any one center to share with your class.) Write a report of your findings.
2. Find out from your local affiliate of NAEYC or local union headquarters the names of local labor unions and their leaders who are involved in contract negotiations. Call and inquire about their interest and involvement in child care as a benefit. (Coordinate with your classmates so only one person makes the request for information to share with your class.)
3. Develop a plan for a consortium of your local small businesses to provide child care for their employees.
4. Research child care provisions in your state to learn how widespread employer-assisted child care is in your state. Discuss with your classmates. Write a report on your findings.
5. Research child care provisions in your state to learn how many labor-management contracts are including child care and other family-related benefits. Discuss with your classmates.
6. Add to your management notebook information on employer-assisted, for-profit, and labor-management support for child care.

STUDY QUESTIONS

1. When was the first industry-financed child care service for workers' children in the United States? What was it called?
2. Explain the trends in workplace child care service.

3. State the seven benefits that employers are finding from workforce child care provisions.
4. List and describe ways that companies are involved with providing child care for their employees.
5. List some examples of for-profit child care corporations.
6. List some examples of labor-management contracts providing child care for employees' children.
7. Describe church involvement in child care.
8. Describe college and university involvement in child care.
9. Describe hospital involvement in child care.

SUGGESTED READINGS

Adolph, Barbara. *The Employer's Guide to Child Care: Developing Programs for Working Parents.* New York: Praeger, 1985.

Berry, Francis Stokes. *On-Site Child Care: New York State's Experiment.* Lexington, KY: Council of State Governments, 1985.

Fernandez, J. P. *Child Care and Corporate Productivity: Resolving Family/Work Conflicts.* Lexington, MA: Lexington Books, 1986.

Friedman, Dana, and Theresa Brothers (eds.). *Work Family Needs: Leading Corporations Respond.* New York: Conference Board, 1993.

Galinsky, Ellen, and Dana Friedman. *Education Before School: Investing in Quality Child Care.* New York: Scholastic, 1993.

Galinsky, Ellen, Dana Friedman, and Carol Hernandez. *The Corporate Reference Guide to Work Family Programs.* New York: Work Family Institute, 1991.

Haas, Karen S. *Child Care Is Good Business: A Manual on Employer Supported Child Care.* Northfield, IL: CBH, 1985.

Maynard, Fredelle. *The Child-Care Crisis: The Thinking Parent's Guide to Day-Care.* New York: Penguin, 1986.

Mitchell, Anne, Michelle Seligson, and Fern Marx. *Early Childhood Programs and the Public Schools: Between Promise and Practice.* Dover, MA: Auburn House, 1989.

National Association for the Education of Young Children. *Employer-Assisted Child Care: Resource Guide.* Washington, DC: Author, 1987.

Reeves, Diane Lindsay. *Child Care Crisis: A Reference Handbook.* Santa Barbara, CA: ABC-CLIO, 1992.

Rooney, Teresa. *Who Is Watching Our Children? The Latchkey Child Phenomenon.* Sacramento, CA: The Office, 1983.

Ruggie, Mary. *The State and Working Women: A Comparative Study of Britain and Sweden.* Princeton, NJ: Princeton University Press, 1984.

Schumer, Fern, and S. Caminiti. "Executive Guilt: Who's Taking Care of the Children?" *Fortune* 115:4 (February 16, 1987), pp. 30–37.

Steele, Dorothy M. (ed.). *Congregations and Child Care.* Washington, DC: National Association for the Education of Young Children, 1990.

Stephens, Keith, and Roger Neugebauer. "How's Business? Status Report #8 on For Profit Child Care." *Child Care Information Exchange* 84 (March 1992), pp. 57–61.

Waxman, Pearl L., "Children in the World of Adults—On-Site Child Care." *Young Children* 46:5 (July 1991), pp. 16–21.

CHAPTER 11

Managing Spatial Resources

••

T he physical facilities of the child development center are part of the human-built environment of the human ecological system. In other words, they are physical structures, like schools, shopping centers, and office buildings, that are created to serve human needs.

As part of the human-built environment, the child development center exists within and has many connections with the natural, physical-biological environment, such as the land on which it is built and the surrounding terrain, the extent and landscaping of the play yard, the fresh air and sunshine, the drainage and wind protection, and so forth. In addition, the natural environment provides fuels for heating and cooling, and sun, which gives the center light and heat indoors and makes playgrounds usable even on cold days.

The child development center that operates as an institution within these environments is a complex social-cultural environment in which humans interact with the purpose of nurturing and educating young children. These interactions reflect the social and cultural context of the center as well as the moment-to-moment personal contacts of the individuals involved. Child development centers in the United States, for example, place a higher priority on teaching children to talk out their conflicts than do child development centers in Japan.[1] And individual children and adults bring different temperaments, learning styles, abilities, cultures, and experiences to their relationships with each other as well as with the tangible environment. Some people feel constricted by an overly neat environment while others crave visual order and symmetry. What

---

[1] See Joseph J. Tobin, David Y. H. Wu, and Dana H. Davidson, *Preschool in Three Cultures* (New Haven, CT: Yale University Press, 1989).

seems like a pleasant hive, humming with activity, to one person can seem like noisy chaos to another.

Ideally, the physical environment (both natural and human built) will foster positive interactions among the children, staff, and families of the center. The impact of the tangible environment on this complex process is illustrated by a study that Abraham Maslow and Norbet Mintz conducted in the 1950s. They arranged three separate rooms: a "beautiful" room with comfortable furnishings, natural lighting, and tasteful decorations; an "ugly" room with "bare light bulbs, grey walls, and torn shades," and an "average" room that was clean and neat but nondescript. Then they asked volunteers to examine photographs of people and decide which showed evidence of "energy" and "well-being." The volunteers, as well as two of the three research assistants who interviewed them, were unaware of the actual purpose of the study, which was to see whether people reacted differently in the three environments.

The findings were striking. Not only did the volunteers find the same pictures more full of "energy" and "well-being" when they viewed them in the "beautiful" room, but the research assistants spent less time on the interviews in the "ugly" room and experienced more negative feelings toward their work there, including "monotony, fatigue, headache, sleepiness, discontent, irritability, hostility, and avoidance." The findings for the "average" room were more like those for the "ugly" room than for the "beautiful" room.[2]

MANAGING SPACE

All aspects of the managerial process are needed for procuring, renovating, arranging, decorating, redecorating, allocating, furnishing, and maintaining space. The policy board usually designates one officer to be specifically responsible for the physical facilities along with the manager. These two will be concerned with both indoor and outdoor space. Management must consider the activities of both children and adults.

The accreditation criteria of the National Association for the Education of Young Children (NAEYC) call for 35 square feet of indoor space per child and 75 square feet of outdoor space; the latter can be calculated on the basis of the number of children using the play yard at a given time.[3]

Some argue that 40 or 50 square feet of indoor space per child would come closer to ideal.[4] If you are fortunate enough to be involved in the planning and

---

[2] Tony Hiss, "Experiencing Places," *New Yorker*, June 22, 1987, pp. 45–68, and June 29, 1987, pp. 73–86; cited in Jim Greenman, *Caring Spaces, Learning Places: Children's Environments That Work* (Redmond, WA: Exchange, 1988).

[3] Sue Bredekamp (ed.), *Accreditation Criteria & Procedures of the National Academy of Early Childhood Programs* (Washington, DC: National Association for the Education of Young Children, 1994), pp. 25–27.

[4] See, for example, Candace H. Bowers, "Organizing Space for Children," *Texas Child Care* 13:4 (Spring 1990), pp. 3–10, 22.

The school provides sufficient space for both quiet and noisy activities, thus reducing conflicts and meeting the children's needs.
Metropolitan State College Child Development Laboratory, Denver, CO

building of a new facility, you will have an opportunity to argue for the larger amount. Most directors, however, must work with existing facilities, and they are usually pressed to stretch available space as far as licensing regulations will allow.

Even then, additional considerations must go into calculating the capacity of a given space. Imagine an empty warehouse with 35,000 square feet. Using the standard of 35 square feet per child, you might conclude that this space could accommodate 1,000 children. But licensing regulations regarding the number of toilets and washbasins, amount of equipment, and number of staff required will add constraints to your total capacity. And, if you are striving for quality above and beyond minimum regulations, you will, of course, be concerned with maximum group sizes. When all these things are taken into consideration, your 35,000-square-foot warehouse—with the addition of a toilet and washbasin—will house no more than 20 children, and those 20 children will be too overwhelmed by the openness of the space to have a high-quality experience. Adding walls and additional bathrooms can increase the capacity, but you will have to plan carefully so that all the new rooms have proper exits and ventilation. In short, managing spatial resources is a complex matter and deserves careful thought.

As you help design and organize space, you will be contributing to the following:

1. Children's learning
2. Children's feelings of independence and competence
3. Children's and adults' security
4. Teachers' positive methods of guidance
5. Accomplishing required tasks
6. Order and beauty for individuals

The arrangement of the space in the child development center can make a difference in how easy it will be for children to learn and become self-directed in the activities planned for them each day. As children leave the car or bus that brings them to school, or as they walk to school from their nearby home, they soon enter the school space. They go through many self-care routines and learning activities before returning home each day. The physical environment in which they find themselves at school will have an effect on their behavior and learning.

A carefully planned environment will support growing, developing children. Arrangement and decoration of space can make a child feel confident or afraid, competent or incompetent, interested or disinterested, intelligent or stupid, secure or insecure, in control or controlled. Managers and teachers should study the organization of the space and how it is being used and at times consider reorganizing space for more effective or interesting uses. Space and its related equipment should be continuously monitored to ensure the health and safety of children and adults.

The Children's Life Space

When children enter their first child development center, they are extending their life space or home range. As infants, children have a very limited life space, focused mostly on their own bodies. When infants are warm, well fed, and comfortable, they are generally satisfied. They are primarily concerned with their immediate environment. As children grow and develop, the home range expands beyond the immediate surroundings. The crib, nursery, and other people begin to have meaning. The child starts to sort out many places and objects in the environment. Walking helps expand the child's home range, eventually taking the child outdoors, beyond the walls of the home. Going to a child development center and then to primary and secondary school further expands a child's home range. This process continues throughout life.

How will the child respond to the new life space found in the child development center? What will be the meaning of this environment for the child? According to Leon Pastalan, an architect-sociologist, "Environment is organized as intricately and systematically as any spoken language. It has a system of cues that tell us how to respond to a particular stimulus."[5] Pastalan says there are a number of dimensions on which the space environment needs to be organized;

---

[5] Leon Pastalan, *How the Elderly Negotiate Their Environment*, paper prepared for "Environment for the Aged: A Working Conference on Behavioral Research, Utilization, and Environmental Policy," San Juan, Puerto Rico, December 17–20, 1971.

for example, space organized to aid (a) mastery, (b) orientation, (c) stimulation, and (d) security. These dimensions will now be explored in some detail.

Space Organized to Aid Mastery

Can children master and independently use the activity spaces in the child development center? Will each child feel competent and capable in this environment? These will be goals to achieve.

All individuals, including young children, need some **personal space** that is theirs to claim and defend, according to Pastalan. In the child development center, this is usually the locker holding the children's personal belongings—their coats, boots, and items they accumulate at school such as paintings. It may also be important that each be given a place at the lunch or snack table and a cot in a certain spot as his or her personal space. According to Pastalan, it should be very difficult for others to infringe on the individual's personal space. He suggests that "possession of a tangible piece of space seems almost essential for one's identity."[6]

With this point in mind, the child development center where there are no lockers and where children's belongings are simply piled in a corner somewhere must be violating the children's sense of personal space and contributing to their insecurity. The teacher who removes a 5-year-old's toy brought from home from his locker and places it on a high shelf is also violating the child's personal space.

Territoriality is an important space concept. In the child development center, territoriality means a child's specific claim to a place in the learning environment—the place at the easel, in the sandbox, or on the carpet in the block room. Teachers often say to young children, when a conflict arises over a piece of equipment or a space on the floor or in the sandbox, that it is "yours while you are using it." This rule may be a source of confusion for some children—those who have had no claim to equipment or space in their prior experience or those who come from small families in large homes where almost all the territory is theirs most of the time. Parents teach children to use their own tricycle and to keep it in their own yard, so the communal use of tricycles at school may be confusing.

Territoriality also refers to how close you like to have others come to you in a social interaction. Variations have been observed in adults and in different cultures. Some North Americans, for example, have experienced discomfort traveling in other countries, where people stand much closer together when commuting on crowded buses or push against each other to get served at train stations or post offices. If they judge these behaviors by their own cultural standards, they might become offended at what they perceive as rudeness when, in fact, their distancing behavior might seem insulting to members of the other culture.

Further complicating these cultural differences are the differences that exist between individuals due to temperament or other personality factors. Some people simply do not like to be touched as much as others. All of these influences impact the behavior of even very young children, as well as the adults in the center.

---

[6] Pastalan, "How the Elderly Negotiate Their Environment."

DECISIONS, DECISIONS . . .

In your observations of child development centers, have you witnessed any conflicts that seemed due to territoriality? Describe what you saw and give suggestions for how a director might manage the space to alleviate the problem.

Pastalan suggests that scale or density—the number of people and their size who use the space—is related to the individual's feeling of mastery. As sensory acuities develop, individuals can cope with larger numbers of people and larger spaces. He warns against high density and overcrowding as producing negative effects on behavior.

The National Day Care Study compared groups of 12 children and groups of 24 children and found that the small groups fostered positive behaviors such as cooperation, reflection, and innovation in the children. The children in the small groups were more verbal, giving opinions and making spontaneous comments. They also were more involved in tasks and were less frequently seen wandering aimlessly than were children in the large groups.[7]

NAEYC accreditation criteria stipulate that infants shall be in groups of six or eight, toddlers and 2-year-olds in groups of six to twelve, 3-year-olds in groups of ten to eighteen, and 4- and 5-year-olds in groups of sixteen to eighteen with the stipulation that large groups are not optimal. In the case of 3- to 5-year-olds, twenty are allowed only if the staff is highly qualified.[8] Of course, each of these groups would have a minimum of two adults present. Thus, the researchers indicate that scale or density is a particularly relevant concept in a child development center.

Teachers have discovered that arranging space so that children are actually working in small groups further facilitates the desired goals for the group and for individuals. Density applies not only to the total space for the whole group but to smaller spaces within the playroom. To keep the density appropriate to prevent crowding, many teachers are posting "tickets" or signs with stick figures showing the number of children the area is prepared to serve. For example, four in the painting area or four building with blocks. The children are expected to learn to read the numbers or count the stick figures, count the children already in the space, and wait their turn if the total is too high.

Teachers who use this method argue that it teaches children one-to-one correspondence, counting skills, and the ability to delay their gratification. The system has drawbacks, however. For it to work, it must be enforced consistently. Children who have difficulty remembering to count themselves in the total, or waiting their turn, are often evicted from a center only to slip back in when teachers are

---

[7] Richard R. Ruopp J. Travers, F. Glantz, and C. Coelen, *Children at the Center: Final Report of the National Day Care Study*, Vol. 1 (Washington, DC: Department of Health, Education, and Welfare, 1978; Cambridge, MA: Abt, 1979).

[8] Bredekamp (ed.), *Accreditation Criteria*, p. 24.

A spacious play yard enables children to enjoy their parachute with the addition of sponge balls for flipping into the air.
Brigham Young Early Childhood Center, Provo, UT

not looking, thus undermining all their prior "learning" of the rule. In some centers, the teachers seem to give as many reminders at the end of the school year as they did at the beginning—a good sign that the rule is either not appropriate or not being learned.

Some teachers question whether they should invest so much time and energy in the role of enforcer and whether children should be taught blind obedience to arbitrary rules. They prefer to manage spatial density more subtly, and more efficiently, through the use of **indirect guidance techniques**.[9] That is, they can arrange the environment to give concrete cues that tell the children something about how many can play in a given area as well as something about why that is so: two pairs of safety goggles in the woodworking area, for example, along with the rule that safety goggles must be worn there in order to protect eyes.

Another important indirect guidance technique that will help teachers manage density is to make sure that enough interesting activities are available in the center at any one time and that popular activities are offered often enough for children to get their fill of them. A sign with four stick figures will not help limit the

---

[9] See Verna Hildebrand, *Guiding Young Children,* 5th ed. (Upper Saddle River, NJ: Merrill/Prentice Hall, 1994), pp. 27–44.

number of children crowded around the play dough table if the dough is made available only rarely and if all the other materials in the room have been there since the center opened its doors.

Whether teachers choose the direct or indirect way of limiting group size, there are at least two good reasons for doing so. Social psychologists have long maintained, on the basis of experiments with adults, that participation in groups of three or four is fairly evenly distributed, but as group size increases to eight, participation is concentrated in fewer persons. Some believe that if the study were done with children, the results would be even more striking; that is, participation would decrease even more with increase in group size.

Social psychologists also indicate that group unity decreases as the size of a group increases. They find that when there is high "goal achievement" in a group, the group is stronger and more unified. They further suggest that control can be maintained over about five adults without resorting to some authoritarian means. Thus, the freedom necessary in a person-centered child development center is facilitated by small groups.

Learning Centers.   To facilitate supervision in the classroom and play yard, teachers usually prefer a large area that is subdivided into learning centers, sometimes called **interest centers**. Learning centers set off by child-high shelves or dividers enable the teacher to observe the entire room at a glance yet encourage children to select an activity and settle down to concentrate on that activity. Learning centers may be set up to enable about four children to play comfortably in one spot, with others getting a turn as soon as one child leaves. The cues for the children are the four chairs around the art table or around the dining table in the housekeeping area.

Learning centers or work areas are popular with teachers in the elementary school as well as in early childhood education. Some teachers need to observe the learning center organization in operation to become convinced that adequate control (discipline) can be maintained and that significant learning takes place. Many teachers who have tried learning centers in kindergartens are glad to relegate desks to less significant places and finally trade them for tables and develop learning centers for small groupings of children. Typically, children flow from one area to another as they finish a project and independently make a decision to move to a new activity. Because independent decision making is important, they are not timed to march lockstep from learning center to learning center.

Rules about the numbers of children in each center can be flexible and limited to those that are necessary for safety. Older children in particular can take part in deciding how to control the traffic flow.

Well-defined areas for activities and arrangements that eliminate paths across these areas make it possible for children to play without undue interference and conflicts. Children begin to know what the appropriate behavior or activity is in each area. For example, the paints stay on hard-surfaced areas where spills will not matter. Blocks stay on carpeted areas where sounds are deadened. Blocks should be out of traffic lanes, so that cherished buildings are less likely to be knocked down accidentally. Some teachers set up a "surprise area" where children can anticipate a new activity each day. This could be a cooking surprise one day and a special musician another. Other areas of interest are manipulable table toys, a music-rhythm area, a literature area, a water play area, and so on. The play yard also needs a number of centers, some for quiet and others for active play, such as areas for sand play, story time, water play, gardening, block building, and gross-motor activity. See Figure 11–1 for a typical classroom with learning areas.

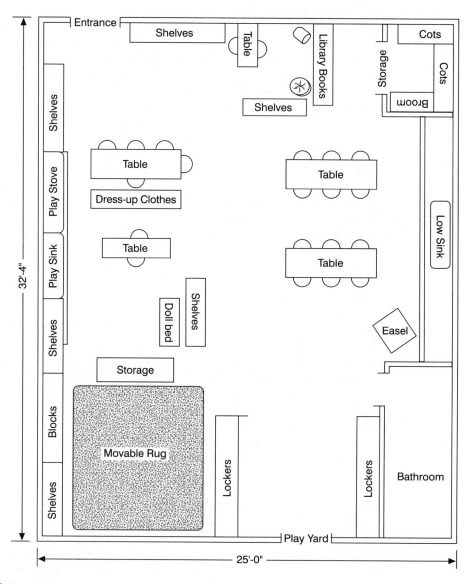

Figure 11–1
Typical classroom with learning areas

Classrooms for the youngest children need to keep the same arrangement for a while to add to children's security. However, for older children, rooms should be reorganized from time to time to stimulate children to combine activities in different ways. For example, moving the blocks near the art table frequently stimulates children to draw tickets for signs for their block highways. Moving the blocks near the housekeeping corner may stimulate children to combine blocks and the dolls or to add to the housekeeping area by using the blocks to build a room. Older children can participate in decisions about these changes and learn a great deal in the process as they discuss the merits of various possibilities or draw proposed floor plans.

Child-Sized Equipment. Child-sized equipment and low latches on doors facilitate mastery—the child controls the environment. Child-high lavatories, toilets, and drinking fountains help children gain control of their own personal care sooner. Low chairs and tables, child-height bulletin boards and easels, and accessible equipment stored on open shelves invite children to get their own learning materials out and to put them away when finished using them. Handrails are needed on all stairs.

A principle called **prepared environment**, applied in the Montessori schools, is that each toy or learning device has its own special space for use. The child is taught where to use the material and to return it to its rightful space on the shelf when finished. The items to be used with a particular activity are often color coded to help with organization: two small blue pitchers with a blue sponge, on a small blue tray, for example, comprise a pouring activity complete with the tool needed for clean up. Additionally, the materials are arranged on shelves in a sequential order of difficulty, so that a child knows that something from the top left, for example, will be easier than something from the bottom right. Small mats are provided for children to spread on the floor and demarcate their work space. These aspects of Montessori's approach to managing spatial resources have been adapted by many teachers in other types of centers to help children work independently and without interference from others.

Mastery of the gross-motor skills is the particular contribution of the playground environment of the school. Outdoor equipment must also be suited to children's sizes and level of development. That is, it should be neither too small nor too large, not too easy or too difficult. There must be sufficient individual play spaces for the number of children using the playground. These spaces can be readily counted—for example, two for a wagon and its puller, two for a push-pull swing, one for a tricycle or two if the tricycle has room for a rider on the back. If there are more than enough places, one can anticipate more harmony on the playground than if there is a shortage of equipment and related play spaces.

Cleaning the Space. Space that is easily kept clean contributes to the child's mastery and eliminates numerous problem areas where children might be admonished to "be careful" or be reprimanded if they spill something. Carpeting has contributed to tension in this regard in many centers. Most teachers do not believe that carpeting is as "washable" as some manufacturers claim it to be. The problem is that janitorial services simply do not clean carpets well. Thus, teachers often firmly caution children when engaged in messy activities. For this reason, carpeting should be eliminated where food, paints, or modeling clay is to be used.

Where it is impossible to eliminate carpet, protective coverings can help alleviate worries about spilled juice or sand. Care must be taken so such coverings do not create hazards that will trip children. One center solved this problem by purchasing rigid vinyl floor pads from an office supply company and placing them under their snack and art tables.

Sufficient storage is closely related to the tidiness of a child development center. Storage should be planned for each area to ensure a place for everything and everything in its place. If the staff notices a large number of items lying around, it may indicate that inadequate storage is provided. Children can be taught to store items if storage is accessible to them. Especially with older children, you can teach them to tidy up and check that everything is orderly before moving on to other activities.

To avoid vandalism, nearly all outdoor equipment that moves freely must be kept under lock and key. In some centers, storage for outdoor equipment is inadequate. Items should be easily moved in and out, or the staff will tend to neglect the task of getting equipment out and children will be unable to help put things away—a task that helps them learn to care for equipment. A wise manager gives full attention to storage, together with children's freedom to use the equipment and staff members' time and energy needed to store it. The center's investment in equipment is at stake.

Space Organized to Aid Orientation

A space that has only one purpose helps people have a better orientation and be better able to predict appropriate behavior, according to Pastalan, who suggests that attention be given to three types of space: personal, social, and public space. But space is expensive and often pressed into multiple duties in child care centers, few of which can afford rooms designated for the sole purpose of eating or napping. Nevertheless, items associated with personal, social, or public uses of space can be color coded to signal these functionally different uses. Centers can, for example, use the same color for lockers, cots, and name tags—all of which are part of the children's personal space. Care is needed, however, to make sure that all the colors harmonize and create an aesthetically pleasing environment. Many centers today are choosing more muted and subtle tones than the garish mixture of primary colors so often associated with children's spaces. The key might be to think of what you would like in your own home rather than limiting yourself to stereotyped images of what children are thought to like.

Texture and sound can also help distinguish the types of space. The same room can signal time for active play, peaceful meals, or napping simply by adjusting the light and adding or removing soft background music. A low-pile area rug on a hardwood or vinyl floor surface creates a well-defined boundary for block building, and the exposed floor on the perimeter suggests a "road" that will steer riding toys away from block structures.

Given boundaries and clues such as these, children can more readily learn the appropriate behavior for each space. With conscious attention being given to space utilization and coding, the staff will be more consistent in teaching what behavior is appropriate for each space. "Don't run" might be unheard in such a space-oriented child development center.

Space Organized to Aid Stimulation

The stimulus dimension of space involves the principle of getting the message across largely through sensory stimulation. Messages that teachers want children to learn to respond to and to learn must be repeated by numerous kinds of sensory stimuli—sight, sound, smell, taste, and touch. According to Pastalan, the environment becomes a meaningful language to people and appropriate responses are feasible. He uses "winter" as an example of how many sensory clues we receive to conceptualize our environment; that is, we see the snow on the ground and ice on the pond, we feel that the air is cold, we hear the wind, and so on.

The **open school concept**, which is typical of child development centers, allows children free movement among learning centers and permits them to respond to stimuli perceived through any sensory mode. It might be the sound of their best friend laughing in the block corner, the sight of a piñata being constructed in the art area, or the smell of cookies baking in the kitchen. As the child responds to a stimulus and moves in any one of these directions, prior experience guides the response or behavior. If help is needed in learning a new behavior, the adults use appropriate guidance techniques.

Space can be beautiful and orderly. It can be clean. These particular qualities can impress young children and aid in their learning. Special attention should be given to lighting, textures, acoustic balance, and density. An orchestration of these various dimensions can produce a supportive environment for a special population. As they strive to create an environment that stimulates all the senses, teachers must take care not to overdo things. Too many early childhood classrooms are visually chaotic, with walls crammed from floor to ceiling with dozens of commercial "decorations" and multiple versions of every craft project from the beginning of the year. Many people in such an environment simply shut out the excess stimulation and stop seeing their surroundings. Some children might not be able to do this and, as consequently, are unable to focus on any one aspect of the environment. If you really intend for children to take in information, you need to provide some blank space around the pictures and symbols you display on the walls.

The same principle applies to sound. Some teachers feel that they are creating an appreciation for music by playing it as a "background" for play. Does the muzak in the shopping mall stimulate an appreciation in adults, or do they simply tune it out? Other teachers use music as a sort of "white noise" to deaden the sound of voices and footsteps in a room with poor acoustic qualities.

A cork strip should be placed at the children's eye level for hanging their paintings and other pictures of interest. Pictures increase the stimulus aspect of space. Pictures need to be changed from time to time to maintain any stimulation.

Care should be taken in the selection of images to display. Of course, the children's work should predominate. Perhaps instead of the mass-produced, cartoon-style images that abound in educators' supply stores, teachers could make their rooms more individually appropriate by displaying photographs of the children, their families, and the community.

A carefully planned play yard can be a very stimulating space for children. Attention should be given to plantings of shrubs and trees to give a variety of foliage and blooms. Some shrubs can serve as windbreaks, making the yard usable for much of the year even in colder climates. They can also serve the same purpose as low dividers inside the classroom: that is, they break up the space into smaller, more intimate areas and help control density. Moreover, they stimulate imaginative play. One little girl in a northern Italian toddler center, for example, invited a foreign guest to visit the "forest" in the corner of the play yard and thoughtfully assured her that she need not worry because there were no wolves in it. A variety of knolls and hills makes the yard more interesting and helps children gain experience in running over uneven surfaces. To help make tricycle riding safer and more organized, a strip of concrete going around a segment of the yard is useful. Children can be taught to ride all in the same direction, thus cutting down on accidents. Lueck suggests making a variety of surface textures for the tricycle riders, such as corrugated cement, bumpy rock surfaces, sand, gravel, and even a low bridge where careful driving is required to make the wheels cross without falling through.[10]

Managers should study carefully before investing in large expensive items for the playground. Items designed for backyard use by one or two children can become unstable and dangerous when subjected to the heavy use of a large group of children. Swings often stimulate little more than constant demands to "Push me!" And large wooden playscapes can quickly become boring. There is need for open spaces for children to run, skip, and pull their wagons. Consequently, all space should not be taken up with fixed equipment.

It is desirable to leave a small area without grass so planting a garden will be easy when spring comes. A few flowers and vegetables with short growing seasons can stimulate children to learn about plants, dig in the soil, and find earthworms.

Coverings on the play yard should be varied, with some grass, sand, and wood chips. Wood chips are good to place under swings and any other places where children might all. Chips cushion falls and absorb moisture where rain water accumulates.[11] It is highly desirable to have a source of water for moistening the sand box, playing in mud, and washing the sidewalk or the tricycles. Drinking water should be available outdoors, too.

---

[10] Phyllis Lueck, "Planning an Outdoor Learning Environment," *Theory into Practice* 12:2 (April 1973), pp. 121–127.

[11] For guidelines established by the Consumer Product Safety Commission regarding the amount of cushioning material, see *Caring for Our Children: National Health and Safety Performance Standards: Guidelines for Out-of-Home Child Care Programs* (Washington, DC: American Public Health Association, 1992), p. 362.

Colorful boxes made of sturdy wood are useful for many of the pretend games that children play outdoors. Frequently the best source of these is a local carpenter. The wood should be smooth and well painted to prevent splinters.

Some movable equipment stimulates children to create their own spaces. Outdoors they may enclose an area with packing boxes or use long planks to wall off an area. Indoors a few lightweight room dividers or hollow blocks often encourage children's spatial creativity. They may create spaces such as an office, a hideout, or an airport. Both teachers and older children will enjoy opportunities to add variety to their room or yard by changing the spatial arrangements from time to time. For the older children who have been in school for a period of time and feel very secure, a reorganization of space often stimulates new ways to play. For example, if the reading area is moved near the blocks, children may use blocks to build a display for the books. If the music area is moved near the blocks, the sight of blocks may stimulate the children to build a stage for an impromptu performance.

Adults are encouraged to be as creative and flexible as the children as they try new ways to organize the available space. If teachers often find themselves carrying certain equipment from place to place, they might question why this is necessary. Could new storage for that equipment be planned nearer to its usual use area? Could carts or dollies be used to save the teacher's energy and give children an experience with energy-saving equipment? Could duplicate items be purchased, if the item is frequently needed in two different locations? Creative solutions to spatial problems can often be found by questioning customary usage and developing alternatives to be tested in your center. Children can help with this problem solving.

Teachers will enjoy making their work environment a stimulating place. One teacher said she knew her classroom had been arranged the same way too long when she could come in at night and find something without turning on a light. Without variety, the environment can be as boring for teachers as it may be to children.

Space Organized to Aid Security

Children must feel secure in their environments if they are to function fully to attain their potential. Parents must feel that everything possible is being done to assure their child's safety and security within the child development center, or they will be unable to leave their child with confidence.

The personal space discussed earlier helps assure the child that he or she will not be left out when it is lunchtime or bedtime. The personal locker ensures a child a place for treasures.

Having easy access to the play yard, lunch room, library, or indoor large-motor area without having to traverse long halls reduces children's anxiety. Adequate lighting can also reduce anxiety. A sturdy 4-foot-high fence around the play yard keeps children safely inside and unwanted intruders outside.

Children's safety from fire, tornado, and other devastations must be paramount in a manager's concerns. All possible precautions are taken to fulfill licensing fire safety requirements. Heat sources such as furnaces and hot water heaters are protected by fire-retardant walls. All exits are kept open and accessible during operating hours. Practice sessions are held with children to reassure teachers and parents that evacuation procedures will work. It is easy to unduly alarm children during a fire or tornado drill; therefore, the drills should be conducted as a routine with a serious but not threatening attitude. Local civilian defense officials can give specific advice for adults conducting fire, hurricane, or tornado drills. It is essential that sufficient staff be always available to evacuate children. All rooms should be equipped with smoke detectors and fire extinguishers. Staff and visitors should not smoke in the center.

Security in the sense of preventing theft and vandalism will be a manager's concern. Locks on windows, doors, storage sheds, and gates must be maintained. Keeping careful account of your center's keys and getting keys back from employees who leave your employment are essential. Using locks and making careful inventories of your supplies helps keep your stored supplies from disappearing.

Employees in the center also need a secure place for their personal effects such as handbags or wallets and clothing. Some locked space for valuables is essential. People cannot do a good job if they are continually trying to keep track of their valuables.

Children should be supervised at all times by a reliable adult. The staff members should be able to see the entire room or yard when the children are using the space. A clear view of all the equipment and corners of the space enables the adult to notice behavior that might become dangerous and thus move quickly to provide closer supervision or take care of an emergency. Any walls or storage should be sufficiently low to ensure good vision. Adequate supervision contributes to children's safety in the environment. It also contributes to the protection of the center's reputation. More than one center has found itself in an uncomfortable investigation of possible sexual abuse when staff failed to notice curious children exploring each other's bodies in hidden corners of a classroom or playground.

Based on a study of sexual abuse in child care centers, Finkelhor et al. recommend that doors and stalls in bathrooms be eliminated along with any other place where a young child could be isolated.[12] Again, this precaution can serve to protect staff from unwarranted accusations, as well as to protect children from harm. A wise manager makes sure that staff are not put in the position of being alone with children.

Space Organized to Meet Special Needs

As discussed in Chapter 1, the Americans with Disabilities Act of 1992, prohibits public accommodations, including child development centers, from discriminating on the basis of disability. This means that child development centers must now

---

[12] David Finkelhor, Linda M. Williams, Michael Kalinowski, and Nanci Burns, *Sexual Abuse in Day Care: A National Study* (Durham, NH: Family Research Laboratory, University of New Hampshire, 1988), pp. 1–16.

make a reasonable effort to accommodate the special needs of children with disabilities. For managers and caregivers who grew up and perhaps began their professional lives in an era of segregation of children with disabilities, this new requirement may be a little threatening. It can be argued, however, that child development centers have been accommodating special needs as long as they have been in existence. After all, what are child-size toilets, or "sippy cups," or wooden puzzles with large knobs on the pieces if not adaptations to the special needs of individuals who are smaller in stature or less physically coordinated than others?

The essence of developmentally appropriate practice is that programs and services for children be *individually appropriate* as well as *age appropriate*, that they begin with a general knowledge of what children are like at various ages but tailor this knowledge to the unique needs of each individual. Accommodating the needs of children with disabilities may take a little extra effort, but it is really a matter of extending the concept of developmental appropriateness to all children.

Managers of child development centers can take further comfort in the fact that they will not be alone as they try to meet the special needs of a particular child with a disability. Recall from the discussion of legislation in Chapter 1 that children with disabilities must be provided with an Individualized Education Plan (IEP) or an Individualized Family Service Plan (IFSP), depending on whether they are over or under 3 years of age.

These plans are the product of collaboration on the part of parents, teachers, therapists, or other specialists. If the child is enrolled in the center as part of a previously formulated plan, the manager and caregivers will certainly want to study the plan and perhaps have a role in subsequent revisions. Sometimes, the planning process results when center staff observe signs of developmental delays and make an appropriate referral for screening. In that case, child development staff may be included in the team from the beginning. The challenge is not for any one member of this team to meet all the child's needs but rather for the team to develop the communication and cooperation needed to make the best use of each individual member's expertise.

One major concern in considering space for meeting special needs is **accessibility**. The center itself must be accessible, as well as the activities within the center. If you are planning a new center or renovating an old one, local building codes may require that you install ramps, wider doorways, larger restrooms, and handrails. Child development centers will already have materials on low shelves, hand-washing sinks at child height, and several other features designed to make things more accessible to children. Will these same shelves and drinking fountains be accessible to children in wheelchairs or walkers? What about the unit blocks? Are they accessible to children who cannot get down on the floor? Or can an elevated platform be installed that will allow everyone to build?

Another important concern is **safety**. For the sake of all children, you will want to eliminate sharp corners on furniture and obstacles that might trip people; these precautions become doubly important when you enroll a child with a vision impairment. You will have a fire drill signal in place when you open your doors, but have you thought about how you will alert a child with a hearing impairment? Is there room on your bus for wheelchairs? Do you have a place to store adaptive equipment? Hearing aids often need replacement batteries that must be stored and disposed of safely out of reach of children. Children with cerebral palsy or other disabilities might have a variety of standers for different positions, and those that are not in use must be stored out of the way so that classrooms are not cluttered.

Space must be managed to provide the additional services that children with disabilities might need. Sometimes this means providing a separate, quiet room, where speech therapy can occur away from distractions. Many therapists, however, are moving toward more integrated ways of delivering services to children. Instead of singling out the child with a disability, they might stay right in the classroom and work either individually with the child with a disability or a small group that includes children who are developing in typical as well as atypical patterns. Some therapists adopt a consultative model, meaning that they discuss the child's needs with the teacher or caregiver and offer suggestions for ways of modifying everyday classroom routines and activities to accomplish therapeutic aims. Typical child development center classrooms and offices can probably meet the spatial needs for these approaches without much alteration.

Some types of disabilities mean that children wear diapers or need help with toilet functions much longer than their age-mates. Thus, diapering areas may have to be enlarged to accommodate the larger bodies. The diapering surface may have to be lowered to reduce the strain on caregivers' backs, or it may have to be relocated to provide privacy for older children whose mental and emotional maturity exceeds their physical capability.

Whatever the challenge, the center manager can probably find help from a number of sources. For one thing, the child's family has probably been finding ways to make an ordinary house meet new and changing needs. Ask what they have done to make it possible for the child to get up close to the table, for example. The other members of the child's IEP or IFSP team can also offer guidance. The suggested readings at the end of this chapter provide a number of resources regarding the topic of inclusion.

Staff Space

The center will require space for business matters to be taken care of. The usual tasks require sitting at a desk, telephoning, filing, and duplicating. Furnishings for these tasks must be located conveniently. Adequate storage should be planned.

The manager needs closed-off office space for working alone and holding one-to-one conferences with parents or staff. This space is often the place where parents come to enroll their child, and thus it provides them with their first impression of your center. Will that impression be one of sterility, with no sign that children live and work here? Will it be cluttered and chaotic? Or will it be peaceful and businesslike, with displays of children's art and photographs of events at the center to convey a sense of the program? Some centers display photographs of each staff member in this space, giving parents the reassurance of being able to recognize the people with whom they leave their child each day. A conference room for larger meetings, such as staff meetings and parent meetings, is desirable. Adults' restrooms should be available nearby.

A teachers' workroom with planned storage for classroom supplies is needed. A washable counter with a sink where children's paints can be mixed is highly desirable; it is very inadequate for teachers to have to mix paints in the children's bathroom. These materials must be kept orderly. Supplies of paper are a fire hazard, as are collections of fabric and paper scrap used for art projects. Any bulk quantities of these materials should be kept in the center's storage room. Fire safety regulations require that storage rooms have fire-retardant walls and that the door remain closed. You can further reduce the fire hazard by keeping these materials well organized and sorted into noncombustible containers. Only the amounts actually in daily use should be brought into the areas of the center used by children. All precautions are needed to prevent fires. Maintenance of the building and equipment requires a separate workroom and an array of supplies. Dangerous cleaning solvents and the like must always be kept locked away from children.

The kitchen and food service areas must meet the state requirements. Careful planning will assure surfaces that are easy to keep spotless. Storage should be adequate for supplies and locked to prevent children and others from entering. Of course, art and cleaning supplies will not be stored in areas designated for food.

A sanitary and safe place for garbage and waste disposal must be provided, along with frequent pickup by a trash collection service. Employees must be expected to keep the area clean and free of odors, insects, and rodents.

Smoking is prohibited everywhere in the center at all times. This prohibition applies especially to bathrooms, conference rooms, and play areas. Prompt all visitors to deposit smoking materials in a receptacle at the door.

CLASSROOM ARRANGEMENTS

A mixture of quiet and vigorous activities goes on in each classroom. Teachers make arrangements to ensure adequate supervision of the many activities. Self-direction is a desired goal for the children; therefore, many learning centers are arranged to encourage the children to get out and put away their own materials. Teachers should be careful to keep spillable items out of traffic lanes. For example, the easels with their bottles of paint should be in a protected area, where a passerby is less likely to catch a sleeve or a foot on the easel leg and spill the whole thing accidentally. Water play should be kept to the hard surface to make mopping up easy.

Breaking up the larger space into smaller learning centers reduces the tendency of children to run or skip around the room. Having a sufficient number of interesting and appealing learning centers reduces congestion. When there is an especially popular center, children are often content to wait if they can put their names on a sign-up sheet and thus be reassured that they will get a turn. Rather than imposing their own arbitrary limits on play in a particular center (e.g., with a cooking timer), teachers can ask the children in the center to tell the next child on the sign-up sheet when they are finished. When given the right to decide for themselves, children often surprise us by relinquishing the spot much sooner than the arbitrary timer would have dictated—and, while in the center, they focus more on their play and less on their impending eviction.

Wide-open spaces where children can run with abandon as they develop locomotion skills should be arranged outdoors. Yet there should also be outdoor places for quiet play, such as the sandbox. Children soon learn to play where their energy needs dictate when there are choices of quiet or active play.

The room arrangement should remain stable, especially for younger children or children with disabilities, to promote feelings of security and the competence that comes from knowing where things are. New materials can be added to existing centers to provide variety, and larger changes can be introduced one at a time, perhaps in consultation with the children. Older children, in particular, might enjoy participating in a major rearrangement of the room: planning it out on paper first, arguing out the various possibilities, and helping with the move.

Equipping Indoor and Outdoor Space

Furnishing the various units of a child development center follows the acquisition and preparation of suitable space for an early childhood program. Numerous commercial companies have booths at most professional meetings where they exhibit and demonstrate their equipment and supplies designed for use in child development centers. Consequently, managers of child development centers are advised to attend professional meetings, not only to hear important workshops and lectures but also to visit the exhibits to learn what equipment is available and to pick up literature and catalogs containing information relevant to their centers—information helpful to wise decision making. Some of the major companies offering equipment are listed at the close of this chapter. Consulting with other managers about their experience in using equipment and dealing with vendors can be helpful.

Managers might want to consider exercising their creativity and having some items custom-built. This approach could have the advantage of saving money and adding a bit of individuality to the center. Of course, care must be taken to ensure quality workmanship with no wobbly joints or protruding bolts.

The Manager's Office.   Organization of the manager's space should be given high priority because many details are related to licensing and reporting that must be taken care of; there are many conferences with parents and staff; and a lot of planning and organizing that must be carried on efficiently if staff members in all the units will be able to function effectively. A virtual blitz of paper seems to enter the center daily. Filing must be carefully done to facilitate the retrieval of the proper materials when needed. A comfortable place must be arranged where a conversation with a visitor or two can be carried on. A convenient space for telephoning and conferring or ordering over the telephone is essential for both the manager and the secretary. To plan for furnishings, equipment, and supplies, you must carefully consider the tasks to be performed in each room.

DECISIONS, DECISIONS . . .

 Consider the tasks to be performed by each of the following staff members: center manager, secretary, cook, custodian. List the furnishings and supplies that should be made available in a work space for each of them. Visit a child development center and compare your lists to the items you observe.

Activity Areas

The sample classroom in Figure 11–1 contains learning centers semi-isolated within the larger playroom by shelves, furnishings, or dividers. The arrangement defines the activity expected to take place and provides shelves with the needed equipment and supplies. For example, the learning center marked "Library Books," with its small table and two chairs and two pillows, sets the stage for a few children to have a quiet time looking at books. The housekeeping area is encircled by the miniature play stove, sink, and shelves, which suggest housekeeping dramatic play. Blocks are wisely stored in an out-of-traffic area on carpeting, to allow for a few children to build creative arrangements with a minimum of interference from other children. Notice that when the blocks are put away, this carpeted area easily serves double duty as a place to hold large-group activities. Tables and chairs close to a low sink allow for activity needing water, including messy activities requiring water for cleanup. Children use the low sink to wash up after fingerpainting. Snacks or meals are served in this area too, confining crumbs or milk spills to one hard-surface area. Adequate shelving enables the teachers to rearrange most areas in numerous ways, thus allowing the learning centers to be changed from time to time to stimulate interest in various activities. Lockers are close to the door, enabling children to deposit their wraps properly before moving farther into the play space.

As discussed in Chapter 2, the theory that undergirds your program will provide guidance in the selection of materials to include in the various centers. Additional ideas are available in most early childhood curriculum books, as well as in some of the suggested readings at the end of this chapter. The following lists contain suggestions to start your own brainstorming process.

Learning Areas

Writing/Communications Area
- Table with seats for about four children
- Working typewriter or computer and printer
- Paper in a variety of sizes, weights, colors
- Envelopes
- Writing implements (pencils, markers, pens)
- Receptacles labeled with each child's name for receiving messages
- Stick-on letters
- Divided trays for sorting letters cut from newspapers

- Old greeting cards
- Stamps, stickers, and reply envelopes from junk mail
- Old checkbooks or check registers
- Blank books

Library Area
- Book display rack
- Appropriate books (including some made by teachers and children)
- Comfortable seating (cushions, soft chairs)
- Adequate lighting
- Tape cassette player and headphones
- Tape recordings of familiar stories (commercial or teacher made)
- Storybook props (puppets, flannel boards, and figures)

Science Area
- Table or cupboard with working surface
- Magnets and objects to pick up
- Magnifying glasses
- Prisms
- Scales
- Thermometer
- Dry cell batteries with hookups for lights and bells
- Bulletin board and display area with interesting items such as photos, insects, acorns, bones, rocks, and so forth, arranged to encourage children to look on their own
- Cages, food, and water for animals if appropriate facilities and care are available for them
- Field guides to birds, minerals, plants, and so forth
- Notebooks and pencils for recording observations
- Various containers for sorting and organizing collections

Block Area
- Unit blocks

	Ages 2–3	Ages 4–5
Half units	40	60
Unit blocks	100	200
Double units	100	200
Quadruple units	40	60
Pillars	20	80
Small columns	20	40
Large columns	20	30
Elliptical curves	5	10
Circular curves	10	20
Pairs of small triangles	5	10
Pairs of large triangles	5	10
Y switches	2	4

- Other blocks of interest
- Block accessories such as plastic or rubber figures of people and animals, small vehicles, markers and tagboard for signs, pipe cleaners and other materials for child-made accessories

- Hollow wooden blocks

	Ages 2–3	Ages 4–5
Squares	6	24
Double squares	3	12
Half squares	3	12
Ramps	1	4
Short boards	2	8
Long boards	2	8

Some teachers prefer reinforced cardboard blocks instead of the hollow wooden blocks for younger children, because they are easier to stack and less likely to cause injury if they fall on a child. Others simply consider them more economical and are disappointed to find that they deteriorate rapidly when older children stand or walk on them.

Art Area
- Table and chairs sufficient for about six children.
- Two easels
- Supplies such as 18" × 24" easel paper (newsprint roll ends often obtainable from newspaper shops), manila drawing paper, construction paper, pastel mimeograph paper, fingerpainting paper, roll of wrapping paper, powdered tempera in many colors including white, wheat paste for mixing fingerpaint, liquid soap for extender, pastel chalk, crayons in large size, felt markers, scissors for both left and right hand, white glue (buy a dozen small bottles, which you will fill from a gallon jug of glue using a plastic squeeze bottle with a pointed tip like a mustard bottle), paste brushes, easel brushes, collage materials (usually "found" materials), stapler, masking tape, paper punch

Table Games
- Table and chairs sufficient for about six children
- Shelves and puzzle racks
- Wooden puzzles from simple to complex designs
- Lotto games
- Sorting games of various shapes, sizes, colors
- Perceptual matching toys
- Parquetry block set
- Dominoes with both numbers and pictures
- Nested toys
- Tinker Toys® and other connector toys
- Beads and strings

- Candy Land® and other games (teacher or child made as well as commercial)[13]

Carpentry
- Work table
- Hammers
- Saws
- Vises
- Nails
- White glue
- Soft wood scraps usually available at cabinet shops
- Safety goggles
- Peg board with space delineated for hanging each tool

Music/Rhythm
- Simple record player that children can operate
- Records
- Illustrated music books
- Rhythm instruments, drums, maracas
- Xylophone

Water Play/Sand Play Table
- Lined table permitting water or sand play for about six children
- Plastic containers for pouring, measuring, comparing amounts of water or sand
- Pipes, pulleys, pendulums

Dramatic Play/Housekeeping
- Child-size stove, sink, refrigerator
- Table and two chairs
- Doll high chair
- Bed, sturdy enough for a child to lie in
- Blanket
- Tablecloth, tableware, dishes
- Cooking utensils
- Grocery items stored in cupboards and refrigerator
- Dolls, male and female, with various ethnic characteristics
- Dress-up clothing including circle skirts, boys' jackets, hats, jewelry, boots, high-heeled shoes
- Several phones
- Literacy items found in homes (newspapers, magazines, telephone books, paper and pencils for grocery lists)

---

[13] See Constance Kamii, *Number in Preschool and Kindergarten* (Washington, DC: National Association for the Education of Young Children, 1982), for suggestions.

- Letters, stamps, and so forth, to play post office
- Pizza pan to play restaurant
- Rollers, razor, combs to play beauty/barber shop
- Tent, suitcases for camping out
- Table and full-length mirrors for beauty shop and dress-up play
- Typewriter, paper, phones for office play

Play Yard
- Sandbox with utensils for filling, shovels
- Jungle gym with various ladders, slide, hideouts
- Jumping boards, sawhorses
- Packing boxes of various sizes
- Wheel toys, tricycles, wagons
- Swings, preferably two-person cooperative type
- Ribbon of cement for tricycles to follow
- Water fountain
- Water faucet and hose
- Balls of various sizes
- Plastic bat
- Acrobat's bar
- Outdoor wooden blocks (large size)
- Garden tools, shovel, rake

In addition to these activity areas, the center will need to provide the following:

Nap Facilities
- Either a separate room where the cots can remain set out or a safe storage area away from children's play
- Enough cots for each child to have one labeled with his or her name, or a number equal to the number of children that will be napping on any given day, which can be sanitized between uses
- A blanket for each child, labeled with the owner's name and stored separately from all the others to avoid cross-contamination. Some centers find bath towels serve the purpose well and are less bulky to store. If the cots are used by the same children each day, the blankets can simply be stored on the individual cots—whether they are left out or stacked away.

The Isolation Space.
A small space equipped to make an ill child comfortable while waiting for a parent to come is needed. Usually a room close to the center office enables the manager or office staff to look in on the child while attending to other duties. This space should include the following items:

- Child's cot, sheet, blanket, pillow
- Child's chair near cot
- Adult chair, perhaps a rocker
- A child's book or two; soft, washable, cuddly toy

Parents' Conference Room or Nook.   The objective is to provide an inviting place for a parent to wait for a child, visit another parent, or select reading material. This room could also serve as a conference room or the policy board room. If the table is large, it could accommodate the staff when assembling booklets, advertising, and so on. The following features should be part of this space:

- Table, chairs
- Bookcase with books to lend
- Bulletin board with educational exhibits
- Wastebasket
- Coffee-making supplies

Classrooms.   Each teacher needs some office supplies to handle the business portions of the job. Lined tablets, scratch pads, memo pads with the center's letterhead and telephone number for notes to parents, stapler, staples, ruler, yardstick, masking tape, Scotch tape, glue, rubber cement, paper clips, scissors, pens, and pencils are necessary. Although teachers in child development centers usually do not have desks to work at as the manager does, they need a cupboard where all of these materials can be organized and readily available. A workroom with adult tables is desirable for planning and preparation.

CONCLUSION

A carefully planned environment will support growing children and their development and learning. Managers and teachers must use space well in organizing the child development center. Four dimensions should guide the planning:

1. Space organized to aid mastery
2. Space organized to aid orientation
3. Space organized to aid stimulation
4. Space organized to aid security

In managing spatial resources, managers must consider the needs of children with disabilities as well as others and plan for accessibility, safety, special services and privacy of older children.

Space and equipment for both quiet and active play have been discussed. In addition, space and equipment for the adults' work activities have been suggested. All are part of the desired balance of the internal ecosystem of the child development center.

EQUIPMENT SUPPLIERS

ABC School Supply, Inc.
3312 N. Berkeley Lake Rd.
Duluth, GA 30136

Addison-Wesley Publishers
PO Box 144
Palo Alto, CA 94303

Childcraft Education Corp.
20 Kilmer Rd.
Edison, NJ 08817

Community Playthings
Route 213
Rifton, NY 12471

Constructive Playthings
1227 E. 119th St.
Grandiew, MO 64030

Creative Educational Surplus
9801 James Circle
Bloomington, MN 55431

Environments, Inc.
PO Box 1348
Beaufort, SC 29901-1348

Hand in Hand
First Step Ltd.
RR 1, Box 1425
Oxford, ME 04270-3841

Kaplan Companies
1310 Lewisville-Clemmons Rd.
PO Box 609
Lewisville, NC 27023

Lakeshore Learning Materials
2695 E. Dominguez St.
PO Box 6261
Carson, CA 90749

Playsystems, Inc.
PO Box 50
Maple Valley, WA 98038

Scholastic, Inc. Pre-K Today
730 Broadway
New York, NY 10003

Teachers' School Supply
PO Box 35126
Los Angeles, CA 90035

Torelli/Durrett
Infant and Toddler Childcare Furniture
1250 Addison St., Suite 113
Berkeley, CA 94702

OTHER USEFUL ADDRESSES

Child Care Law Center
22 Second St., Fifth Floor
San Francisco, CA 94105

Consumer Product Safety Commission
Washington, DC 20207

APPLICATIONS

1. Evaluate the indoor environment of a selected child development center classroom using the four dimensions suggested by Leon Pastalan. Discuss your findings with your classmates or the staff of the center.
2. Evaluate the outdoor environment of a selected center using the four dimensions suggested by Pastalan. Discuss your findings with your classmates or the staff of the center.
3. Get permission, if needed, then place all movable equipment in the center of the classroom. Discuss with a classmate where new learning centers might be arranged. Analyze the pros and cons for making a new arrangement. Try out one arrangement that seems to meet this book's criteria. If you are able to observe children using the center, discuss what happens.

4. Make a drawing of a classroom on quarter-inch squared paper. Cut furnishings templates to scale. Use a catalog to find dimensions. Consider different ways of organizing the environment. Discuss with your classmates.

5. Discuss with your classmates and make a list of exhibits of artifacts that would make beautiful, interesting, stimulating items for children to see in a center.

6. Add information on equipment, spatial arrangements, decorating and redecorating, safety, and the like, to your management notebook.

STUDY QUESTIONS

1. State the required space allocations per child for (a) indoors and (b) outdoors.

2. Given a class of 18 children, calculate the required total square feet of indoor space and outdoor space.

3. State the six ways that designing and organizing space facilitates the child's growth.

4. Discuss the meaning of the concept "the child's life space."

5. Researcher Leon Pastalan states that space environment should be organized in four ways to aid the individual using the space. List the four ways and give examples of each for a child development center.

6. Define and give examples of territoriality.

7. Tell how the Montessori system helps a child define his or her territoriality.

8. How does the concept of density apply in a child development center?

9. Define a learning center and give examples of how they are used in child development centers.

10. Discuss and give examples of the following:
    a. soundproofing
    b. personal space
    c. color coding of space
    d. staff space

SUGGESTED READINGS

Bowers, Candice H. "Organizing Space for Children." *Texas Child Care* 13:4 (Spring 1990), pp. 3–10, 22.

Cartwright, S. "Learning with Large Blocks." *Young Children*, 45:3 (March 1990), pp. 38–41.

Child Care Law Center. "Implications of the Americans with Disabilities Act on Child Care Facilities," March 1993.

Cohen, Stewart. "Children and the Environment: Aesthetic Learning." *Childhood Education* 70:5 (Annual Theme 1994), pp. 302–304.

Cohen, Uriel, Ann B. Hill, Carol G. Lane, Tim McGinty, and Gary T. Moore. *Recommendations for Child Play Areas*. Milwaukee: Center for Architecture and Urban Planning, University of Wisconsin, 1983, updated 1991.

Cohen, Uriel, Jeffrey Beer, Elizabeth Kidera, and Wendy Golden. *Mainstreaming the Handicapped: A Design Guide*. Milwaukee: Center for Architecture and Urban Planning, University of Wisconsin, 1979.

Community Playthings. *Criteria for Play Equipment*. Rifton, NY: Author, 1990.

David, T., and C. Weinstein. *Spaces for Children: The Built Environment and Children's Development*. New York: Plenum, 1987.

Dodge, D. T. "Making Classrooms Work for Children and Adults." *Child Care Information Exchange* 83 (January/February 1992), pp. 21–26.

Doggett, Libby, and Jill George. *All Kids Count: Child Care and the Americans with Disabilities Act*. Arlington, TX: The Arc, 1993.

Forman, George. "Different Media, Different Languages." In Lilian Katz and Bernard Cesarone (eds.), *Reflections on the Reggio Emilia Approach* (pp. 41–54). Urbana, IL: ERIC Clearinghouse on Elementary and Early Childhood Education, 1994.

Frost, J., and S. Sunderlin. *When Children Play*. Wheaton, MD: Association for Childhood Education International, 1985.

Frost, J. L. "Playground Equipment Catalogs: Can They Be Trusted? *Texas Child Care* 14:1 (Summer 1990), pp. 3–12.

Gandini, Lella. "Not Just Anywhere: Making Child Care Centers into 'Particular' Places." *Child Care Information Exchange* 96 (March/April 1994), pp. 48–51.

Greenman, Jim. *Caring Spaces, Learning Places: Children's Environments That Work*. Redmond, WA: Exchange, 1988.

Harms, Thelma, and R. M. Clifford. *Early Childhood Environment Rating Scale*. New York: Teachers College Press, 1980.

Harms, Thelma, and R. M. Clifford. *The Infant-Toddler Environment Rating Scale*. New York: Teachers College Press, 1988.

Hildebrand, Verna. *Guiding Young Children*, 5th ed. Upper Saddle River, NJ: Merrill/Prentice Hall, 1994.

"Hollow Blocks: How to Make and Use Them." *Texas Child Care* 17:1 (Summer 1993), pp. 26–31.

"Is Your Center Secure? Twenty Questions You Need to Ask." *Child Care Information Exchange* 104 (July/August 1995), pp. 38–39.

Jones, Elizabeth. "Making the Most of the Best Play Materials." *Child Care Information Exchange* 94 (November/December 1993), pp. 45–47.

Kamii, Constance, and Rheta DeVries. *Physical Knowledge in Preschool Education: Implications of Piaget's Theory*. New York: Teachers College Press, 1993.

Knight, Diane and Donna Wadsworth. "Physically Challenged Students." *Childhood Education* 69:4 (Summer 1993), pp. 211–215.

Kritchevsky, S., E. Prescott, and L. Walling. *Planning Environments for Young Children: Physical Space*. Washington, DC: National Association for the Education of Young Children, 1977.

Loughlin, Caherine E., and Mavis D. Martin. *Supporting Literacy: Developing Effective Learning Environments*. New York: Teachers College Press, 1987.

Lovell, Penny, and Harms, Thelma, "How Can Playgrounds Be Improved? A Rating Scale." *Young Children* 40:3 (March 1985), pp. 3–8.

Moore, Gary T., Carol G. Lane, Ann B. Hill, Uriel Cohen, and Tim McGinty. *Recommendations for Child Care Centers*, rev. ed. Milwaukee: Center for Architecture and Urban Planning, University of Wisconsin, 1994.

Moyer, Joan (ed.). *Selecting Educational Equipment and Materials for School and Home*. Wheaton, MD: Association for Childhood Education International, 1995.

Myhre, Susan M. "Enhancing Your Dramatic-Play Area through the Use of Prop Boxes." *Young Children* 48:5 (July 1993), pp. 6–11.

National Association for the Education of Young Children. *Facility Design for Early Childhood Programs: NAEYC Resource Guide*. Washington, DC: Author, 1987.

"Playground Equipment You Can Build." *Texas Child Care* 18:3 (Winter 1994), pp. 34–37.

"Playing Together: Ideas for Adapting Materials to Include All Children in Play." *Texas Child Care* 17:4 (Spring 1994), pp. 32–37.

Prescott, Elizabeth. "The Physical Environment—A Powerful Regulator of Experience." *Child Care Information Exchange* 100 (November/December 1994), pp. 9–15.

Readdick, Christine. "Solitary Pursuits: Supporting Children's Privacy Needs in Early Childhood Settings." *Young Children* 49:1 (November 1993), pp. 60–64.

Readdick, Christine A., and Connor Walters-Chapman. "Welcoming Environments: Promoting Attachments." *Texas Child Care* 18:2 (Fall 1994), pp. 2–7.

Smith, Dennis G. "Have You Explored Leasing as a Vehicle for Equipping Your Center?" *Child Care Information Exchange* 58 (September 1987), pp. 29–30.

Stephens, Keith. "Leasing Commercial Space for Your Child Care Program." *Child Care Information Exchange* 58 (November 1987), pp. 15–18.

Warren, Deborah. "Outdoor Play Spaces of Wonder and Beauty: A Tour of the Playgrounds of the University of British Columbia Child Care Services." *Child Care Information Exchange* 103 (May/June 1995), pp. 6–9.

CHAPTER 12

Managing Health
and Safety Needs
of Children

W ith happy abandon and energy, young children enter your child development center each day, ready for the day ahead. With unspoken trust, parents leave children under your watchful care, believing that until they return some hours hence their children will remain safe and healthy. Yours is a serious responsibility.

POLICIES AND PRACTICES

From the very beginning you will be concerned with health and safety policies and practices in your child development center. You will ponder children's health and safety while designing and erecting a new building or while renovating an older one long before children ever enter.

The facility's structure, layout, equipment, finishes, and furnishings will all contribute to the health and safety of children entrusted to you by their parents and society. Maintaining a child's health, avoiding exposure to unhealthful conditions, and protecting the child from harm are major items in the licensing regulations.

The American Public Health Association and American Academy of Pediatrics have developed national guidelines for health and safety in child care programs.[1] Licensing regulations in some states, though not all, conform to the guidelines' recommendations regarding such things as adult-child ratio (see Appendix A). Success-

---

[1] See *Caring for Our Children: National Health and Safety Performance Standards: Guidelines for Out-of-Home Child Care Programs* (Washington, DC, and Elk Grove, IL: American Public Health Association and American Academy of Pediatrics, 1992).

ful managers often have new employees read and discuss these guidelines as a group to have full understanding of what licensing requires—and to affirm the seriousness with which the manager regards the center's compliance with the requirements.

Furthermore, the health and safety of children are significant aspects of the accreditation criteria established by the National Association for the Education of Young Children.[2] Careful reading of this chapter and familiarity with the national guidelines will prepare you to meet the health and safety standards of the accreditation process.

The health system is part of the human-built environment. As manager of a child development center, you will establish close ties with the health care system. You will use the public health system for information and referrals and the physicians and nursing personnel for referrals and advice. Maintaining close links will enable you to serve children and families better.

Above all else, parents and society trust you to keep children safe while they are in your care. It is a trust for you and your staff members to assume with a deep sense of responsibility. As you plan your facility's structure, decor, staffing, operation, and maintenance, you will give full attention to factors that contribute to children's safety. From childproof gates to attention to splinters on wooden furniture, you will be constantly aware of children's safety.

You will equip your center with alarm systems that signal evacuation in case of fire, tornado, other weather emergency, or earthquake. You will have ample smoke detectors and a battery-operated radio that will enable you to receive emergency directions from your civil defense authorities if a disaster or a power failure occurs. Flashlights for use when the power is off and in storm shelters are essential. Many people now consider a cordless telephone a vital piece of equipment. You practice emergency drills and procedures to help reduce confusion and stress in children and staff that any real emergency would create. You inform parents what your procedures are and where their children would be. As one mother of an infant said, "I heard the emergency sirens from a 23rd-floor city office building, and I had to believe, as I made my way to the basement of the office building, that the infant care center would take good care of my baby."

Liability insurance does not protect the health and safety of children; only staff members following sound procedures can do that. Insurance simply protects the owners and operators from financial devastation. Most charges of liability will come as a result of problems in the health and safety arena. See Chapter 9 for more discussion of insurance.

PLANNING FOR A HEALTHFUL ENVIRONMENT

From the inception of a plan for a child development center, the policy board and the manager will be considering ways to make their center a healthful environment for children and the staff. A center's good reputation is fostered if the

---

[2] Sue Bredekamp (ed.), *Accreditation Criteria & Procedures of the National Academy of Early Childhood Programs* (Washington, DC: National Association for the Education of Young Children, 1991), pp. 47–56.

Providing plenty of drinking water for children is an important health measure.
Louisiana State University Child Development Laboratory, Baton Rouge

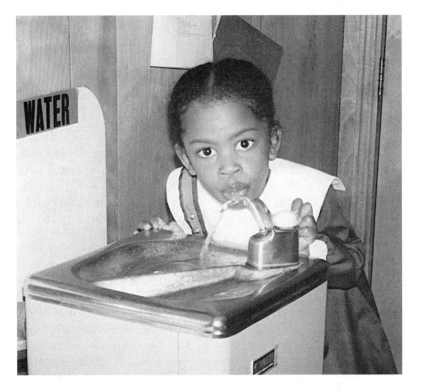

general perception is that children in this center are healthy, energetic learners and seldom ill. The reputation of the center is hurt if the word is out that children there have frequent illnesses.

Minimum standards and requirements for record keeping and reporting are set by licensing agencies. Such requirements are established in cooperation with public health officials, with the goal of preventing harm to children. Parents, who usually are not knowledgeable about such details, depend on centers to maintain high health protection standards. Included in licensing standards are items such as the following:

1. Certification that all staff members are free of tuberculosis
2. Permission from parents for the center to seek emergency medical care for their child
3. Requirements for immunizations, medical checkups, and statements of good health from physicians for each child
4. Prior written permission from each parent to give prescription medication to a child
5. A policy requiring a doctor's prescription for a special diet for a child to be on file
6. A plan for health care services in the center
7. Individual records on children's health indicators

8. A plan for reporting child abuse, protections from abuse occurring within the center, and compliance with regulations preventing hiring of staff with records of child abuse
9. A plan for medical and safety emergencies
10. A plan for training staff and communicating with parents on health and safety matters

Medical Advice and Referral

In planning the center's health care services, the manager will work closely with health professionals. You will arrange for sources of medical information and advice that can be contacted whenever questions arise. For instance, should a child develop an undiagnosed rash while at school, you may call the prearranged medical information source for advice. This could be a pediatrician or a public health clinic. In addition, the staff should be well informed of the closest source of emergency medical treatment and the procedures for calling for help.

Some centers establish contacts with the nearest hospital in anticipation of future emergencies. In this way they can be sure that the records they keep on file will meet the hospital's requirements should a child need emergency treatment when a parent cannot be reached. Some hospitals require specific wording on permission forms, for example, or they might expect the center to provide health insurance information for the injured child. A manager who keeps these links open can serve children better. Phone numbers for emergency medical service should be posted at each phone.

INDIVIDUAL RECORDS

Teachers and caregivers are in a unique position when it comes to protecting children's health. With their broad knowledge of child development and direct experience with many children, they have a basis for comparison when a particular child's behaviors stand out for some reason. Without such a background, parents might miss important cues that their child is having a problem. Then, as teachers come to know a particular child more fully over time, they become sensitized to changes in appearance or behavior that signal potential problems. Observant, sensitive caregivers who keep careful records become valuable team members, cooperating with parents and medical professionals to safeguard children's health.

Records of a child's baseline health condition can be started when the child enrolls. The physician's report will show the immunizations record, height, weight, and basic health condition. Your staff can routinely record height and weight. Children love to learn they are taller or heavier.

Teachers can observe for vision problems. Evidence may be that the child insists on sitting very close to the book during story time, for example. This behavioral evidence can be reported to parents with the suggestion that they have the child's vision checked.

Alert teachers may notice physical anomalies when the child plays with others on the playground, such as when he or she runs and falls more than others. Further observation may show orthopedic problems that should be checked by a specialist. Some children might exhibit several unusual behaviors that, when taken together, warrant further evaluation for possible genetic conditions. Lead poisoning is estimated to affect 15% of U.S. children.[3] Caregivers might be the first to notice subtle signs of unexplained hyperactivity or lethargy, either of which can be symptoms of this problem.

Hearing may be a problem for a few children who seem to misbehave—they simply do not hear the teacher's directions. Look for such a child, or one who breathes through the mouth or eats noisily due to trying to eat and breathe through the mouth at the same time.

Children in group care are known to suffer from more middle-ear infections than children who stay home. These infections sometimes produce fluid in the middle ear, which makes it difficult for the child to hear well, especially in a noisy environment such as the child development center. Although long-term effects of such infections are rare, some experts think that impaired hearing during early childhood may lead to language delays. An observant caregiver can watch for signs of such delays and alert parents to seek medical opinion.

Having a baseline of the general health condition of each child in mind, the teachers and caregivers can then gauge when the child shows symptoms of ill health. They can make recommendations to parents to have the child checked by a physician. When orienting a new staff member, the manager should be especially careful to help the new person understand the special health factors relating to individual children.

This is especially true for infants and toddlers, who are unable to tell you when they do not feel well. Assigning a **primary caregiver** who has responsibility for no more than four infants or toddlers provides a real opportunity for that caregiver to get to know those children. This approach not only helps meet the mental health needs associated with attachment but gives a caregiver plenty of opportunity to become familiar with the way a particular child looks and acts when he or she is healthy. Then, changes in activity level or appearance can be checked out as possible signs of illness. Another good reason for assigning primary caregivers is that it limits the number of children that any one caregiver will come into contact with, thereby limiting the potential for spreading contagious diseases from a sick child to all the other children in the center.

CHILD CARE FOR SICK CHILDREN

One of the more recent developments in the child care arena has been the development in some communities of care for sick children. This care is a response to working parents' needs. Of course, this type of care is beyond many teachers' professional expertise and thus requires specialized personnel. Many

---

[3] "Lead! No. 1 Environmental Pediatric Health Problem," *Young Children* 49:4 (May 1994), p. 9.

of these programs are established in health care facilities yet are available for the entire community on an emergency basis. Meeting standards for the programs will be essential.

The Methodist Hospital Child Development Center in Lubbock, Texas, has specially designed small isolation rooms for sick children. The rooms are designed with glass walls enabling a centrally located nurse to monitor all of the children and provide them with appropriate play activities during the day. The rooms are equipped with audio and video outlets, allowing children to watch special videos and hear story and music tapes.

Sick-child care is an expensive service because of the special facilities and personnel needed. Few child development centers have the luxury of extra space or staff to care for recuperating children. Some communities are experimenting with a system in which family day care providers are paid to reserve a certain number of spaces for sick children. Parents pay to enroll their children in the network, and families meet with providers in advance. Then, when an illness arises, parents have the peace of mind that comes with knowing that there is a place for their child, and the children are not faced with a total stranger while feeling sick and vulnerable.

Center managers could form their own network of such homes in communities where it does not already exist. Another option might be for a center manager to maintain a list of caregivers (perhaps a substitute list, or applicants waiting for full-time openings at the center) who could be sent into the sick child's home to provide care.

Some health professionals are arguing that mildly ill children who are no longer contagious should be cared for in their regular center. They reason that the sick child has probably already infected others during the disease's incubation period and that excluding the child from the regular center only increases the chances that a desperate parent will simply take the child to another (unsuspecting) center and infect more children.

NAEYC accreditation criteria stipulate that a written policy specifying limitations on admitting sick children should be established for your center. The criteria indicate that children with a fever of 101°F, diarrhea, contagious illness, and head lice should be excluded from regular centers. However, the criteria indicate that the children may no longer be contagious once symptoms appear. Thus, if a center has appropriate staff to care for such children, they could be admitted.[4] Such discretionary decision making requires medical consultation with local health authorities as well as your licensing agency.[5]

Children who become sick during the day need to be isolated from other children until their parent can arrive to care for them. They often need special attention from a staff member who can help them feel loved and protected, not alone and forgotten, at this time.

---

[4] Bredekamp (ed.), *Accreditation Criteria*, p. 49.

[5] More detailed guidelines regarding reasons for exclusion and conditions for readmitting children to care can be found in *Caring for Our Children*, pp. 80–82.

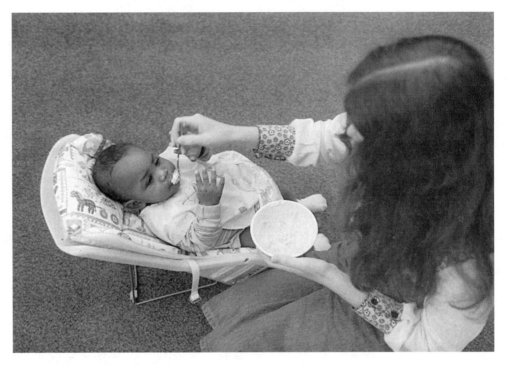

Meeting the food needs of children is an important health measure in any center.
Westview High School Child Care Center, Wichita, KS

ORGANIZING A SYSTEM FOR MEETING HEALTH REQUIREMENTS

A number of routine health forms may be developed and presented to parents for signatures when a child is enrolled. Contact your licensing agent and legal advisers to be certain that your forms meet the legal requirements of your community and state. Forms similar to Figure 12–1, which gives the center consent to obtain emergency medical care for the child, should be in the file. Figure 12–2 gives permission for giving prescription medication. Figure 12–3 shows that a child's immunizations are up-to-date and that the physician has declared the child healthy.[6] Figure 12–4 is obtained by employees when they are declared free of tuberculosis. A folder for each child and each employee should contain needed signed forms.

A small note to send home with the child with the child's name and fill-in blanks for times of feedings, bowel movement(s), sleeping, and so forth, can be a routine procedure. It is especially helpful with infants and young toddlers. In addition to these routines, the note could report to parents special milestones their child had reached (e.g., stood alone, spoke a new word, walked 10 feet). In some states, these and other written records are required by licensing regulations.

---

[6] See *Caring for Our Children*, p. 372, for a recommended schedule of immunization.

Dear Parent or Guardian:

This form is provided to you to leave with those responsible for your child in your absence. If your child needs emergency medical treatment during your absence, the completed form should be presented to the attending physician. Individual hospitals and medical personnel may require additional authorization. Please return this form to the XYZ Child Development Center. Report any changes to the center office.

Child's name _____ Birth date _____

Address _____

Father's name _____ Place of employment _____

Home phone _____ Work phone _____

Mother's name _____ Place of employment _____

Home phone _____ Work phone _____

Child's physician _____

Office phone _____ Home phone _____

Preferred surgeon (if any) _____

Office phone _____ Home phone _____

List any respiratory illnesses or medication allergies the child has _____

_____

List any medications the child is now taking _____

_____

List any other special illnesses (epilepsy, diabetes, etc.) _____

_____

Date of last tetanus shot _____ / _____ /   Blood type _____

Number at which parent can be reached _____

Friend or relative that can be contacted _____ Phone _____

Insurance company _____ Policy number _____

Authorization

I hereby authorize the treatment of my minor child _____
in the event of an emergency situation occurring in my absence. This authorization extends to any hospital and both physician and nursing personnel within the hospital. I release from medical responsibility and liability the hospital medical authorities and physicians for perfoming medical procedures acting on the authority of this medical treatment consent form which are deemed necessary for my minor child. If I cannot be reached in case of an emergency, please allow

_____ to act in my behalf.
(Name of Center)

_____   _____
Signature of Parent or Legal Guardian   Date

_____   _____
Witness   Date

Figure 12–1
Emergency medical treatment consent for minors

The XYZ Child Development Center is hereby given permission to give prescription

medication to my child _____

The medication was prescribed by Dr. _____

whose phone number is _____ . The container containing the medication is the original one. It is clearly marked with the time of day and amount of
medication required.

Signed _____   Parent or guardian _____

Address _____   Phone: Home _____

                                          Work _____

Date _____   Effective until: _____

This form received by _____

Date   Signature of person giving medication   Time   Amount

_____

_____

_____

Figure 12–2
Permission form to give prescription medication

A special form for reporting a child's minor blows and abrasions to parents
should be devised. Make the report, complete with date and signature, the day, and
time the mishap occurred. Keep a copy for your file. In a large center, perforated
carbonized reporting forms can be kept in a looseleaf notebook. The teacher tears
off the small note (about a quarter page in size) and sends it home; the second sheet
holding carbons of four reports remains in the notebook. Making written reports
and keeping copies are essential procedures. Staff members cannot be expected to
recall accurately the dates, times, or names after a short interval of time passes.

Basic first aid training is needed for all staff members. This training is generally available from public health services or the Red Cross. Each classroom should
have the emergency telephone numbers for the children enrolled there. Having
these numbers only in the office could cause unnecessary delay in reaching parents, especially at the end of the day when office staff has gone home.

Cardiopulmonary Resuscitation (CPR)

Training for CPR is obtained from the American Heart Association and the
American Red Cross. It is essential to have one individual in the center at all
times who can administer CPR. The most practical way to meet this standard is to
routinely give staff members this training or a refresher in CPR and first aid.

Name of child _____

Parents _____

Address of parents _____

_____

Phone _____

The XYZ Child Development Center requests that physicians give the child an overall physical examination and state below whether the child is healthy and can benefit from an early childhood program. Physician's statement:

Restrictions (if any):

Signed _____ Date _____
          Physician

Immunization Dates

DTP   _____ _____ _____ _____ _____

OPV/IPV   _____ _____ _____ _____

HbCV   _____ _____ _____ _____

MMR   _____ _____

I certify that the above records are accurate.

_____   _____
Signature of Physician or Nurse   Date

Figure 12–3
Medical checkups and immunizations

EMPLOYEES' HEALTH

Most states require an up-to-date tuberculosis test for employees in a child development center of any kind. The employee should otherwise be in good health, with physical strength to do the lifting and other physical activities required in the job. It is desirable for centers to have health insurance for workers to enable them to consult a physician regarding their health and provide paid sick leave to prevent ill staff members from exposing others because they cannot afford to miss a day's pay.

Name _____

has been tested for tuberculosis on _____

Findings are _____

Signed _____ Date _____

Address _____

_____

This form shall be filed in the office of the center.

Figure 12–4
Employees' tuberculosis test

CHILDREN WITH DISABILITIES AND CHRONIC MEDICAL PROBLEMS

As a manager of a child development center, you will not only be concerned with protecting the health and safety of children in general; you will also be faced with the special health needs of children with disabilities or chronic medical problems. The key to your success in responding to this challenge will be in your ability to form a partnership with parents and health professionals as you educate yourself and your staff and establish procedures for making your center a safe and healthy place for *all* children. Your greatest asset as you strive to achieve this ideal is knowing and trusting that others will help you out. The burden is not yours alone.

The national health and safety standards[7] provide guidelines for developing a service plan for children with special needs and coordinating services among the various components of the health, education, and social services systems involved. Some considerations regarding special equipment and space needs have been discussed in Chapter 11.

Once the plan has been made and space and equipment have been provided, it will be up to you to see that your staff have the knowledge and skill necessary to accommodate special feeding, toileting, or respiratory needs. Some disabilities involve difficulty with swallowing, and staff will have to be alert for choking. Other conditions might involve catheterization or suctioning, and staff will need training to carry out these procedures. Depending on the nature of the disabilities involved, staff may also need to know how to handle seizures, remaining calm and removing hazards from the child's vicinity, and when to call for medical help when the seizures become uncontrollable.

---

[7] *Caring for Our Children*, pp. 243–256.

Estimates vary regarding the number of children in the United States afflicted with chronic medical problems, but all agree that the likelihood of your having such children in your center is very high.[8] As a manager, therefore, you will want to ensure that your staff recognize the signs of an asthma attack and know how to help a child calm down and regain control of his or her breathing. With a diabetic child, staff must be alert for symptoms of low blood sugar and be prepared to assist with sugar cubes, fruit juice, or hard candies and to call for medical help if the child does not respond to these interventions. Children with sickle cell anemia are subject to painful episodes that can be triggered by exertion. When an attack occurs, teachers need to comfort and quiet a child until parents can be summoned.

The key to handling all these situations lies in planning. Decide ahead of time, and make sure your staff members know who will be responsible for helping the child in crisis, who will go or call for help, and who will attend to the other children.

With more than 1 in 10 newborn babies having been exposed to drugs or alcohol during pregnancy,[9] you will very likely have to deal with the consequences of such exposure in some of the children at your center. Like all children, they will exhibit individual differences and not conform to stereotyped preconceptions. Some infants will need to be swaddled and held or rocked in special ways; some young children will have a greater need for stability and predictability in their environment. Careful consultation with families and medical professionals will help you and your staff learn the most effective ways of assisting each child.

Acquired immune deficiency syndrome (AIDS) is another health problem that early childhood professionals will be confronting in growing numbers. National estimates indicate that the number of children with AIDS increased almost 20-fold between 1984 and 1992, and for every diagnosed case, there are likely to be as many as 10 HIV-infected children. Each year, 1,800 infected infants are born in this country.[10] Even if no child in your center is infected, you may encounter the disease in one of your caregivers or a family member of one of the children enrolled.

Hepatitis B is another virus, transmitted via blood or infected bodily fluid, that is of growing concern to public health officials because of increasing numbers of carriers, particularly among children adopted from parts of the world where the virus is widespread.

Your role as manager will be to seek out accurate, up-to-date information to combat the fear and ignorance that surround these diseases. Train your staff to practice **universal precautions**—in other words, to assume that every person might be infected: wear gloves whenever handling bodily fluids (i.e., blood, urine, feces, saliva, nasal or eye discharge, injury or tissue discharges, vomit), and wash hands thoroughly after any contact with bodily fluids. A solution of a quar-

---

[8] Barry B. Frieman and Joanne Settel, "What the Classroom Teacher Needs to Know about Children with Chronic Medical Problems," *Childhood Education* 70:4 (Summer 1994), p. 196.

[9] California Department of Education, *Just Kids: A Practical Guide for Working with Children Prenatally Substance-Exposed* (Sacramento, CA: Author, 1994), p. 1.

[10] Peggy O. Jessee, M. Christine Nagy, and Deborah Poteet-Johnson, "Children with AIDS," *Childhood Education* 70:1 (Fall 1993), p. 10.

ter cup of chlorine bleach in a gallon of water can be used to disinfect surfaces after spills of such fluids are cleaned up.

Staff and families may worry about the risk that ill children pose to others at the center. Although the child with hepatitis B who bites other children does pose a health risk, it is more likely that adults or children with HIV infection will need extra protection from exposure to the normal childhood illnesses because of their depressed immune systems. If they are exposed to measles or chicken pox, for example, they should be immediately referred to their health care provider for administration of immune globulin.[11]

A large part of your center's responsibility will involve helping all the children and families understand and respond appropriately to children with disabilities or chronic medical problems. Of course, confidentiality must be protected, and unless you are able to ensure that it will be, families will not be likely to share needed information with you. In some cases, however, when a disability or medical problem is visibly obvious, caregivers may forbid children from mentioning it, in a misguided attempt to spare someone's feelings or (more likely) to avoid dealing with their own discomfort. For the same reasons, adults sometimes ignore or gloss over a child's comments about his or her own disability, illness, or fears. It will be much more helpful for all concerned to acknowledge these comments openly and to discuss the various conditions matter-of-factly with all the children. Parents might benefit as well from such a discussion at parent meetings.

Sooner or later, all early childhood professionals are called on to respond to children's feelings and questions about the death of a pet or the classroom guinea pig. Someone may lose a grandparent while enrolled in your center. Somehow, these losses seem part of the natural scheme of things. In the case of AIDS or other serious illnesses, however, you and your staff may be challenged to help children and families confront the death of a child or family member. As in the case of disabilities or illnesses, you will have to confront your own feelings first, and then provide the necessary factual information, reassurance, and comfort. You may wish to report to parents what you are saying to children, so they can give the same information at home if the child asks.

Consult the agencies and suggested readings listed at the end of this chapter for additional information regarding disabilities and chronic medical problems. As the manager of a child development center, you will be in a unique position to provide needed education and model compassion and common sense for your entire community in the face of these challenges.

PARENTAL RESPONSIBILITY FOR CHILDREN'S HEALTH

Parents must be helped to appreciate their obligation to their own child's health and also to the health of all the children in the group. Children are generally exposed to many groups and go shopping in public places in addition to attend-

---

[11] *Caring for Our Children*, p. 233.

ing a center. Therefore, a center cannot be held responsible for all the children's illnesses. However, it is imperative that health rules be enforced to eliminate as much contagious illness as possible.

National health and safety standards specify that children should not be at the center when they are too sick to join in the activities; when caring for them makes it impossible to care for the other children adequately; or when any of the following conditions exist: fever over 101°, indications of severe illness such as lethargy or wheezing, uncontrolled diarrhea, repeated vomiting, mouth sores with drooling, rash with fever or behavior change, conjunctivitis with discharge, scabies or head lice, tuberculosis, impetigo, strep infections, chicken pox, mumps, pertussis, or hepatitis A. Once the child has received treatment or the infectious period has passed, as confirmed by medical personnel, the child may be readmitted.

Even parents who want to cooperate with these prohibitions, however, may be tempted to claim a fever is due to teething, for instance, or diarrhea to too many blueberries the night before, if their job hangs in the balance. You can help prevent these occurrences by making your policies regarding exclusion clear at the time of enrollment and working with each family to devise a plan for what they will do in case of the child's illness. In two-career families in which each parent has adequate leave time, the plan may involve their sharing the responsibility of coming to pick up their ill child. In other cases, the parent may be able to enroll the child in a service such as the network of family day care providers or the hospital-based center mentioned earlier. The Community Coordinated Child Care Association or a similar agency in your locale may be able to provide a variety of resources that you can share with parents.

As you discuss this plan with parents, you should also make clear to them your center's policy regarding the child's return after an illness. Some conditions require a medical evaluation. Although some centers routinely require a physician's statement before they will readmit a child, this practice could place an undue burden on the time and finances of working parents. National standards as well as some states' licensing regulations require that each center work with consultants from the medical profession to establish practices and policies. Your health consultant will be able to help you decide exactly what is needed to readmit a child after various illnesses.

In spite of your best precautions, you will eventually be faced with a child who becomes ill at the center. While traditional nursery schools—and the public schools of yesteryear—often had a nurse on staff who could conduct daily health inspections, few of today's centers have that luxury. Therefore, your staff will have to be trained to recognize signs and symptoms of illness, such as fever or unexplained rashes and lethargy. A 3-year-old might be able to tell you that he or she vomited all last night, but an infant must rely on your powers of perception. Ongoing training in these skills is required by the national health and safety standards.

In addition, once a child becomes ill at the center, you will need two things: a quiet, secluded place where the child can wait to be picked up by parents, and up-to-date, accurate information for reaching parents or an other emergency contact person. You will have to be sure that the child is supervised while isolated,

Name of child _____

Name of parent or guardian _____

Address _____   Home phone _____

_____   Work phone of mother _____

_____   Work phone of father _____

The following persons have agreed to serve as emergency caregivers in the event that our child gets sick at school:

Name _____   Name used by child _____

Address _____   Phone _____

_____   Relation to child? _____

A second emergency caregiver:

Name _____   Name used by child _____

Address _____   Phone _____

_____   Relation to child? _____

These persons have been asked and have agreed to serve as emergency care-givers for my child.

_____   _____

Signature   Date

Figure 12–5
Emergency contact persons

and you will have to impress upon parents the need for them to inform you of any changes in the location, schedule, or telephone number of their place of employment, as well as any changes in the emergency contact information. Obsolete information in this regard is as good as no information at all, as is information that is locked in a file cabinet in your office and inaccessible to staff who might be faced with a sick child at times when you are not there.

If the illness becomes serious or a child is injured, you will need a plan for getting the child to the nearest hospital or emergency facility, having a staff member stay with the child until the parents arrive, and providing back-up care for the children who remain at the center. Figure 12–1 shows one format for parental permission to obtain emergency medical care. Figure 12–5 is a typical form used by centers to record the names, addresses, and telephone numbers of emergency contact persons.

CONFIDENTIAL FAMILY INFORMATION

During your orientation families should be encouraged to report to the teacher any family happening, event, or crisis that could make a change in the child's behavior. These can be happy occurrences, such as a visit from grandparents, or a sad situation, such as a divorce or death in the family. Whoever receives calls from parents and learns this information must relay it to the teachers or caregivers to help them judge the appropriate manner of interacting with the child as incidents arise. Thus, child development center personnel receive many bits of information that should be held in confidence among the staff who deal with the child.

The person answering the phone should be knowledgeable about the teachers and caregivers—their names and the specific groups they work with. The person should write down what the parent says over the phone to be sure to record the information correctly. When parents call and cannot talk to the teacher or caregiver because she or he is involved with the children, it is frustrating to have to give a message to a clerk who appears not to have enough information to understand what the parent is relating.

As manager, you and your staff should use personal information from families as any professional would—in confidence and only for the benefit of the parent or child. You should nip in the bud gossip among staff members about confidential information concerning families. Right-to-privacy laws should be kept in mind as you make any records. You should act as though you expect parents to read your notes and records eventually and refrain from writing down anything you would not want them to read. Direct, dated observational notes should be acceptable. These notes should remain without interpretation unless you are an expert. Any information about a parent's child should be available to that parent, especially if the parent asks.

PRESCRIPTION MEDICATIONS AND DIETS

Being responsible for giving prescription medication to a child is a task to take seriously. A policy should be developed and procedures written to ensure protection of the child and the teacher or caregiver. Only prescription medication should be given, to guarantee that a real medical need for the medication exists. Your center must develop a method of recording the time, the amount given, and the person who gives the medication. Designating only one person to give medications helps assure adherence to standards. Checking your policy statement with your medical adviser is essential. Because giving too much medication and missing a dose of essential medication are both hazardous for a child, many careful procedures must be established. Refer to Figure 12–2 for a permission form for giving prescription medication.

Some parents who become concerned for their own diets may institute a diet plan for their child that is quite unhealthful. The young child who is growing and highly active needs calories and nutrients for these activities that an unknowing parent may attempt to deny. For a center to be on the safe side, a doctor's prescription should be required for a child's special diet. On the other hand, centers need to be sensitive to cultural or religious preferences of the families who entrust their children to them. This may mean teaching your cook to read package labels to avoid purchasing graham crackers made with pork lard, for example. This sort of accommodation should not require a note from the family doctor.

MEETING CHILDREN'S PHYSIOLOGICAL NEEDS

All human beings have basic physiological needs that must be met daily. The management and staff of every child development center must ensure that all of each child's physiological needs are met as they arise during the time the child is in the center. In addition, the staff must be helpful to parents by reporting to them details of how their child's needs were met throughout the day and by giving suggestions for the child's hours at home as well.

Physiological needs of special concern are nutrition and digestion, elimination, respiration, and circulation. All of these systems are interrelated within the body, requiring an equilibrium or balance. For example, the body needs adequate and appropriate food to be well nourished. The timing, amount, and type of food eaten; fresh water intake along with other beverages; and the amount of exercise are related to digestion and elimination. Exercise, fresh air intake, and rest are related to respiration and circulation, and so on.

Routines of eating, resting, eliminating, and exercising help children develop habits that contribute to their overall physiological health and well-being. Teachers quickly become aware of the individual differences in children's physiological functioning and set the stage so that children can independently take care of their own needs as soon as they are ready. Equipment, both indoors and outdoors, is developmentally appropriate and challenging enough to encourage children to take healthy risks rather than to use inappropriate equipment in unsafe ways. If you find yourself constantly reminding your 4-year-olds to "go down the slide on your bottom," it could be because they are bored with the toddler-sized climber you have provided and are simply trying to create a more interesting challenge for themselves. On the other hand, because the children are young, the teachers and caregivers must be prepared to help when needed.

For example, to help children rest and recuperate after a period of active play, a restful activity such as story time is planned. Plenty of time is allowed for outdoor play every day so that children can breathe fresh air and exercise their lungs and muscles. Parents are reminded to provide appropriate clothing for such play, and reasonable guidelines (such as wind-chill factor and not mere staff preference) determine when to stay inside. A nutritious snack replenishes energy needs after a busy hour or two of play. Because energy levels differ among children, teachers' expectations should be flexible, allowing one child to engage in a restful activity, such as listening to records, while another climbs on the jungle gym.

Children's health habits are important. Teaching them to wash their hands thoroughly can help reduce the spread of germs.

Special plans should be made for removing toys that have been mouthed by children. This precaution is of special concern in infant and toddler groups where mouthing is an expected behavior. One center has colorful plastic buckets suspended out of children's reach where a staff member can quickly put a mouthed toy until it can be removed and put through the dishwasher or disinfected before use by other children. Such procedures reduce the spread of germs and increase the alertness of staff members to health conditions.

DIAPERING INFANTS

When centers enroll infants, certain requirements must be met with regard to diapering. Chapter 13 discusses diseases that are spread through feces, and that information applies in infant care centers and especially in the diapering area.

The issue of the type of diapers to use in child development centers has come into question. Environmentally conscious people are worrying about disposable diapers filling landfills. Disposable diapers are costly, and depositing untreated feces in landfills is being questioned. Considering that each infant uses about 10,000 diapers from birth through toilet training, diapers are a very considerable expense for parents and a center. For a fee, commercial diaper services regularly deliver hygienically laundered cloth diapers in appropriate sizes to homes or centers. Whether diapers are disposed or laundered, they do represent an environmental problem.

National standards for health and safety stipulate that either disposable diapers with an absorbent filling or cloth diapers with a waterproof covering are acceptable—if the cloth diaper and waterproof covering are removed together and neither part is used again before being sanitized. In other words, caregivers should not put the same pair of plastic pants back on the child after they change the diaper underneath.[12] Therefore, center managers can take other factors, such as cost or environmental concerns, into consideration as they decide between these two alternatives.

DECISIONS, DECISIONS . . .

 Compare the cost of disposable diapers for four infants with what a commercial diaper service would charge for the same number of children in your community. Discuss the alternative you would use in your center, giving your rationale.

The diapering table, not the carpet or any other surface, should always be used for diapering. The surface of the table must be cleaned and disinfected after each use, whether or not a disposable paper cover is used. If you do use such a covering, check with the health department to make sure you are using an appropriate material and disposing of it properly. Caregivers should wipe their hands clean with a premoistened towelette or paper towel after removing the soiled diaper and before handling the clean one.

After changing the diaper, the caregiver must wash his or her own hands thoroughly, as well as wash the child's hands. You can avoid recontaminating your hands by using a paper towel to turn off the faucet or, better yet, by installing a faucet that is operated by a foot pedal. The contents of dirty diapers may be

---

[12] *Caring for Our Children*, pp. 68–69.

flushed down a toilet, but the diapers themselves must be placed in a sealed container (for laundry pickup or for disposal) immediately.

Be sure that caregivers realize how important it is for them to talk to infants and respond to communication cues from the babies while they are diapering them. This eye-to-eye contact gives an opportunity to help the infant gain trust in caregivers. It helps babies feel important to those caring for them and to practice communicating with others.

Imagine the situation in one large center where two individuals were assigned to do all the diapering of the infants. Thus, all day long they changed diaper after diaper. In addition to exposing themselves to possible contamination from the dozens of children they handled and risking the transmission of diseases from one child to many others, these individuals became very mechanical in their approach to the infants. With training and firmer understanding regarding the importance of their personal interaction and conversation with the babies, they soon were talking and smiling with the babies and appeared to enjoy their jobs more. They were certainly being more helpful to the babies. On further consideration, the manager trained the individuals to do some additional tasks, and other caregivers also shared the diapering responsibility. Children are not machines, and assembly-line techniques that seem efficient on the surface may actually be counterproductive. How much more efficient to meet a child's needs for intimacy, attachment, language stimulation, and cleanliness—all in the simple act of diapering. How inefficient to have to close a center because one child's shigella diarrhea has been spread to everyone, staff and children alike!

TOILET TRAINING

For toddlers, the manager and staff must confer with parents to plan how to aid children in learning acceptable toilet habits. Coordination with parents is absolutely essential so that parallel home training can be carried out. Agreement should be reached on when the child is ready to be toilet trained and the techniques to be used. Even words used for urinating and defecating need to be discussed. Some family words are so unique that it is difficult to guess what they mean. Most professionals feel that if toilet training is begun only after the muscle and nervous systems are sufficiently mature, a child can become responsible for independent toileting faster and more easily. Parents may push for toilet training before you feel it is developmentally appropriate. They may believe it is an adult's responsibility to anticipate a child's need to urinate or defecate and get the child on a potty chair in time. They may not realize that what is possible when caring for one child that you have known since birth is more difficult when caring for four (or more) children with whom you are less familiar. You will need to be sensitive to their concerns as you try to reach a consensus about what is appropriate for their child.

Helping children accept and adjust to their changing bodies is a basic developmental task that continues from birth through life. Children are very interested in learning about their bodies and how to take care of themselves. Good health habits concerning urinating, defecating, washing hands, and eating must be established during the early years. In the course of these routines, questions about the genitalia may arise. These questions should be accepted and answered at the child's level of understanding. No shame should be attached to a child's questions or explorations. Self-manipulation of genitalia is a common behavior among young children. It is also harmless; thus, the child should not be admonished for doing it. At times, there may be chapping or rash in the genital area, which needs a simple cleaning and baby lotion to heal. Staff members sometimes need help in understanding these issues because old myths and practices may be part of their upbringing. Be sure they are not shaming the children.

DECISIONS, DECISIONS . . .

A 4-year-old boy in your center has toilet accidents several times each week. The lead teacher in his room has begun confining him to a time-out chair after each incident. What do you think of this method of discipline? Discuss with your classmates.

RESTING AND SLEEPING

A high-quality program allows for resting the children by balancing active, less active, and quiet play. Within such a plan, individual children can choose the activity most suited to their need of the moment.

In a short-day program, the needs for rest are usually met by having a quiet snack, story time, or singing time. Making children lie down on their rugs is not recommended because the time spent getting them prone is often less than restful. However, in full-day programs, a planned resting period is needed and will be a sleeping period for most children. Many full-day children arrive early and are ready for a nap by noon or a little after. To be refreshed and restored for another round of play and interaction, they need an hour or so of sleep about midday.

The nap room must be equipped with washable individual cots and sheets and blankets of appropriate size for the exclusive use of each child. Sheets should be laundered each week, or whenever they become wet or soiled.

Some centers use different rooms for children who sleep from those who only rest quietly. This practice applies especially where older children are in attendance. All children need a quiet period to rest and recuperate from a busy morning; however, the amount of actual sleep required is largely related to how much sleep the child gets at home at night and some individual differences. Caregivers and parents should confer regarding the amount of sleep a child needs and gets. Some parents would like to have a child awakened after an hour so an earlier bedtime can be planned.

Managers must give special attention to adequate supervision for napping children. Staff on duty should always be sufficient in numbers and well prepared, and they should know plans for evacuating sleeping children in case of a fire or tornado. All cribs and cots and other furnishings must be placed in a manner that leaves fire exits free. Rooms must be fully provided with smoke detectors.

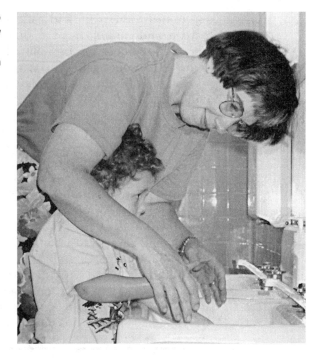

Children may need assistance to learn the proper hand-washing technique for good hygiene.
Early Learning Center, Appalachian State University, Boone, NC

Cribs for infants should have railings that keep the child safe if he or she should stand up. Mattresses are firm and protected with a washable cover or coating. Cribs should be small enough to be pushed out a door in case of emergency evacuation. Several sleeping infants could be moved this way. (See Chapter 11 for further details regarding the arrangement of space for safety.)

Usually nap time follows immediately after lunch and toileting. Keeping a low-key atmosphere in a darkened room helps children sense the quiet behavior expected. By receiving quiet personal attention, each child is encouraged to get ready for a nap without dawdling. Teaching children to breathe deeply with eyes closed and think about what they will do after "resting" usually is all that is needed to get them to relax and fall asleep. Some caregivers sing a personalized song to a child as soon as he or she arrives on the cot, which makes a positive reward for getting ready quickly. In other centers, caregivers gently rub children's backs or softly stroke their heads to help them relax. Nap time should never become a time of battle but rather a pleasant respite for children and staff alike. If problems occur, the manager should make observations and develop suggestions immediately to help the situation. Bed-wetting should be handled individually without admonition.

HEALTH EDUCATION FOR CHILDREN

Teachers should include health education in their planned curricula, helping children appreciate their responsibility for their own health. Learning about washing hands after going to the toilet and before eating is helpful to good health. Learning to brush the teeth and eat nutritious foods can also be planned. Supporting parents and guiding them as they also help teach children good health habits is part of the center's responsibility. The dramatic play area offers children an opportunity to play out health worker roles and to be cared for when playing "sick."

Because of high rates of dental caries, most child care centers are requiring children to brush their teeth after meals. Toothbrushes are labeled with children's names and stored in sanitized racks. Toothpaste is not necessary, but, if used, it should be used sparingly and never squeezed directly onto the individual brushes. Small dots of toothpaste can be squeezed onto the edge of a paper plate, for example, so that it can be transferred to the brush without contaminating the contents of the tube. This routine helps parents establish the routine at home. Children like to do things their friends are doing.

Careful washing of hands should be frequently scheduled for children and explained often to help them understand and develop the habit. Children and staff should always wash hands before handling food, after toileting, after sneezing or blowing noses, and after handling pets. Health authorities believe that extra hand washing with soap greatly reduces the transmission of colds from child to child. Help your staff learn that using soap increases the cleansing quality of water. They should use soap for their own hygiene as well as encouraging its use by children. Children can easily use a liquid soap dispenser.

DECISIONS, DECISIONS . . .

 Try spreading some Vaseline or other clear petroleum jelly on your hands. Then try washing with just water. Now try washing with soap or detergent. What happens? What principle is learned?

Also, to help keep germs from spreading, health authorities encourage parents and caregivers to teach children to cough into their shoulder by turning their head aside and bringing their sleeve-covered shoulder to their mouth. Contrasted with covering your mouth with your hand when you cough, this procedure helps keep cold germs off children's hands where they can more readily be transmitted to toys and people. Centers can further reduce transmission of germs by using a bleach solution to sanitize faucet handles, toys, and table surfaces at least daily. The solution recommended by the Centers for Disease Control is a quarter cup of chlorine bleach per gallon of water, or one tablespoon of bleach per quart of water. The solution should be mixed fresh daily, stored in a labeled container, and kept out of children's reach.

SAFE ARRIVAL AND DEPARTURE

Parents are usually responsible for children as they are transported to and from centers. Parents and any transportation the center supervises should be meticulous regarding the use of proper restraint seats and seat belts, as is usually required by licensing standards.

Sanitizing faucet handles regularly with a bleach solution is an important means for reducing colds in centers.
Kansas State University Hoeflin Child Care Center, Manhattan

Organizing a safe procedure for parking is essential. It is best if children do not have to walk in parking lots. They are so short in stature that people may not see them from their rearview mirrors. A one-way traffic circle is often helpful.

Your records should show to whom each child is to be released, and staff members should be familiar with those individuals. Parents should know the procedure for informing the center in writing when someone different is going to pick up the child. Young children cannot be expected to know who is allowed to pick them up, especially if the person is an estranged though familiar parent or grandparent. Staff should know procedures for checking before releasing a child to a person who is not listed.

DECISIONS, DECISIONS ...

? It is late afternoon at your center and a woman you have never seen comes in, asking to pick up her niece. She shows you her driver's license, which indicates that she has the same last name as the 1-year-old girl. Her name does not appear on the list of persons authorized to pick up the child, however. What should you do?

SAFETY PROTECTION FOR CHILDREN

Being responsible for the safety of other people's children is an awesome task. Both accreditation and licensing standards help centers double-check the most likely avenues for danger to children. Staff members should be especially prepared to follow the standards and respond to emergencies. As manager, you must monitor compliance closely.

The adult-child ratio is in part a safety standard. Sufficient supervision by qualified adults is expected by parents and the community to ensure the safety of children enrolled in centers. Children must be supervised by an adult at all times. The nature of supervision is determined by the children's ages. Infants and toddlers require immediate supervision; older children may do some things alone, with adults being completely aware of where they are and what they are doing.

Licensing regulations require centers to secure a parental release for taking children on supervised field trips. Before each trip, parents are informed specifically when and where children will be going. Liability insurance and safety precautions must be assured.

Making specific plans for fire safety is essential. Frequent drills will help ensure that each staff member should know what to do in case of a fire. Tested smoke alarms should be located in each room. If a fire breaks out, children should be removed from the building immediately. Their safety is your number one priority. Adults must maintain self-control because the children's lives are depending on them. Adequate training for your staff will help them remain calm during emergencies. The children should be counted several times by different people and checked against attendance records to be sure no one is missing. Reporting the fire is second in importance. In calling the fire department, be sure they verify the address. All should be aware of the location of the nearest fire alarm box.

DECISIONS, DECISIONS . . .

 You have been told that monthly fire drills are recommended to ensure that all staff and children become thoroughly familiar with the routine. Four weeks have passed since your last drill and you want to have another, but it has been cold and snowing nearly all month. What you should do, and why?

In any emergency, it may be useful to know where the electricity breakers, water valve, and gas valve are located so these can be turned off. Keep a flashlight handy in a convenient place to use in case the electricity goes off, and test it regularly to be sure the batteries work.

A similar plan should be in place in case of a tornado or hurricane alarm. You can request advice for your specific situation from your local civil defense authorities. Generally the rule is to go to a basement and get near inside walls such as halls away from windows. Remember that if a tornado alarm (or other weather emergency alarm) sounds, the children's parents will likely be miles away. They will have to seek shelter where they are. They must depend on the center staff to give their child the best possible protection. Parents should be aware of the emergency plans. They may arrive at school and will want to know where to expect to find the children and teachers. Your original parents' orientation should give them this information.

CHILD ABUSE

Managers must cope with several aspects of child abuse. In the first place, you are legally required to report any evidence of a child's having been abused at home or on arrival at your center. You must inform your staff members regarding the signs of abuse and how to report those to you and to public authorities. Most child abuse occurs in children's homes. Not every bump or bruise is caused by abuse, but a pattern of recurring bumps and bruises, without plausible explanations for their sources, may be sufficient cause to suspect abuse. Keeping a dated record of each time you observe such marks on a child, as well as any explanation you are given, is the only way you will be aware if such a pattern develops. Some centers keep such a record in a spiral-bound notebook (in which pages cannot be inserted or rearranged), which can serve as evidence to clear center staff when abusing parents falsely accuse them of causing injury to a child.

Children who have been abused will require special concern. You may wish to secure the advice of the mental health center personnel or other professionals if a child in your center has been abused. Such children may have greater need for relating to a consistent caregiver and extra patience to help them reestablish trust in adults. They may have trouble controlling their impulses and need continued, firm reminders of center limits. They may make caregivers uncomfortable as they work through their concerns in dramatic play. Some drop-in centers are organized expressly to take in children whose parents are prone to child abuse and are in treatment. The parent may secure counseling nearby while the child plays in the center.

A few recent, highly publicized cases of child abuse in child care centers and family day care homes have been horrifying to the child care community, and managers are taking extra precautions to ensure that such acts will never occur in their centers. States have instituted clearance procedures for teachers, caregivers of young children, and family day care operators to keep convicted child abusers from entering child care work. Your role is to know and follow the law carefully in this regard. Ask your licensing office for information if you do not know.

Within the operation of a center, many managers have clearly stipulated that all doors will always remain open in their centers, enabling teachers to monitor each other. Abuse can occur physically, mentally, and sexually. Although some groups question the legal prohibition against corporal punishment, no high-quality center would ever consider such punishment as a form of discipline. Other, more effective ways are possible to work with children who may be acting out. Any teacher or caregiver who cannot handle a group of children without resorting to punishment should immediately be removed from contact with children. Mental punishment in the form of teasing, scolding, or shaming a child should not be allowed.

Some center staff members have been accused of sexual abuse. Of course, no qualified manager would knowingly permit such behavior to occur. Your role is to hire staff capable of proper conduct toward children and monitor each employee sufficiently to be assured that such behavior does not arise. One advantage of having a period of probation for a new employee is for you to have an opportunity to see whether the person's temperament and methods of dealing with children are compatible with high-quality standards. The probationary period is one for you to use wisely and well to evaluate a new employee.

Finkelhor and his colleagues completed a nationwide study of sexual abuse in family and center day care, focusing on reported cases from 1983 through 1985. They write, "We estimate the risk to children is 5.5 children sexually abused per 10,000 enrolled." The report puts this figure in the perspective of the estimated 8.9 per 10,000 children under 6 who were sexually abused in their own homes in the same period. Other findings show that 60% of the sexual abuse in day care is done by men even though men represent only an estimated 5% of the staff. Perpetrators were caregivers, volunteers, janitors, bus drivers, family members of staff, and outsiders. In two-thirds of all cases, sexual abuse occurred in the bathroom of the facility. Therefore, the researchers recommend removing partitions and stalls that create private areas where children can be isolated and suggest that managers may need to establish better controls over who takes children into the toilet areas and when this is done. Emphasis is placed on the need for parents to have open access to the center and be alert to changes in children's behavior or complaints.[13]

TRANSPORTING CHILDREN

Safety precautions are essential whenever your center is responsible for transporting children. Some centers transport children to and from school each day. Others transport children only occasionally, for example, on field trips. In every case, transporting children requires special preparations and precautions. Adequate restraint seats and seat belts appropriate for the age of the children must be provided. Well-qualified, licensed drivers must do the driving and a sufficient number of adult assistants must be present to ensure that children are under control and the driver can concentrate on driving. There should never be more passengers (adult or children) than the vehicle is designed and equipped to hold. This generally means no more passengers than available seat belts.

Each vehicle should be provided with a list of children as well as emergency information for each child. Careful accounting procedures are needed to make sure that no child is left in an unattended vehicle. This is especially crucial when transporting infants or children with disabilities who may not be able to make their presence known. More than one tragic news report has concerned the death of a child left in a parked bus all day long in stifling heat. The same type of accounting should be used to ensure that no child is left behind on field trips. When parent volunteers drive, make sure each small group of children stays with the same car and driver

---

[13] David Finkelhor, Linda M. Williams, Michael Kalinowski, and Nanci Burns, *Sexual Abuse in Day Care: A National Study* (Durham: Family Research Laboratory, University of New Hampshire, 1988), pp. 1–16.

going and returning. When children are taken home, drivers should be certain that they are received by authorized persons and not left on a corner or allowed to walk unaccompanied into an empty house or other potentially unsafe situation.

MONITORING HEALTH AND SAFETY CONDITIONS

Managers and staff must keep closely in touch with all health routines because neglect could be harmful to many. Leadership among parents, staff members, and children can help improve the health and safety of the center environment. To assess the health and safety performance of your center, you should make a list such as that shown in Figure 12–6, adding other items as they are relevant to your center.

Reporting a Serious Accident or Fire

Whenever a child has an accident, an accident report must be filed immediately giving details of the time, place, and persons present at the time of the accident. In addition to a copy for the manager's office, the center's insurance company and the licensing agency will require these reports.

Fires resulting in the loss of life or property must be reported immediately to the appropriate state official—probably the state fire marshal. See your state's licensing regulations regarding reporting of fires.

Meeting Children's Mental Health Needs

A discussion of managing a child development center to meet the health needs of children would not be complete without mentioning children's mental health needs. Clearly, in establishing the programmatic goals for children and interacting with the children throughout the day, the emotional or mental health needs must be foremost in everyone's mind. Achieving a positive self-concept is an important developmental task of the early years. Fostering a child's sense of security and trust facilitate this task. Appropriately designed learning activities will contribute to a child's positive self-concept. Guidance, which may be defined as anything the adult does to influence the behavior of the child, must be planned with this long-range goal in mind, not simply as a means of controlling children.

Self-efficacy is an individual's belief in his or her own ability to perform a behavior, according to social psychologist Albert Bandura. Most children will develop a high level of self-efficacy if parents and caregivers learn how to take advantage of the teachable moments when each child is interested in learning. Self-efficacy applies to such tasks as eating, toileting, and dressing—all tasks related to the health of the young child. Older infants and toddlers are in a critical stage of self-efficacy and need the support and guidance of center staff. Maintaining self-efficacy in each child should be an important goal of teachers and caregivers.[14]

---

[14]Verna Hildebrand, "Young Children's Self-Care and Independence Tasks: Applying Self-Efficacy Theory," *Early Child Development and Care* 30, 1988, pp. 199–204.

Yes	No		Date _____	Checked By _____
( )	( )	1.	Is the center's health plan prepared?	
( )	( )	2.	Are health policies written?	
( )	( )	3.	Has fire inspection been carried out?	
( )	( )	4.	Have all recommendations of the fire marshal been carried out?	
( )	( )	5.	Are smoke detectors in place and checked?	
( )	( )	6.	Are fire extinguishers in place and checked?	
( )	( )	7.	Is an evacuation plan ready in case of fire?	
( )	( )	8.	Is a shelter plan ready in case of a tornado or hurricane?	
( )	( )	9.	Have parents been informed about the fire, tornado, and hurricane plans?	
( )	( )	10.	Have all rooms been checked for improperly stored combustible materials?	
( )	( )	11.	Are addresses and phone numbers of parents' homes and places of work on file and accessible?	
( )	( )	12.	Are names, addresses, and phone numbers of each child's substitute caregiver on file and accessible?	
( )	( )	13.	Has each parent signed a form allowing emergency medical treatment for his or her child?	
( )	( )	14.	Has each child's medical checkup form been filed?	
( )	( )	15.	Has each child's immunization form been filed?	
( )	( )	16.	Are prescription medication forms available for parents needing them?	
( )	( )	17.	Are all employees' TB tests up-to-date and filed?	
( )	( )	18.	Have teachers carried out units to teach health?	
( )	( )	19.	Have teachers carried out units to teach safety?	
( )	( )	20.	Are the center's "No Smoking" signs posted?	

Figure 12–6
Monitoring health and safety conditions

The book *Guiding Young Children* describes in considerable detail a system of interacting with or guiding infants and young children to help them become independent individuals with a happy approach to life.[15] Given what is known about guiding children, a positive approach works best in almost every instance. Punitive measures are not used in high-quality child development centers. Most punishment is in outright violation of licensing standards.

[15]Verna Hildebrand, *Guiding Young Children* (Upper Saddle River, NJ: Merrill/Prentice Hall, 1994).

In this regard, it is often helpful to provide parents with ideas for improving their interaction processes with young children. They have many questions and enjoy the chance to share with other parents who have children about the same age as their own. Teachers, through their contacts with parents, can often help parents appreciate their child more as they learn to recognize his or her increasing abilities. Teachers assist parents by letting parents know that they really appreciate and enjoy their child.

CONCLUSION

Parents are usually very concerned that children remain healthy when they are in a child development center. Both parents and society trust that you will keep children safe from harm. This chapter has discussed the health of teachers and caregivers and the ways that centers can protect the health and safety of all children, as well as the ways they can work with families and other professionals to meet the needs of children with disabilities or chronic health problems. Policies and practices regarding immunizations, medical examinations, medications, observations and record keeping, and the exclusion and readmission of ill children have been suggested. Safety precautions for transportation of children were outlined, as well as measures for preventing and reporting child abuse.

RESOURCES

The following organizations can provide additional information regarding children's health and safety needs.

American Academy of Pediatrics
141 Northwest Point Blvd.
PO Box 927
Elk Grove Village, IL 60009

American Public Health Association
1015 15th St., NW
Washington, DC 20005

Centers for Disease Control
U.S. Department of Health and Human Services
National AIDS Information and Exchange Program
Atlanta, GA 30333

Division of Services to Children with Special Health Needs
Bureau of Maternal and Child Health and Resource Development
Department of Health and Human Services
Washington, DC 20202

Epilepsy Foundation of America
4351 Garden City Drive
Landover, MD 20785

Juvenile Diabetes Foundation International
432 Park Ave. South
New York, NY 10016

Lung Line Information Service
National Jewish Center for Immunology and Respiratory Medicine
1400 Jackson St.
Denver, CO 80206

Office of Public Affairs
U.S. Department of Education
AIDS and the Education of Our Children
400 Maryland Ave., SW
Washington, DC 20202

Sickle Cell Disease Branch
National Heart, Blood, and Lung Institute
National Institutes of Health
9000 Rockville Pike
Bethesda, MD 20892

APPLICATIONS

1. Write a sample health policy with regard to giving medication to children in a center.
2. Make a checklist of health forms a center must collect from each parent. Design the list to go in the front of each child's folder of information.
3. Make a list of local phone numbers that might be needed in emergencies.
4. Draw up an evacuation plan for a child development center you know.
5. Locate in the library or elsewhere recommended health and safety practices for a children's center. Place a copy or photocopy of relevant pages in your management notebook.

STUDY QUESTIONS

1. Where do health and safety fit in the human ecological system of a community?
2. What safety and emergency preparations are required for licensing a child development center?
3. What plans must the manager have in place that protect children's health?
4. Name and describe the special forms parents must sign that give center staff permission to serve children's medical needs.
5. State the available choices for providing hygienic diapers for infants in a center. Discuss the issues involved.
6. List the physiological needs of children that staff in a children's center must provide for. Give related precautions regarding serving these needs.
7. Discuss child abuse and the recommendations for protection for children that must be followed.
8. Discuss precautions and requirements in transporting children.
9. In what ways may children's mental health be protected in a center?

SUGGESTED READINGS

American Academy of Pediatrics. *1994 Red Book: Report of the Committee on Infectious Diseases.* Elk Grove Village, IL: Author, 1994.

American Public Health Association and American Academy of Pediatrics. *Caring for Our Children: National Health and Safety Performance Standards: Guidelines for Out-of-Home Child Care Programs.* Washington, DC, and Elk Grove, IL: Authors, 1992.

Aronson, Susan S. "CMV (Cytomegalovirus) and Child Care Programs." *Child Care Information Exchange* 59 (January 1988), pp. 25–28.

Aronson, Susan. "Early Childhood Safety Checklist #4: General Indoor Areas and Hall-
     ways and Stairs." *Child Care Information Exchange* 96 (March/April 1994), pp. 90–92.

Aronson, Susan. "Early Childhood Safety Checklist #5: Playgrounds." *Child Care Informa-
     tion Exchange* 99 (September/October 1994), pp. 64–66.

Aronson, Susan S. "Exclusion Criteria for Ill Children in Child Care." *Child Care Informa-
     tion Exchange* 49 (May 1986), pp. 30–35.

Aronson, Susan. "Going Barefoot and Having Animals in Child Care." *Child Care Informa-
     tion Exchange* 91 (May/June 1993), pp. 57–58.

Aronson, Susan S. "Health Update: AIDS and Child Care Programs." *Child Care Informa-
     tion Exchange* 58 (November 1987), pp. 35–39.

Aronson, Susan S. "Health Update: Coping with the Physical Requirements of Caregiv-
     ing." *Child Care Information Exchange* 55 (May 1987), pp. 39–40.

Aronson, Susan. "Meeting the Health Needs of Children with Asthma." *Child Care Informa-
     tion Exchange* 101 (January/February 1995), pp. 59–60.

Aronson, Susan. "Updates: Infectious Diseases, SIDS, HIV/AIDS." *Child Care Information
     Exchange* 103 (May/June 1995), pp. 59–61.

Brown, Janet F. "Annotated Bibliography on Preschool Child Transportation Safety." *Young
     Children* 40:4 (May 1985), pp. 16–17.

California Department of Education. *Just Kids: A Practical Guide for Working with Children
     Prenatally Substance-Exposed*. Sacramento: Author, 1994.

Coleman, Jeanine G. *The Early Intervention Dictionary*. Rockville, MD: Woodbine House,
     1993.

DeHaas-Warner, Sarah. "The Role of Child Care Professionals in Placement and Program-
     ming Decisions for Preschoolers with Special Needs in Community-Based Settings."
     Young Children 49:5 (July 1994), pp. 76–78.

Dixon, S. "Talking to the Child's Physician: Thoughts for the Child Care Provider." *Young
     Children* 45:3 (March 1990), pp. 36–37.

Essa, Eva L., and Colleen I. Murray. "Young Children's Understanding and Experience
     with Death." *Young Children* 49:4 (May 1994), pp. 74–81.

Essa, Eva L., Colleen I. Murray, and Joanne Everts. "Death of a Friend." *Childhood Educa-
     tion* 71:3 (Spring 1995), pp. 130–133.

Finkelhor, D., L. M. Williams, and N. Burns. *Nursery Crimes: Sexual Abuse in Day Care*. New-
     bury Park, CA: Sage, 1988.

Fredericks, B., R. Hardman, G. Morgan, and F. Rodgers. *A Little Bit under the Weather: A
     Look at Care for Mildly Ill Children*. Boston: Work/Family Directions, 1986.

Frieman, Barry B., and Joanne Settel. "What the Classroom Teacher Needs to Know about
     Children with Chronic Health Problems." *Childhood Education* 70:4 (Summer 1994), p.
     201.

Goldberg, Ellie. "Including Children with Chronic Health Conditions: Nebulizers in the
     Classroom." *Young Children* 49:2 (January 1994), pp. 34–37.

"Hearing Loss: Detect It Early." *Texas Child Care* 17:4 (Spring 1994), pp. 14–19.

Henniger, Michael. "Planning for Outdoor Play." *Young Children* 49:4 (May 1994), pp.
     10–15.

Honig, Alice Sterling. "The Shy Child." *Young Children* 42:4 (May 1987), pp. 54–64.

Honig, Alice Sterling. "Stress and Coping in Children" (Part 1): "Research in Review."
     Young Children 41:4 (May 1986), pp. 50–63.

Honig, Alice Sterling. "Stress and Coping in Children" (Part 2): "Interpersonal Family
     Relationships." *Young Children* 41:5 (July 1986), pp. 47–59.

Hrncir, E. J., and C. E. Eisenhart. "Use with Caution: The 'At Risk' Label." *Young Children*
     46:2 (January 1991), pp. 23–27.

Kendrick, A. S., R. Kaufmann, and K. P. Messenger (eds.). *Healthy Young Children: A Manual for Programs*. Washington, DC: National Association for the Education of Young Children, 1995.

"Lead Poisoning: A New Crisis for Child Care?" *Texas Child Care* 17:1 (Summer 1993), pp. 2–8.

Mazur, Sally, and Carrie Pekor. "Can Teachers Touch Children Anymore?" *Young Children* 40:4 (May 1985), pp. 10–12.

Mazzocco, Michele, and Rebecca O'Connor. "Fragile X Syndrome: A Guide for Teachers of Young Children." *Young Children* 49:1 (November 1993), pp. 73–77.

Meddin, Barbara J., and Anita L. Rosen. "Child Abuse and Neglect: Prevention and Reporting." *Young Children* 41:4 (May 1986), pp. 26–30.

National Association for the Education of Young Children. *Child Care Center Diseases and Sick Child Care: NAEYC Resource Guide*. Washington, DC: Author, 1987.

NAEYC Information Service. *Child Care and Ill Children and Healthy Child Care Practices*, rev. ed. Washington, DC: National Association for the Education of Young Children, 1994.

Rab, Victoria Y., and Karren Ikeda Wood. *Child Care and the ADA: A Handbook for Inclusive Programs*. Baltimore: Brooks, 1995.

Scott, Dana K. "Child Safety Seats—They Work!" *Young Children* 40:4 (May 1985), pp. 13–15.

Skeen, Patsy, and Diane Hodson. "AIDS: What Adults Should Know about AIDS (and Shouldn't Discuss with Very Young Children)." *Young Children* 42:4 (May 1987), pp. 65–71.

Watt, Margaret R., Joanne E. Roberts, and Susan A. Zeisel. "Ear Infections in Young Children: The Role of the Early Childhood Educator." *Young Children* 49:1 (November 1993), pp. 65–72.

Weiser, M. G. *Group Care and Education of Infants and Toddlers* Upper Saddle River, NJ: Merrill/Prentice Hall, 1990.

Winter, Suzanne M., Michael J. Bell, and James D. Dempsey. "Creating Play Environments for Children with Special Needs." *Childhood Education* 71:1 (Fall 1994), pp. 28–32.

CHAPTER 13

Managing Food Service

∙∙

Ironically, in a country where millions of children live in poverty and go to bed hungry at least part of the time, millions of others are either obese or somewhat overweight. Whether you are dealing with homeless and hungry children or children at risk for health problems because of obesity, as the manager of a child development center, you will need to devote considerable attention to providing the food that children need today and fostering the healthy eating habits that they will need for a lifetime.

Meal service is one provision that characterizes full-day child development programs. Short-day programs typically serve only a midmorning or midafternoon snack. Providing young children with adequate nutrition for growth, body maintenance, and repair is essential. Proper nutrition is required for all areas of a child's development—physical, mental, social, and emotional. Parents and teachers generally hold a number of goals for each child:

1. To eat a well-balanced nutritious meal
2. To enjoy mealtime among friendly people
3. To taste and ultimately enjoy a wide variety of foods
4. To learn to eat independently
5. To sit at the table and develop acceptable table manners
6. To develop an understanding that good food is related to growing and being strong and healthy
7. To see a relationship between foods eaten at home and those eaten at school

PLANNING MEAL SERVICE

Many considerations must be taken into account when planning a good food service program. Time is required to do adequate planning. National health and safety standards[1] and center accreditation criteria of the National Association for the Education of Young Children (NAEYC) follow the U.S. Department of Agriculture (USDA) recommendations for nutritional requirements of foods served in child care centers.[2]

DECISIONS, DECISIONS . . .

 Locate copies of the nutrition and food service guidelines in NAEYC's *Accreditation Criteria* and *Caring for Our Children.* Compare these guidelines to your state's licensing regulations, listing similarities and differences.

FEDERAL SUBSIDIES FOR FOOD PROGRAMS

Child development centers and family day care homes may qualify for federal reimbursement for meals and snacks served in the center if 25% of the children are needy. The U.S. Department of Agriculture (USDA) manages the food program although it is administered locally by state or regional agencies. In some states, for example, the Department of Education administers the Child Care Food Program. If you do not know who administers the program in your state, write to:

Child Care and Summer Programs Division
Food and Nutrition Service
USDA
3101 Park Center Drive, Room 416
Alexandria, VA 22302

Centers must apply and document the income levels and family size of needy children. The center will receive more monies for the needy children and a small amount for moderate- and higher-income children. One report states that an average center serving 30 children could receive $200 to $2,500 per month in reimbursement. The federal funds do not totally pay for the food service program, but they are of sufficient help that most centers participate in spite of the

---

[1] *Caring for Our Children: National Health and Safety Performance Standards: Guidelines for Out-of-Home Child Care Programs* (Washington, DC, and Elk Grove Village, IL: American Public Health Association and American Academy of Pediatrics, 1992), pp. 115–139.

[2] Sue Bredekamp (ed.), *Accreditation Criteria & Procedures of the National Academy of Early Childhood Programs* (Washington, DC: National Association for the Education of Young Children, 1991), pp. 57–58, 69–72.

Mealtime in a full-day program is an important time for conversation as well as a nutritious meal.
Howard University Preschool Center, Washington, DC

extra effort required. The USDA also subsidizes milk as a beverage for all children in schools and centers, on request.

The calculations for receiving the reimbursements are somewhat complex, and records must be kept for each meal. Some reimbursement is available to pay personnel for taking the training, doing the bookkeeping, and filing the reports. Computer software companies that have prepared programs for record keeping in child care centers have developed a program specifically for keeping records for USDA food reimbursements.

The USDA has established guidelines for each age group of children that specify the amounts and types of foods that must be included in each meal or snack (see Figures 13–1 and 13–2).

Of course, having highly nutritious menus and meals does not guarantee that each child has eaten a nutritious meal. Careful guidance of children will help them learn to eat and eventually enjoy a variety of foods. Eating a range of foods is considered an important factor in being well nourished throughout life. Research has shown that when children are given a wide variety of appropriate foods from which to choose, they will eat a balanced diet. They may need as many as 10 times to taste a new food without being forced or coaxed to eat it, before deciding they like it.[3]

---

[3] Leann L. Birch, Susan L. Johnson, and Jennifer A. Fisher, "Children's Eating: The Development of Food-Acceptance Patterns," *Young Children* 50:2 (January 1995), pp. 71–78.

0–3 Months	4–7 Months	8–11 Months
	MORNING	
4–6 fluid oz. breast milk or iron-fortified formula	4–8 fluid oz. breast milk or iron-fortified formula	6–8 fluid oz. breast milk, iron-fortified formula, or whole cow's milk
	0–3 tablespoons dry, iron-fortified infant cereal (optional before 6 months, but introduce by 6 months)	1–4 tablespoons fruit of appropriate consistency
		2–4 tablespoons dry, iron-fortified infant cereal
	MIDDAY	
4–6 fluid oz. breast milk or iron-fortified formula	4–8 fluid oz. breast milk or iron-fortified formula	6–8 fluid oz. breast milk, iron-fortified formula, or whole cow's milk
	0–3 tablespoons dry, iron-fortified infant cereal (optional—see above)	1–4 tablespoons fruit *and/or* vegetable of appropriate consistency
	0–3 tablespoons strained fruit and/or vegetable (optional, but if introduced, introduce as close to 6 months as possible)	2–4 tablespoons dry, iron-fortified infant cereal *and/or* 1–4 tablespoons fish, lean meat,* poultry, or cooked dry beans or peas (all of appropriate consistency), *or* ½–1½ oz. cheese *or* 1–3 oz. cottage cheese *or* 1 egg yolk (introduce at 11 months of age)
	SUPPLEMENT SNACK	
4–6 fluid oz. breast milk or iron-fortified formula	4–6 fluid oz. breast milk or iron-fortified formula	2–4 fluid oz. breast milk, iron-fortified formula, or whole cow's milk, *or* 2 oz. full-strength fruit juice
		0–½ slice hard toast or 0–2 crackers or teething biscuits (optional) suitable for infants, made from whole-grain or enriched flour

Note—On the infant's arrival at the facility, the caregiver must ascertain what foods and/or formula the infant was fed at home in order to determine the infant's nutritional needs.

* Lean meat is beef, pork, or veal without visible fat. Luncheon meats and frankfurters are high in fat and are *not* considered lean meat.

Figure 13–1

Food components for infants

Source: Caring for Our Children: National Health and Safety Performance Standards (Washington, DC, and Elk Grove Village, IL: American Public Health Association and American Academy of Pediatrics, 1992), p. 352. Copyright 1992 by the American Public Health Association and the American Academy of Pediatrics. Reprinted with permission.

Foods for Children Ages 1 to 12	Ages 1–3	Ages 3–6	Ages 6–12
Breakfast			
Milk	1/2 cup	3/4 cup	1 cup
Juice or fruit or vegetable	1/4 cup	1/2 cup	1/2 cup
Bread or bread alternate	1/2 slice	1/2 slice	1 slice
including cereal, cold dry	1/4 cup or 1/3 ounce	1/3 cup or 1/2 ounce	3/4 cup or 1 ounce
or cereal, hot cooked	1/4 cup	1/4 cup	1/2 cup
Snack (supplement) Select 2 out of the 4 components:			
Milk	1/2 cup	1/2 cup	1 cup
Juice or fruit or vegetable	1/2 cup	1/2 cup	3/4 cup
Meat or meat alternate	1/2 ounce	1/2 ounce	1 ounce
Bread or bread alternate	1/2 slice	1/2 slice	1 slice
including cereal, cold dry	1/4 cup or 1/3 ounce	1/3 cup or 1/2 ounce	3/4 cup or 1 ounce
or cereal, hot cooked	1/4 cup	1/4 cup	1/2 cup
Lunch or Supper			
Milk	1/2 cup	3/4 cup	1 cup
Meat or poultry or fish	1 ounce	1 1/2 ounces	2 ounces
or egg	1	1	1
or cheese	1 ounce	1 1/2 ounce	2 ounces
or cooked dry beans or peas	1/4 cup	3/8 cup	1/2 cup
or peanut butter	2 tablespoons	3 tablespoons	4 tablespoons
Vegetables and/or fruits (to total) (2 or more)	1/4 cup	1/2 cup	3/4 cup
Bread or bread alternate	1/2 slice	1/2 slice	1 slice

Figure 13-2
Food requirements for children ages 1 to 12
Source: U.S. Department of Agriculture, 1985.

Observing and recording what a child eats helps nutritionists determine a child's intake. Reports should be made to parents about a child's eating, perhaps with suggestions of how parents can assist the child at home. If children particularly like a food, you might share a recipe with parents for making the food at home. Stating the nutritional quality of a food to parents may help them understand why you include it on the menu. Accreditation criteria as well as national health and safety standards require that parents be informed of what food is served at the center. The national standards have the additional requirement of a nutrition education program for parents.

Cultural Diversity

Managers will need to consider the cultural diversity of their families. Some groups have strong prohibitions against eating certain foods, which must be understood and honored by food service personnel. For example, many Hindus do not eat beef, many Muslims and Jews do not eat pork, and some groups are vegetarian; thus, substitutes for meats must be available.

Some groups do not typically serve a food in their homes, but they do not object if their children learn to like that food at the center. For instance, Chinese typically do not serve raw vegetables, but their children can eat raw carrots, broccoli, or cauliflower at school if they like. People from Germany may consider corn a food only for pigs, but they often learn to enjoy corn when they come to the United States. Some groups use hot chili or fried foods, yet they can learn to taste foods that are bland or cooked without much fat. Such differences should be kept in mind as menus are planned and meals served. Guiding children to try foods they have never seen at home will take patience.

Facilities for Preparation and Serving

As manager, you may have the opportunity to plan an ideal new kitchen and serving area. Or you may have to accept space and equipment that someone else has planned or spend some time planning a renovation program. Adequate equipment and space for preparation and storage of food, dishwashing, and serving meals are essential for high-quality meal service.

Your state's minimum child care licensing standards must be applied from the very beginning, and you may be able to obtain technical assistance and consultation from your licensing agency as you make your plans. Institutional dishwashers and other equipment may be required by the licensing standards. Proper finishes for cabinets and floors make keeping up the sanitation standards rather simple. A manager is wise to visit a number of centers and food service programs and to question the dietitians, cooks, and managers regarding the latest and best arrangements or the best equipment to buy. Getting advice from persons who have recently made similar decisions or who are involved with a food service program daily may help eliminate some costly mistakes as decisions are made.

Always compare information you obtain informally from colleagues with the specific written standards for food service equipment. You can obtain this information by writing to:

National Sanitation Foundation
3475 Plymouth Road
PO Box 1468
Ann Arbor, MI 48106
or
USDA Food Safety and Inspection Service
Facilities and Equipment Sanitation Division

14th and Independence Avenues, SW
South Building, Room 1142
Washington, DC 20250

Even the most modern facilities for preparing and serving food will be of little use if you have not provided appropriate storage and the equipment and supplies needed to keep the facilities clean. Shelves where food items are stored, for example, should have hard-gloss finishes that can be easily cleaned. Crates or cans of food should never be stored on the floor. Refrigerators and freezers should be equipped with thermometers so that temperatures can be monitored.

A separate sink for hand washing must be stocked with soap and paper towels. Disposable gloves are needed for handling food. A vacuum cleaner makes it possible to pick up quickly bits of debris that might attract rodents or insects. Screens in windows let fresh air in and keep insects out. Trash cans need covers as well as disposable liners, and garbage should be stored in a covered dumpster or can and removed at least weekly to discourage proliferation of pests.

FOOD SERVICE PERSONNEL

In initially planning the food service, the manager and the board may come to some agreement on the staff that they can afford to hire to provide the service. They might hire a dietitian or nutritionist in a very large center but may decide in a smaller center to hire a dietician on a consultative basis a day or two a month to help plan menus and give advice when problems arise. Or the manager may have enough knowledge to carry out the nutritionist's role and therefore only need to hire a cook. Carefully writing a job analysis, job specification, and job description will be required (see Chapter 6 for more information on hiring staff). Food service personnel are usually responsible for the following tasks:

1. Planning menus with proper nutritional content
2. Buying foods
3. Checking in food ordered and keeping track of inventories
4. Operating and maintaining the kitchen and dining rooms
5. Maintaining high sanitation standards for all food handling and preparation, dishwashing, and garbage disposing
6. Monitoring costs, reporting to the manager, and helping make USDA reports
7. Cooperating with the teaching staff to help provide any food product learning material such as play dough or foods needed for learning projects in the classrooms
8. Preparing foods using appropriate methods that maintain nutritional quality
9. Getting to know children, their individual needs, and the appropriate guidance methods for interacting with them—especially related to eating
10. Appreciating families' needs and cultural diversity, which may affect meal service

The food service personnel who work in the kitchen will be responsible for following the menus and organizing the food, equipment, and human labor to get the meals on the table on time. Each task requires the ability to think through the steps and carry out the tasks. Once items appear on the menus, the organizing begins. The food service director must consider the feasibility of each menu in terms of equipment, utensils, and help available. For example, an oven main dish and an oven dessert may not both be feasible on the same day unless the dessert is cooked early before the main dish has to go into the oven.

Food service workers must know, or be willing to learn quickly, proper methods of cooking to preserve nutrient qualities. A reputable quantity-cooking recipe book is essential. If staff members follow the suggested methods and temperatures, the products should remain nutritious. Vegetables, for example, generally cook quickly; prolonged cooking destroys the very vitamins the vegetables are expected to provide for children.

Understanding children is desirable in food service staff members; at a minimum, they should be willing to learn about children's development, nutritional needs, and typical behaviors related to food. Ideally, food service staff will be included in all professional development activities, and nutrition education for the entire staff should include information about the ways children develop healthy eating habits and appropriate guidance techniques for helping them. No staff member should ever admonish a child for not eating, cajole a child to entice him or her to eat, or talk across the child as though he or she were not present. For help with nutritional questions, managers might consciously recruit a board member with a dietetics or home economics background who could be helpful and inspirational for the nutrition work your center needs to do. Teachers often need support and encouragement to plan and carry out nutrition education activities.

PREVENTION OF FOOD POISONING

Food-handling staff members must be fully aware of their responsibility in preventing food poisoning of children and staff members. An outbreak of food poisoning among children or staff can severely damage your center's reputation. Each staff member should read and understand the following quotation regarding transmission of bacteria and work to prevent contamination of food in the center. According to USDA's Food Safety and Inspection Service:

> Prevention of food poisoning becomes a matter of stopping the growth of bacteria or killing them at the proper time to prevent their causing food poisoning. Four organisms—*Staphylococcus aureus*, a large group of bacteria lumped under the general category, *Salmonella, Clostridium perfringens*, and *Clostridium botulinum*—are sources of most food poisoning cases.
>
> Salmonella bacteria occur frequently in the intestinal tracts of humans and other animals. They are shed in feces from both sources, and for that reason, a cycle of infection is always present in the environment. The organisms are found in raw meats, poultry, eggs, milk, fish, and products made from them. Other sources of the organisms are food handlers and pets, including turtles, birds, fish, dogs, and cats. Insects and rodents are also sources of the bacteria. Food contaminated by salmo-

nella bacteria does not change in taste, odor, or flavor, so the presence of the organisms is not apparent. Salmonella is killed by proper cooking.

If food containing viable salmonella bacteria is eaten, the organisms multiply rapidly in the intestine, causing headache, diarrhea, abdominal discomfort, and, occasionally, vomiting. These symptoms appear within 24 hours after eating contaminated food. Most people recover in 2 to 4 days. Children under 4, elderly people, and people weakened by disease sometimes become seriously ill. Death from the disease may occur.[4]

Other food poisoning bacteria cause similar symptoms; however, botulism can be fatal in very small doses. Therefore, home canned foods or foods from damaged or unlabeled cans should never be used.

The Food Safety and Inspection Service (FSIS) of the USDA offers guidelines and an Information Hot Line for anyone with questions ([800] 535-4555, 10 A.M. to 4 P.M. EST). The FSIS recommends the following procedures to help you maintain food purity:

1. Maintain extra care with food handlers' personal cleanliness—wash hands *with soap* after using the toilet, wear clean clothing and aprons, and keep hair pinned back.
2. Keep utensils clean. Do not use wooden cutting boards.
3. Cook foods thoroughly; especially, cook high-protein foods, beef, and chicken to well-done stage. Serve foods hot.
4. Avoid keeping food at room temperature. Cool or freeze foods promptly after preparation to prevent the multiplication of all bacteria.
5. Make one or two small pans of an item rather than a very large one; then, you can put out a small amount toward the end of a meal to take care of seconds, rather than having a large amount exposed to contamination and incubating the bacteria. Only uncut casseroles can be served another day.
6. Reheat thoroughly all stored foods to destroy bacteria. Use a thermometer.
7. Do not taste partially cooked foods for seasoning.

As the manager of a child development center, you will be responsible for making sure that staff understand the importance of good hygiene practices. Posting signs over sinks and in lavoratories may help remind some to wash their hands. Simple training exercises can be conducted at staff meetings to emphasize the importance of thorough hand-washing practices. The experiment with petroleum jelly, described in Chapter 12, can convince skeptical members of the value of soap and water.

Staff should never work with food if they have symptoms of illness such as diarrhea or vomiting, or cuts or sores on their skin that cannot be covered with disposable gloves. The use of disposable gloves should not be allowed to lull staff into laxness about washing their hands. Ideally, staff responsible for changing diapers should not also be responsible for preparing food. In smaller facilities, where such double duty might be unavoidable, staff members must be even more

---

[4] U.S. Department of Agriculture, *Food-Borne Bacterial Poisoning* (Washington, DC: Author, 1985), pp. 1–4.

scrupulous about washing their hands with soap and running water each time they move from caregiving to food preparation.

Perhaps one way to help you and your staff conceptualize the sanitation aspects of your center's food service would be to ask yourselves if you would feel comfortable eating in a restaurant whose kitchen resembled yours. Sometimes in their effort to create a homelike atmosphere, child care providers forget that they are feeding a public clientele and need to exercise every precaution to protect the health and safety of their "customers."

MENU PLANNING

Infant Formula and Food

Requirements for infant feeding are noted in Figure 13–1. Licensing standards give important details for managing the feeding of infants. Each baby's needs are very special and likely to be very different from those of the baby in the next crib. The proper amount and kind of formula is essential to the health and well-being of the infants. Some centers provide infant formula, and some rely on the parents to bring it. In either case it must be handled properly. That means that each bottle must contain only enough for one feeding, be labeled with the child's name and date, stored in the refrigerator. Formula left in a bottle after feeding should be discarded.

Infant caregivers should hold the baby warmly while giving the bottle. One reason for the three- or four-to-one infant-adult ratio recommended in infant centers is this need for the babies to have one-to-one contact with the same caregiver. Security and trust are fostered in both infants and parents by this arrangement. Many personal interactions between an infant and its caregiver should occur during the day. In addition to meeting psychological needs, holding babies while feeding them avoids choking, ear infections, and dental caries that can result when babies are put to bed with bottles in their mouths.

Breast-feeding mothers are encouraged to return to the center to feed their infants or to leave expressed breast milk in the bottle for the caregiver to give. Because of the special benefits for infants of being breast fed, even for a few months, the center should assist mothers who desire to feed their infants in this way. One way to do this is to provide a comfortable rocking chair in a quiet, private room or corner so mother and baby can enjoy a relaxing time together. If a mother is planning to leave expressed milk for her baby, you might want to recommend that she try using the bottle at home a few times before you try it at the center. That way the baby will not have to adapt to too many changes all at once.

Of course, refrigerate breast milk as you do any milk. It can be stored in the refrigerator for up to 48 hours, in the freezer for 2 weeks. Frozen breast milk should be thawed in the refrigerator. Warm all baby bottles by putting them in pans of hot (not boiling) water for 5 minutes. Never use the microwave because it heats foods unevenly, and even a bottle that feels lukewarm can contain liquids that will scald a baby's mouth.

Solid foods are started around the 6th month and in consultation with the child's parents. Introduce foods one at a time and carefully observe the child for

---

XYZ Child Development Center

Caregiver _____

Baby's Name _____ Date _____

Food: Times for bottle _____

         New foods _____

         Unusual _____

Sleeping: A.M. _____ P.M. _____

         Unusual _____

Bowel Movements _____

         Unusual _____

New Motor Skills _____

New Words _____

Other _____

Note: Parents, please feel free to discuss any item with your baby's caregiver.

Figure 13–3
Sample report to parents

possible allergic reactions before introducing another food. Since babies have grown accustomed to using a different type of tongue movement for sucking, they may need some time to learn the finer points of taking and swallowing food from a spoon. Pushing food out of the mouth with the tongue may be part of this effort and not necessarily a sign of dislike. Be alert for possible choking.

All foods should be of high quality, unsalted, and kept covered and fresh. Never feed a child directly from a jar of baby food. The saliva on the spoon can carry bacteria that will multiply in the jar and cause illness the next time you use it. Use a clean spoon to place a small amount of food in a clean dish for each feeding—and for each baby you might be feeding at one time. Replace the cover on the jar and refrigerate it immediately. Discard any food left in the dishes at the end of the feeding.

At about 6 months of age, the infant will begin self-feeding and will enjoy a graham cracker while sitting in the feeding table. It is the beginning of independence! Make sure that you do not provide foods that can cause choking: avoid grapes, pretzels, popcorn. Slice hot dogs in half lengthwise before cutting them into small chunks.

Your center will usually be required to keep records on individual infants showing food intake, sleeping patterns, bowel movements, and developmental milestones. Copies of such reports should be sent home with parents daily. Parents must also be encouraged to report to the center staff any unusual changes in their baby's food intake, sleeping patterns, or bowel movements. A sample report form appears in Figure 13–3.

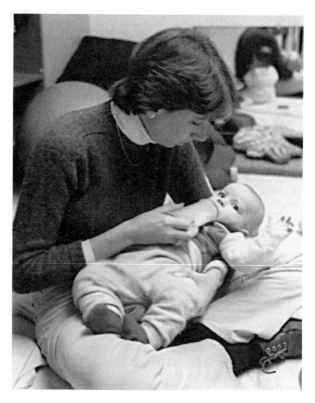

Infants are always held while being fed, to give each baby security and individual attention. University of Missouri Child Development Laboratory, Columbia

Meals and Snacks

Menus of meals and snacks served to children in group care must be planned to meet daily nutritional standards. Foods planned should be colorful and interesting in texture and flavor. The USDA publishes nutritional standards and other helpful meal planning information for centers and for families.[5] Figure 13–2 shows the nutritional standards for children ages 1 to 12 years.

When developing menus for meals and snacks, the USDA daily nutritional standards should be followed (see Figure 13–4 for sample menus that follow these standards). While you may remember "the four basic food groups" from your elementary school days, the USDA and the Department of Health and Human Services have recently updated the way we conceptualize a balanced diet. "The Food Guide Pyramid" takes into account the proportion as well as variety of foods that

---

[5] These materials are available from the Child Care Food Program, U.S. Department of Agriculture, Washington, DC 20250, and from your local Cooperative Extension Service or land-grant university's nutrition department. Computer programs are also available to help you manage all aspects of your food service program: menu planning, shopping lists, recipe analysis for cost and nutritional content, food inventory. Write to The Center for Science in the Public Interest, 1875 Connecticut Ave., NW, No. 300, Washington, DC 20009. See *Texas Child Care* 19:1 (Summer 1995), p. 15, for more information.

Milk Irish stew Buttered carrot slices Parsley garnish Lime Leprechaun cottage cheese mold Hot rolls Shamrock cookies Butter/margarine	Milk Fish sticks Stewed tomatoes Cabbage slaw Old fashioned bread pudding with lemon sauce	Milk Roast pork Candied yams Chopped buttered spinach Hot cinnamon apple-sauce Cornbread Butter/margarine	Milk Macaroni and cheese casserole Butter green beans Celery sticks Chilled fruit mix Brown bread Butter/margarine	Milk Baked meat loaf Diced beets Bread Vanilla ice cream with peach slices Butter/margarine
Milk Porcupine meat balls in gravy Green beans/carrot slices Bread Cranberry crunch Chocolate chip pudding Butter/margarine	Milk Baked chicken legs Mashed potatoes Emerald salad Biscuit Honey Butter/Margarine	Milk Bologna and cheese sandwich Scalloped potatoes Fresh fruit platter Apple wedges, grapes, cherry tomatoes Split pea soup	Milk Hearty bean & frank bake Zucchini squash Hot rolls Orange gelatin with fruit Butter/margarine	Milk Turkey and ham sandwich Buttered cauliflower Hot cinnamon applesauce with cherry
Milk Tacos/lettuce/meat Green beans Ice cream	Milk Braised beef liver Orange beets Buttered corn Cinnamon muffin Butter/margarine	Milk Spaghetti with ground beef Tomato sauce Bread sticks Seedless grapes	Milk Chicken salad sandwich French fries Fresh vegetable relishes Chocolate chip cookie	Milk Barbecue beef on bun Peas Cole slaw Banana cake

Figure 13–4

Cycle menus for lunches—15 days

Source: Menus provided by Dr. Jean McFadden, dietitian, Michigan State University, Lansing. Requirements for lunch include fluid milk, meat or alternate, vegetables or fruit (two servings), and bread or equivalent. Other food is optional. See Figure 13–2 for details on requirements.

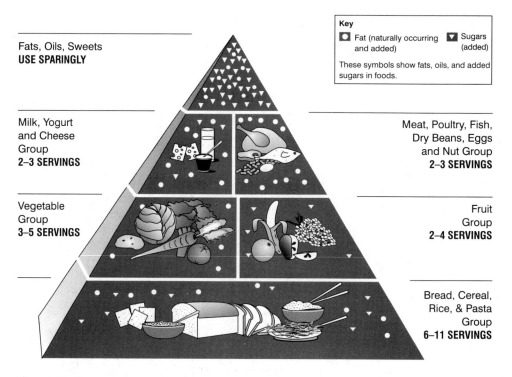

Figure 13–5
Food Guide Pyramid: A guide to daily food choices
Source: U.S. Department of Agriculture, 1992.

constitute a healthy diet (see Figure 13–5). The grain group forms the base of the pyramid and should provide the highest number of servings in the daily diet. Next comes the fruit and vegetable section, which provides vitamins, minerals, and fiber with few calories. Next is the group that provides protein iron and calcium: meats, poultry, fish, dairy products, nuts, and beans. The tip of the pyramid represents the fats and sweets—lots of calories but few nutrients—which should be used very sparingly. A healthy diet contains the appropriate number of servings from each section of the pyramid each day.

Several considerations can guide the choices of foods. As mentioned earlier, the combination of foods must fit the quantity and type of equipment available. Children's likes should also guide menu planning. Though it is highly desirable to introduce children to new foods, it helps their transition from home to school to be served some familiar foods. Foods from various ethnic groups are often desirable for this reason.[6] All children can learn to enjoy foods from a variety of ethnic groups.

---

[6] See Jeannette B. Endres and Robert E. Rockwell, *Food, Nutrition, and the Young Child* (Upper Saddle River, NJ: Merrill/Prentice Hall, 1990), Chapter 6, for suggestions for ethnic foods in meals and snacks.

Milk	Milk	Hot chocolate	Milk	Hot chocolate
Applesauce	Pineapple	Stewed prunes	Baked apples	Orange juice
Hot biscuits	Cinnamon rolls	Toast	Grits	Oatmeal
Milk	Milk	Milk	Milk	Milk
Apple juice	Grapes	Grape juice	Orange slices	Apples
Toast	Rice w/butter	Pancakes, butter/	Cinnamon roll	Grits
Boiled egg		syrup		
Hot chocolate	Milk	Milk	Milk	Milk
Sliced peaches	Pineapple juice	Prune juice	Orange juice	Blueberries
Cinnamon toast	Toast w/cheese	Cream of Wheat	Oatmeal cooked	Waffles
		cooked in milk	in milk	

Figure 13–6

Cycle menus for breakfast—15 days

Source: Menus provided by Dr. Jean McFadden, dietitian, Michigan State University, Lansing.
Requirements for breakfast include milk; juice, fruit, or vegetable; and bread or bread alternate,
including cereal. See Figure 13–2 for details on requirements.

Cycle menus provide a shortcut to menu planning. The cycles are often a 15-
or 20-day sequence of menus repeated throughout a season with minimum
changes. New cycles can be planned for a new season. Once checked by the
dietitian, the combinations should not be changed without checking the nutritional content of the substitute food. To keep a balanced diet, it may be better to
substitute a whole day's menu if you have a shortage of some crucial item. See
Figure 13–4 for sample cycle lunch menus, Figure 13–6 for sample cycle breakfast
menus, and Figure 13–7 for sample snack menus.

Milk	Orange juice	Applesauce	Milk	Milk
Banana nut bread	Cheese and	Zucchini bread	Peanut butter	Raisin cookies
	crackers		sandwiches	
Carrot	Pineapple	Grape juice	Milk	Milk
Oatmeal cookie	Triscuit	Toast strips	Corn muffin	Celery with
				peanut butter
Mixed fruit	Grapefruit juice	Bananas	Milk	Apple butter
Corn Chex	Cookies	Cookies	Potato bread	Peanut butter
				cookies

Figure 13–7

Cycle menus for midmorning or midafternoon snack—15 days

Source: Menus provided by Dr. Jean McFadden, dietitian, Michigan State University, Lansing.
Requirements: Select two of these four components: Milk; juice, fruit, or vegetable; meat or meat
alternate; bread or bread alternate, including cereal. See Figure 13–2 for details on requirements.

Good nutritional practice requires counting the dessert in the recommended daily allowance (RDA). Dessert is not planned as a reward for a clean plate, nor should it be withheld as punishment or used as reinforcement in any way. In fact, research has demonstrated that children who receive food as a reward for eating another food, increase their preference for the "reward" food and learn to dislike the food they were rewarded for eating.[7]

Children who have been allowed to follow their own body's signals have been shown to be able to adjust their intake of food to meet their caloric needs. Since these needs will vary from day to day, and since adult interference reduces children's capacity to recognize their own bodily signals, adults should not be concerned or call attention to the fact if a child happens not to eat very much at any given meal.[8] One good reason for serving family-style is that you can allow children to serve themselves second helpings. This approach helps children learn to make their own decisions. It will help to make the serving bowls small enough for children to manipulate, thereby reducing the risk of contaminating large quantities of food should a child lick a serving spoon, for example, or handle all the toast on the plate. Adults who sit and eat with small groups of children can provide the needed supervision so that centers can meet socialization goals without sacrificing sanitation.

Increasingly, nutritionists are questioning the need to give supplementary vitamins to children who receive well-rounded diets. Excessive vitamin supplements may be hazardous. Vitamin D supplement is being questioned, especially because it is added to many foods. Children can get enough Vitamin D by spending a few minutes in the sunshine a few times a week and never need supplements. Managers should watch for more developments in this regard in order to make decisions and advise parents regarding supplementary vitamins.

Managers should feel free to consult the home economist who is part of the Cooperative Extension Service in the local county. This service is typically paid for by local, state, and federal funds. The home economist is backed up by nutrition specialists at each state's land-grant university. Other services may be available from the state department of education. These departments have been assuming responsibility for assisting with the federal government's food programs in cooperation with the USDA.

Vegetarian Diets

Nutritionists are concerned about vegetarian diets, because giving young children enough complete and tasty protein without giving them meat, poultry, or fish requires concerted attention. Centers enrolling vegetarian children must give special attention to their dietary need for protein.

A growing child needs protein for growing, which in part means building a mass of muscle tissue that is composed largely of protein. Milk, cheese, egg, whole-grain cereals, dry beans, soy products, and peanut butter are the protein foods that appear in vegetarian diets.

---

[7] Birch et al., "Children's Eating: The Development of Food-Acceptance Patterns," p. 74.
[8] Birch et al., "Children's Eating: The Development of Food-Acceptance Patterns," p. 77.

Energy Foods

Children need lots of energy for their activities and should not be highly restricted from eating energy foods containing fat and carbohydrates. Concentrated sweet desserts and drinks are typically avoided in menu planning because children will often prefer them to milk and the vitamin-rich fruits and vegetables that are better for them.

Prescription Diets

Of course, centers must be cooperative when children have allergies or other special dietary needs. Managers can develop a policy that requires the parents to bring a physician's request for a diet, just as they would ask for a prescription for medication. This policy keeps managers from being part of a diet fad and leaves the physician responsible. Some parents who are highly conscious about dieting for themselves are minimally informed about nutrition and could jeopardize their child's health through diet restrictions. Where diet restrictions may make sense for sedentary or weight-conscious adults, they generally do not make sense for active, growing children. Managers will want to weigh and measure children's growth from time to time, especially children on restricted diets.

SEATING AND SERVING CHILDREN

Large lunchroom situations are frustrating for young children. They do better in small-table settings with an adult and about four other children. Planning children's places at the meal tables is necessary so that children who need help can be located where an adult can reach them. It is also desirable to locate the independent eaters among the more dependent ones. Children learn from peer role models. Name cards or a regular seat at the tables assure each child that he or she is planned for and has a place to sit.

The teacher sitting with a small group will serve children family-style and grow accustomed to each child's likes and dislikes. Volunteers can be very helpful at mealtimes to help keep the adult-child ratio appropriate. School-age children and high school students could be pressed into service to be helpers at the young children's tables. They learn a lot about children and can be a big help at the same time. The server gives each child a serving to get the eating started. Seconds can be served by the children themselves. They often eat more when they can serve themselves. Adults and children alike should keep servings small until it is known that a child likes a food very much. A small pitcher that will hold just a cup of milk that the children can pour alone will entice many of them to drink "seconds." Adults should remember that children like lukewarm food—not very hot or cold—and not be bothered when the soup gets cold and the ice cream gets mushy. That is the way most children like soup and ice cream!

Except for infants who are not yet ready to feed themselves, a child should be encouraged to become self-sufficient. Even infants may enjoy a cracker to nibble on. Bite-size pieces of meat or other foods are easier for small fingers to grasp.

Remember that circles of hot dogs should not be served to children because of a danger of choking. Have the hot dogs sliced lengthwise, then cut in two. As children get a little older, they can manage small spoons and forks. A stick of toast used as a pusher is useful for getting food onto their spoon. Rather than resorting to the fingers, children can be reminded to "Use your toast pusher." Children should be taught to keep foods on their plate rather than strewing them around the table.

Observing other children independently serving themselves and eating helps encourage a more dependent child to assume the same responsibility. Parents who visit at lunchtime are often very amazed at the maturity of their own child who "acts like a baby at home!" Teachers and caregivers should avoid bribing or cajoling a child to eat. If the child is too tired to eat, it may be helpful to schedule a resting time just before mealtime or to eat a little bit earlier.

Young children have quite a bit of concentrating to do as they eat, and after a busy morning they usually are hungry. However, as they grow in independence, they become more sociable during meals. They can talk about food they may have helped prepare, milk making their teeth grow, or the source of a food they are eating. The conversations should be kept low, just among those at one table without between-table conversations, to reduce noise levels. But children should never be told to "Be quiet and eat," if a pleasant mealtime atmosphere is desired. Caregivers should take care not to detract from the pleasure of the occasion in their zeal to make it a learning experience for children.

Parents, board members, and others can be invited to eat with children when convenient. Having a parent drop by is a very nice surprise for a child, and managers should make efforts to make it happen. You can avoid making children whose parents cannot come at lunchtime feel left out by extending the invitation to breakfast or snack as well. Adults will learn to appreciate their child's eating habits as they see him or her functioning with other children. They may also gain additional respect for the teaching staff as they realize how much effort and organization a simple meal requires. If you are encouraging children to invite parents for meals, remember that children with divorced parents may want to invite each parent on a different day. Or the child can be encouraged to invite a grandparent, aunt, or special family friend. A child should be helped to feel included in a special event even if a parent cannot come.

Children should be encouraged to sit at the table until they have finished eating, carry their plate to a serving cart for their dessert, and remove their dishes when finished. If a child wants to get up and down frequently, he or she may not be hungry and should be excused to go to the toilet and get ready for nap time. Of course, an adult would need to be ready to guide the child in the next steps toward bathroom and nap room. The person responsible for other children at the table should not have to leave them to tend to a child who is ready to leave early.

It can be tiring for teachers and aides who have worked all morning with children also to eat their lunch with them. Yet, children really do better at eating and feeding themselves if these familiar people guide their mealtime. Managers and food service staff must be aware of teachers' needs and be sure that they get adequate food as they supervise children's mealtimes. With adequate support people in the dining room, the teacher who eats with the children will not have to jump up and get items or tend to emergencies—interruptions that interfere with a teacher's resting and eating an adequate meal.

PLANNING THE MIDMORNING OR MIDAFTERNOON SNACK

Snacks should be considered a nutrition break to help restore children's energy after a busy period of play. Sitting at the table for a short time will rest the children. Snack time is usually a social time of day, with conversation about activities the children have been involved in. Only highly nutritious foods should be served. The emphasis should be on vegetables, fruits, cereal, and protein foods. Foods with high sugar content should be avoided. As you may note, in Figure 13–2 the snack requirement calls for any two of the four food categories: (a) milk, (b) juice or fruit, or vegetable, (c) meat or meat alternate, or (d) bread or cereal. For example, milk and apples, juice and sandwiches, or carrots and meat sticks all would be adequate snacks. Excellent arguments can be made for using milk as a beverage a large portion of the time. Seeing their friends drink milk often helps some children learn to drink this highly nutritious and essential food.

Children need plenty of drinking water throughout the day. A small cup of water is preferred by younger children, and older children can usually manage a drinking fountain. Many do not like ice water.[9]

FOOD AND CURRICULUM

Food provides more than just nourishment for the body. Because it involves so many sensory modalities and offers such immediate gratification, it is very engaging for young children. It also provides a rich source of topics to investigate because it is so much a part of daily life, culture, and commerce. Projects and investigations concerning food production, distribution, and preparation help children become aware of all aspects of the human ecological system, providing what Katz and Chard call "horizontal relevance"—connections between school life and life in the everyday world outside.[10]

Food is integrally bound up with culture, making it an excellent means of cultivating an appreciation for diversity. Breads and noodles, for example, appear in many guises in various cultures of the world, and often the forms these items take are associated with particular stories or beliefs. Young children could begin by thinking about all the forms of bread they have eaten and eventually be helped to branch out into the breads of other cultures.[11] Such a study would have the addi-

---

[9] For suggestions for food projects that make good snacks, see Verna Hildebrand, *Introduction to Early Childhood Education* (Upper Saddle River, NJ: Prentice Hall, 1991), pp. 441–465.

[10] Lilian Katz and Sylvia Chard, *Engaging Children's Minds: The Project Approach* (Norwood, NJ: Ablex, 1989), p. 4.

[11] See Anne Mitchell and Judy David (eds.), *Explorations with Young Children: A Curriculum Guide from the Bank Street College of Education* (Mt. Rainier, MD: Gryphon House, 1992).

Time for snacks is handled in a variety of ways, such as this booth designed to "sell" cookies and juice.
Kansas State University Child Development Laboratory, Manhattan

tional advantage of avoiding a "tourist" approach in which children are exposed only to exotic aspects of other cultures.

DECISIONS, DECISIONS . . .

 List the pros and cons of fingerpainting with chocolate pudding as an art activity for 2-year-olds. Would the list be the same if you considered the activity for 4-year-olds?

In thinking about learning goals for young children in connection with food, teachers might consider the four categories of learning goals suggested by Katz and Chard:

1. Knowledge (factual information; content)
2. Skills (actions that can be taught and practiced)
3. Dispositions (mental habits or tendencies, such as curiosity, creativity)
4. Feelings (emotional states, such a feeling of belonging or competence)[12]

Thus, in the realm of knowledge, we might want children to know things about various foods, such as their names, sources, or value for growing healthy bodies;

---

[12]Katz and Chard, *Engaging Children's Minds*, pp. 20–41.

or we might want them to know things in general that they can learn through the medium of food, such as colors, shapes, size comparisons, or the meaning of print labels. With regard to skills, we expect children as they become progressively more mature, to be able to drink from a cup; eat finger foods; use spoons, forks, and simple food preparation tools; chew with their mouths closed; and observe the table manners appropriate to their culture. We want to cultivate a disposition in children to eat healthy foods and only as much as they need to satisfy hunger. Finally, we want to nourish feelings of belonging to a culture, competence at being able to meet one's own needs, and friendliness toward meal companions.

If we keep these aims in mind, as well as what we know about the development of children's cognitive abilities and food acceptance patterns, we can avoid guidance techniques that work at cross purposes to our aims. For example, the lessons about "the four food groups," favored by so many teachers, are probably ineffective for two reasons. First, the content is too abstract for young children really to comprehend which foods go together. They are much more likely to categorize food in ways that are personally meaningful: liked and disliked foods, for example, or foods at home and foods at restaurants. One classification scheme to be avoided is "good" and "bad" foods. Most nutritionists counsel that there are no bad foods and that the important thing is balance among all the foods we eat. Second, the ultimate goal of such lessons probably lies more in the realm of dispositions than of knowledge. After all, how many adults do you know who are perfectly capable of reciting all the components of the food pyramid but subsist on a diet of fast-food sandwiches and soft drinks?

DECISIONS, DECISIONS . . .

 Keep a record of everything you eat for 1 week. Compare your findings with the recommendations in the Food Guide Pyramid in Figure 13–5. Are there one or more categories in which you consume more or less than the recommended number of servings?

According to Birch et al., research has shown that the best way to cultivate a disposition toward healthy eating habits and openness to new food experiences is by providing "children with a variety of healthful foods in a positive social environment and then allowing children the freedom to eat what they wish."[13] Children also seem more disposed to eat foods that they have helped prepare, so wise managers include frequent opportunities for children to help peel carrots for snack, for example, or slice and assemble fruit kabobs. Modeling is another factor: children who think they do not like a food are often persuaded to try it when they see another child enjoying it. On the other hand, adults who encourage children to take a bite of green beans, when they do not eat any themselves, will probably meet with little success.

---

[13] Birch et al., "Children's Eating: The Development of Food-Acceptance Patterns," p. 78.

DECISIONS, DECISIONS . . .

Is there a particular food that you eat too much of? Or one that you intensely dislike? Think about your childhood experiences with that food. Can you see any connection between those experiences and your attitude toward that food today? Discuss your conclusions with your classmates.

Field trips to the dairy, orchard, or grocery store are all concrete ways for children to gain knowledge about the food they eat. Teachers need to prepare the children for such visits by encouraging them to think of questions they want to have answered and then giving them plenty of time at the site to explore. It helps to prepare the people you will be visiting so they have an idea of what to tell children. One group of 4-year-olds paid little attention as the orchard owner told their teacher and parents all about his modern farming methods, but they became very excited when the teacher asked the age of a particular row of young trees and was told they were 4 years old—"just like us!" The conversations at the snack table as they enjoyed their apple slices the next day contained many references to the 4-year-old trees.

Volunteers and visitors can help you meet many nutrition-related goals. Parents might make family or ethnic specialties for the children or, better yet, come in and make them with a small group of children. Older children can come in to help with meal service and eat with the children so that more of them can have individual attention. Boy or Girl Scout groups, 4-H Clubs, and home economics classes all provide potential sources of volunteers to share information or conduct food-related activities. A dentist or hygienist could demonstrate toothbrushing techniques. The possibilities are limited only by your own creativity.

COMMUNICATING WITH PARENTS ON FOOD MATTERS

Meeting children's food needs is of primary concern to parents. The center should encourage them to report on any special problems their child has or might have as a result of some home experience. Their report could include such events as a digestive upset in the night or having a relative in for a big supper the night before, which kept the child eating fancy food at all hours. Either episode may make a significant impact on the child's food intake the next day.

Parents like to know what children are eating at school to avoid duplicating the menu at home in the evening and getting a negative response from the family members. Menus can be posted where parents can see them as they drop off or pick up the child. The local paper or radio in some communities reports the public school menus for parents' benefit. Some schools report to parents exactly what their child ate, using a daily checksheet.

When a child is on a special diet or allergic to certain foods, such information should be given in detail to the food service staff and posted where a substitute cook can easily find it. Older children soon realize what foods they can or cannot have, but younger children have to be watched closely. Some very much like the food that they must leave out of their diet for medical reasons. Some children may be unable to eat certain foods for religious or philosophical reasons. Food service staff thus have another item to keep track of. When the teacher eating with these children understands their special problem, it is easier to explain factually each child's special case to the other children when they wonder why the child is getting a special dish.

MONITORING AND CONTROLLING FOOD PROGRAMS

Monitoring the menus, food shopping lists, specials in the supermarkets, and the center's storage systems will help managers get the most food service for their food dollars. To prevent food service personnel from intentionally mixing up too much food, a policy of not allowing anyone to take leftover food home is essential. Keeping freezers and storerooms locked is advisable. A large inventory is costly when interest rates are high; thus, keeping an inventory beyond reasonable amounts for emergencies is a questionable practice. Managers have found it essential to count the cans in cases of foods delivered, after some boxes were found to be short.

Be sure to check on the hygiene habits of staff members who in any way handle or serve food to be sure they are washing their hands frequently with soap to help prevent transmission of bacteria.

Besides costs, the nutritional content of meals should be regularly checked by the dietitian. This measure is essential for federally funded programs.

Staff need to watch the amount of food left on plates as children finish their meal. Occasionally the waste can be explained by its being a new food or a different recipe, but it is still wasted food. You should plan to serve that food in smaller quantities until children develop a taste for it through repeated exposure.

Parents may give you helpful feedback by the questions they ask and the recipes they request after their children report to them about the foods they are eating at school.

Managers may use the evaluation form in Figure 13–8 to keep check on the food system.

CONCLUSION

Meeting children's food needs requires all steps in the managerial process—planning, organizing, staffing, leading, and controlling. In full-day programs, meal service is essential. In short-day programs, a midmorning or midafternoon snack of highly nutritious foods is recommended. Licensing and accreditation standards apply to food service. Because of the integrated, holistic nature of young children's thinking and learning, food is viewed as part of the curriculum. Whether they are making a special snack as a science experience or enjoying a healthy lunch with their friends, children at the center are acquiring knowledge,

Rating Scale:

4—Very Satisfactory	2—Unsatisfactory
3—Satisfactory	1—Very Unsatisfactory

Personnel

( ) 1. Dietitian or home economist plans menus with adequate nutritional quality?

( ) 2. Food service director takes adequate leadership to ensure high-quality service?

( ) 3. Food service assistants are trained to do their jobs adequately?

( ) 4. Food service personnel are appropriately clean, with hair nets and clean aprons, and hands washed with soap?

( ) 5. Food service personnel are at work on time?

( ) 6. Food service personnel have required health checks?

Facilities

( ) 7. Is the food service space adequate in size?

( ) 8. Is the food service equipment operating appropriately?

( ) 9. Is the storage space adequate in the food service area?

( ) 10. Is the refrigeration space adequate?

( ) 11. Personnel keep the kitchen, appliances, and counter spotless?

( ) 12. Children's chairs and tables are adequate in number and size?

( ) 13. Dishes, utensils, and glasses are safe and adequate in number?

( ) 14. Appropriate dishwashing procedures are used?

Menu Planning

( ) 15. Menus for meals meet minimum USDA standards?

( ) 16. Menus for snacks meet minimum USDA standards?

( ) 17. Records for federal funding are kept daily (if applicable)?

( ) 18. Are cycle menus being used appropriately?

( ) 19. Are menus posted for parents and others to read?

( ) 20. Are copies of menus made available to parents?

( ) 21. Are records of individual children's intake recorded?

( ) 22. Are children's prescriptions for special diets posted where a substitute cook could easily find them?

Preparation and Service

( ) 23. Do food service personnel know appropriate cooking methods for each type of food?

Figure 13–8
Food service monitoring guide

( ) 24.	Is food served in a very sanitary manner?

( ) 25.	Is food served on time?

( ) 26.	Is food service well organized, with each worker knowing required tasks and doing them well?

( ) 27.	Is food regularly served family-style?

( ) 28.	Is adequate attention given to individual children's needs?

( ) 29.	Does each teacher who sits with children have good rapport with the group of children?

( ) 30.	Does each teacher get enough to eat?

( ) 31.	Is a worker ready to take care of emergencies so the teacher does not have to leave the table?

( ) 32.	Are procedures known to children who have been in attendance for a while?

Interpersonal Climate

( ) 33.	Do children seem to be happy and enjoying the meals?

( ) 34.	Are voices quiet and pleasant?

( ) 35.	Do children seem adequately rested to facilitate eating?

( ) 36.	Are children regularly given a quiet restful period just prior to meal-time?

( ) 37.	Are parents invited to attend a meal periodically?

Nutrition Education

( ) 38.	Do teachers tell children about foods that are good for them?

( ) 39.	Do children demonstrate an interest in foods?

( ) 40.	Are food projects offered in the curriculum?

( ) 41.	Are parents informed about food projects?

Budgetary Matters

( ) 42.	Is cost-consciousness adequate among food service staff?

( ) 43.	Is the amount of wasted food reasonable?

( ) 44.	Is leftover food appropriately stored and utilized?

( ) 45.	Does the food service staff plan adequately to avoid running out of needed commodities, calling for quick trips for supplies?

( ) 46.	Are orders placed and deliveries made on time?

( ) 47.	Are deliveries checked for correct quantities?

( ) 48.	Is petty cash disbursement monitored?

Figure 13–8, *continued*

skills, dispositions, and feelings related to healthy nutrition. Careful monitoring of expense, waste, and leftovers is essential to get the most nutrition for the food dollar in the child development center. Federal subsidies can help centers meet food expenses, if they serve 25% or more needy children and complete the required records and reports.

APPLICATIONS

1. Refer to Chapter 6, Figure 6–3, which is a job analysis for a cook in a child development center.
   a. Evaluate this job analysis on the basis of information in Chapter 13.
   b. Write a job description for a child development center cook.
   c. Write a job specification for a cook in a child development center. (See Figure 6–5 for sample job specification.)
2. Write a 15-day cycle of menus for lunches based on requirements listed in Figure 13–2.
3. Write a 15-day cycle of menus for snacks based on requirements listed in Figure 13–2.
4. Brainstorm with your classmates all the things that children might know or like to find out about bread. Create a concept web showing how these ideas are related to each other.
5. Make a list of experiences (classroom activities, field trips, visitors, family participation activities) that could help children explore the ideas in the concept web created in number 4.
6. Copy Figure 13–8 ("Food Service Monitoring Guide"). Visit a children's program where food is being served.
   a. Confer with the head of food service and check against Figure 13–8 as you observe the food service.
   b. Write an essay summarizing your observation of the food service.
   c. Evaluate Figure 13–8 as a useful tool for monitoring food service.
7. Add information related to food service and meal planning to your management notebook.

STUDY QUESTIONS

1. State the goals for each child's food habits and education.
2. What are the sources of standards for meal service in a children's center?
3. What criteria are used for a child care center to receive federal funds for meals and snacks?
4. Read your state's licensing rules and list rules for food service you find there. Do any appear that are not mentioned in this chapter? Discuss.
5. Discuss cultural diversity and tell how it can be handled comfortably in a center with several cultures represented.
6. State recommendations for:

     a. feeding infants,

     b. feeding 2- to 5-year-olds, and

     c. seating children at meals.

7. Why is it recommended to get a doctor's prescription if parents want to put children on a diet?

8. Explain the concept of cycle menus. Describe a sample cycle menu.

9. Explain the role of personal hygiene of employees in the prevention of the spread of harmful bacteria through food.

10. List 10 tasks that food service personnel are responsible for in a full-day children's center.

11. List the suggested ways that the center can:

     a. inform parents about their child's eating habits and

     b. enlist parents' help in their child's nutrition education.

SUGGESTED READINGS

American Academy of Pediatrics. *Pediatric Nutrition Handbook.* Elk Grove Village, IL: Author, 1985.

Aronson, Susan. "Early Childhood Safety Checklist #3: Kitchen and Food Preparation and Storage Areas." *Child Care Information Exchange* 95 (January/February 1994), pp. 78-79.

Birch, Leann, Susan L. Johnson, and Jennifer Fisher. "Children's Eating: The Development of Food Acceptance Patterns." *Young Children* 50:2 (January 1995), pp. 71–78.

Endres, J. B., and R. E. Rockwell. *Food, Nutrition, and the Young Child,* 4th ed. Upper Saddle River, NJ: Merrill/Prentice Hall, 1994.

Hildebrand, Verna. *Guiding Young Children.* Upper Saddle River, NJ: Prentice Hall, 1990.

Hildebrand, Verna. *Introduction to Early Childhood Education.* Upper Saddle River, NJ: Prentice Hall, 1991.

"Infant Nutrition: Drinking from a Cup, Eating from a Spoon." *Texas Child Care* 18:2 (Fall 1994), pp. 12–14.

"Mastering the Recipe Rebus." *Texas Child Care* 15:4 (Spring 1992), pp. 27–31.

"Menu Plans: Maximum Nutrition for Minimum Cost." *Texas Child Care* 19:1 (Summer 1995), pp. 10–17.

Morris, Sandra L. "Supporting the Breastfeeding Relationship during Child Care: Why Is It Important?" *Young Children* 50:2 (January 1995), pp. 59–62.

Newman, Rita. "Bringing the Classroom into the Kitchen: Lessons Learned at Home." *Childhood Education* 71:2 (Winter 1994/95), pp. 107–108.

"Putting the Pyramid into Practice." *Texas Child Care* 17:4 (Spring 1994), pp. 29–31.

Rogers, Cosby S., and Sandra S. Morris. "Reducing Sugar in Children's Diets." *Young Children* 41:5 (July 1986), pp. 11–16.

Satter, Ellyn. *Child of Mine, Feeding with Love and Good Sense,* expanded ed. Palo Alto, CA: Bull, 1986.

Satter, Ellyn. *How to Get Your Kid to Eat—But Not Too Much.* Palo Alto, CA: Bull, 1987.

Shugart, G., and Mary Molt. *Food for Fifty.* Upper Saddle River, NJ: Prentice Hall, 1989.

"Too Many Cooks? No Way!" *Texas Child Care* 15:4 (Spring 1992), pp. 3–5.

U.S. Department of Agriculture. *Building for the Future: Nutrition Guidance for the Child Nutrition Programs.* (Food and Nutrition Service Publication FNS-279). Washington, DC: Author, 1992.

U.S. Department of Agriculture. *Feeding Infants—A Guide for Use in the Child Care Food Program* (Food and Nutrition Service Publication FNS-258). Washington, DC: Author, 1988.

U.S. Department of Agriculture. *Nutrition Education for Preschoolers*. Washington, DC: U.S. Government Printing Office, 1983.

U.S. Department of Health and Human Services, Office of Human Development Services, Administration for Children, Youth and Families and the Head Start Bureau. *Head Start Nutrition Education Curriculum*. Washington, DC: Author, 1988.

Wanamaker, N., K. Hearn, and S. Richarz. *More Than Graham Crackers: Nutrition Education and Food Preparation with Young Children*. Washington, DC: National Association for the Education of Young Children, 1979.

CHAPTER 14

Children's Programs: The Manager's Role

• •

The facility for your child development center is ready. The inspections have been passed. A license has been granted. The staff is in place. Children have been enrolled with all the proper forms completed. The innumerable preliminary steps have been completed. "Whew!" Managers who develop new programs often feel breathless as they move toward a grand opening. Waiting for the children's arrival is full of excitement.

CENTER ACCREDITATION

High-quality children's programs went largely unrecognized until 1984 when the National Association for the Education of Young Children (NAEYC) launched the center accreditation program.[1] Instituting accreditation gave teachers, caregivers, and managers a goal to work toward after meeting the minimum licensing standards. Because of accreditation, parents are being reassured that their child is receiving developmentally appropriate opportunities to learn cognitively, motorically, socially, and emotionally. Society at large has begun to recognize the important difference between the minimum program allowed for licensure and an accredited program. Accreditation has many aspects, as you have learned throughout other chapters.

---

[1] Sue Bredekamp (ed.), *Accreditation Criteria & Procedures of the National Academy of Early Childhood Programs* (Washington, DC: National Association for the Education of Young Children, 1991), pp. 15–25, 61–63.

Age	Adult-Child Ratio	Group Size	No. of Adults
Infants (birth–12 months)	1:4	8	2
Toddlers (12–24 months)	1:4	12	3
24–36 months	1:5	10*	2
24–48 months	1:6	12*	2
3's	1:9	18*	2
4's	1:9	18*	2
5's	1:10	20	2
6's–8's	1:12	24	2

*NAEYC accreditation allows centers to have two additional children only in cases where staff are highly qualified.

Figure 14–1
Recommended group sizes

MANAGER'S ROLE IN PROGRAM DEVELOPMENT

As with all the other aspects of your managerial role, program development calls for planning, organizing, staffing, leading, and monitoring and controlling. With your staff in place, you have already delegated responsibility for organizing each classroom to the teachers involved. You will now use your leadership skills as you focus on being supportive, facilitating staff members' work, and troubleshooting. You will be monitoring all the programs to be certain that the goals you set in your planning sessions become realities and meet high standards.

GROUP SIZE

You will have organized your child development center into appropriate size groups depending on children's ages and the requirements of the licensing authority. Experience shows that if groups are kept small, teachers can plan for and interact more effectively with children and do the extra work with parents that makes a significant difference, leading to higher-quality programs. The National Day Care Study found that a group size of eighteen for 3- and 4-year-olds was optimal. NAEYC accepts a group size of two additional children with the important proviso that the group has highly qualified staff. In addition, some add volunteers, parents, or others to assist the two teachers in the rooms and thereby enrich the children's experience. (See Appendix A for minimum state standards.) Recommendations for high-quality programs are shown in Figure 14–1.

Painting is one of the most widely used activities for children, offering them a wealth of opportunity for creativity.
Southeast Oakland Vocational Technical Child Care Center, Royal Oak, MI

PRELIMINARY ORGANIZATION

Long before opening day, your spaces for children may have been filled. Or, if you are a new center, you may start with a small group and build to licensed capacity as your reputation becomes known. Centers that operate on a school-year calendar advertise, accept, and take deposits from new enrollees in the spring for fall term openings. Centers that operate year-round continuously accept new children as enrollment fluctuates.

Interviewing parents who wish to enroll their child will take lots of time. When you are feeling overwhelmed with your other duties, it will be tempting to rush through this phase or perhaps skip it entirely and just hand a brochure and enrollment forms to inquiring parents, with directions to return the signed forms on their child's first morning at your center. But the groundwork you lay in your initial contacts can become the foundation for a long, cooperative relationship if you give it the time and attention it deserves. Parents wisely do considerable shopping around for their child development services. One director says that she will not enroll a child in her center *unless* the parent has visited at least one other center. Instead of fearing the loss of a potential customer to her competition, she wants to be sure that the parent has done some comparison shopping and selected her center over other options. Teachers must often be involved in the interviews because parents like to know which teacher will be working with their child as he or she is launched into a preprimary program. It is a big step for both the child and the parents.

Parents seeking child development services should be encouraged to come without the child to the center for a conference and a tour of the facility. They should be encouraged to sit comfortably and observe children and teachers in action. Such observation often dispels anxieties they may have or raises questions they might like to ask.

Parents usually feel better satisfied with their choice of a center when they are treated individually during the decision-making stage, rather than being part of a large group of parents. It is generally recommended that parents bring their child on a second visit to the center after their decision to enroll has been made. Then the child can become acquainted with the playrooms, playground, toilet rooms, and locker areas. Often, less confusion arises if the child visits after regular hours when he or she can try out all the equipment without distraction from other children.

Arranging a visit to the child's home before the child begins attending helps strengthen the home-school bond. A short visit is all that is needed to give the child a more secure feeling and provide the teachers with bits of information, such as about siblings, pets, and parental attitudes. This visit assists teachers in helping the child adjust to being without the family in the new environment. It is fun to snap a picture of the child to use in the child's locker, on the bulletin board, or in a book about the children.

During these initial meetings between parents and the teachers, the stage can be set for the cooperation desired throughout the child's enrollment. Information that midyear conferences are routine and that spontaneous visits and consultations are welcome can be given to parents, helping them realize that interaction with the teachers and manager is planned to be ongoing.

If your center operates on a school-year schedule, you can phase in the start-up, having a few children arrive with their parents each day until maximum capacity is achieved, perhaps by the end of the week. Phasing in helps the staff work out problems under less pressure than if large groups of children were in attendance on opening day. Children can receive more individual attention. Parents can observe their child playing with children and interacting with teachers until the child feels comfortable enough to be left at the center for an hour or longer. Managers should encourage parents in full-day programs to phase in their child gradually, too. Dropping a child at the center, then hurrying off to work the child's first day should be seriously discouraged by managers and teachers. Of course, parents do occasionally drop off children and rush away, but, if at all possible, more gradual means should be employed. Children's feelings of security and their attitude toward school are at stake. Perhaps with the Family Leave Act mentioned in Chapter 1, more parents in the United States will be able to follow the example of a father in Sweden who accompanied his son for the first month at the toddler center. He said he considered it an investment in his future relationship with his child.

DECISIONS, DECISIONS . . .

Discuss with your classmates or the manager of a child development center the idea of having parents spend the first month with their child at the center. Would you be comfortable doing your job with parents present? How would you make them feel welcome? How would you structure a gradual transition to the point where the child attends the center alone?

Some differences among early childhood programs arise because the leaders have differing philosophies. (A scheme for clarifying philosophies was presented in Chapter 7.) Certainly all professionals want children to learn and to reach their highest human potential. The philosophical label on an early childhood program may not be as important as whether the interactions are growth producing in all areas of development. A holistic approach that incorporates into the planning the child's needs for physical, cognitive, social, and emotional development is basic. A brief review of developmental principles may be helpful.

DEVELOPMENTAL PRINCIPLES TO KNOW

To plan the high-quality and appropriate programs desirable for children, the manager and staff need to understand principles of child growth and development. **Growth** refers to the increasing size and weight of the child's body. **Development** describes to the child's increasing complexity in locomotor, language, cognitive, social, and emotional skills. **Maturation** refers to the timetable or sequences and stages that growth and development typically follow.

1. All human development is based on a physiological foundation determined genetically at conception and nurtured during the prenatal period and thereafter. Later development builds on early development; that is, nurturing and education must build on this early genetic base and on each preceding stage of development.

2. Development follows a predictable sequence that is very orderly, provided that the environment permits. That is, children walk before they run, babble before they speak, and scribble before they draw faces.

3. Children have individual timetables for moving through the sequences in physical, social, cognitive, and emotional development. That is, one child may walk at 8 months, another at 15 months; one gets a first tooth at 4 months, another at 12 months; one speaks a first sentence at 16 months, whereas another is twice that age, yet all are within a normal range of development.

4. From large, global patterns of behavior, more specific and more complex patterns emerge. New patterns are combined to form increasingly specialized abilities and skills. For example, the child develops from holding a large crayon in a fisted grasp to using fingers and thumb in opposition. Writing, typing, or perhaps playing the violin follows. Each skill is increasingly complex, requiring integration with other skills. Similar examples could be given for development with respect to reasoning, speaking, or getting along with others.

5. Development is influenced by internal and external factors, as well as by interactions between the two. A child may be delayed in walking, for example, because of internal factors, such as neural or muscular disorders, or because of external factors, such as lack of opportunity. A child who has both the physical disability and an unsupportive environment will probably have greater delays.

6. There are dynamic interrelations among areas of development. For example, with the increase in speech development comes increased ability to play with other children, showing a relationship between speech and social development. With increased motor control and ability to hold a crayon, pencil, or paintbrush, the child can demonstrate an ability to think and reason through drawings and paintings.

7. Various critical periods have been identified in development that, if certain conditions exist, would inhibit or prevent the child from proceeding to more advanced levels of development. For example, because the first year of life is so important for brain development, good nutrition and freedom from disease are essential at this critical period. Motor performance studies by Seefeldt and Haubenstricker indicate that skills such as running, jumping, and skipping must reach a certain level by age 6, or individuals are very likely to experience difficulty with the games of school age and adolescence.[2]

8. Individuals generally behave as though they are striving to reach a maximum potential. When deprivation, nutritional or otherwise, is severe, the body shows a strong drive to overcome the deficiency. For example, some reports state that a child needing Vitamin D craves cod liver oil, a source of Vitamin D. When avenues for growth are blocked, many individuals find ways around those roadblocks. For example, a sightless child uses all other senses to compensate for the deficit. Thus, the individual strives toward health and independence, rather than illness and dependence.

With these principles of child development as guides, the management and staff of a child development center will work together to build the best environment for enhancing the potential of each child. Because the field of child development is continuously benefiting from new research, managers and staff members must continue to grow and develop in their knowledge through reading, lectures, conferences, and the like. Raising questions and participating in research will help add to present knowledge about children.

Each age group in a child development center has some particular characteristics. Descriptions of children of various ages are available in readings listed at the close of this chapter.[3] Reference books should be readily available to teachers as they plan programs and encounter behavior that they need to understand more fully.

---

[2] Vern Seefeldt and John Haubenstricker, "Patterns, Phases, or Stages: An Analytical Model for the Study of Developmental Movement," in J. A. Kelso and J. E. Clark (eds.), *The Development of Movement Control and Coordination* (New York: Wiley, 1982), pp. 309–318.

[3] For details on children of various ages, see Verna Hildebrand, *Guiding Young Children* (Upper Saddle River, NJ: Prentice Hall, 1990), Chapter 15.

In addition, NAEYC has published a helpful booklet that should also be in every teacher's room, *Developmentally Appropriate Practice in Early Childhood Programs Serving Children from Birth through Age 8*, edited by Sue Bredekamp (1987). The general age characteristics of children should be as familiar to teachers and caregivers as the back of the hand. The accreditation criteria are based on an understanding of these developmental characteristics.

BASIC GUIDES TO PROGRAM DEVELOPMENT

Keeping developmental principles and the developmental tasks presented in Chapter 7 in mind, you can plan an effective program for young children if teachers have adequate training, take sufficient time to plan carefully, and have the support and encouragement of the manager of the child development center. Teachers plan for the assigned age group, then observe and seek additional information to understand the individual development of each child within the group. The following 18-point guide gives teachers and managers a framework for planning and later for evaluating their programs.

Program Guide

1. A good program is planned from the point of view of the whole child in the immediate environment. Whether the child is from a small or large family, the city or country, an advantaged or disadvantaged home, ongoing experiences are the basis for all planning. The child is observed, then guided through sequential steps to new heights of accomplishment.

2. A good program accepts and treats all children with respect, regardless of race, gender, or ability. Adults teach children to value who they are, show empathy for those who are different from them, and recognize and stand up against unfairness toward themselves or others.

3. A good program values the child's healthy, happy, responding, secure approach to living. The teacher expects the children to respond fully and learn appropriately for their age. An important goal is for them to learn to love school and learning, teachers, and other children. Developing a self-confidence that says, "Whatever there is to do, I can do it," is very important.

4. A good program provides for the emotional growth of the child. It accepts the child as he or she moves from the protected, individualized home experience to a group experience. Every effort is made to give a feeling of security in the new setting—this goal being paramount for some time, depending on the child's need. Parents are helped and guided during this transitional period.

5. A good program balances active and quiet activities. Within large time blocks, the child has freedom to select the type of activity preferred. The teacher's schedule balances routines and learning experiences in a logical sequence of events. Extremes of both prolonged sitting and prolonged physical exertion are avoided. Tensions build up during enforced sitting, and fatigue contributes to lack of inner control that interferes with maximum learning.

The boat inspires dramatic play, as well as singing "Row, Row, Row Your Boat" and other rhythmic songs when the whole class gets in the boat and rocks!
Family Life Center, Georgia Southern College, Statesboro

6. A good program provides appropriate opportunities for children to grow in self-direction and independence. It provides an opportunity for them to learn to make choices through experience. Each child gains in self-understanding.

7. A good program establishes and maintains limits on behavior for the protection of individuals, the group, and the learning environment. By helping a child learn the reasons for various rules, the teacher encourages self-discipline.

8. A good program is challenging to children's intellectual powers. They are encouraged to think, reason, remember, experiment, and generalize. The laboratory rather than the lecture method is used almost exclusively.

9. A good program provides media of self-expression. Creativity is valued, fostered, and recognized in every learning center. Art, literature, and music are part of every day's activity.

10. A good program encourages children's verbal expressions. To learn words and sentence structure, children must have an opportunity to talk. Being quiet is not necessarily valued.

11. A good program provides opportunities for social development. The child learns through experience to share, take turns, and interact with individuals and groups. He or she learns to choose friends and to be chosen. Yet the program also allows time to be alone if desired.

12. A good program encourages children to learn about and care for their bodies. A routine of washing, eating, resting, and eliminating is established. Safety training has priority, both to protect children and to teach them to protect themselves.

13. A good program provides opportunities for each child to exercise the whole body in a daily period of outdoor activity. When bad weather prevents going outdoors, adequate provision is made for gross-motor activities in semi-sheltered or indoor areas.

14. A good program is action packed. It is frequently noisy compared to traditional upper-age classes. The reasons action, noise, and talking are permitted may have to be explained to administrators and others so that programs for children are not curtailed unnecessarily. Carpeting, draping, or other soundproofing should be provided in classrooms to cut down the noise level.

15. A good program engages children's minds with topics and materials that are both attractive to children and meaningfully connected to children's lives and the world they inhabit. Teachers observe carefully and follow up on children's interests as they plan activities.

16. A good program engages teachers' minds so that they become learners alongside the children, discovering new ideas about the topic at hand as well as about the children in their care.

17. A good program includes parents in partnership with teachers and children, recognizing parents' primary importance to their children's growth and development. Communication is two-way, with the center actively soliciting and accepting parents' opinions and ideas, as well as offering support, advice, and appropriate referrals as needed.

18. A good program empowers children, parents, and staff members to become competent members of the human ecological system.

TEACHERS' PLANNING AND SCHEDULING

In the process of planning, the teachers will set up a schedule or sequence of events that they expect to follow in their groups. Schedules help teachers and aides know what to expect as they work together. Schedules help the children gain a sense of security as they come to realize that the sequence of events is the same every day; thus, they add to their confidence as they know what to do without being told.

A general schedule should be posted where parents can see it. They like to know what children do and about what time they do it. Usually a **time block plan** is used where large blocks of time are set aside for certain types of activity. Figure 14–2 is a sample time block plan with approximate times noted for each block. Short-day programs would utilize Time Blocks II, III, and IV; full-day programs would follow all the blocks. Note that the self-selected activity period lasts 60 minutes. This recommended time period is reinforced by recent research by Christie and Wardle, who learned that when longer play periods were planned, children had "higher social and cognitive forms of play. Extra play time prompted children to engage in more complex, productive play activities."[4]

---

[4] James F. Christie and Francis Wardle, "How Much Time Is Needed for Play?" *Young Children* 47 (March 1992), pp. 28–32.

Time Block I	**Greeting Children**
6:30–8:30 or 9:00 A.M.	Breakfast for those desiring it
	Self-selected activity in multiage groups for early arrivals
	Move to own groups as teachers arrive and are ready for children

Time Block II	**Self-Selected Activity (Indoors)**		
9:00–10:00 A.M.	(Arrival time for short-day children)		
	Art	Music	Blocks
	Science	Dramatic play	Books
	Table games	Small, wheeled objects	Language arts

Time Block III	**Teacher-Instigated Activity**
10–10:45 A.M.	Cleanup
	Toileting, washing hands
	Snack
	Quiet time: looking at books, music
	Storytime and discussions

Time Block IV	**Self-Selected Activity (Outdoors)**	
10:45–11:30 A.M.	Climbing	Riding tricycles
	Swinging	Sand play
	Running	Science activity

Time Block V	**Lunch Period**
11:30–12:15 P.M.	Washing hands, toileting, resting
	Eating
	Washing hands
	Preparing for nap (going home if short-day program)

Time Block VI	**Nap Time**
12:15–2:30 P.M.	Dressing for nap
	Sleeping
	Toileting
	Dressing

Time Block VII	**Self-Selected Activity**
2:30–6:00 P.M.	New activities
	Snack
	Outdoor play or indoor motor activity
	Set up morning activities
	Multiage groups as children go home
	Saying good-bye

Blocks II and IV can be interchanged for variation and to meet children's needs for activity. Times are approximate.

Figure 14–2
Time block plan

Week of _____			Teacher _____		
	Monday	**Tuesday**	**Wednesday**	**Thursday**	**Friday**
Art:					
Science:					
Dramatic play:					
Literature-language area:					
Music area:					
Group time:					
Outdoor activity:					
Transition:					
Snack:					
Trips:					
Planning notes:					

Figure 14–3
Weekly activity plan

As they gain experience and skill at facilitating the children's play, some teachers find that 1 hour is not enough, and they extend this period even further. Careful observation of children, reflecting on these observations, and discussing them with colleagues is the best way for teachers to learn to see the possibilities inherent in play. Therefore, managers need to make sure that teachers have adequate protected time to carry out this important aspect of planning.

DECISIONS, DECISIONS . . .

 What would you say, as a manager of a child development center, to parents who complain that all their children do at your center is play? Role play this situation with a classmate.

In weekly planning sessions, teachers will write out plans using a form such as Figure 14–3. For the teacher's daily plan, the planning should be shown on a form such as Figure 14–4. List here the items you expect to present to children in

---

Date _____   **Teacher** _____

Activity   **Who Is Responsible?**

Things to remember:

Art projects:

Science projects:

Dramatic play:

Literature-language area:

Music area:

Group time:

Outdoor activity:

Transition:

Snack menu:

Diary:

Figure 14–4
Daily plan of activities

addition to the equipment and materials offered by the room and play yard. Reminders can be noted along with assignments of each person. People like to know where they are expected to be stationed in the room or yard, even though they can move to where the children are if no children are in their assigned area. Designated responsibilities help the teacher in charge know that each area is supervised and that someone is guiding the children there. Room is left at the bottom of the daily plan sheet to add a short diary. Especially useful is information about interactions that have occurred that day.

Figure 14–5 shows an activity plan for a single activity—using parquetry blocks. Note that several different plans could have been written for using the same materials to meet other kinds of objectives. For example, a teacher might choose to focus on an aesthetic goal and provide the blocks without the forms, asking children to form patterns of shapes and colors that are pleasing to them. Each teacher should be able to think through each activity presented to children. The less experience the teacher has, the more writing of plans that should be done. A notebook of activity plans can be developed. These written plans are handy to give to substitute teachers or volunteers who might help with an activity. The manager should encourage the development of long-range plans and short-range plans. The forms printed here are short-range plans.

Name of Activity: Parquetry blocks

Development Goal:
1. Vocabulary development
2. Perceptual development

Objectives:
Given a set of parquetry blocks with matching forms the child will, each time,
1. Match colors
2. Match shapes
3. Name colors
4. Name shapes

Materials Needed: 3 parquetry sets

Procedure:
Place parquetry sets in an inviting location in the room.
Sit with children. Observe their use of the sets.
Let them discover and teach each other.
Answer any questions. Note their use of vocabulary.
Encourage naming of shapes and colors.

Guidance Suggestions, Including Limits:
Play a game: "Show me the (red square)."
Encourage them to make their own designs after they accomplish matching.

Special Objectives:
To see if Amanda is able to name colors.
To see if John can count to four. Encourage his practice.

Evaluation:
Hide shape and/or color—ask child to name it when it is uncovered. Check chart to see which ones they know.

Suggestions for Future Use:

Figure 14–5
Sample activity plan

PARENTAL CONCERN FOR QUALITY

Some parents will enroll their children in your center reluctantly, feeling forced by the demands of earning a livelihood to forego precious moments with their children during their formative early years. Others will be eager to give their children the advantage of early educational opportunities and social experiences with peers. All parents will expect you to treat their children kindly, protect them from harm, and help them develop to their fullest potential.

A recent study confirms the value that parents place on good-quality care for their children; it also reveals, however, that parents consistently overrate the quality of care their children are receiving. Nine of 10 parents gave their centers "very good" ratings, while professional observers found the same centers to be "poor" or "mediocre."[5] Thus, it seems, while parents want the best for their children, they lack the information necessary to help them judge what is best. Perhaps they have not observed enough programs to have a basis for comparison; perhaps they have never seen a really high-quality program in operation; perhaps they have been seduced by glossy brochures and an attractive surface appearance, never actually seeing what happens at their center while they are at work.

This is where the NAEYC center accreditation process can be helpful. In addition to setting the criteria and administering the process of accreditation, the NAEYC has undertaken a public awareness campaign to alert parents and others to the components of high-quality children's programs and the significance of accreditation as a mark of excellence. As a manager of a child development program, you can contribute to this effort by pursuing accreditation for your program and proudly displaying your certificate of accreditation when you have earned it.

You will also need to contribute continually to the education of parents and the public about the components of high-quality early education. Adults who have not studied child development often rely on their own memories of school to form images of what teaching and learning should look like. They may pressure you and your teachers to provide evidence of such "learning" in the form of worksheets, memorized ABCs, rote counting, and a daily "art" project. Depending on the level of their professional backgrounds, your own staff may either share these beliefs themselves or feel coerced by parent demands to resort to these stereotyped substitutes for genuine learning experiences.

Many teachers have found, however, that when they provide the parents with other kinds of evidence of children's learning, the demands for worksheets and rote skills are replaced by a new enthusiasm for more appropriate experiences. Chapter 15 contains specific suggestions for approaching this issue. Managers who see this kind of public education as part of their job and plan for it accordingly will be far less likely to feel burned out at the prospect of facing each year's new group of well-intentioned but uninformed critics.

---

[5] Cost, Quality, & Child Outcomes Study Team, *Cost, Quality, and Child Outcomes in Child Care Centers, Executive Summary,* 2nd ed. (Denver: Economics Department, University of Colorado, 1995), p. 9.

A Manager's Inputs into Curriculum and Interaction

To fulfill the public trust invested in a child development center, the children in the center must be treated humanely in a growth-producing way and must receive a high-quality educational experience suited to each child's individual characteristics. What part can the manager play in curriculum development and teachers' interpersonal interactions with children? Ten major ways managers can be supportive of teachers who are delegated the task of producing high-quality programs follow.

1. Know High Quality in Programs and Interaction Processes

The manager must be well informed regarding the components of a high-quality program. This is technical information that will give the manager credibility with the professional teaching staff. If managers have climbed the career ladder via the teaching route, such credibility will be attained more easily. However, if the manager arrived at the managerial role via another route, such as through training in business, considerable effort toward understanding quality in programs will be needed. Even managers who have been in the field for years will need to invest time and effort in staying abreast of the rapidly expanding knowledge base. Basic principles of child development may have stayed the same for many years, but our ideas of how those principles should be applied undergo constant transformation as new information becomes available.

Not long ago, for example, early childhood teachers believed that reading and writing were matters for elementary school and bemoaned the "pushed-down" curriculum that brought workbooks into programs for young children. Then we learned that children are aware of print well before they go to kindergarten.[6] Teachers who were stuck in their earlier (justified) resistance to workbooks did not want to hear about writing centers for young children, but teachers who kept abreast of new developments found that supporting literacy acquisition could be very appropriate—and lots more exciting than "teaching prereading skills."

A similar tension exists today between those who feel computers have no place in early childhood programs and those who believe that the child development program that does not offer this experience is failing to prepare its children for life in the 21st century. Just as we learned that *appropriate* literacy activities had their place in programs for young children, the resolution to this debate may have more to do with *how* rather than *whether* computers are used. True, much of the software available for young children has offered little more than an animated workbook exercise. It is also true that even the most up-to-date computer will never replace paints, blocks, dramatic play, or the other traditional early childhood materials that belong in all good programs. And it is especially true that

---

[6] See, for example, Lois Bader and Verna Hildebrand, "An Exploratory Study of 3- to 5-Year-Olds' Responses on the Bader Reading and Language Inventory," *Early Child Development and Care* 77, pp. 83–95.

even the most user-friendly computer cannot replace complex interactions with living, breathing human beings. But increasingly convincing arguments are being made for the computer's place *alongside* these time-tested elements of high-quality programs. Resources regarding appropriate use of technology in early childhood programs are included in the Suggested Readings at the end of this chapter.

Attending workshops and visiting many centers help managers appreciate the breadth of curricular possibilities available. Curriculum activities and interaction processes are discussed in many books and journals; several are listed at the close of the chapter. Books on the early childhood curriculum need to be available in your center to serve as guides for curriculum development and as inspiration and reminders for teachers. As new professional literature comes out, teachers will appreciate having it readily available to them. As manager, you can make it your center's policy to maintain an up-to-date collection of professional literature available to staff and to interested parents. Many parents will recognize such a library as one indication of excellence. Certainly an image of excellence is one that you will want to create and merit.

2. Hire Staff Prepared to Provide High-Quality Programs

The children's specific learning activities are primarily the responsibility of the teachers and caregivers in the child development center. The employment of persons who have adequate professional preparation and know-how for planning a high-quality program is where the manager's role begins. Securing adequate funding, analyzing each job and writing related job specifications and job descriptions, and hiring well-prepared people are all very important steps toward a high-quality children's program.

Some managers find it desirable to hire people on a trial basis for several weeks to see how they operate within the center. Some make it a policy to require that potential staff members work first on a substitute basis for several months before being hired as a permanent employee. This gives each side a chance to get to know the other without a firm commitment. Common sense suggests that attributes that appear one way in an interview situation may be supported or discounted in the actual situation.

Every teacher should carry out specific personal monitoring and controlling of his or her program as it evolves. Evaluations should be an everyday occurrence. When an individual teacher is conscientiously evaluating performance daily, the evaluations that might be done by a manager or some outsider generally bring no surprises. Actually, evaluation should go on from moment to moment. Time should be set aside every day to reflect on how standards were or were not met. Revisions in procedure can be suggested and tested during the ensuing days. As teachers see things that are not going well, they make changes right away. In a postsession conference among teachers and all support persons who have been involved, a pleasant and useful evaluation in a give-and-take format can be carried out, which can be very helpful in improving programs. Both good results and those not so good can be talked over with an eye toward improvement.

At the end of each day, it helps recall if the teacher writes down on the planning form a short diary of particular events that occurred, such as "Johnny talked for the first time. He said, 'I want some milk.'" Or you might record that Peter bloodied Jackie's nose. Such records help in later evaluation. A summary of curricular ideas presented each day can be tallied to show the variety of activities offered the children. The teachers or manager might use an evaluation sheet similar to Figure 14–6 to evaluate the plans for a term or a year. A parents' program rating sheet was shown in Figure 8–2.

3. Provide Paid Planning Time

Paid planning time is one of the criteria in the NAEYC accreditation project.[7] Careful planning and preparation for each day are hallmarks of high-quality programs, help ensure variety in activities, and increase each teacher's ability to be relaxed and responsive to children's needs and interests. When planning and preparation are adequately done, children will be busy and productive in their classrooms and play yards. They will be learning well and will be adequately meeting the developmental tasks of their ages.

When there is a lack of productive learning, many professionals believe that lack of planning is often to blame. Far too many teachers in today's child care centers must do the little planning that gets done after working 8 hours with children. They plan for tomorrow's activities in the kitchen while they prepare supper or after they put their own children to bed. Of course, overworked teachers are forced to draw on ideas that have worked in the past, taking little time to develop new ideas or improved approaches. Many do not have much time to confer with their coworkers, sharing ideas and insights. A great deterrent to high quality in some child development center programs is the fact that teachers are often not given paid time to make definite curriculum plans or reflect together on what they have seen the children do.

Managers who really want a high-quality program must find some way to relieve teachers from classroom responsibility with children for a few hours each week to allow them to plan learning activities and prepare materials. Teachers simply need time away from children to think, read, organize, confer with colleagues, and develop challenging ideas for programs. Managers might consider the following alternatives:

1. Provide a block of planning time for the teacher by hiring adequate substitute teachers during the lunch and nap periods one or more days per week.
2. Offer a block of planning time for the teacher by hiring adequate substitute teachers for the last hour or two of the teacher's day for one session each week.
3. Have paid planning sessions for the whole staff for an hour or two in the evening or on weekends.

---

[7] Bredekamp (ed.), *Accreditation Criteria,* p. 37.

4—Very Satisfactory   2—Unsatisfactory
3—Satisfactory   1—Very Unsatisfactory

Rating   Program Guidelines

The program:

(   ) 1.   Was planned from the point of view of the whole child in the immediate environment

(   ) 2.   Respected cultural differences and fostered participation by all children, regardless of gender or ability

(   ) 3.   Valued the child's healthy, happy, responding, secure approach to living

(   ) 4.   Provided for the emotional growth of the child

(   ) 5.   Balanced active and quiet activities

(   ) 6.   Provided appropriate opportunities for children to grow in self-direction and independence

(   ) 7.   Established and maintained limits on behavior for protection of individuals, groups, and the learning environment

(   ) 8.   Challenged children's intellectual powers

(   ) 9.   Provided media of self-expression

(   ) 10.   Encouraged children's verbal expressions

(   ) 11.   Provided opportunities for children's social development

(   ) 12.   Helped children learn to understand their bodies

(   ) 13.   Provided opportunities for each child to play outdoors daily

(   ) 14.   Provided opportunities for vigorous motor activities

(   ) 15.   Appeared to engage children's interests and thinking processes

(   ) 16.   Involved learning and growth on the part of teachers as well as children

(   ) 17.   Considered the interests and needs of parents as well as the children

(   ) 18.   Helped children and adults to form meaningful connections with and become more competent in the larger world

Remarks: _____

_____

_____

Evaluator _____ Date _____

Figure 14–6
Program evaluation

Musical teachers and guests are popular in any group of children. Children's lives are enriched by exposure to a variety of musical experiences.
University of Illinois Child Development Laboratory, Urbana

4. Take time as manager to take over each classroom for an hour or two each week to personally relieve each teacher to do planning. (This suggestion has the important advantages of helping the manager keep up professional skills, maintain credibility with the staff, become better acquainted with the children, and understand program problems and needs.)[8]

After you have arranged for teachers and caregivers to have time set aside for planning, you may have to help some staff members use the time effectively. Especially beginning staff may need help locating books with ideas. Or several teachers may need to brainstorm together to generate curriculum ideas. Teachers often need help focusing on specific children and developing a program that especially fits their needs.

---

[8] See Vincent L. Lombardi and Verna Hildebrand, "Modernizing Administration" *Education* 101:3 (Spring 1981), pp. 270–272, concerning the importance of managers' or administrators' maintaining their professional competence in the classroom or laboratory.

More experienced teachers may be helpful to less experienced teachers as mentors—a role that can be formalized if you, the manager, specifically assign a present teacher to help a new teacher get started. Also, through this process, you may be helping the present teacher avoid feeling competitive with the new one. Sometimes teachers have become rigid or less spontaneous after they have worked with children for a number of years. Your efforts as manager should be diagnostic in that you observe where and what help is needed and seek to provide it. By observing teachers as they plan, you may learn where inservice efforts need to be focused.

While encouraging regular planning, the manager will also need to require teachers to make a plan for an emergency, such as when they might be ill and unable to attend school. If regular teachers post plans in their rooms that can easily be followed by substitute teachers, there is less confusion for children and learning can continue. Figure 14–7 shows a set of basic plans containing the main components of a program. The plan assumes a well-equipped room and play yard from which the children also choose activities. Set aside an "emergency cupboard" that is well supplied with some outstanding paperback books, song-sheets of words to familiar songs, and ideas that can be carried out on the spur of the moment. With this preplanning, the emergency can be an accepted change for children.

The need for "one-size-fits-all" emergency plans can be reduced in two ways. First, as teachers develop more collegial relationships with other teachers and assistants, planning becomes more of a shared process, and everyone in the center knows the daily routine as well as the current topics or projects underway. Thus, a substitute filling in for an ill teacher has many sources of information and support in addition to the written plans. In some centers, the classroom assistant (who has taken part in the planning) moves into the lead teacher's position during her absence, and the substitute fills the assistant role.

Second, as programs move more toward a play-based program, with large blocks of time during which children carry out projects and activities that they have initiated, the need for adult direction becomes less and less. One first grade teacher reported with pride that, when she returned from a brief illness, the principal (who had substituted for her in her absence) remarked that the children did not seem to need him at all! They entered the room, marked their name on the attendance chart, put a token in the appropriate container to indicate whether they wanted to order a hot lunch, and went to work in the learning centers according to their individual weekly plans. Obviously, routines have to be well established in advance for children to function so efficiently in such a program.

Another aspect of planning involves coordination among the various programs that might serve the same children. Children with disabilities, for example, might spend mornings in special educational or therapeutic settings and afternoons in your child development center. School-age children often move within the same building, from their regular classroom and teacher to another room with another adult for after-school programs. Too frequently, the staff in one program have no idea what happened in the other—whether it is down the hall or across town.

Day 1
Easel painting
Crayons
Magnets

Read:
Harry the Dirty Dog
Angus and the Ducks

Songs:
Comin' Round the
Mountain

Day 6
Easel painting
Playdough
Grocery store
Peg boards

Read:
Curious George
Tim Tadpole and the
Great Bullfrog

Songs:
Row, Row Your Boat
Yankee Doodle

Day 2
Easel painting
Fingerpainting
Scales

Read:
The Snowy Day
Busy Timmy

Songs:
Twinkle, Twinkle
Wheels on the Bus

Day 7
Easel painting
Mud clay
Water play
Making pudding

Read:
The Circus Baby
Bread and Jam for
Frances

Songs:
I'm a Little Teapot
Hokey Pokey

Day 3
Easel painting
Playdough
Geo-board

Read:
Make Way for Ducklings
Blueberries for Sal

Songs:
Eency Weency Spider
This Old Man

Day 8
Easel painting
Crayons
Sorting bolts
Puzzles

Read:
Muffin in the City
Where Does the Butter-
fly Go When It Rains?

Songs:
Monkey See, Monkey Do
Paw Paw Patch

Day 4
Easel painting
Wet chalk
Magnifying glasses

Read:
Ask Mr. Bear
Curious George Rides a
Bike

Songs:
Where Is Thumbkin?
Pop! Goes the Weasel

Day 9
Easel painting
Fingerpainting
Typewriter
String wooden beads

Read:
The Noisy Book
Muffin in the Country

Songs:
Old MacDonald
Hush Little Baby

Day 5
Easel painting
Collage
Prism

Read:
Two Roses for Harry
Madeline

Songs:
Little Red Caboose
Brother John

Day 10
Easel painting
Wet chalk
Scales—weigh fruit
Cut fruit for snack

Read:
Millions of Cats
Caps for Sale

Songs:
Farmer in the Dell
Mulberry Bush

Figure 14–7
Emergency plan

High quality demands that all the adults in a child's life collaborate to provide the best possible program wherever it happens to occur.

Managers should appreciate the fact that planning for children and relating to them and their parents requires knowledge and lots of teacher time and patience. The less experienced the teacher, the more time and support are needed. No program can maintain high quality without careful planning. Surely, creative managers can help solve the problem of providing adequate time for planning, which would increase teachers' ability to deliver a high-quality program to children.

4. Keep Classes Small

Span of control was discussed in the section on organization, with support cited favoring small groups of children because a teacher or caregiver can more productively relate to a few children and achieve higher levels of quality in interpersonal interaction and programming. The manager who carefully controls the assignment of children, keeping the classes small, enables teachers to do a more adequate job. Class size is one avenue by which a high-quality program can be facilitated by management.

5. Provide Support Staff

Some support staff are professionals who render specific professional services to children and parents of the center. Some may be contracted for short-time services. They may be a nurse who helps with particular health problems, a psychologist who helps with a certain behavior problem, or a family-life educator who plans and chairs a series of parent meetings on topics that parents face in their child rearing.

A volunteer or support person could do a number of routine chores, which would extend the energies of the teaching and caregiving staffs, thus enabling the latter to provide higher-quality programs. The manager can initiate ways to supplement the staff—perhaps through volunteers, students from high schools or universities, or paid labor. These persons will need training to be really helpful, a responsibility that the management must assume. In addition, recognition and rewards must be provided, especially to unpaid volunteers. Chapter 6 included a discussion of specific ways that managers can cultivate this precious resource.

Following suitable planning, volunteers or support staff can make preparations for activities such as mixing fingerpaint or play dough, cutting collage materials, buying groceries for a food experience, or the like. Some managers have been successful in getting the late-afternoon staff to set up the classroom for the following day's activity—especially for that early morning period that can be so hectic in a full-day child development center. It really is nice for the morning teacher to walk into a room set up with puzzles out, an art project invitingly displayed, and the housekeeping corner organized for the first tea party. The morning teacher can provide a list of suitable activities to the late-afternoon staff.

6. Provide Adequate Equipment and Supplies

Child development centers require equipment, games, books, and materials arranged in inviting ways that entice children to explore, discover, try out, talk about, think about, question, and grow in ability to understand and control many aspects of their world. As manager, you can facilitate the educational program by having the appropriate items available in sufficient quantity and at the time and place where needed, to enable teachers to plan and carry out high-quality programs. Knowing what high-quality standards are and interpreting those standards to the staff, keeping abreast of new materials and equipment, and seeking ways to add to your present stock of equipment will all be part of your job. Teachers can be helpful and should always be consulted for their advice.

At times teachers need encouragement to daydream creatively about what improvements could be made in their programs. A manager's leadership can encourage this creativity. The attitude of "making do" with the present situation may be necessary during periods of financial crises to help ensure survival, but that attitude is not one that moves a center's program ahead in quality during more normal times. If an attitude of curtailment prevails, the manager might question whether this is necessary. A teacher's creativity can be released during brainstorming. A manager might say, "If you didn't have to worry about lack of money or staff, what would you really like to be able to do with your group of children?" Write every idea down on the board—even the "crazy" ideas. Finally, reality will return, but the ideas received will be useful, and maybe some of the "farfetched" ideas are not impossible after all. The manager may see ways that some of the daydreaming can become a reality.

7. Provide Opportunities for Professional Development

Every employee you hire should be expected to have potential for growth. Potential growth should be one criterion for employee selection. No job stands still, and everyone should be expected to learn and improve. That is why it is suggested that all job descriptions include a statement that the candidate is expected to continue learning through courses, workshops, and other professional development activities.

Through their own professional growth (discussed in Chapter 6), teachers become motivated to plan more variety in learning activities. A cooperative spirit can develop in which generous sharing is promoted among all units in a center. For example, if a magician comes for one group, other children are generously included, or arrangements are made for the magician to visit other groups. Education may be needed to increase teachers' understanding of children's behavior and help discover appropriate responses to behaviors. Teaching is far less lonely if others lend support. Depth in psychological understanding can grow as staff members study and help each other more fully understand a child that needs help.[9]

As manager, you can help teachers increase their skills and knowledge through one-to-one sessions, small-group sessions, or total staff sessions. You may hire an outside consultant to observe and evaluate. You may send staff members to

---

[9] Productive staff inservice workshops might focus on topics such as "Appreciating Positive Behavior," or "Understanding Negative Behavior," as discussed in Chapters 16 and 17 of Verna Hildebrand, *Guiding Young Children*, pp. 290–322.

appropriate professional meetings. The dynamic learning program desired for children must have management's psychological and financial support. The manager's monitoring and controlling function requires evaluating the programs and interactions taking place with each group of children and making efforts to keep professional standards high.[10]

8. Run Interference

To facilitate the high-quality learning activities that your teachers provide, you may have to run interference defending programs occasionally with a principal, a president of the board, a parent, or a custodian who inappropriately complains, for example, that activities are "noisy, messy, and smelly," as in the case of animals, or "junky" as in the case of some art projects. By countering the complaints with reasoned, logical explanations you can reduce the dissonance before difficult confrontations develop. Having full knowledge of a teacher's curriculum innovations will help the manager answer critics. Thus, having teachers share plans is an excellent communication arrangement.

9. Give Positive Feedback

As you, the manager, move around the building behavioral evidence of a high-quality program will surely catch your attention. Wonderful drawings, joyous music, hilarious laughter, and energetic, talkative children will pour out of playrooms and play yards. Letting teachers know that you approve and appreciate the learning activities that produce such behaviors will motivate teachers to continue their efforts. Of course, you will not want teachers to do things just to please you. Your goal as a manager is to provide the kind of feedback that will foster their feelings of confidence and competence and encourage them to be self-motivated. Routinely assuring people that they are "doing a fine job" gives them more information about your opinion than about what they are doing or how it fits with what they think they are doing.

This assumes, of course, that staff have had a say in setting goals for their program and for themselves. Suppose, for example, that you and your staff have decided to use displays of photographs and transcriptions of children's comments to convey information about your curriculum to parents. Instead of telling teachers that they made a "great bulletin board," you might want to let them know that you are aware of the hours of work that went into it and tell them that you have seen several parents stop to look at the photographs and read the captions. Some writers refer to this sort of feedback as "encouragement," as distinguished from "praise."[11]

---

[10] For assistance with early childhood curriculum development, see Verna Hildebrand, *Introduction to Early Childhood Education* (Upper Saddle River, NJ: Prentice Hall, 1991). For your staff members who prefer to read in Spanish, it may be helpful to refer them to the Spanish translation of this work, titled *Fundamentos de Educación Infantil: Jardin de Niños y Preprimaria*, available from Editorial Limusa, S.A., Balderas 95, Mexico City, Mexico 06040.

[11] See Randy Hitz and Amy Driscoll, "Give Encouragement, Not Praise," *Texas Child Care* 17:4 (Spring 1994), pp. 2–11.

You can give positive feedback indirectly, as well, by suggesting that parents stop by a classroom to see the work that a teacher has been doing with children, or by suggesting that one teacher consult another because of some particular expertise the latter has to offer.

You may have chances to show children how you value their creativity as you take notice of their paintings or listen to their songs. Providing space for displays of children's work helps this recognition and brightens the building. Another form of positive feedback is recommending staff members to represent your center on a program, for an office in a professional organization, an honor, or a professional advancement. Such recognition will be helpful to the center and everyone related to it.

10. Interpret to Parents

Helping parents appreciate the available experiences in your child development center will be high on your agenda. Many parents have little background for evaluating the program their child is receiving. They may welcome reassurance from you. As parents are being oriented, you can begin to inform them what to expect and what they should appreciate about the type of program you offer. They will not mind paying the tuition if they feel and see evidence of high-quality learning in their child.

Sometimes a high-quality program is messy, and parents may criticize the mess until it is pointed out to them how the activity is helping their child learn. Children may become more outspoken, and parents may need to learn that for a child to verbalize and support an opinion is desirable growth. A child's creative artwork may not be valued by parents because it does not fit coloring book stereotypes that they may have in mind. The manager can help interpret children's drawings to parents, helping them value creativity and the fact that prereading and prewriting skills are being practiced as the child does free painting and drawing. Illustrations could go on and on. Managers need to be alert to the many opportunities they have to interpret components of a high-quality program to parents and to relieve the teachers of unwarranted criticism that might discourage improved programs. Chapter 15 gives more information on planning and interacting with parents.

CONCLUSION

Serving children in the child development center is the basic reason for a center's existence. The manager plays a key role in determining the quality of that service.

Programming for children must be based on sound developmental principles. An 18-point guideline has been presented to serve as a basis for program planning and evaluation.

Ten ways that managers can be supportive of teachers who plan and carry out children's programs have been presented under these headings:

1. Know high quality in programs and interaction processes.

2. Hire staff prepared to provide high-quality programs.
3. Provide paid planning time.
4. Keep classes small.
5. Provide support staff.
6. Provide adequate equipment and supplies.
7. Provide opportunities for professional development.
8. Run interference.
9. Give positive feedback.
10. Interpret to parents.

APPLICATIONS

1. Make a list of 10 art experiences, involving different combinations of media, that teachers could rotate through their plans.
2. List 10 science projects that teachers could rotate through their plans.
3. Describe 10 musical activities that teachers could rotate through their plans.
4. What are 10 outdoor activities that teachers could rotate through their plans?
5. Make a list of five storybooks appropriate for each age group as follows: 2- to 3-year-olds, 3- to 4-year-olds, and 4- to 5-year-olds. Prepare illustrative materials for at least one story.
6. Make a list of five food-related nutrition projects that teachers could rotate through their plans.
7. Put these plans together in a handbook suitable for use in a center.
8. With another person, plan a presentation on curriculum innovations for presenting to a center's staff as an inservice education program. Give the presentation to your class, encouraging suggestions for improvement. Improve the presentation further for a larger audience, and propose your workshop for a conference of teachers.
9. Add materials on curriculum development and evaluation to your management notebook.

STUDY QUESTIONS

1. Discuss high-quality programs from a manager's perspective with respect to decisions concerning age of children, group size, and adult-child ratio.
2. Outline steps, in order of occurrence, from the point where a parent inquires about your center to the point where a child begins school.
3. Define and give an example of children's growth, development, and maturation.
4. List the 18 guides to program development given in this chapter, and write an example of each guide based on your information from a child development center.
5. State the 10 ways a manager can be supportive of high-quality programs.

SUGGESTED READINGS

Albrecht, K. M., and M. C. Plantz. *Developmentally Appropriate Practice in School-Age Child Care Programs*. Alexandria, VA: American Home Economics Association, 1991.

Albrecht, K. M. *Quality Criteria for School-Age Child Care Programs*. Alexandria, VA: American Home Economics Association, 1991.

Ambery, Mary Elizabeth. "The Case of Seymore: How Long Does It Take for a Beginning Teacher to Be So Shaped by the Pressures of a School That Best Practice Gets Lost?" *Young Children* 50:5 (July 1995), pp. 22–26.

Ard, Linda Gifford. "Dittos? But Parents *Want* Dittos." *Texas Care Quarterly* 11:3 (Winter 1987), pp. 10–14.

Blakley, B., R. Blau, E. H. Brady, C. Streibert, A. Zavitkovsky, and D. Zavitkovsky. *Activities for School-Age Child Care*. Washington, DC: National Association for the Education of Young Children, 1987.

Brooke, Gretchen E. "My Personal Journey Toward Professionalism." *Young Children* 49:6 (September 1994), pp. 69–71.

Carter, Margie. "Building a Community Culture among Teachers." *Child Care Information Exchange* 101 (January/February 1995), pp. 52–54.

Carter, Margie. "Developing Strong Self-Images—It's Important for Teachers, Too!" *Child Care Information Exchange* 104 (July/August 1995), pp. 60–62.

Clements, Douglas H., Bonnie K. Nastasi, and Sudha Swaminathan. "Young Children and Computers: Crossroads and Directions from Research." *Young Children* 48:2 (January 1993), pp. 56–64.

Daily, Janice. "Science for Toddlers: The Teachable Moment." *Texas Child Care* 15:4 (Spring 1992), pp. 22–26.

Dennis-Willingham, Carolyn. "Do We Practice What We Teach?" *Texas Child Care* 15:3 (Winter 1991), pp. 3–6.

Dodge, Diane Trister, and Laura J. Colker. *The Creative Curriculum for Early Childhood*, 3rd ed. Washington, DC: Teaching Strategies, 1992.

Gonzales-Mena, Janet. "Taking a Culturally Sensitive Approach in Infant-Toddler Programs." *Young Children* 47:2 (January 1992), pp. 4–9.

Harris, V. J. "Multicultural Curriculum: African American Children's Literature." *Young Children* 46:2 (January 1991), pp. 37–44.

Hildebrand, Verna. *Fundamentos de Educación Infantil: Jardin de Niños y Preprimaria*. Mexico City: Limusa, 1987.

Hildebrand, Verna. *Guiding Young Children*, 5th ed. Upper Saddle River, NJ: Merrill/Prentice Hall, 1994.

Hildebrand, Verna. *Introduction to Early Childhood Education*, 6th ed. Upper Saddle River, NJ: Merrill/Prentice Hall, 1997.

Hitz, Randy, and Amy Driscoll. "Give Encouragement, Not Praise." *Texas Child Care* 17:4 (Spring 1994), pp. 2–11.

Jones, Elizabeth, and Louise Derman-Sparks. "Meeting the Challenge of Diversity." *Young Children* 47:2 (January 1992), pp. 12–18.

Katz, Lilian. "What Should Young Children Be Learning?" *Child Care Information Exchange* 100 (November/December 1994), pp. 23–25.

Kostelnik, Marjorie J. (ed.). *Teaching Young Children Using Themes*. Glenview, IL: Good Year Books, 1991.

Kostelnik, Marjorie J., Anne K. Soderman, and Alice P. Whiren. *Developmentally Appropriate Programs in Early Childhood Education*. Upper Saddle River, NJ: Merrill/Prentice Hall, 1993.

Lakin, Mary Beth. "Observing from a Different Point of View." *Child Care Information Exchange* 95 (January/February 1994), pp. 65–69.

Malaguzzi, Loris. "Your Image of the Child: Where Teaching Begins." *Child Care Information Exchange* 94 (March/April 1994), pp. 52–61.

Meisels, S. J. *Developmental Screening in Early Childhood: A Guide*. Washington, DC: National Association for the Education of Young Children, 1985.

Melson, Gail F., and Alan Fogel. "The Development of Nurturance in Young Children." *Young Children* 43:3 (March 1988), pp. 57–65.

Neugebauer, Bonnie (ed.). *The Wonder of It: Exploring How the World Works*. Redmond, WA: Exchange, 1989.

Papert, Seymour. *The Children's Machine: Rethinking School in the Age of the Computer*. New York: Basic Books, 1993.

Powell, Douglas R. "Effects of Program Models and Teaching Practices: Research in Review." *Young Children* 41:6 (September 1986), pp. 60–67.

Ramos-Ford, Valerie. "Redirecting Aggressive Play." *Texas Child Care* 19:1 (Summer 1995), pp. 2–7.

Ramsey, P. *Teaching and Learning in a Diverse World: Multicultural Education for Young Children*. New York: Teachers College Press, 1987.

Rogers, Dwight L., and Dorene D. Ross. "Encouraging Positive Social Interaction among Young Children." *Young Children* 41:3 (March 1986), pp. 12–17.

Soderman, Anne K. "Dealing with Difficult Young Children: Strategies for Teachers and Parents." *Young Children* 40:5 (July 1985), pp. 15–20.

Wadlington, Elizabeth. "Basing Early Childhood Teacher Education on Adult Education Principles." *Young Children* 50:4 (May 1995), pp. 76–80.

Waring-Chaffee, Marty B. "'RDRNT . . . HRIKM' ('Ready or Not, Here I Come!'): Investigations in Children's Emergence as Readers and Writers." *Young Children* 49:6 (September 1994), pp. 52–55.

Weiser, M. G. *Group Care and Education of Infants and Toddlers*. Upper Saddle River, NJ: Merrill/Prentice Hall, 1986.

Wittmer, Donna S., and Alice S. Honig. "Encouraging Positive Social Development in Young Children." *Young Children* 49:5 (July 1994), pp. 4–12.

Wright, June L., and Daniel D. Shade (eds.). *Young Children: Active Learners in a Technological Age*. Washington, DC: National Association for the Education of Young Children, 1994.

Wyde, Joan S. "Creative, Constructive, and Concept Art." *Texas Child Care* 16:2 (Fall 1992), pp. 18–22.

York, Stacey. *Roots and Wings: Affirming Culture in Early Childhood Programs*. St. Paul, MN: Redleaf, 1991.

Ziemer, Maryann. "Science and the Early Childhood Curriculum: One Thing Leads to Another." *Young Children* 42:6 (September 1987), pp. 44–56.

CHAPTER 15

Communicating with Parents and the Public

• •

A child development center is an organization designed to provide a service to families. It is part of the social-cultural environment of the human ecological system described in Chapter 2. One way of looking at the social-cultural environment is to envision a vast network of many interconnecting parts. The child development center has a connection with each family whose child is enrolled. Those families have connections to each other, partly as a consequence of their involvement with the center. Both the center and the families have specific connections with agencies and institutions outside the center, as well as more general connections with society as a whole.

Maintaining these relationships is essential to the survival of individuals, families, and institutions, and communication is vital to any relationship. One of your major functions as director of a child development center will be to manage the communication among your center, the families whom you serve, and the rest of your community. In doing so, you will use the managerial processes that have been discussed throughout this book: planning, organizing, leading, staffing, monitoring, and controlling for quality. Your success will benefit the children in your care, their families, your center, and your community. This chapter examines aspects of your communication with parents who are part of your program and with the larger community, as well as the links between the two.

COMMUNICATION WITH PARENTS

To be approved for accreditation by the National Association for the Education of Young Children (NAEYC), your center must have a functioning system for parents' involvement in their young child's care and education. The NAEYC advocates orientation visits, conferences with parents, daily reporting to keep parents informed

<table>
<tr><th>Communication with Parents</th><th>Communication with Community</th></tr>
</table>

Communication with Parents

As prospective customers
As consumers of service
- Direct care
- Assistance with family functions

As partners in child's education
- Home visits
- Orientation
- Conferences
    Formal meetings
    Day-to-day encounters
- Newsletters
- Parent group meetings
- Home activities

As human resources for program
- Staff members
    Employees
    Volunteers
- Consultants, special services
- Leaders, board members
- Ambassadors, advocates

Communication with Community

Marketing
- Potential customers
- Funding agencies
- Advocates

Linkages with agencies
- For the center (e.g., licensing, health agencies, funding sources, child care referral systems)
- On behalf of children and families

Promoting public awareness
- Existence of center
- Characteristics of high-quality child care
- Benefits of high quality
- Risks of poor quality
- Staffing dilemma
    Quality
    Compensation
    Affordability

Informing policy makers
Connecting with colleagues

Figure 15–1
Purposes of communication with parents and community members

about their child's progress, and telephoning parents so the staff can gain information regarding parental experience, observations, and wishes. In fact, the NAEYC's assessment of how well your center performs these functions will include input from the parents. As part of your self-study for the accreditation process, you will survey parents for their evaluation of your center's parental involvement component.[1]

Parental involvement is thus a mark of quality in a child development program. Your center's job is not to supplant parents but rather to supplement families' efforts and support them as they nurture and educate their children. This is only possible if you have open communication with each family and strong links with the community in which you and those families participate. Figure 15–1 outlines examples of the various purposes you might have as you communicate with the parents in your program and other members of your community. You will no doubt be able to add to the list as you think of each category.

You will also be able to envision how the various purposes overlap and interconnect: your public relations efforts in recruiting families lays the foundation for later parent involvement when those families become part of your center; your

---

[1] Sue Bredekamp (ed.), *Accreditation Criteria & Procedures of the National Academy of Early Childhood Programs* (Washington, DC: National Association for the Education of Young Children, 1991), pp. 6, 21, 25–26.

efforts to involve parents is repaid in the public relations that those parents help you cultivate. For example, when you do a good job communicating with parents of children in your center about the ways in which you provide high-quality care, those parents become ambassadors for your center and an effective marketing vehicle for getting the word about your center out to other parents who may be looking for a good child development center. We will now consider the types of communication appropriate to each of these purposes.

Communicating with Parents as Prospective Customers

If people are going to enroll their children in your center, they will need to know, first, that you exist and, second, enough information to suggest that your center might match their needs: location, price, hours, services, and indicators of quality. To be effective, that information must be brief, accurate, and positive. You will probably want to consider all the avenues available as you plan this phase of your public relations strategy: printed material, mass media, and person-to-person oral communication.

Brochures.   Printed brochures can give parents of prospective enrollees information that will be helpful in making a decision. These brochures need to be carefully planned. The information must be up-to-date and accurate. The material must be clearly and interestingly written; that is, your center should sound like a stimulating place to be. A legal-sized colorful page printed on both sides with a space left for a mailing address is very convenient for brochures. A few pictures from your center can give the information piece some sparkle. You might ask your entire staff to brainstorm concerning ideas for a logo and content to be covered in publicity efforts. Have your staff and policy board help in final editing. Remember to give specific, concrete information and to avoid as far as possible the abstract vocabulary of the educator.

The brochure should state center name, address, and telephone number. It could include a brief description of age groups served, prices of the service, hours the center is open, availability of part-time enrollment, philosophy, typical activities, transportation provided (if any), and bus routes nearby that can be useful to nondriving parents. The parents may wish to know about the facility or the number of classrooms in the center, qualifications of the staff, availability of food service, after-school care, and so on.

Brochures can be placed with Welcome Wagon, the Chamber of Commerce, pediatricians' offices, businesses, churches, and other places of public access. Your objective in any printed matter is to provide accurate information that will create interest and make friends for your center.

DECISIONS, DECISIONS . . .

 Collect brochures from several child development centers in your community. Analyze them according to the criteria for brochures discussed here. Would you recommend any changes?

Advertisements.   Here is an example of an advertisement for a center that is brief and to the point:

> The Edgewater Little People's Child Development Center, an NAEYC-accredited center, is enrolling 3- and 4-year-old children for fall term. Call 555-1111 to learn more about this innovative child development program.

Information such as this notice may appear in a newspaper classified advertisement, on a TV or newspaper community calendar, or on a laundry room bulletin board. It tells parents of an available service. It tells them where to get more information. Using the term *innovative child development program* helps indicate that there are quality differences among centers that parents may wish to investigate.

Another form of public relations information can be demonstrated by the following notice:

> TALK ON PARENTING: The Central Michigan Association for the Education of Young Children (CMAEYC) meets on April 15 at 8 P.M. at the Edgewater Little People's Child Development Center. Dr. James Service, noted child development specialist, will discuss "Problem-Solving Techniques to Use with Your Young Child." All community parents are invited. Edgewater Child Development Center, 123 Child Way, Watertown, Michigan. Child care is provided for young children during the meeting. Call 555-1111 for more information.

Public relations objectives of the Edgewater Child Development Center are served in several ways through the simple act of hosting a public meeting on a topic of interest to parents. The notice does the following:

1. It lets people know the center exists.
2. It tells parents and others there is a connection between your center and a professional group—CMAEYC. This point may properly give the center prestige in parents' eyes.
3. Edgewater Center's phone number is displayed, giving parents an opportunity to call for information about the center. Some may preserve the number for future reference.
4. It draws attention to the Edgewater Center and identifies it with a worthwhile community service—the parent meeting.

You will also want to make sure that up-to-date information is listed with the child care information and referral service, if your community has one, in the yellow pages of your telephone book and in any other type of community directory that parents might consult.

Telephone Inquiries.   Your center's telephone offers a window to the world. People who call you will be favorably impressed by a pleasant, courteous, and professional manner. While the sounds of children laughing and playing in the background may be appealing, the sounds of children crying or adults yelling will certainly have the opposite effect. Having space and staff available to answer the telephone in an office, away from center noises, is desirable. Some center managers, who do not want to draw staff away from their primary responsibility for supervising children, have installed automatic answering machines to handle calls that come in during peak operating hours. If you choose this option, you will be wise to state your reason for doing so in the recorded message, and be certain to return all calls promptly. You will also need to provide an alternate number that parents can call to reach a human being in the event of emergency.

Staff should be instructed in telephone etiquette, including a proper greeting, knowing which questions they can answer and which should be referred to someone with more authority, and making sure that the message gets to the intended person for follow-up. This training is important for all staff, but perhaps especially so for the less experienced or substitute staff who may be present at the center.

Many centers routinely take a name and address and mail a brochure to anyone who telephones. In addition, a caller might request, or you might suggest, that they come in for a tour to see the center for themselves. Parents seeking child development services may be unskilled in requesting the information they need. The way you handle their call will give them a lasting impression regarding your center's helpfulness; it is up to you whether that impression will be positive or negative.

Parents Visiting the Center.   Parents searching for a suitable center for their child may simply drop by your center. Or their visit may be arranged by the secretary. Are you prepared to be cordial on a moment's notice? Confidence in your center will be built through open-door policies. You must have a procedure worked out that helps the parent receive answers to questions and see the center without disrupting ongoing work with children. Clearly, the teachers cannot leave their children unattended to talk with parents of prospective enrollees. Therefore, it must be made clear that to talk with the child's potential teacher a later time must be arranged, unless a qualified substitute is available for the teacher's class. Most visiting parents will be happy to cooperate if you explain the reason for your policy of avoiding disruption.

Frequently parents bring their child along. Depending on the activities under way, it may be unwise to take a visiting child into an ongoing group of children. The children may resent a visitor disrupting ongoing activity. Occasionally, children will call a strange child names or make negative or teasing comments that could be taken as unfriendly by both the child and parents. Thus, waiting until the children have gone outdoors may work best. Alternatively, another time could be arranged for the child's visit, such as after hours or on a weekend. With no other children in the room, the child can explore the environment uninhibited, without the added need to adjust socially to numerous unfamiliar children. Such exploration generally leaves a favorable impression and the child and parent become eager to enroll the child.

Prospective parents may wish to visit the center for several hours. This is wise from their point of view for they can see more clearly how children are treated and how problems are handled than if they make only a hurried visit. As manager, you should be open to such a visit, even suggest it, especially if parents come without their child.

Communicating with Parents as Consumers of a Service

Once parents do enroll their children in your center, they become consumers of your service. The most obvious example of such service is the direct care and education you provide for children, supplementing parents' time, energy, and know-how. Depending on your program's funding source and mission, you will also provide information, advice, and, when appropriate, referrals to other agencies to assist families as they fulfill the functions that are essential to society. Berns[2] identifies functions common to all families, though they may vary widely in the form they take, as reproduction, socialization, assignment of social roles, economic production and consumption, and emotional support.

Reproduction consists of more than just having babies. In order for society to survive, those babies must be cared for and kept healthy and safe so that they can replace members lost through death. Keeping children healthy and safe is the prime function of child development centers and a major concern of managers. The center might also impact the reproduction function of families in at least two other ways. First, the existence or lack of high-quality child care may influence a couple's decision to have a child. Second, the child development center might provide some families with the links that they need to access other community services, such as family planning, prenatal care, and well-baby clinics—all of which contribute directly to the family's ability to raise healthy, functioning members of society.

Socialization is the process by which "society's values, beliefs, attitudes, knowledge, skills, and techniques" are passed on to children.[3] Child development centers assist with this function in ways that are perhaps too numerous to list. The curriculum at the center, with its specific objectives for helping children acquire knowledge and skills, is only the most obvious example of its socialization function. All the other aspects of the environment and interactions at the center also embody and pass on certain beliefs and attitudes to children—from the tidy shelves that tell children how materials are to be valued and treated, to the way that caregivers foster independence and competence by encouraging toddlers to pull up their own pants after diaper changing.

For this very reason, centers must take care to ensure that a dominant culture, with its values, beliefs, knowledge, skills, and techniques, does not obliterate or teach children to devalue these same aspects of their home cultures. This means that center managers and staff must continually educate themselves about today's family forms and lifestyles and about all the cultures with whom they come in contact.[4] Only through open and honest communication will centers be able to be a help instead of a hindrance for families in the socialization of their children.

---

[2] Roberta M. Berns, *Child, Family, Community* (Fort Worth, TX: Harcourt, Brace, Jovanovich, 1989), p. 76.

[3] Berns, *Child, Family, Community,* p. 76.

[4] See Verna Hildebrand, Lillian A. Phenice, Mary M. Gray, and Rebecca P. Hines, *Knowing and Serving Diverse Families* (Upper Saddle River, NJ: Merrill/Prentice Hall, 1996). Also see the March 1995 issue of *Parenting* magazine for a special report on "The New American Families," which includes several articles and a resource guide pertaining to the variety of family forms in existence today.

Regarding the **assignment of social roles**, Berns states that families pass on to their children racial, ethnic, religious, and socioeconomic identities, consisting of behaviors and obligations. Just as with socialization, centers must take care to respect the diversity of social roles that children bring to the center with them. Centers might have a positive impact on this family function by helping parents of children with disabilities, for example, see potentials that they had not previously recognized.

Economic production and consumption are vital concerns for your center. Obviously, the existence of high-quality child development centers makes it possible for parents to work and thereby participate to a greater extent in the community's economic life. Centers might also provide information that enables families to become wiser consumers of everything from laundry detergent to television shows and toys.

Emotional support arises from relationships. Relationships at the center build on and extend the relationships that children have formed with their immediate families, fostering trust, independence, and competence. Parents, too, receive emotional support through their interactions with center staff and other parents. All parents go through feelings of being inadequate and overwhelmed by the enormous job of child rearing. In the past they received support from extended families and close neighbors. In today's mobile society, the child development center becomes, in the words of Ellen Galinsky, a prominent early childhood professional, "the new extended family."[5]

Communicating with Parents as Partners in Their Child's Education

A growing body of research demonstrates that the involvement of parents, regardless of their wealth or education, is the single most important factor for a child's success in school.[6] This involvement begins with the family's first encounter with the educational system. For many of today's children, that means when they are carried into the infant room at their child development center. The way that first relationship between parent and educator is handled can color the entire educational career—and thus, the entire life—of that child.

Unfortunately, few states require early childhood professionals to have course work or training in parent involvement skills.[7] This places a heavy responsibility on the manager of the child development center to help staff members develop these skills. Care must be taken to avoid several pitfalls. Some parents may have had bad experiences during their own schooling and, as a result, may feel intimidated or hostile toward representatives of "the system." Others might have the opposite reaction and, relinquishing their own role, depend on you to make all

---

[5] Ellen Galinsky and William Hooks, *The New Extended Family: Day Care That Works* (Boston: Houghton Mifflin, 1977).

[6] U.S. Department of Education, *Strong Families, Strong Schools*: *Building Community Partnerships for Learning* (Washington, DC: Author, 1994).

[7] See "FYI: Professional Preparation and Family Involvement," *Young Children* 50:3 (March 1995), p. 9.

1. Brief history of the center, including accreditation
2. A welcome to parents and families
3. A statement of philosophy
4. A statement regarding discipline
5. Policies regarding fees, absences, illnesses, continuing enrollment, immunizations, withdrawal, safety, storm warnings, and emergency shelter
6. Administrative structure
7. Daily routine, program for children
8. Meal and snack quality, birthday celebrations
9. Parent involvement, contacts, visits, conferences, meetings, newsletters, reporting family emergencies, and special events
10. Phone numbers for special people and agencies

Figure 15–2
Typical contents of a parent handbook

decisions as the omniscient expert. Still others might feel that they must compete with center staff for their child's affection and respect.

All of these pitfalls hamper the creation of the kind of partnership that will work best for all parties involved. The following are some concrete steps you can take, from the beginning of your relationship with each family, to help establish that partnership.

Home Visits.   A home visit is the single most effective act that can be performed for developing your center's harmonious relationship with children and their families. Home visits are common in many programs that operate on a school-year calendar. The practice is much more rare among full-day, year-round programs, whose budgets are more typically based on what parents can pay and that, therefore, seldom have the luxury of extra staff members to supervise children while directors or lead teachers make home visits. If home visits are impossible, every effort must be made to establish the same sound basis for an ongoing relationship through other means. But if home visits have been so helpful for 3- and 4-year-old children in adjusting to half-day programs, how much more beneficial might they be to the even younger child who is about to spend so much more of his or her life in your center over the next few years?

If it is financially impossible for centers to release teaching staff for such visits or to expect them to devote hours outside their already long days, perhaps a center could hire a person whose specific role is to visit the home of each new child, getting acquainted with the child, the family, and the neighborhood. This same staff member could make it a point to visit the child's classroom at the center a few times, providing a familiar face to help bridge home and center. Snapshots from home can help the child in the same way.

Orientation. This is the get-acquainted period for your center and the new family. Ideally, parents will have already visited the center to observe the program and discuss it with you and the teachers. They will have received a copy of the center's parent handbook to read at their leisure, and someone will have explained the content and purpose of the various application and permission forms that parents are asked to sign.

Phasing in new children was discussed in the preceding chapter. It simply means that parents are encouraged to bring their enrolled child and remain for part of the first several days, helping their child's adjustment to the new environment. Working parents should make this effort just as do the parents who have more free time. The child's feelings of security and happiness are at stake. Once the child has adapted and the parents and teachers agree that it is time for the parents to leave, the parents can be reassured that the staff will call the parents if the child seems to need them. Often the parents have some anxiety themselves that should be recognized. Such procedures may take a lot of effort and coordination, but they pay off in better adjustment of children and good publicity for your center, because parents will tell others that you are a person-centered manager who really has the child's and parents' interests at heart.

After a child is enrolled, parents should be encouraged to visit whenever it is convenient, without calling. In addition, you may also plan specific times for parents to visit—such as inviting mothers, dads, or a substitute parent to lunch on separate occasions. Centers often hold potluck meals in early evenings where parents bring a dish to share and have the opportunity to meet other parents at the center with their child. The children can proudly show off "my school" to parents and siblings during these times.

Conferences. Once the child has begun attending the center, you will need a system for maintaining the partnership that you have begun with the family. Many people think of parent conferences as those hurried, somewhat formal events, scheduled at the end of each semester, where teachers go over children's grades and point out areas where improvement is needed. Too often, any conferences that occur at other times are precipitated by some misbehavior or serious difficulty the child is having. How can conferences be used more positively? It helps to put the idea of conferences into a broader context and realize that every contact you or your staff has with a family can be a "mini-conference"—an opportunity to exchange information that will help you both do a better job of nurturing and educating the child.

Of course, such exchanges cannot occur unless family members and your staff speak the same language—both literally and figuratively. If you are unable to hire staff who share a language with the families you serve, perhaps you can find volunteers from the community to serve as interpreters. These same volunteers might be willing to perform the same service with any written materials you send home. Teachers and caregivers must refrain from jargon when they communicate with family members.

As a director, you can set an example for your staff by making it a point to know each child's family members well enough to greet them by name and make

Understanding each family's composition helps serve parents adequately. Including the baby during a parent's visit is usually essential.
Fran Kertez, photographer

pertinent comments or inquiries when you see them casually. "How do you like your new job?" or "Is Melinda's grandmother feeling better?" These things make the family feel welcomed and provide you with valuable information that might explain why Melinda has seemed so fretful lately.

By scheduling adequate staff and assuring staff members that relationships with families are part of their job and not just idle chatter, you can make sure that primary caregivers have a moment or two for informal sharing of information at drop-off and pick-up times. You can encourage staff to call families or send notes home to share bits of their child's daily life at the center. And, of course, you can provide paid time for staff to plan and carry out regular, more formal conferences at times when parents are available.

Comfortable, adult-size seating, a quiet corner, and perhaps some coffee or fruit juice will all set the stage for a relaxed, friendly conversation. Some teachers find it helpful to send a note to families, explaining what they hope to discuss in the conference and asking families to write down any particular questions they might have. When both parties have given thought to the conference beforehand, precious time is not wasted.

Many teachers and parents are finding it useful to have actual examples of things that illustrate the child's growth. For infants, this might be an album or diary, including photographs taken at the center, and written anecdotes about specific incidents. For slightly older children, these materials can be augmented by drawings and writing samples, photographs of block constructions or dramatic play episodes, or lists of favorite books. These concrete examples are more meaningful to parents than abstract developmental checklists, which can be unconvincing if teachers happen not to have noticed a child doing something that he or she does quite well at home. This **portfolio method** of assessing and recording children's development was described in Chapter 8.[8]

Sometimes families may want to discuss some concern or complaint with you, and you need to make it clear that you are available for this. It is essential that you express an openness to listen to parents' views without becoming defensive, on the one hand, or prejudging your staff, on the other. Assure the parent that you will investigate and take action if necessary. Follow through as quickly as possible, taking care to express the same openness and willingness to listen to the staff members involved, and report back to the parent.

DECISIONS, DECISIONS . . .

The mother of a 3-year-old requests a conference. She indicates that she feels that the children in her son's group are not being intellectually challenged. She says she has done some reading and that children should have a story time everyday. She believes her son's teachers are overlooking this need. What would you say to her? What would you say or do next?

Newsletters.   A newsletter is a useful communication device for many centers. It can come out weekly, biweekly, or less often. In a page or two, you can give short accounts of class activities and can update parents on future plans and events. A page of the children's favorite songs and poems helps get parents involved with reading and singing with their children. Hints can be given for holiday activities or places they can take children to visit, such as a local dairy or cider mill. Of course, secretarial help and some expenses will be related to these activities and must be arranged by the manager.

The computer and printer and copying machines are very helpful in producing newsletters as well as staff handbooks, parent handbooks, and any printed material that needs to be developed. Several software programs provide interesting headlines and custom formatting. Many centers now have this technology or

---

[8] See Cathy Grace and Elizabeth F. Shores, *The Portfolio and Its Use: Developmentally Appropriate Assessment of Young Children* (Little Rock, AR: Southern Association on Children under Six, 1992).

can get a friend or parent to use their equipment to produce newsletters. The computer's facility for storing materials—allowing them to be revised, added to, and moved from page to page in subsequent printings—makes short work of what used to be time-consuming typing and repeated proofreading. Even novice typists can produce professional-looking materials.

Parent Meetings.   Parents like to meet with their child's teacher for answers to certain types of questions. Teachers and caregivers can become more personally acquainted with parents if the groups are kept small. In large centers serving many children, general meetings of parents are often poorly attended simply because parents realize that specific information about their child cannot be given.

The manager's role is to establish a policy of holding parent meetings, giving teachers guidance and support as they plan for the meetings, and assigning support staff to provide logistical services, such as arranging the seating, preparing snacks and beverages, and cleaning up afterward. A manager wisely stays in the background, encouraging the teachers and caregivers to strengthen their ties with parents.

Parent meetings have a number of functions in the child development center. Parents can be called together to receive general information on center procedures and policies. Meetings can facilitate parents' getting acquainted with each other. An outgrowth of this objective is that many parents become support persons for each other—for example, baby-sitting for each other, sharing a car pool, or teaching a skill such as sewing.

Some meetings are especially designed to give parents information on parenting and child development. In addition, in some centers an extension-type program includes classes in English as a second language, nutrition lessons and cooperative food buying, driver's education, and cultural renewal—history of the parents' culture. Meetings may serve to update parents on recent activities in the center, perhaps to see the children's art exhibits or hear a singing presentation by the children.

The value of having a well-organized parent group has been felt by a number of early childhood educators who have found their programs on the list for reduced or eliminated funding. Head Start actually survived during the Nixon administration thanks to the countrywide outcry by parents who rallied to Head Start's support. Although parent groups are organized for reasons such as those stated here, one cannot discount the political strength of an already functioning parent group when a threat arises to their children's child development center.

The parents in parent cooperatives are a well-organized group because they actually operate the school. Other centers may have ad hoc committees that function in a more or less formal way speaking for parental concerns, planning programs, and advising the manager or policy board.

Parents should be encouraged to take part in conferences related to children, families, and early childhood education. Participation in their child's parent group has opened new career vistas for many parents, especially as parents attended conferences and began to see the breadth and depth of the field of early childhood education.

Including parents in a variety of events helps them see other children's behavior—thus, increasing understanding of child development.
Parent-Child Development Center, Houston, TX

With parents doing the planning for educational meetings, the topics are far more likely to fit parents' needs. A designated parent educator may help plan some meetings or the regular staff may help with plans. Parents generally wish for the teacher of their child to be present at meetings even when general topics are on the agenda. Though personal counseling cannot take place at a public meeting, a casual conversation may solve a problem, or an appointment can be made for future individual conferences.

Home Activities. Home activities have long been prescribed by child development centers, often as a way of influencing parents to spend more time and energy with their children or teaching them ways of interacting with children that are considered more appropriate or beneficial for the children than the things the parents are already doing. Some families may be unaware of the need or too busy to read to their children, for example. In that case, a workshop on effective ways of reading to children, along with a book-lending program, can be helpful. Several articles and books in the reading list at the end of this chapter contain suggestions for other ways to share appropriate activities with families.

Care must be taken, however, to avoid creating undue stress for children or parents by asking families to spend precious time on activities that are, at best, trivial and, at worst, so much like school that parents resort to the methods they remember being used with them as young children in school. They might feel pressured to send back completed "homework" and therefore demand that their children take part in activities that hold no interest for either the children or the parents.

Far more helpful is providing tactful suggestions for ways that families can enhance learning by including their young children in their daily lives. You might suggest that they ask a 4-year-old to find the items that match cost-saving coupons when they go to the grocery store, for example, or that toddlers be given a collection of clean empty margarine or yogurt containers to stack while the older family members prepare a meal. Perhaps you and your staff could brainstorm such a list simply by thinking about every room in a house and imagining the kinds of learning experiences a child could have there. Water play in the bathtub, for example, is a sound way of learning about objects that float and sink.[9]

Communicating with Parents as Human Resources for the Center

Communications and relationships are two-way affairs. The child development center is a resource for the families whose children are enrolled, and those family members are a rich source of human capital for the center. As mentioned earlier, programs such as Head Start have long made a practice of hiring staff members from within the population that they serve. What better way of making sure that your center's policies and practices are in tune with the cultural backgrounds of the children in the center? In some centers, such as parent cooperatives, the staff consists almost entirely of unpaid parent volunteers who take turns assisting the paid teacher.

Even when they are not regular staff members, parents provide valuable information and support for teachers and caregivers. Child development staff may know a lot about children in general, but usually the family knows more about any particular child. Furthermore, the burden of being the all-knowing "expert" can be a heavy one for anyone who assumes it. When center staff members value the contributions that family members can make, everyone stands to gain.

In addition to the expertise they bring with regard to their own children, families can provide a center with a rich pool of professional expertise from which to draw. Perhaps someone with advanced computer skills can help you set up a system for maintaining your center's health and financial records and train a staff member to use that system. Carpenters, plumbers, electricians, landscape gardeners, or carpet cleaners might contribute a few hours to a special improvement project. People who do not work outside their home might agree to sew new curtains or make a slipcover for the easy chair in your reading corner. A corporate executive might agree to provide consultation on some aspect of your center management. The list of possibilities is limited only by your own imagination.

Besides contributing directly to your center's day-to-day operation, family members can serve the center as leaders and policy makers. In addition to all the professional skills they might bring, parents can help you see things from the perspective of your customers, which is a key element of today's quality management. (The makeup of policy boards and advisory boards was discussed in Chapter 4.)

---

[9] See Dorothy Rich, *Megaskills* (Boston: Houghton Mifflin, 1992), for suggested activities that are age-appropriate and related to important life skills.

Finally, satisfied customers, who are informed about the elements of high-quality child development programs, can serve as ambassadors in your community. Many centers ask new parents to tell how they heard about the center, and often the most common answer is that they have a friend, neighbor, or coworker who uses the center and is highly satisfied with its service. Furthermore, when you have informed your satisfied customers about the value of highly qualified staff and better adult-child ratios, they can help prospective customers understand why the lower rates at another center are not necessarily a better bargain. Satisfied parents also become advocates when, for example, a building owner moves to evict a center or when funding and licensing safeguards are threatened by government cutbacks. Advocacy is discussed in greater detail in the following chapter.

Family members as well as centers derive benefits when they contribute human capital in this way. In addition to immediate recognition and approval, some might gain valuable experience that can be used in their own careers. For some, what is gained is a new level of confidence that comes from being appreciated. One mother, who volunteered in her son's early childhood classroom many years ago, still credits that experience with restoring her self-image and enabling her to find the rewarding work that she enjoys today.

COMMUNICATION WITH COMMUNITY MEMBERS

Children grow up and families move on, regardless of how well you have cultivated your relationship with them during the time that they were with you. To remain viable, you will need a continual flow of new families into your center. You will also need to establish good relations with others in the community in order to provide high-quality services for the families of children in your care. Thus, as you plan your communications program, you will want to take these other elements into account.

Marketing

Marketing is the process by which you inform the community about the benefits and desirability of your services. You may do this to attract new customers and use all the techniques described earlier for relating to prospective customers. You may use marketing strategies to convince a corporation to purchase your services for its employees or a charitable agency to fund a scholarship program for homeless children to attend your center. More general marketing strategies can create an informed body of potential advocates to come to your assistance when you need them.

More than one child development manager has been faced with disgruntled neighbors who would like to see the center shut down or moved. They might be neighbors who object to noise from the playground or church members who resent what they see as messy rooms. Wise managers see to it that as many or more people have been informed of all the good that their program accomplishes. Good publicity can help you with all these marketing objectives.

Publicity

Every center appreciates good publicity. You might get acquainted with a reporter who likes to do stories about children and give a standing invitation to him or her to visit your center. Or, if your groups of children will be doing an interesting project or field trip, you might inform your local newspaper. The editor might send a photographer or reporter for a human interest piece.

One of the best publicity stories of all for your center will be when you become fully accredited by the NAEYC. You can plan that story well in advance, having photos available and topping the story off with a photo of your certificate! Of course, you will frame the certificate and place it in a conspicuous place in your center. You will want the interested editors of newspapers and TV to know that accreditation signifies that you have met the criteria for recognition as an out-standing child development center with a high-quality program for young children. And, thereafter, remember to add a note about accreditation to your public relations materials, brochures, and, perhaps, even your letterhead.

You can also write stories when really newsworthy items arise. These should be written like any news story, with the basic information in the lead paragraph, followed by supporting details. This form allows the paper to use as much of the story as space allows. Deleting material from the end of the story, if necessary, will not hurt the basic information. Be sure that all names and dates are precisely correct. Mail the typed, double-spaced story to the appropriate editor.

Publicity for your center also comes when you or your staff members participate with or appear before other groups. Say, for example, that you talk to a church group about child care. The people will gain impressions about you and about your center from how well you are prepared and the manner of your presentation. Be sure to share opportunities with your staff to represent your center. This approach makes them feel good and also shows the public how you value your teachers' abilities. This holds, too, for encouraging your staff to be active in local, state, and national professional associations. Thus your center gains professional recognition.

You and your staff can initiate appearances on conference programs by following procedures outlined. The NAEYC, for example, publishes a call for presentation proposals in *Young Children* about a year before its annual meeting. Your state and local associations may work in the same way, perhaps within a shorter time frame. A presentation has most of the same components suggested for writing a good feature article.

Even if you do not choose to present a topic, you can tell conference planners the topics and presenters that you would like to see on the program. Some conferences schedule "work-alike" groups, which give each category of professional a chance to meet with people with similar interests and problems—for example, managers, teachers, cooperative centers, private centers, public centers, employer-operated centers, and laboratory schools.

You or your teachers may wish to publish articles in local, state, or national journals. Many practitioners have innovative ideas that would be useful to others.

You or your teachers could write up the innovation in an article and submit it to a journal read by other teachers.

Writing good feature articles entails four steps, according to Richardson and Callahan, as adapted by Burckhardt.[10] They are (a) visualize your audience, (b) analyze your problem, (c) organize your thinking and material, and (d) dramatize your presentation. Before you start to write, study issues of the magazine or journal to determine the nature, style, and length of its articles. Prepare your article, writing and rewriting until it is clear and interesting. Type it neatly, double-spaced. Professional journals want names of authors on a separate page from the article. They may want two or three copies of each article to speed up the review process.

Magazines require that you enclose a self-addressed return envelope and postage, to facilitate the article's return should the editors find it currently not suitable for their publication. If the article is returned, look it over for errors or outdated material, improve wording where possible, and submit it to another magazine or journal. Persistence pays off, so never give up on the first rejection slip. Your byline can include information about your center, which adds to public recognition of your center.

Linkages with Agencies

Your success in cultivating linkages with agencies in your community can benefit your center in numerous ways. Licensing representatives can often offer advice and information that will help you meet or even exceed regulatory requirements. Centers that have established good contacts with their community health services will have experts to call when, for example, an outbreak of head lice occurs. Networking with other agencies in your community puts you in position to hear about new sources of funding or requests for proposals that might be put out by corporate or charitable foundations. And, of course, you will want to maintain ties with your local resource and referral agency, which is your link to a large pool of prospective customers, as well as a possible resource for staff training.

The same networks that benefit your center can benefit the families and children you serve. Many centers keep a file of community agencies and resources to which they can refer families as needs arise. Such referrals will be much more productive if you have established contacts in the various agencies and can suggest that families ask for a particular person by name. Your agency contacts might also bring specific resources to the center where they are more accessible to families. Some centers have health department representatives offer immunization clinics on site at certain times during the year. Others might invite a parenting expert from the community mental health clinic to conduct workshops for interested family members. Perhaps you can think of other ways that child development centers might help families access the services that are available in your community.

---

10 Ann Burckhardt, *Writing about Food and Families, Fashion and Furnishings* (Ames: Iowa State University Press, 1984), p. 8.

Promoting Public Awareness

Promoting public awareness of the existence of your center for marketing and public relations purposes is only one benefit of your communications program. As a leader in the early childhood profession, you will also want to promote public awareness of the benefits of high-quality programs for children, the risks of poor-quality care, and the dilemma faced by managers who try to balance high quality of care with affordability for parents and fair compensation for their staff.

This awareness will benefit children, families, and early childhood professionals in general as people become more willing to invest personal and government resources in paying for high-quality care. One of the findings of the four-state study of *Cost, Quality and Child Outcomes in Child Care Centers* was that "inadequate consumer knowledge . . . reduces incentives for some centers to provide good-quality care."[11] In other words, parents, although they value good-quality care, do not have sufficient information about what constitutes high quality in a center. One effective method of conveying this information to parents is the NAEYC's accreditation system: according to the study, accredited centers were able to charge more for their services than other centers.[12]

In general, however, neither parents nor government agencies pay rates that reflect a quality difference between centers. This means that, as a manager striving to provide high-quality care for children and fair compensation for your staff, you will have a harder time making ends meet than the manager who is less conscientious.

Stronger licensing regulations could reduce this financial advantage for mediocre centers. According to the Cost, Quality, and Child Outcomes Study, "states with more demanding licensing standards have fewer poor-quality centers."[13] But it takes an informed public to demand those stronger standards and to be willing to invest the resources necessary for their consistent enforcement.

---

[11] Cost, Quality, and Child Outcomes Study Team, *Cost, Quality and Child Outcomes in Child Care Centers: Executive Summary* (Denver: Economics Department, University of Colorado, 1995), p. 9.

[12] Roger Neugebauer, "Public and Private Purchasing Practices Drive Quality Down," *Child Care Information Exchange* 103 (May/June 1995), p. 14.

[13] Cost, Quality, and Child Outcomes Study Team, *Cost, Quality and Child Outcomes in Child Care Centers*, p. 4.

As you work toward accreditation and inform the public about your center, you are helping raise awareness of all these issues. In this way, you can have positive effects for children, families, and child care professionals far beyond those directly involved in your center. Fortunately, you are not alone in this endeavor. You are part of a community of professionals who are working on a variety of fronts to achieve the goal of high-quality care for all children. The NAEYC provides an example.

THE NAEYC'S CHILD CARE INFORMATION SERVICE

The NAEYC has an information service available through the (800) 424-2460 phone number at their Washington, DC, headquarters. The service is designed to help anyone needing information on children, child care, and early childhood education. They have a computerized "Quick Facts" database. Managers and others can receive some information over the phone and leads for locating published information. One objective of the service is to facilitate networking among individuals in the early childhood community—that is, helping people find others who can provide the help or information desired. Information is available on topics such as the following:

- People to contact in local and state affiliate groups
- National child-related issues and legislation
- Standards for child care centers
- Center accreditation
- Names of accredited centers in a locality of interest
- Demographics related to children's needs for care
- Affordability of child care

DOUBLE DUTY IN PUBLIC RELATIONS

Developing a sound public relations strategy pays off in numerous ways. Preparation of one type of information may be useful as you develop some other types of public information. For example, carefully prepared talks to parents can form the nucleus for professional articles, or vice versa. Carefully stated objectives can enhance your written reports to the policy board as well as serve as key statements on a public information brochure. Pictures taken for publicity pieces make delightful books for children in a classroom. They can be arranged on tough cardboard and labeled with short descriptive phrases that children will soon be "reading."

Many materials serve several purposes; therefore, you must develop a system for carefully filing all the materials you develop. With an adequate filing system you will be able to locate quickly a previous piece that might serve a present need when updated.

CONCLUSION

Child development centers, as organizations designed to provide a service to families, comprise part of the social-cultural environment of the human ecological system. To provide high-quality programs, center managers must cultivate effective communication and positive relationships with the families of children they serve, as well as with people and institutions in the larger community. Centers relate to families as prospective customers, as consumers of services, as partners in their children's care and education, and as potential human capital resources.

High-quality child development centers put a high priority on the involvement of parents. The NAEYC center accreditation program calls for evidence of involvement of parents. Parents who ultimately enroll their child are extended the hand of friendship and encouraged to participate in orientation processes for their child, home visits, conferences, parent meetings, and evaluation of the center's program. Parents are encouraged to drop in on a moment's notice or talk with the teacher or manager about issues for improving the service. Teachers need to be involved directly with the parents of a child enrolled in their group to coordinate the efforts of home and school in the child's development. Newsletters, parents' handbook, and other printed matter are used to help inform parents.

In their relating to the larger community, centers use marketing strategies to broaden their customer base, attract funding sources, and develop a pool of potential advocates. Centers form linkages with community agencies to help themselves operate more smoothly and effectively, as well as to create a network of resources to which families can turn for assistance. Finally, centers promote public awareness of the hallmarks and advantages of high-quality care, as well as the liabilities of mediocre care and, in so doing, help create a demand for excellence in all programs for young children.

APPLICATIONS

1. Make a file of newspaper articles on child development centers. Include feature articles, enrollment announcements, and classified advertisements. Discuss these with your classmates, especially evaluating the benefit for the center of feature articles.
2. Study several professional articles on a favorite curriculum area; then write a 500-word article for parents encouraging them to use that curriculum area, say, art media, at home. Have your classmates review the article and offer suggestions. Work on it until it is well done and find a magazine to submit it to.
3. Read articles in the local or regional professional publication of the NAEYC. Prepare an article from your experience that would help other teachers or managers. Have classmates make helpful suggestions.
4. Plan a meeting for parents of a center. Ask for their input in planning, write out the plan, and carry it out, if possible. Evaluate the meeting.
5. Place materials about recruiting, publicity, and parent communication in your management notebook.

STUDY QUESTIONS

1. Why might parents hesitate to interact voluntarily with teachers?
2. Discuss who is responsible for making the contacts with parents whose children are enrolled in early childhood programs.
3. Why do authorities believe interaction with all parents is essential?
4. Give the five functions of families as identified by Berns, and indicate how teachers or managers may be helpful or involved with each function.
5. How do communication with parents and public relations relate to each other?
6. Discuss the importance of the role of the person answering the center's phone.
7. List and describe in detail at least five ways teachers and managers can interact with parents.
8. Describe how a news item is written about an event at your center.
9. List the four steps for writing good feature articles as discussed in this chapter.

SUGGESTED READINGS

Albrecht, Kay. "Helping Teachers Grow: Talking with Parents." *Child Care Information Exchange* 82 (November/December 1991), pp. 45–47.

Albrecht, Kay (ed.). *Quality Criteria for School-Age Child Care Programs*. Alexandria, VA: American Home Economics Association, 1991.

Aspen Institute. *The Challenge of Parenting in the '90s*. Washington, DC: Author, 1995.

Barclay, Kathy, and Elizabeth Boone. *Building a Three-Way Partnership: The Leader's Role in Linking School, Families, and Community*. New York: Scholastic, 1995.

Berger, Eugenia H. *Parents as Partners in Education: Families and Schools Working Together*, 4th ed. Upper Saddle River, NJ: Merrill/Prentice Hall, 1995.

Brazelton, T. Berry. *Working and Caring*. Reading, MA: Addison-Wesley, 1987.

Brazelton, T. Berry. *Touchpoints: Your Child's Emotional and Behavioral Development*. Reading, MA: Addison-Wesley, 1992.

Brock, Dana R., and Elizabeth L. Dodd. "A Family Lending Library: Promoting Early Literacy Development." *Young Children* 49:3 (March 1994), pp. 16–21.

Bundy, Blakely. "Write an Article for *Young Children?* Who, Me?" *Young Children* 49:5 (July 1994), p. 87.

California Department of Education. *A Guide to Creating Partnerships with Parents*. Sacramento: Author, 1990.

Davidson, D. H. "Child Care as a Support for Families with Special Needs." *Young Children* 45:3 (March 1990), pp. 47–48.

Dinkmeyer, Don. *The Parent's Handbook: Systematic Training for Effective Parenting (STEP)*. New York: Random House, 1982.

Dodge, Diane Trister. "Sharing Your Program with Families." *Child Care Information Exchange* 101 (January/February 1995), pp. 7–11.

Dreikurs, Rudolf, and Lawrence Zukerman. *Children—The Challenge & Parent's Guide*. New York: Dutton, 1987.

Foster, Suzanne M. "Successful Parent Meetings." *Young Children* 50:1 (November 1994), pp. 78–80.

Galen, H. "Increasing Parental Involvement in Elementary School: The Nitty Gritty of One Successful Program." *Young Children* 46:2 (January 1991), pp. 18–22.

Galinsky, Ellen. *The Six Stages of Parenthood*. Reading, MA: Addison-Wesley, 1987.

Galinsky, Ellen, and Judy David. *The Preschool Years: Family Strategies That Work—from Experts and Parents*. New York: Ballantine, 1988.

Gargiulo, Richard M., Katie Sefton, and Stephen B. Graves. "Writing for Publication in Early Childhood Education." *Childhood Education* 68:3 (Spring 1992), pp. 157–160.

Gestwicki, Carol. *Home, School and Community Relations*. Albany, NY: Delmar, 1992.

Gordon, Joel. "Separation Anxiety: How to Ask a Family to Leave Your Center." *Child Care Information Exchange* 59 (January 1988), pp. 13–15.

Greenman, Jim. "It Seemed to Make Sense at the Time: Stupid Child Care Tricks." *Child Care Information Exchange* 96 (March/April 1994), pp. 19–22.

Greenman, Jim. "No Surprises: Reducing Staff-Parent Tensions." *Child Care Information Exchange* 103 (May/June 1995), pp. 29–31.

Hale, Janice. *Black Children: Their Roots, Culture, and Learning Styles*. Baltimore: Johns Hopkins University Press, 1986.

Hatcher, Barbara (ed.). *Learning Opportunities beyond the School*. Wheaton, MD: Association for Childhood Education International, 1987.

Helm, Jeanne. "Family Theme Bags: An Innovative Approach to Family Involvement in the School." *Young Children* 49:4 (May 1994), pp. 48-52.

Hildebrand, Verna. *Introduction to Early Childhood Education*, 6th ed. Upper Saddle River, NJ: Merrill/Prentice Hall, 1997.

Hildebrand, Verna. *Parenting and Teaching Young Children*. New York: McGraw-Hill, 1990.

Johnston, Lynne, and Joy Mermin. "Easing Children's Entry to School: Home Visits Help." *Young Children* 49:5 (July 1994), pp. 62–68.

Kasting, Arlene. "Respect, Responsibility and Reciprocity: The 3 Rs of Parent Involvement." *Childhood Education* 70:3 (Spring 1994), pp. 146–150.

Kokoski, Teresa M., and Nancy Downing-Leffler. "Boosting Your Science and Math Programs in Early Childhood Education: Making the Home-School Connection." *Young Children* 50:5 (July 1995), pp. 35–39.

Leach, Penelope. *Your Baby and Child from Birth to Age Five*. New York: Knopf, 1989.

Lee, Fong Yun. "Asian Parents as Partners." *Young Children* 50:3 (March 1995), pp. 4–8.

Miller, Karen. "The Dual Challenge: Meeting the Needs of Parents and Babies." *Child Care Information Exchange* 92 (July/August 1993), pp. 56–58.

National Commission on Children. *Strengthening and Supporting Families*. Washington, DC: Author, 1993.

National Task Force on School Readiness. *Caring Communities: Supporting Young Children and Families*. Alexandria, VA: National Association of State Boards of Education, 1991.

Neugebauer, Bonnie (ed.). "Beginnings Workshop: Working with Parents of Children with Differing Abilities." *Child Care Information Exchange* 88 (November/December 1992), pp. 25–40.

Neuman, Susan B., and Kathy Roskos. "Bridging Home and School with a Culturally Responsive Approach." *Childhood Education* 70:4 (September 1994), pp. 210–214.

"Parent Involvement: It's More Than Baking Muffins." *Texas Child Care* 18:1 (Summer 1994), pp. 10–15.

Powell, Douglas R. *Families and Early Childhood Programs*. Washington, DC: National Association for the Education of Young Children, 1989.

Schon, Isabel. "Hispanic Books: Libros Hispanicos." *Young Children* 43:4 (May 1988), p. 85.

Shiff, E. (ed.). *Experts Advise Parents: A Guide to Raising Loving Responsible Children*. New York: Delacorte, 1987.

Stipek, Deborah, Linda Rosenblatt, and Laurine DiRocco. "Making Parents Your Allies." *Young Children* 49:3 (March 1994), pp. 4–9.

Stone, Jeannette G. *Teacher-Parent Relationships*. Washington, DC: National Association for the Education of Young Children, 1988.

Studer, Jeannine R. "Listen So That Parents Will Speak." *Childhood Education* 70:2 (Winter 1993/94), pp. 74–76.

Tiger, Fern. "The Art of the Brochure." *Child Care Information Exchange* 102 (March/April 1995), pp. 24–29.

U.S. Department of Education. *Strong Families, Strong Schools: Building Community Partnerships for Learning*. Washington, DC: Author, 1994.

Washington, Valora, Valorie Johnson, and Janet Brown McCracken. *Grassroots Success! Preparing Schools and Families for Each Other*. Washington, DC: National Association for the Education of Young Children, 1995.

Wassom, Julie. "Prospect Follow Up Pays Dividends in Enrollment." *Child Care Information Exchange* 92 (July/August 1993), pp. 5–9.

Wassom, Julie. "Turning Bad Press into Prestige." *Child Care Information Exchange* 101 (January/February 1995), pp. 69–72.

Wickens, Elaine. "Penny's Question: 'I Will Have a Child in My Class with Two Moms–What Do You Know about This?'" *Young Children* 48:3 (March 1993), pp. 25–28.

CHAPTER **16**

Advocacy and Professionalism

• •

Y ou can be an advocate for children. Advocacy is a natural outgrowth of managerial leadership and your professionalism. By virtue of your role in providing child development services, you are in a pivotal position to advocate for children. You have seen lots of families firsthand. You are in touch with them and are aware of their needs and concerns. You have credibility and expertise because your child development center is an important support service for families in your community. Yes, you can be a strong advocate for children and their families. As many people would say, free competition in the marketplace of ideas is what makes the democratic system work well. Will you add your voice to the marketplace of ideas and help create a better world for children and families of the 21st century?

DECISIONS, DECISIONS . . .

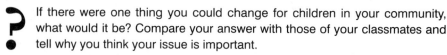
? If there were one thing you could change for children in your community, what would it be? Compare your answer with those of your classmates and tell why you think your issue is important.

GOALS OF CHILD ADVOCATES

An **advocate** is defined as one who works hard to promote a cause—in this context, promoting programs and actions improving life for children and families. The **child advocate** builds linkages between children and their families and other systems in their local and global environments with the goal of making significant improvements in the lives of children. A child advocate also works indirectly to improve children's lives through higher professional standards and better working conditions for the people who staff child development centers.

By using the human ecological system framework, as has been done throughout this book, you can visualize where linkages between various systems would be advantageous, even essential, to a child individually or to children as a group. The human ecological system framework helps us think of the various systems and issues that overlap and influence children's well-being. One begins to see how the ripple effect works: when you change one factor in the system, it affects and changes other things. Here are just three examples: An increase in unemployment rates quickly causes children to drop out of child development centers because parents cannot pay tuition when they are unemployed. A rise in the cost of living causes more women to seek employment outside their homes, thus influencing them to seek child care. The need to make child care affordable means lower wages for staff, which means that as soon as they acquire some expertise, many workers leave the field for better paying jobs. Thus, centers must perpetually divert energy and other resources to recruiting and training staff, and children are continually in the position of being "practiced on" by neophytes in the profession.

WORK OF THE ADVOCATE

Advocacy means that you become committed to joining in discussions and actions supporting a cause that you think needs community attention. You learn about it, work for it, and persuade others to join you. As a child advocate, you attempt to understand situations from the child's point of view, and you decide to do something specific to improve the conditions of a child or a group of children. You acquire this insight from your professional education and experience and your daily interactions with the families your center serves. You see parents in happy and depressed moods. You see them hurrying to work and hurrying home. You see children who have just become comfortable and happy in your center having to leave because their parents can no longer afford the tuition, and your center cannot make ends meet without it. You see caregivers in your center working hard to provide a high-quality program for other people's children, yet earning a salary that does not allow them to provide the same experience for their own children.

You also have a broad perspective arising from your philosophy, education, and experience with many children and parents over the years. You have a strong belief that something can be done about most things if enough ideas and energy are brought to bear on them. As you advocate for an individual child, a group of children, or all children in our global village, you show your optimistic view that, with effort, a better future is possible. You will be adding your voice to those of a long line of visionary leaders throughout history and around the world, using the time-honored democratic process to bring about the kinds of progress that modern societies increasingly seek to provide. Most importantly, keep in mind that using the talents and ideas of everyone leads to more progress.

You may assume because our state and federal governments have departments appropriately labeled mental health, public health, social services, education, and so on, that children will receive the services they need from these departments. Unfortunately, even though well-intentioned individuals head and serve in those agencies, budget constraints, bureaucracy, and the sheer size of the workload often hamper them, causing children's concerns and problems to be pushed aside.

STEPS IN ADVOCACY

At a workshop for women leaders, *advocacy* was defined as "pursuing specific activities to reach a vision."[1] Potential advocates were encouraged to follow five steps toward reaching that vision:

1. Know what you want to say about an important issue.
2. Decide who needs to hear your message.
3. Decide how to say it in a way that will capture attention and promote positive responses.
4. Get help from groups with common goals.
5. Develop a plan of action.

DECISIONS, DECISIONS . . .

With a small group of your classmates, choose one topic from the list of changes needed for children in your community. Apply the five steps of advocacy described here. Develop a brief statement of what you would like to see happen. Decide who needs to hear your message for the change to happen, and then tailor your message for each specific audience. Brainstorm a list of groups or individuals who might be your allies in this issue, and, finally, try to anticipate roadblocks you will encounter and think about how you will surmount them. Present your plan to the entire class.

EXAMPLES OF ADVOCACY

Advocates are sensitive to how treatment, services, or conditions appear to the children and families. They are aware that high-quality child development programs cannot exist without well-trained and fairly compensated professionals to staff them. Therefore, advocates for children and families work at the following:

1. Waking up complacent agencies
2. Forging linkages among systems on behalf of children and child care professionals

---

[1] Nicole Etchart, "Cairo, Beijing & Beyond!" *Association for Women in Development Newsletter* 9:3 (June 1995), p. 15.

3. Resolving all conflicts peacefully
4. Providing or locating information
5. Getting people to work together
6. Protecting constitutional and legal rights of children and parents
7. Helping parents enjoy their children
8. Encouraging needed new services to be developed
9. Providing publicity on issues related to children
10. Improving children's lives now for future payoffs
11. Improving the lives of child care workers

Examples of each of these areas of advocacy follow.

Waking Up Complacent Agencies

Advocating for elementary education, a group of parents persuaded the principal of a school to put monitors on the school yard to keep children safe. A group of parents of children with disabilities advocated among the legislators for provisions for special education for their children. Decision makers' attention must become focused on what constituent members consider problems. When the governor of one state, as part of a budget-cutting measure, proposed cutting out child care center licensing, the child care community advocates went into immediate action. They provided decision makers with information about the need for licensing to protect children, and—perhaps more importantly from the governor's point of view—about federal child care legislation that required that federal funds be allocated only to licensed centers.

Forging Linkages Among Systems on Behalf of Children

Parents and teachers, who have become increasingly concerned about the warlike toys being sold for children, have banded together to protest to toy manufacturers and distributors. This effort links the home, school, and business communities. Some advocates may seek to use legal means to regulate the sale of war toys, arguing for renewed restrictions on advertising during children's television.

Other types of linkages are being forged in states throughout the country as community colleges and 4-year institutions seek to establish articulation agreements that will allow child development professionals to move on to higher levels of education without starting over. In the same vein, advocates are calling for the agencies that confer teaching credentials to coordinate their requirements with those that license child care centers, recognizing that all young children need nurturing *and* education, whether their child development center goes by the name of school or day care.

Resolving All Conflicts Peacefully

Conflict may involve children, or children and their families. It might include neighborhoods represented in your center. Using your conflict resolution skills, you help children learn to talk over their differences. With elementary school playground conflicts becoming more aggressive, one group of parents helped persuade administrators to initiate a conflict resolution scheme. Specialists taught the children to become negotiators. When a problem occurred, the negotiators went immediately to the site of the conflict and prompted the participants to talk over their problem. Similarly, you may hold meetings in your center to help resolve a neighborhood conflict or disagreement. Conflict resolution strategies are needed, and they are effective from the individual level to the global level.

Providing or Locating Information

One important role of the advocate is to provide information essential for wise decision making. You should be comfortable with this role, especially when it comes to facts about children's development and the early childhood profession. You know about information sources and where to look for them. You can help your staff keep open minds and a willingness to listen and accept new facts and ideas. You may use many means for getting facts to people. Suggestions range from one-to-one conversations to the use of various types of mass media.

Getting People to Work Together

Leadership is required in advocacy. Many shy people have come out of their psychological shells when they have found a cause to work for. Cooperation grows when people know each other. Within your center you can facilitate social exchange among families to aid their working together. First, parents must become acquainted with each other and must become aware of their common concerns. They must realize where time, energy, or money can be invested most effectively to serve their children better. Many of your activities and arrangements will involve specific goals to help people become acquainted and cooperate. Parents, who work together in the parent cooperative early childhood program, often baby-sit for each other and even vacation together because they have children of the same age and have become acquainted on an equal basis. You can facilitate the growth of similar cooperation in your center.

Protecting Constitutional and Legal Rights of Children and Parents

Rights of parents and children should be paramount in all you do within your center. From your admission and staffing policies onward, everything should be done from an individual rights point of view. All civil rights must be protected at all times.

The goals of the antibias curriculum advocated by the NAEYC might be viewed as a proactive approach toward protecting the civil rights of children and families. They include fostering the healthy self-image of all children, as well as cultivating empathy and respect for others, the ability to recognize unfairness, and the willingness to stand up for oneself and others when unfairness exists.[2]

---

[2] Louise Derman-Sparks, "Reaching Potentials through Antibias, Multicultural Curriculum," in Sue Bredekamp and Teresa Rosegrant (eds.), *Reaching Potentials: Appropriate Curriculum and Assessment for Young Children* (Washington, DC: National Association for the Education of Young Children, 1992), pp. 114–127.

Clearly, the center that embraces these goals is contributing toward the protection of civil rights in ways that will reach far beyond the center's walls.

The Americans with Disabilities Act requires that your center make reasonable effort to accommodate the special needs of children with disabilities whose parents may want to enroll them in your school. Here again, as a leader and advocate, you can take a proactive stance and make the extra effort needed to access community resources and devise creative solutions to meeting those special needs. You can enthusiastically encourage the enrollment of children with special needs, knowing that all children—not only those with disabilities—benefit from such inclusion.

Helping Parents Enjoy Their Children

Helping parents appreciate their children and learn more about how to enjoy them may be part of your advocacy work. Simply by sharing news of the child's accomplishments you can inspire parents to look more closely and notice things that they might have taken for granted. Many centers have discovered that parents are fascinated by attractive displays documenting children's work with photographs, drawings, and samples of their conversations. An added benefit of such displays is that parents gain new respect for children's thinking and the work that teachers and caregivers do.

At every stage of life, children have some negative characteristics that may bother parents, especially those who do not understand children's growth and development very well. However, if you teach them about child development and how to cope with the various stages, you will be making life in many homes less stressful for both parents and children. The hours in the child development center each day relieving parents of caregiving can help them be more relaxed and loving when they take the child home at the end of the day. You help the children by serving their needs and sending them home with interesting ideas and new skills to share with their families.

Encouraging New Services to Be Developed

Being aware of children's needs helps you make recommendations for important new services. In recent years, children's science museums have developed that provide hands-on activities helping children learn more than they could ever learn just by looking and listening. Drop-in child care in churches, airports, and shopping centers is a response of sensitive businesspeople who realize that being a child tagging along after parents in these settings is tiring and not much fun. Businesses are persuaded that children's needs are served better in a child-appropriate playroom that provides a place to rest, a snack, and other children. It takes creative people to conceptualize helpful new services, and it takes people knowledgeable about child development to make sure that they are appropriate places for children, not just brightly decorated parking lots.

Providing Publicity on Issues Related to Children

You can advocate among parents, through various media, the activities that children and their families would find enjoyable and educational. For example, you

The teacher has a goal of helping children understand other children with disabilities by using dolls, stories, and discussions.
University of Georgia Child Development Laboratory, Athens

can let parents know when the library story hours are held, when a children's symphony is playing, or when a parade will be held. Giving this publicity to your parents fosters their parenting skills and is an important part of your job. You can extend your horizons more widely and consider all children in the local or global community. For instance, you can encourage a television station to run a special series for parents—and you can even organize discussion groups around the series. You can inform parents and the public when one of your staff members completes a new credential or college degree. You can participate in and spread the word about national celebrations of the Week of the Young Child or Worthy Wage Day. You can encourage the various media organizations in their coverage of programs appropriate for families by calling or writing them or by encouraging parents to comment to the media.

Improving Children's Lives Now for Future Payoffs

Many people are very concerned about their own children but are not strong advocates for other people's children. You, with a broader view, can help people in your community and beyond realize that the future depends on everybody's children. What we do or fail to do for children today will come back to repay us in the form of their behaviors as youth and adults. It is really in our collective local and global self-interest to do well by all children when they are young.

UNICEF, the United Nations Children's Fund, takes the position that the needs and rights of children should, in fact, be the centerpiece of all other development strategies. Its report, *The State of the World's Children 1995*, states the case eloquently:

> This argument is based neither on institutional vested interest nor on sentimentality about the young; it is based on the fact that childhood is the period when minds and bodies are being formed and during which even temporary deprivation is capable of inflicting lifelong damage and distortion on human development. It follows that, whether the threat be war and conflict or economic marginalization, children should, as far as is humanly possible, be protected from the worst mistakes and malignancies of the adult world. . . . [T]he vital, vulnerable years of childhood should be given a first call on societies' concerns and capacities, and this commitment should be maintained in good times and in bad. A child has only one chance to develop normally; and the protection of that one chance therefore demands the kind of commitment that will not be superseded by other priorities. There will always be something more immediate; there will never be anything more important.[3]

The UNICEF report summarizes 10 goals for the year 2000 that have been agreed to by almost all the world's governments.[4] The goals set specific targets for the following issues:

1. Lower infant and child mortality rates
2. Lower maternal mortality rates
3. Reduced rates of malnutrition, fewer incidences of low birthweight, and increased support for breastfeeding
4. Increased immunization rates and the elimination of or reduction in deaths due to preventable childhood illnesses
5. Reduction in deaths caused by diarrheal disease
6. Reduction in deaths due to acute respiratory infections
7. Increased access to education for all children
8. Clean water and safe sanitation for all communities
9. Universal acceptance in all countries of the Convention on the Rights of the Child
10. Availability of high-quality family planning information and services for all[5]

These goals may seem to focus only on distant, Third World countries, but the UNICEF report indicates that the United States is behind several other industrialized societies in infant mortality rate. The report also points out the ways that poverty, population growth, and environmental degradation are interrelated with each other and with political and social instability. Thus, advocates in the United States have plenty of reasons to concern themselves with the state of the world's children.

---

[3] James P. Grant, *The State of the World's Children 1995* (New York: Oxford University Press, 1995), pp. 9–10.

[4] As of this writing, President Bill Clinton has signed but the U.S. Senate has not ratified the UN Convention on the Rights of the Child. For a copy of the convention, write to UNICEF, Division of Public Affairs, UNICEF House, 3 United Nations Plaza, New York, NY 10017.

[5] Grant, *The State of the World's Children 1995*, p. 10.

Improving the Lives of Child Care Workers

Advocating to improve the lives of child care workers is a logical extension of your work on behalf of children and families. Unless child care workers receive adequate salaries and recognition of the importance of their work, we will continue to see annual staff turnover rates of crisis proportions. Only by making it possible for dedicated people to stay in the field without sacrificing the welfare of their own families can we make it possible for children to have the consistency and continuity of care that we know they need.

Advocates in this important area are working toward breaking the link between what families can pay and what child care workers should earn. They argue that every part of society—government, corporations, and the citizenry—should help bear the cost of providing high-quality child development centers for all our children. They argue that licensing and certification requirements should establish training requirements for each level within the child development profession. And they argue that child care workers should receive additional compensation and responsibility as they obtain additional training.

REACHING DECISION MAKERS

Your target population for advocacy is usually the public, business, and government decision makers. It will be the general public, as influenced by prominent decision makers, in the case of passing school bond issues, for example. Decision makers are usually political beings, responsive to a constituent group. These decision makers need solid information, and often advocacy groups can provide it. Advocates must also analyze the power dynamics of any organization they wish to influence. Getting the support of only one powerful leader may be all that is necessary to get a policy changed. Advocates must take the time to analyze the dynamics of situations to know who the leaders are and to seek the best people to influence those leaders. Advocates can telephone the NAEYC's Public Affairs Division at (202) 328-2605 for information that will be helpful in this process.

LINKING ADVOCACY TO OTHER PROFESSIONAL ROLES

Advocacy can be carried on by many people. As a professional, you will likely be involved with many aspects of advocating for children and parents wherever you go. Through other professional avenues, you will have additional opportunities for advocacy.

Speaking, Writing, and Research

You can see that advocacy really means taking leadership in speaking, writing, and researching—all in the interest of children and families. Advocacy requires many aspects of leadership. Advocacy requires you to make public presentations, conduct meetings, meet others, and use your ability to express your ideas on behalf of children and families.

Writing and researching are important professional contributions you can make as an advocate. Writing can start with newsletters to your parents and memos to your staff. In addition to information regarding coming events, you can write feature articles for the community media on topics you believe would interest readers. For example, developmental stages that are very familiar to you as a manager of a child development center may be less understood by some segments of your community. You may be able to enlighten others by writing a short article about children's development. With the availability of word processors, newsletters can easily be attractively produced.

You may also write articles for teachers or other managers that you submit to journals and magazines. Writing articles makes a fine contribution to the vitalization of your profession. Each new generation of teachers and managers needs the practical and theoretical information found in articles published in professional and lay journals. If you have ever had a long conversation with another teacher or a manager about a topic of mutual interest, that subject could easily be appropriate for an article that many others would read and learn from. Directions for prospective authors to follow when submitting material are found in the particular publication or may be obtained upon request. Figure 16–1 lists some of the many issues that would benefit from informed advocacy.

Communicating Your Advocacy Message

Imagine you have decided to work for curricular improvement in the early childhood programs in your state. How would you start a campaign to advocate for your position? Whom do you think it is important to persuade? Where do fundamental changes in curriculum get made?

Shepherd suggests six principles of message construction to aid persuasive communication.[6]

1. *Knowing your audience.* Who will you write for and speak to? What do they do for a living? Where will you meet them? What type of language and examples will they understand?
2. *Capturing attention.* Analyze the audience to determine what will appeal to them. Can they identify with your topic and approach from their personal perspective? Can they translate their own experience into the experience of their children? How can you make a strong argument for a beneficial outcome?
3. *Enhancing comprehension.* Small bites of information are remembered better than large ones. Think of the short sound bite of the television world. Thus, break your large message into many smaller messages. Give the "how to" examples from everyday life.
4. *Promoting acceptance.* Show how people with credibility are advocating this approach. Use some local leaders' opinions or experiences. The medical authorities are usually among the most credible. Be sure you address and

[6] Sandra K. Shepherd, "Principles of Message Construction," *Food and Nutrition News* 63:5, November/December 1991, pp. 1-3.

Adoption
AIDS prevention
Before- and after-school care
Bilingual education
Blended or step families
Bottle feeding
Breastfeeding
Career education
Child abuse
Child sexual abuse
Childbirth preparation
Children with disabilities
   AIDS
   autism
   blindness
   cerebral palsy
   chronic illness
   Down syndrome
   fetal alcohol syndrome
   mental retardation
   orthopedic problems
   prenatal drug exposure
   speech impairment
Children's libraries
Children's museums
Children's television
Computer-assisted education
Computer games
Curriculum areas
Diets/prenatal/children
Disciplinary methods
Displaced homemakers
Diversity
   ability
   economic
   ethnic
   gender
   racial
   religious

Educational reform/child care
Emerging literacy
Exercise/aerobics
Expanding Head Start
Family medical leave
Family planning
Family privacy rights
Family sports
Family wellness
Fathers as primary caregivers
Foster care
Friend of the Court
Full-day kindergarten
Gender roles
Goals, values and ethnic/racial
   group
Homeless children
Hunger
Immigrant children
Immigrants' rights
Immunization campaigns
Inclusion of children with
   disabilities
Infant care
Kindergarten curriculum reform
Lamaze/other birth
   preparation
Legal rights of a child
Licensing standards
Lifestyles of families
Little League sports
Locomotor skills
National health insurance
National language policy
Nonviolent conflict resolution
One-child family
Parent workshops
Peace education
Population/ecological balance

Prenatal care
Prenatal diagnosis
Preventing teen pregnancy
Professional recognition for
   child care workers
Programs for teen fathers
Programs for teen mothers
Quality, compensation and
   affordability in child care
Reproductive rights
School-age child care
Second language education
Sexual abuse
Sick-child care
Single adoptive parents
Single-parent fathers
Single-parent mothers
Staffing crisis in child care
Teen fathers' responsibility
Teen mothers in school
Teenage mothers
Testing children
Toddler care
United Nations children's
   programs
Values clarification
Violence in children's lives
   communities
   domestic
   television
Working mothers
Year-round school
Zero population growth and
   environment

Figure 16–1
Sample advocacy issues

work through the points of resistance in your community. Tailor your messages to anticipate and respond to opposing arguments.

5. *Remembering techniques.* High-imagery words arouse your audience to see your point and remember that point. To help stir readers' reactions, use good true-to-life examples of the type that might have occurred down the street. Organize information so it is easily recalled. You can use a poem, joke, or gimmick that ties several points together and aids memory.

6. *Deciding and acting.* You want the audience to decide and to act on the information you have provided. Chart their actions step-by-step; tell them precisely what their choices are. Walk them through it verbally. Like the television marketeer, tell them to "Go to the phone, dial the number, and ask for. . . . " Discuss the great outcomes if everyone listening decides and acts. Be persuasive, positive, and pleasant.

These principles of persuasive communication can be used for articles, talks, brochures, and books, and even for preparing testimony before a community or legislative body. If you are thinking about writing a book to submit to a publisher, you can start by requesting a format for a book proposal from the publishers you are considering. In addition to a proposal outline, most publishers will require that you submit a chapter or more of the manuscript for them to evaluate before they will contract with you to publish it. You can learn about magazine, journal, and book publishing by reading the magazines *The Writer* and *Writer's Digest*, found in most libraries and on newsstands. *The Writer's Market* and *Literary Marketplace*, annual reference books available in most libraries, contain helpful advice and information on places, articles, and books on almost any subject imaginable that might be published.

CONCLUSION

Advocacy and professionalism go hand in hand. Your educational experience, professional work with children and their families, and commitment to children and families prepare you well for becoming an advocate on some aspect of children's lives that you recognize as needing improvement. You can select many avenues of advocacy, from the neighborhood to the world level. You can join with other like-minded advocates and work for causes helping children and families.

Principles for getting your message across have been indicated. Shepherd identifies (a) knowing your audience, (b) capturing attention, (c) enhancing comprehension, (d) promoting acceptance, (e) remembering techniques, and (f) deciding and acting.

APPLICATIONS

1. Select an advocacy issue of importance in your community (perhaps from the list given in Figure 16–1) that interests you very much. Outline an advocacy program you and your professional association might present to a local or regional decision-making body.

a. Define the issue and goal or outcome desired.

b. Describe the audience.

c. Describe the steps for getting your message across.

d. Outline the decision-making process.

e. Propose the action desired.

2. Collect three articles from recent issues of *Young Children* and *Child Care Information Exchange* on topics where the author is advocating action. Write an analysis of the articles using Shepherd's criteria.

3. Write a 250- to 500-word magazine article advocating that parents provide some special learning experience at home for their child. Select some activity you feel is very important. Use the Shepherd criteria in this chapter and the Richardson/Callahan/Burckhardt steps discussed in Chapter 15 to help you professionalize your writing and your advocacy.

4. Add articles on advocacy to your management notebook.

STUDY QUESTIONS

1. Define advocacy. Explain how advocacy is part of professionalism.

2. State the goals of advocacy for children and families.

3. List the likely targets of advocacy efforts.

4. Give 10 examples of what advocacy groups and individuals do. Relate each example to advocacy work in a child development center.

5. State Shepherd's six principles of message construction and relate each principle to advocacy in a child development center.

SUGGESTED READINGS

Annie E. Casey Foundation. *Kids Count Data Book: State Profiles of Child Well-Being*. Baltimore: Author, 1995.

Association for Childhood Education International. "The Banning of Corporal Punishment." *Dimensions of Early Childhood* 23:3, pp. 36–37.

Bundy, Blakely F. "The Winnetka Alliance for Early Childhood: One Community's Collaboration on Behalf of Its Young Children." *Young Children* 50:5 (July 1995), pp. 84–85.

Carnegie Corporation of New York. "Starting Points: Executive Summary of the Report of the Carnegie Corporation of New York Task Force on Meeting the Needs of Young Children." *Young Children* 49:5 (July 1994), pp. 58–61.

Children's Defense Fund. *The State of America's Children Yearbook 1995*. Washington, DC: Author, 1995.

Daniel, Jerlean. "NAEYC's Contractual Commitment to Children." *Young Children* 50:3 (March 1995), p. 2.

Elkind, David. *Ties That Stress: The New Family Imbalance*. Cambridge, MA: Harvard University Press, 1994.

Feeney, Stephanie, and Kenneth Kipnis. "A New Code of Ethics for Early Childhood Educators." *Young Children* 45:1 (November 1989), pp. 24–29.

Fennimore, Beatrice S. *Child Advocacy for Early Childhood Educators*. New York: Teachers College Press, 1989.

Galen, H. "Increasing Parental Involvement in Elementary School: The Nitty Gritty of One Successful Program." *Young Children* 46:2 (January 1991), pp. 18–22.

Galinsky, Ellen. "The Costs of Not Providing Quality Early Childhood Programs." In Barbara Willer (ed.), *Reaching the Full Cost of Quality Early Programs* (Washington, DC: National Association for the Education of Young Children, 1990), pp. 27–40.

Goffin, Stacy G., and Joan Lombardi. *Speaking Out: Early Childhood Advocacy*. Washington, DC: National Association for the Education of Young Children, 1988.

Greater Minneapolis Day Care Association. "The High Cost of Waiting for Child Care Assistance." *Young Children* 50:5 (July 1995), pp. 47–49.

Hildebrand, Verna, Lillian Phenice, Mary M. Gray, and Rebecca Peña Hines. *Knowing and Serving Diverse Families*. Upper Saddle River, NJ: Merrill/Prentice Hall, 1996.

Hine, C. "What Does It Take to Become a Consultant?" *Child Care Information Exchange* 82 (November/December 1991), pp. 51–54.

Jensen, Mary A., and Zelda W. Chevalier. *Issues and Advocacy in Early Education*. Boston: Allyn & Bacon, 1990.

Johnson, Julienne and Janet B. McCracken (eds.). *The Early Childhood Career Lattice: Perspectives on Professional Development*. Washington, DC: National Association for the Education of Young Children, 1994.

Kamii, Constance, Faye B. Clark, and Ann Dominik. "Are Violence Prevention Curricula the Answer? *Dimensions of Early Childhood* 23:3 (Spring 1995), pp. 10–13.

Kozol, Jonathan. *Savage Inequalities: Children in America's Schools*. New York: Crown, 1991.

Leach, Penelope. *Children First*. New York: Knopf, 1994.

Levin, Diane E. "Power Rangers: An Explosive Topic." *Child Care Information Exchange* 102 (March/April 1995), pp. 50–51.

Moore, Evelyn K. "Mediocre Care: Double Jeopardy for Black Children." *Young Children* 50:4 (May 1995), p. 47.

Neugebauer, Roger. "Child Care and the Global Economy." *Child Care Information Exchange* 104 (July/August 1995), pp. 9–16.

Odland, Jerry. "Children's Rights and the Future." *Childhood Education* 71:4 (Summer 1995), p. 224-B.

Osofsky, Joy D., and Emily Fenichel. *Caring for Infants and Toddlers in Violent Environments: Hurt, Healing, and Hope*. Arlington, VA: Zero to Three/National Center for Clinical Infant Programs, 1994.

Pelo, Ann, Jim Morin, Margie Carter, Deb Curtis, Walter Draude, and Marcy Whitebook. "From Our Readers . . . Thoughtful Letters on the Subject of Worthy Wages for Child Care Workers." *Young Children* 50:2 (January 1995), pp. 3–4, 82–83.

Reed, Sally, and R. Craig Sautter. "Children of Poverty: The Status of 12 Million Young Americans." *Phi Delta Kappan,* June 1990, pp. K1–K12.

Slaby, Ronald G., Wendy C. Roedell, Diana Arezzo, and Kate Hendrix. *Early Violence Prevention: Tools for Teachers of Young Children*. Washington, DC: National Association for the Education of Young Children, 1995.

"25th Celebration of the Week of the Young Child Focuses Public Attention on the Rights and Needs of Young Children." *Young Children* 50:3 (March 1995), p. 46.

Van Deusen, Jenifer. "Community Schools: A Vision of Equity and Excellence for Young Children." *Young Children* 46:5 (July 1991), pp. 58–60.

Whitebook, M., C. Howes, and D. Phillips (eds.). *Working for Quality Child Care: An Early Childhood Education Text from the Child Care Employees Project*. Berkeley, CA: Child Care Employee Project, 1989.

Whitebook, Marcy. "What's Good for Child Care Teachers Is Good for Our Country's Children." *Young Children* 50:4 (May 1995), pp. 49–50.

Wishon, Phillip M. "On Our Watch: Connecting across Generations of Early Childhood Advocates." *Young Children* 49:2 (January 1994), pp. 42–43.

Zeisler, Laura M. "Twenty-five Ways to Celebrate the Week of the Young Child." *Young Children* 49:3 (March 1994), p. 48.

PART IV

Conclusions

CHAPTER 17

Children: Our Future

• •

Children are particularly fragile human beings. They and their families are vulnerable to innumerable risks within the human ecological system. Degradation of the natural environment reduces the availability of resources needed for survival, creating health hazards particularly dangerous for children and ill or elderly people. Some human-built environments that leave no room for play drive children to less socially acceptable outlets for their energies and stresses.[1]

A social-cultural environment can exploit children with violent television shows. It can ignore them with economic policies that give corporate tax breaks a higher priority than immunization and nutrition programs. Changes in the social-cultural environment can mean that families no longer live near enough to grandparents or other relatives to seek their aid and advice or that the adults in the family must devote energy to work or study instead of children.

For all these reasons, child development centers that help care for and educate children are crucial necessities for today's families. Yet children are also competent and powerful beings, full of potential and deserving of the best that the world has to offer. For this reason, those child development centers should be not just adequate, they should be ideal. Is this a dream? We think not. Skillful managers who apply the principles of child and family development and early childhood education, as well as principles of sound management, can create such ideal

---

[1] Joe L. Frost and Paul J. Jacobs, "Play Deprivation: A Factor in Juvenile Violence," *Dimensions of Early Childhood* 23:3 (Spring 1995), pp. 14–20, 29.

places. But, in addition to their knowledge and skill, they will need certain personal qualities. Just as there are two sides to our image of the child as vulnerable yet competent, there are two sides to each of the personal qualities essential for managers of child development centers.

DECISIONS, DECISIONS . . .

 Think of your image of children and families. Do you see them as vulnerable and helpless, or as competent and strong? Can you think of any recent items in your local news media that might illustrate examples of the natural, human-built, or social-cultural environment contributing to this vulnerability or competence?

DEDICATION . . . AND ENLIGHTENED SELF-INTEREST

People who work in child development centers are entrusted with the task of helping parents nurture and educate their children. You are expected to love and care for these children as though they were your own beloved offspring.

Offering nurturing and educational services in a community, whether under private or public auspices, requires dedication to fostering the growth and development of each child, helping families succeed at their parenting tasks, and providing the highest-quality service possible. The challenges are many. You, as manager, and your staff can serve families well, sharing your love, knowledge, and abilities. Developing a climate of enhancing common human concern, caring about each individual, working to allay conflict, and struggling to make your services the best possible are charges that you as a manager are expected to assume. Peace, love, security, trust, respect, and wisdom are attributes that should be connected with your services to children and families.

To accomplish this enormous responsibility, you will need the professional dedication to view your work as more than "just a job," continually seeking new information and new ideas that help you make your center a better place for children, families, and staff. You will need more than dedication, though; you will need the enlightened self-interest that will enable you to reach out for help and nurture yourself.

Your policy and advisory boards, your staff members, outside consultants, families, community members, and the children themselves are all potential sources of new ideas and creative solutions to the challenges you face. One of your tasks as manager will be finding ways to tap those sources. You will also need to remember that your own energy needs replenishment from time to time. A healthy diet, exercise, time with family and friends, hobbies, and outside interests will all help you give your best. The trick is to give your best when you are at work and then leave that work behind at the end of each day. Remember that, while your work is important, it is not the only important thing in your life.

Children may feel pensive or tired as they await their parents. Teachers should make every effort to understand their feelings and meet their needs.
Bill Mitcham, photographer

HUMILITY . . . AND PROFESSIONAL PRIDE

Keep humble as to what you know about human growth and behavior. In dealing with humans young or old, little if anything can be said with absolute certainty. The sciences of understanding children and families are infant sciences with much to be discovered. Help your staff and the children's parents think of themselves as searchers on a treasure hunt for truth and understanding that will yield solutions to problems in the social-cultural, human-built, and natural physical-biological environments that support children and parents wherever they happen to reside.

While you are humble about the limits of your knowledge, however, you can cultivate a healthy pride in your accomplishments and the wonderful profession you have chosen. As you struggle with a shoestring budget and the mundane daily realities of lost mittens or clogged toilets, remind yourself that the work you do has a ripple effect in society that is more far-reaching than that of many corporate executive officers. Your service, in fact, may be what enables that corporate executive to get to her office every day and her employees to keep their minds on their work. Providing high-quality child care has been demonstrated to be one of the best investments societies can make, saving many dollars in social, legal, and educational services for every dollar spent. Be proud to be part of such worthwhile work.

PATIENCE . . . AND RIGHTEOUS IMPATIENCE

Patience may be your ultimate virtue as a manager or staff member in any human service. You need patience in encouraging children, parents, and others to search to learn rather than directly providing ready-made, but perhaps inadequate, solutions to existing problems. As you gain experience, you will realize more and more that each generation must in some ways rediscover the "wheel" that works. People feel really good and motivated about using their own discoveries.

If you have patience you will not expect instant results from children, families, staff, or yourself. You will endeavor to make realistic timetables and will adjust timetables when you see that they are unrealistic or impossible. Pressure to fit someone else's timetable may bring inordinate stress. The psychological response to stress is often to screen out some of the pressure, disengage oneself, and simplify one's life. Children need time and space to be alone, just watch, or sit quietly, not constant demands to keep up with the group. Parents, who are pressured by their work roles, scarcely need the extra pressure of unrealistic demands from their child development center. Staff members need time away from children and your understanding when they do not always implement new center policies as perfectly as you would like. You need to realize that you cannot change the world in a day . . . or even a few years.

But, if you must be patient with people, you must also be impatient with ignorance and poor policies that put children last time after time. Every week that a needy child has to wait to enter your program because there are more children needing services than funding to subsidize those services is a week lost forever in that child's lifetime. Every year that goes by without programs to ensure adequate prenatal care for every mother means that thousands of new babies are at risk for birth complications and possible life-long problems. All the hours that caregivers "donate" to child development centers (because their education and skills earn them less money there than the same education and skills would earn them elsewhere) add up to a childhood of good-byes and readjustment for too many children when those caregivers have to leave the field to support their own families. As an advocate for children, your righteous impatience with these conditions will move you to speak out for change.

THOUGHTFULNESS . . . AND THOUGHTFUL ACTION

Knowledge is powerful. Knowledge and information are costly. It is also costly if people attempt to operate without knowledge and accurate information. Problems arise when people believe things that are not true. As the famous homespun philosopher and comedian, Will Rogers, was fond of saying, "It ain't ignorance that does so much damage in this world, as knowin' so darn much that ain't so." Libraries are full of information about every conceivable subject. Any of this information needs thoughtful evaluation before applying it to the human experience—past and present.

As a manager of a human service organization, you are obligated to be aware of information in many areas—for example, in child development, family relations, education, psychology, sociology, business organization, employee relations, family and business law, art, literature, music, and current worldwide political and economic thought and activity. These topics are only a sample of the breadth of your needed education and continued self-education as you tackle the job of preparing children for the 21st century.

A democratic society requires thoughtful, educated people who continually strive to discover a better way to care for and educate children. This means that the status quo must be challenged. We cannot wait until we have all the answers before we take action. We must always admit that what we think we know and what we consequently do at the present time may require modifications in the future as new scholars learn more about children's growth, development, care, and education. This realization of fallibility should promote continuous studying, testing, and challenging of the ideas implemented with every day. In this manner, the best possible programs for children will be developed year by year as the tools and information that make up the present state of the art are continuously updated and used.

SERVICE ORIENTATION . . . AND HEALTHY ASSERTIVENESS

Institutions should serve people—never use them. As manager of the child development service, your ultimate goal should be to strengthen children and their families. Your role is to supplement, never supplant, the care that families give their children. You must avoid putting yourselves ahead of the people you serve or assuming unwarranted power over people. Many individuals are in weak positions. Some parents need your child development services desperately, yet the day you take advantage of their weakness and vulnerability is the day you break the trust they and society place in you. You and your staff are taking advantage of your power over people who need you:

> . . . if your center demands that children arrive by 9:00 A.M. or be turned away, when the parent has to take another child to school several blocks away and cannot get to your center before 9:30.
> . . . if only a particular type of blue tennis shoes are acceptable for gym and even the small amount that such shoes costs is a burden on the family's budget.
> . . . if all the children at your center are expected to participate in a religious observance and not all families share that particular religious orientation.

You can accommodate families' needs, however, without being taken advantage of. Clearly formulated policies, discussed with each family at enrollment, will

Children who become absorbed in their activities develop powers of concentration that will help them tackle challenges throughout life.
Early Learning Center, Appalachian State University, Boone, NC

avoid situations in which parents decide to do a few errands on their way to pick up their child, causing tired caregivers to be even later than usual in getting home to their own children. Setting fees at a level that allows you to pay your staff a living wage requires no apology—although it may require effort to locate financial assistance for families who cannot afford those rates. These are simply examples of healthy assertiveness, without which you will be less able to fulfill your mission of service.

A GLOBAL VIEW . . . AND A LOCAL AGENDA

"Think globally, act locally" is a current slogan being applied in areas such as business, cultural exchange, education, and international relations. Like the human ecological system framework, this slogan helps individuals realize that their actions at the home and community level have ramifications for the entire global community. The world sorely needs a generation of happy children with the ability to think broadly and creatively. Children need to develop trust in other human beings. They need the ability for friendly interaction with—and to feel their oneness with—people everywhere. Understanding, love, and kindness from those who care for children will play a significant role in developing children's healthy attitudes. Children need to develop self-assurance, feel good about themselves, and be convinced that they can deal creatively with new problems as they arise. Knowledge, trust, and self-assurance are worthy goals for each child in every child development center.

Many children throughout the world are being cared for and educated in child development centers. All parents and children everywhere are part of the global interdependent human family with responsibility toward improving the social-cultural environment, the human-built environment, and the natural physical-biological environment. Today, environmental degradation, population pressures, political turmoil, and anxieties about nuclear weapons threaten the global human ecological system as never before. It is fitting to hope that competent managers at work in child development centers everywhere will help each child and each parent feel a part of the larger human family, responsible in some individual way for the security, peace, and happiness of every person throughout our planetary home.

A Pledge to Children

I am somebody.
I am somebody who cares.
I am somebody who cares about children.

A child is somebody.
A child is somebody who cares.
A child is somebody who cares to learn.

I am somebody.
Each child is somebody.
We each have talents and energy.

I promise to try.
I promise to help each child try.
Together we shall build a better world.

—Verna Hildebrand

APPLICATIONS

1. Interview two or more sets of parents who have a child enrolled in some type of child development center. Ask them these questions:
   a. How does the child development center in which your child is enrolled alleviate pressure on your family system?
   b. How does the child development center put roadblocks in the path of achieving full success in your parenting role? That is, are there any parts of the service that would be more helpful if changed or altered?
   Compare notes with your classmates and analyze the factors that are positive and negative about the child development services that parents are experiencing.
2. Collect news stories depicting young families and their children and ways in which they are using community institutions to help with their parenting roles. Compare notes with other classmates and make a list of community resources for parents.
3. Look up a reading in the library through the *Reader's Guide* to learn about child development services in a country other than your own. Write an

abstract and share the information with your classmates. Can you draw any conclusions from this bit of research?

4. Locate and report in class on studies about child development centers that were published by agencies of the United Nations. You may want to look particularly for items related to the 1979 United Nations International Year of the Child. An excellent film to use with this project would be *What Rights Has the Child?* distributed by the United Nations. For information, write to United Nations Publications, A-3307, New York, NY 10017

5. Add information on child development centers and services from around the country and the world to your management notebook.

STUDY QUESTIONS

1. Describe the following manager's personal qualities and relate each to specific behaviors in a child development center.
   a. Dedication and enlightened self-interest
   b. Humility and healthy pride
   c. Patience and righteous impatience
   d. Thoughtfulness and thoughtful action
   e. Service orientation and healthy assertiveness

2. Using the human ecological system framework, write an essay that relates each of the following global conditions to the development of children in a child care center in your local community:
   a. Environmental degradation
   b. Population pressures
   c. Political unrest
   d. Nuclear weapons anxieties

SUGGESTED READINGS

Baldwin, Sue. *The Early Childhood Super Director*. St.Paul, MN: Redleaf, 1991.

Carlsson-Paige, Nancy, and Diane Levin. *The War Play Dilemma: Balancing Needs and Values in the Early Childhood Classroom.* New York: Teachers College Press, 1987.

Carlsson-Paige, Nancy, and Diane Levin. *Who's Calling the Shots: How to Respond Effectively to Children's Fascination with War Play and War Toys.* Philadelphia: New Society, 1990.

Carter, Margie. "Honoring Diversity: Problems and Possibilities for Staff and Organization." *Child Care Information Exchange* 59 (January 1988), pp. 43–47.

Deep, Sam, and Lyle Sussman. *What to Say to Get What You Want.* Reading, MA: Addison-Wesley, 1992.

Duff, Carolyn S., and Barbara Cohen. *When Women Work Together: Using Our Strength to Overcome Our Challenge.* Emeryville, CA: Conari, 1993.

Edelman, Marian Wright. *The Measure of Our Success: A Letter to My Children and Yours.* Boston: Beacon, 1992.

Hildebrand, Verna. "Third World Children: Promise and Problems." *Early Child Development and Care* 30, 1988, pp. 200–215.

McCracken, Janet Brown. *Valuing Diversity: The Primary Years.* Washington, DC: National Association for the Education of Young Children, 1993.

Neugebauer, Bonnie (ed.). *Alike and Different: Exploring Our Humanity with Young Children.* Washington, DC: National Association for the Education of Young Children, 1992.

Schorr, Lizbet B., and Daniel Schorr. *Within Our Reach: Breaking the Cycle of Disadvantage and Despair.* New York: Doubleday, 1988.

Zigler, Edward, and Sally J. Styfco. *Head Start and Beyond: A National Plan for Extended Childhood Intervention.* New Haven, CT: Yale University Press, 1993.

Comparison of State Licensing Requirements for Child Care Centers

State	Maximum Number of Children per Caregiver								Inservice Hours/Year	Director Qualifications
	0–12 mo	12–24 mo.	24–36 mo.	36–48 mo.	48–60 mo.	60–72 mo.	6–8 yr.	9–12 yr.		
Alabama	6	8	12	12	20	20	22	25	4–8	Educ. + exper.
Alaska	5	6	6	10	10	15	20	20	12	9 hr. college
Arizona	5	6	8	13	15	20	20	20	12	Educ. + exper.
Arkansas	6	6	9	12	15	18	20	20	10	H.S. = 4 yr. exper.
California	4	4	12	12	12	14	14	14	0	Educ. + exper.
Colorado	5	5	7	10	12	15	15	15	0	Educ. + exper.
Connecticut	4	4	4	10	10	10	10	10	1% hr. worked	Educ. + exper.
Delaware	4	7	10	12	15	25	25	25	15	Educ. +/or exper.
District of Columbia	4	4	8	8	10	15	15	15	As needed	Educ. +/or exper.
Florida	4	6	11	15	20	25	25	25	8	CDA (1/20 children)
Georgia	6	8	10	15	18	20	25	25	10	Educ. +/or exper.
Hawaii	3	4	8	12	16	20	20	20	0	Educ. + exper.
Idaho	*	*	*	*	*	*	*	*	4	None
Illinois	4	5	8	10	10	20	20	20	15	Educ. +/or exper.
Indiana	4	5	5	10	12	15	20	20	12	Educ. + exper.
Iowa	4	4	6	8	12	15	15	15	6	Educ. + exper.
Kansas	3	5	10	12	12	12	16	16	10	Educ. +/or exper.
Kentucky	5	6	10	12	14	15	15	25	12	Educ. +/or exper.
Louisiana	6	8	12	14	16	20	25	25	12	Educ. + exper.
Maine	4	5	8	10	10	10	10	10	12 or 24	Educ. +/or exper.
Maryland	3	3	6	10	10	15	15	15	3–6	Educ. +/or exper.
Massachusetts	3	4	4	10	10	13	13	13	20	Educ. +/or exper.
Michigan	4	4	10	10	12	12	20	20	0	CDA or 2 yr. college
Minnesota	4	4	7	10	10	15	15	15	2% hr. worked	Educ. +/or exper.

	3–5	7–9	10–12	12–14	14–16	14–20	14–20	14–20	14–20	
Mississippi	4	4	8	10	10	16	16	16	15	Educ. + exper.
Missouri	4	4	8	10	10	14	14	14	12	Educ. + exper.
Montana	4	4	6	10	10	12	15	15	8	CDA + 3 yr. exper.
Nebraska	4	4	6	10	12	12	15	15	12	Educ. +/or exper.
Nevada	*	*	*	*	*	*	*	*	3	Educ. + exper.
New Hampshire	4	5	6	8	12	15	15	15	0	Associate's degree
New Jersey	4	7	10	10	15	15	18	18	0	Educ. +/or exper.
New Mexico	6	6	6	12	12	15	15	15	24	Educ.
New York	4	4	5	6–7	7–8	8–9	10	10	7.5	Educ. + exper.
North Carolina	5	6	10	15	20	25	*	*	Varies	Educ. +/or exper.
North Dakota	4	4	5	7	10	12	18	18	10	Educ. +/or exper.
Ohio	5–6	5–6	7–8	12–14	12–14	18–20	18–20	18–20	15	Educ. + exper.
Oklahoma	4	6	8	12	15	15	20	20	12–20	Educ. + exper.
Oregon	4	4	4	10	10	15	15	15	15	Educ. or 1 yr. exper. or training
Pennsylvania	4	5	6	10	10	12	15	15	6	Not specified
Rhode Island	4	4	6	9	10	12	13	13	Required	Educ. + exper.
South Carolina	6	6	10	14	19	22	24	24	10–15	H.S. + 3 yr. exper.
South Dakota	5	5	5	10	10	10	15	15	20	Educ. +/or exper.
Tennessee	5	7	8	10	15	20	25	25	6–12	H.S. + 2 yr. exper.
Texas	5	6	9	13	16	20	22	25	15–20	AA or CDA
Utah	4	4	7	12	15	20	*	*	20–40	CDA + 1 yr. exper.
Vermont	4	4	5	10	10	13	13	13	6–9	Educ. + exper.
Virginia	4	5	10	10	12	20	20	20	8	Educ. +/or exper.
Washington	4	4	7	10	10	15	15	15	Required	Educ. + exper.
West Virginia	4	4	8	10	12	15	16	16	Required	H.S. + 9 college credits + exper.
Wisconsin	4	4	6–8	10	17	17	18	18	39	Educ. + exper.
Wyoming	5	5	8	10	15	20	25	25	8	Educ. +/or exper.

* Not specified

Source: Children's Defense Fund and *1995 Child Care Center Licensing Study* (Washington, DC: The Children's Foundation, 1995).

State Agencies Responsible for Licensing Child Care Centers

• •

Assistant Director
Department of Human Resources
Division of Family and Children's Services
Office of Day Care and Child Development
50 Ripley St.
Montgomery, AL 36130

Licensing Specialist
Division of Family & Youth Services
PO Box 110630
Juneau, AK 99811-0630

Health Program Manager
Office of Child Care Licensure
Department of Health Services
1647 E. Morten Ave., Suite 230
Phoenix, AZ 85020

Administrator
Child Care Unit
Division of Children & Family Services
PO Box 1437/Slot 720
Little Rock, AR 72203-1437

Deputy Director
Community Care Licensing Division
Department of Social Services
744 P St., M.S. 19-50
Sacramento, CA 95814

Licensing Administrator
Office of Child Care Services
Department of Social Services
1575 Sherman St.
Denver, CO 80203-1714

Program Supervisor
Public Health & Addiction Services
150 Washington St.
Hartford, CT 06106

Administrator
Office of Child Care Licensing
Department of Services for Children,
    Youth, & Their Families
1825 Faulkland Rd.
Wilmington, DE 19806

Administrator
Service Facility Regulation Administration
Department of Consumer & Regulatory
    Affairs
614 H St., NW
Washington, DC 20001

Chief
Child Care Unit
Department of Health & Rehabilitative
    Services
2811-A Industrial Plaza Dr.
Tallahassee, FL 32301

Director
Department of Human Resources
Child Care Licensing Section
Two Peachtree St., NW
20th Floor
Atlanta, GA 30303-3167

Child Care Program Administrator
Office of Human Services
PO Box 339
Honolulu, HI 96809

Deputy Administrator
Department of Health & Welfare
Division of Family & Community Services
450 W. State St.
Boise, ID 83720

Licensing Specialist
Office of Child Development
Department of Children & Family Services
406 E. Monroe St.
Springfield, IL 62701

Director
Day Care Licensing
Division of Family & Children
402 W. Washington St.
Third Floor
Indianapolis, IN 46204

Program Manager
Child Day Care Services
Department of Human Services
Hoover State Office Building
Fifth Floor
Des Moines, IA 50319

Director
Child Care Licensing & Registration
    Section
Department of Health & Environment
Mills Building, Suite 400-C
1095 SW 9th St.
Topeka, KS 66612-2217

Child Care Program Specialist
Division of Licensing & Regulation
Office of the Inspector General
CHR-DL & R, CHR Building, 4-E
275 E. Main St.
Fourth Floor East
Frankfort, KY 40621

Director
Bureau of Licensing
Department of Social Services
PO Box 3078
Baton Rouge, LA 70821

Supervisor
Child Care Licensing
Department of Human Resources
State House Station 11
Augusta, ME 04333

Assistant Director of Licensing
Child Care Administration
Department of Human Resources
311 W. Saratoga St.
First Floor
Baltimore, MD 21201

Director of Field Operations
Group Day Care Licensing
Office for Children
1 Ashburton Place
Boston, MA 02108

Division Director
Child Day Care Licensing
Department of Social Services
235 S. Grand Ave.
PO Box 30037
Lansing, MI 48909

Unit Manager
Division of Licensing
Department of Human Services
444 Lafayette Rd.
St. Paul, MN 55155-3842

Director
Division of Child Care
Department of Health
PO Box 1700
Jackson, MS 39215-1700

Child Care Supervisor
Child Care Licensing Unit
Department of Health
1728 Plaza, PO Box 570
Jefferson City, MO 65102

Day Care Program Officer
Department of Family Services
PO Box 8005
Helena, MT 59604

Administrator
Child Care & Development Division
Department of Social Services
PO Box 95026
Lincoln, NB 68509

Licensing Bureau Chief
Child & Family Services
711 E. Fifth St.
Carson City, NV 89710

Licensing Supervisor
Bureau of Child Care Licensing
Department of Health and Human Services
Division of Public Health Services
6 Hazen Dr.
Concord, NH 03301

Chief
Bureau of Licensing
Division of Youth & Family Services
CN 717
Trenton, NJ 08625

Bureau Chief
Child Care Licensing Bureau
Department of Children, Youth and Families
PO Drawer 5160
Santa Fe, NM 87502

Director of Regional Operation
Bureau of Early Childhood Services
Department of Social Services
40 N. Pearl St.
Albany, NY 12243

Director
Division of Child Development
Department of Human Resources
PO Box 29553
Raleigh, NC 27626-0553

Department of Human Services
Children & Family Services Division
State Capitol Building
Bismarck, ND 58505-0250

Chief
Child Day Care Licensing Section
Department of Human Services
65 E. State St.
Fifth Floor
Columbus, OH 43215

Office of Child Care
Department of Human Services
PO Box 25352
Oklahoma City, OK 73125

Licensing Manager
Child Care Division
Employment Department
575 Union St., NE
Salem, OR 97311

Program Specialist
Bureau of Child Day Care Services
Department of Public Welfare
PO Box 2675
Harrisburg, PA 17105

Child Development Specialist
Division of Community Services
Department of Children, Youth & Families
610 Mt. Pleasant Ave.
Providence, RI 02908

Director
Division of Child Day Care Licensing &
    Regulatory Services
PO Box 1520
Columbia, SC 29202

Program Specialist
Office of Child Care Services
Department of Social Services
700 Governors Dr.
Pierre, SD 57501-2291

Coordinator of Day Care Licensing
Social Services Division
Department of Human Services
Citizen's Plaza
400 Deaderick St.
Nashville, TN 37248-9800

Standards Specialist
Child Care Licensing Consultant
Licensing Division
Department of Protective & Regulatory
    Services
PO Box 149030
Austin, TX 78714-9030

Director
Office of Licensing
Department of Human Services
120 N. 200 West
Salt Lake City, UT 84106

Chief, Children's Day Care Unit
Division of Licensing & Regulation
Department of Social and Rehabilitation
  Services
Agency of Human Services
103 S. Main St.
Waterbury, VT 05671-2401

Program Development Supervisor
Division of Licensing Programs
Department of Social Services
Theater Row Building
730 E. Broad St.
Richmond, VA 23219-1849

Licensing Program Manager
Office of Child Care Policy
Department of Social & Health Services
PO Box 45710
Olympia, WA 98504-5710

Director
Department of Health & Human
  Resources
Capitol Complex, Building 6
Room 850-B
Charleston, WV 25305

Director
Office of Regulation & Licensing
Department of Health & Social Services
PO Box 7851
Milwaukee, WI 53707

Social Services Consultant
Day Care Licensing
Department of Family Services
Hathaway Building
Cheyenne, WY 82002

Name Index

Adolph, B., 253
Albonese, R., 167
Albrecht, K., 30, 75, 94, 163, 192, 210, 369, 391
Alexander, N., 188
Almy, M., 48
Ambery, M. E., 369
Andrews, M., 47
Ard, L., 241, 369
Arezzo, D., 407
Aronson, S., 26, 312, 313, 341
Axinn, N., 61, 71
Azer, S., 164

Bader, L., 357
Baldwin, S., 417
Barcher, A., 142
Barclay, K., 391
Barrett, B., 13
Beer, J., 281
Belensky, M., 70
Bell, M., 314
Bellm, D., 251
Benham, N., 163
Berger, E., 391
Berk, L., 47
Berns, R. M., 376
Berry, F. S., 253
Birch, L. L., 317, 330, 335, 341
Bittel, C., 27
Black, C., 184
Black, J., 211
Blakely, B., 369
Blau, R., 369
Bloom, B., 32, 47

Bloom, P., 210
Boje, D. M., 188
Boone, E., 391
Boss, P .G., 36
Boswell, C., 241
Bowers, C. H., 255, 280
Brady, E. H., 369
Brazelton, T. B., 391
Bredekamp, S., 30, 34, 70, 75, 94, 98, 117, 174, 178, 192, 210, 255, 259, 284, 288, 316, 343, 359, 372, 398
Brett, A., 188
Breunig, G. S., 251
Briggs, B., 26
Briggs, P., 189
Brock, D. R., 391
Bronfenbrenner, U., 26, 32, 47
Brooke, G. E., 369
Brothers, T., 253
Broussard, A .M., 210
Brown, B., 26
Brown, J. F., 313
Brown, M. H. 210
Bubolz, M., 36, 47,
Bundy, B., 391, 406
Burckhardt, A., 387
Burns, N., 268, 308, 313

Cadden, V., 219
Caldwell, B., 26, 173
Caminiti, S., 253
Carlsson-Paige, N., 417
Carter, M., 144, 157, 163, 369, 407, 417

Carton, R. S., 49
Cartwright, C., 168
Cartwright, S., 280
Caruso, J. J., 26, 210
Casper, L. M., 215
Certo, D., 205
Cesarone, B., 157, 164, 281
Chandler, P., 26
Chard, S., 189, 333, 334
Cherry, C., 70, 94, 164, 241
Chevalier, Z. A., 407
Childs, G., 47
Christie, J. F., 351
Clark, F. B., 407
Clark, J. E., 348
Clements, D. H., 369
Cleverly, J., 48
Clewett, A. S., 164
Click, P., 70
Clifford, R. M., 113, 210, 281
Clinchy, B., 70
Coelen, L., 27, 42, 102, 134, 259
Cohen, B., 417
Cohen, S., 280
Cohen, U., 280, 281
Coleman, J. G., 313
Colker, L. J., 48, 210, 369
Condelli, L., 13
Connor, M. W., 26
Costley, J., 164
Covey, S., 167, 189
Curtis, D., 163, 407
Curtis, F., 119

Daily, J., 369
Daniel, J., 406
David, J., 48, 333, 392
David, T., 281
Davidson, D. H., 189, 254, 391
Decker, C. A., 70
Decker, J. A., 70
Deep, S., 417
DeHaas-Warner, S., 313
Dennis-Willingham, C., 369
Dempsey, J. D., 314
Derman-Sparks, L., 174, 187, 192, 369, 398
DeVries, R., 281
Diamond, K. E., 26
Dinkmeyer, D., 189, 391
DiRocco, L., 393
Dittman, L. L., 210
Divine-Hawkins, P., 27
Dixon, S., 313
Dodd, E. L., 391
Dodge, D. T., 48, 210, 281, 369, 391
Doggett, L., 48, 281
Doherty, R., 36, 47
Dominik, A., 407
Doud, J. L., 26
Downing-Leffler, N., 392
Draude, W., 407
Dreikers, R., 391
Dressler, G., 51, 61, 74
Driscoll, A., 366, 369
Duff, C. S., 417
Duff, R. E., 210
Duncan, S., 87

Eckstein, R.M., 241
Edwards, C., 48, 137
Edelman, M. W., 417
Eheart, B., 164, 189, 210
Eisenhart, C. E., 313
Elkind, D., 210, 406
Endres, J., 113, 328, 341
Engelhart, M. D., 47
Epenter, S., 189
Erikson, E., 32, 48
Essa, E. L., 313
Etchart, N., 396

Everts, J., 313
Eyer, D., 94

Farquhar, E., 27
Feeney, S., 70, 406
Fenichel, E., 407
Fennimore, B. S., 406
Fernandez, J. P., 253
Filippini, T., 137
Finkelhor, D., 268, 308, 313
Fisher, J. A., 317, 341
Fisher, R., 179, 189
Flippo, E., 48
Fogel, A., 370
Forman, G., 48, 137, 281
Foster, S. M., 391
Fox, L., 30, 48, 192
Fredericks, B., 313
Friedman, D., 253
Frieman, B. B., 294, 313
Fritz, R., 70
Frost, J., 210, 281, 410
Fulmer, R. M., 43–44, 88

Galen, H., 392, 407
Galinsky, E., 120, 164, 253, 377, 392, 407
Gallant, K. R., 30, 48, 192
Gandini, L., 48, 137, 281
Ganson, H., 13
Garbarino, J., 26
Gardner, H., 70
Gargiulo, R. M., 392
Gartrell, D., 189
Genser, A., 164
George, J., 48, 281
Gesell, A., 48
Gestwicki, C., 392
Gilmore, J., 189
Glantz, F., 27, 42, 102, 134, 259
Gnezda, T., 251
Godwin, A., 94, 241
Goffin, S., 48, 113, 181, 407
Goldberg, E., 313
Goldberger, N., 70
Golden, W., 281
Goodman, I., 164
Gonzales-Mena, J., 71, 94, 369

Gordon, J., 392
Gordon, T., 154, 181, 189
Grace, C., 210, 381
Granger, R., 165, 241
Grant, J. P., 401
Granucci, P. L., 164
Graves, S. B., 392
Gray, M., 11, 144, 376, 407
Green, M., 164
Greenman, J., 94, 189, 241, 255, 281, 392
Gunzenhauser, N., 26

Haas, K. S., 253
Hale, J., 392
Hall, O., 61, 71
Hanline, M. F., 30, 48, 192
Hardman, R., 313
Harkness, B., 70, 94, 164, 241
Harms, T., 113, 210, 281
Harris, V. J., 369
Hartman, B., 48, 71, 241
Hatcher, B., 392
Haubenstricker, J., 348
Havighurst, R., 32, 48
Hayden, J., 96
Hayes, C. D., 26
Hearn, K., 342
Helms, J., 392
Hendrick, J., 164
Hendrix, K., 407
Henniger, M., 313
Hernandez, C., 253
Hestenes, L. L., 26
Hewes, D., 45, 48, 71, 241
Hildebrand, V., 11, 26, 48, 94, 113, 144, 178, 210, 260, 281, 309, 310, 333, 341, 348, 357, 362, 365, 366, 369, 376, 392, 407, 417
Hill, A. B., 280, 281
Hill, L., 164
Hill, W. W. 47
Hine, C., 407
Hines, R. P., 11, 144, 157, 376, 407
Hiss, T., 255
Hitt, M. A., 137
Hitz, R., 366, 369

Hodson, D., 314
Hofferth, S. L., 27
Hoffman, C., 241
Hohmann, M., 48
Honig, A. S., 94, 313, 370
Hooks, W., 377
Howes, C., 165, 241, 407
Hrncir, E. J., 313
Huss, R., 184

Inhelder, B., 48

Jacobs, P., 410
Jalongo, M. R., 26
Jensen, M. A., 407
Jessee, P. O., 294
Johnson, J., 164, 407
Johnson, S. L., 317, 341
Johnson, V., 393
Johnston, L., 392
Jones, E., 157, 164, 184, 189,
    281, 369
Jorde-Bloom, P., 164, 189

Kagan, S. L., 26, 189
Kahn, A., 17, 22, 26
Kahn, R. L., 167
Kalinowski, M., 268, 308
Kamerman, S., 17, 22, 26
Kamii, C., 33, 48, 189, 210, 276,
    281, 407
Kaplan-Sanoff, M., 135
Kasting, A., 392
Katz, D., 48, 167
Katz, L. G., 135, 157, 164, 189,
    210, 281, 333, 334, 369
Kaufman, R., 314
Kelso, J. A., 348
Kendrick, A. S., 314
Khokha, E., 241
Kidera, E., 281
Kipnis, K., 70, 189, 406
Kisker, E. E., 27
Klass, C. S., 164
Klein, T. C., 27
Knight, D., 281
Kohn, A., 119
Kokoski, T. M., 392
Kontos, S., 27, 163
Koralek, D., 210

Kostelnik, M., 27, 34, 48, 210,
    369
Kozol, J. 407
Krathwohl, D. R., 47
Kritchevsky, S., 281
Kuschner, D., 48
Kuzma, K., 70, 94, 164, 241

Lakin, M. B., 370
Lane, C. G., 280, 281
Lang, M. E., 24, 27
LaRossa, W. R., 36, 47
Lazar, I., 13
Leach, P., 392, 407
Leavitt, R.L., 164, 189, 210
Lee, F. Y., 392
Levin, D. E., 407, 417
Lilienthal, J. W., 178
Linder, E. W., 27, 85
Lippitt, R., 168
Logue, M. E., 164
Lombardi, J., 164, 241, 407
Lombardi, V., 362
Loughlin, C. E., 281
Lovell, P., 281
Lucas, M.-A., 251
Lueck, P., 266
Lukaszewski, T., 241

Malaguzzi, L., 370
Mali, P., 88
Mallory, B., 34, 48
Margulis, N., 188
Martin, M. D., 281
Marx, E., 241
Marx, F., 253
Maslow, A. H., 48, 117
Massarik, F. 188
Mathis, R., 137
Mattiss, M. C., 27, 85
Maynard, F., 253
Mazur, S., 313
Mazzocco, M., 314
McConkey, C., 13
McCracken, J. B., 164, 393, 407,
    417
McDowelle, J. O., 27
McFadden, J., 327, 329
McGimsey, B., 164
McGinty, T., 280–281

McKay, R. H., 13
Meddin, B. J., 314
Meisels, S. J., 370
Melson, G. F., 370
Mermin, J., 392
Messenger, K. P., 314
Middlemist, D., 137
Miller, K., 392
Miller, P., 27, 164
Miller, T., 163
Minick, B., 49
Mitchell, A., 48, 253, 333
Modigliani, K., 164
Moen, U. P., 26
Molnar, J., 27
Molt, M., 341
Monighan-Nourot, P., 48
Montessori, M., 31, 48
Moore, D., 94, 189
Moore, E. K., 407
Moore, G. T., 280, 281
Morado, C., 27
Morgan, G., 164, 313
Morin, J., 407
Morris, S. L., 341
Moyer, J., 281
Murray, C. T., 313
Myers, I. B., 71
Myers, P. B., 71
Myhre, S. M., 282

Nagy, M. C., 294
Nastasi, B. K., 369
Neisworth, J. T., 48
Neugebauer, B., 164, 370, 392,
    418
Neugebauer, R., 27, 91, 94,
    108, 141, 164, 216, 236,
    241, 243, 250, 253, 388,
    407
Neuman, B., 392
New, R. 34, 48
Newman, R. 341
Nimmo, J., 189

O'Connor, C. E., 26
O'Connor, R., 314
Odland, J., 407
O'Malley, E. T., 94
Osofsky, J., 407

Paley, V., 189
Paolucci, B., 47, 61, 62, 65, 71
Papert, S., 32, 48, 370
Pastalan, L., 257, 258
Pekor, C., 314
Pelo, A., 407
Pence, A. R., 48
Perreault, J., 141, 142, 164
Perrin, M. S., 211
Perry, K. S., 243
Peters, D. L., 48
Pettygrove, W., 241
Phair, M. A., 165
Phenice, L., 11, 144, 238, 376, 407
Phillips, C. B., 164
Phillips, D. A., 27, 164, 165, 407
Phillips, D. C., 48
Piaget, J., 31, 48
Plantz, M. C., 13, 30, 75, 94, 192
Popham, W., 211
Porter, S., 222, 223
Poteet-Johnson, D., 294
Powell, D. R., 26, 27, 370, 392
Prescott, E., 281, 282
Puckett, M., 211

Rab, V.Y., 314
Ramos-Ford, V., 370
Ramsey, P., 370
Ranck, E., 141
Readdick, C. A., 282
Reed, S., 407
Reeves, D. L., 253
Rich, D., 384
Richarz, S., 342
Rieber, R. W., 49
Rinaldi, C., 157, 164
Roberts, J. E., 314
Rockwell, R. E., 113, 328, 341
Rodgers, F., 313
Roedell, W. C., 407
Rogers, C. S., 341
Rogers, D. L., 211, 370
Rogers, J. R., 27, 85
Rooney, T., 94, 253
Rosegrant, T., 174, 192, 398
Rosen, A. L., 314
Rosenblatt, L., 393
Roskos, K., 392

Ross, D. D., 370
Ross, S. D., 142
Rothenberg, D., 183
Rubin, D., 142
Ruggie, M., 27, 253
Ruopp, R. R., 27, 42, 102, 134, 138, 259
Ryan, S., 13

Satter, E., 341
Sautter, R. C., 407
Scales, B., 48
Scallan, P., 164, 165, 241
Schiamberg, L., 48
Schon, I., 392
Schorr, D., 418
Schorr, L. B., 418
Schrag, I., 94, 241
Schumer, F., 253
Schumm, W. R. 36, 47
Schweinhart, L. J., 27, 115
Scott, D.K., 314
Seefeldt, C., 238
Seefeldt, V., 348
Sefton, K., 392
Seligson, M., 253
Settel, J., 294, 313
Shade, D. D., 370
Shepherd, S. K., 403
Shiff, E., 393
Shores, E. F., 210, 381
Shugart, G., 341
Simon, H. A., 61
Skeen, P., 314
Skinner, B. F., 32, 48
Slaby, R. G., 407
Smith, D. G., 282
Smith, E., 205
Smith, S., 71
Soderman, A., 27, 34, 210, 369, 370
Sontag, M. S., 36, 47
Spodek, B., 189
Spratling, C., 247
Staley, C., 141
Stanley, S., 211
Stanton, S., 241
Stayton, V., 164
Steele, D. M., 253
Stein, L., 27, 210

Steiner, R., 31
Steinmetz, S. K., 36, 47
Stephens, K., 165, 241, 253, 282
Stine, S., 71
Stipek, D., 393
Stone, J. G., 393
Storm, S., 71
Streibert, C., 369
Studer, J. R., 393
Styfco, S., 418
Sunderlin, S., 281
Sussman, L., 417
Swaminatham, S., 369

Tannenbaum, R., 188
Tarule, J., 70
Thomas, R. M., 34
Thornton, D., 87
Tiger, F., 393
Tobin, J., 189, 254
Travers, J., 27, 42, 102, 134, 259
Travis, N., 142
Tryon, C., 178
Tull, C. Q., 113

Ulrich, D., 188
Uphoff, J. F., 189
Ury, W., 179, 189

Vail, C. O., 30, 48, 192
VanDusen, J., 407
VanHoorn, J., 48
VanScoy, I., 210
Venditti, P., 165
Vygotsky, L. S., 32, 48, 49

Wadlington, E., 370
Wadsworth, D., 281
Waller, C. B., 211
Walling, L., 281
Walters, C., 26
Walters-Chapman, C., 282
Wanamaker, N. K., 342
Ward, E., 189
Wardle, F., 351
Warger, C., 27
Waring-Chaffee, M. B., 370
Warman, B., 238
Warren, D., 282
Washington, V., 393

Wassom, J., 393
Watt, M. R., 314
Waxman, P. L., 253
Weber-Schwartz, N., 165
Weeks, E., 241
Weikart, D. P., 27, 48, 180
Weinstein, C., 281
Weinstein, D. T. 281
Weiser, M. G., 95, 314, 370
Weissbourd, B., 26
Whiren, A., 27, 34, 210, 369
White, B. P., 165
White, R., 168
Whitebook, M., 164, 165, 241, 251, 407

Wickens, E., 393
Widoff, E., 164
Wilbers, J., 21, 95
Willer, B., 10, 27, 117, 121, 232
Williams, L. M., 268, 308, 313
Winsler, A., 47
Winter, S. M., 314
Wishon, P. M., 408
Wittmer, D. S., 370
Wolery, M., 21, 95
Wood, K. I. 314
Workman, S., 241
Wright, J. L., 370
Wu, D., 189, 254
Wyde, J. S., 370

Yablans-Magid, R., 135
Yawkey, T. D., 48
York, S., 189, 370

Zander, A., 168
Zavitkovsky, A., 369
Zavitkovsky, D., 369
Zeece, P., 211,
Zeisel, S. A., 314
Zeisler, L. M., 408
Zemel, B., 165
Ziemer, M., 370
Zigler, E. F., 24, 26, 27, 418
Zukerman, L., 391

Subject Index

ABC Task Force, 189
Abuse, 307
Accreditation
    of centers, 58, 168, 191, 288,
        343, 359
    group size, 344
    and parents, 371 59
    space requirements, 255
    validation, 59
Active listening, 154
Activity areas, 273–278
Activity plans, 355
Adult-child ratios, 104, 105
Advertising
    center services, 374
    job openings, 139
Advisory board, 76
Advocacy, 394
    examples, 396–402
    goals, 394
    issues, 404
    public awareness, 388
    steps in, 396
AIDS, HIV, 294
American Academy of Pediatrics,
    104, 113, 191, 283, 312,
    316, 318, 341
American Consumer Protection
    Society, 191
Americans with Disabilities Act
    (ADA), 21, 268
American Public Health
    Association, 104, 113, 191,
    288, 312, 316, 318
Antibias Curriculum, 174

Assessment, portfolios, 197
Association for Childhood
        Education International,
        94, 406
Authority
    decentralized, 100
    plan, 99

Bathroom design, 268
Before and after school care,
        16
Behaviorist theory, 33
Brochures, 373
Budgeting, 230
Building and grounds, 254–278
Burn-out, 182
Bylaws, 76, 77–78

California Department of
        Education, 294, 313, 391
Carnegie Corporation of New
        York, 406
Career ladder, 132
Career lattice, 117
Carpeting, 263–264
Cash, petty, 235
CDA, 17, 133, 191
Center for Science in the Public
        Interest, 326
Central concept, 51
Certification, 134
Characteristics of professionals,
        411–416
Child abuse, 307
Child advocate, 394

Child care
    church sponsored, 215, 250
    demand for, 6
    for profit, 216
    history, 17
    hospital sponsored, 251
    infant-toddler, 11
    labor negotiations, 246–250
    latchkey, 16
    military, 251
    partial day, 10
    public schools, 10
    quality, 190, 356
    remedial, 21
    sick children, 11
    as social utility, 17
    subsidies, 217–220
    substitute for parents, 22
    supplemental, 16
    teacher preparation, 22
    university supported, 250–251
Child Care and Development
        Block Grant of 1990, 217
Child Care Employee Project,
        165
Child Care Food Program, 316,
        326
Child Care Information Exchange,
        26, 69, 245
Child Care Law Center, 280
Child Care Quarterly, 69
Child Development Associate,
        17, 133
Child development center,
        defined, 2

Child development centers, types, 12–22
Child Welfare League of America, 26
Children data, 5–6
Children of immigrants, 6
Children's Congress, 218
Children's Defense Fund, 10, 104, 219, 406
Children with disabilities, 21, 268–270, 293, 362
Children's Foundation, 70, 113, 191
Chronic medical problems, 293
Church-supported centers, 215, 250
Classroom arrangement, 271
Cleaning service, 111
Cleanliness, 263
Communication
  advocacy message, 403
  purposes, 372
  with parents, 336, 367, 371
  with staff, 181
Community Coordinated Child Care (4C), 17, 296
Competitive bidding, 236
Computers
  and children, 357
  newsletters, 381
  record keeping, 107
  systems, 235
Conferences
  professional groups, 160
  with parents, 379
  with staff, 156
Confidentiality, 297
Constitutional rights, 398
Constructivist theory, 31
Cook's responsibility, 110
Coordination among programs, 362
Corporate child care, 216, 242
Cost, Quality, and Child Outcomes Study, 190, 210, 215, 230, 356, 388
Costs
  calculating, 230
  equipment, 227
  opportunity, 231

per child, 103
personnel, 231
space, 227
CPR, 291
Criteria for play equipment, 281
Cultural diversity, 59, 376
  food, 320
Curriculum
  coordinator, 136
  manager's role, 357
Custodial service, 111

Data
  child care arrangements, 9
  children, 5–6
  corporate child care, 12, 216–217, 243
  workforce, 6–7
Day Care and Early Education, 69
Death, 295
Decentralized authority, 100
Decision making, 61, 62–65
Decision types, 61–62
Developmental principles, 347–348
Developmental task theory, 178
Developmental theory, 29
Developmentally appropriate practices, 30, 34, 178, 192
Diapering, 300
Disabilities, 27
Dismissing staff, 151

Ecological model, applications, 42
Ecological system, 29, 35
Efficiency Rule, 232
Emergency contact person, 297
Emergency plans, 362, 363
Emergency procedures, 306
Emergency services, 111
Emergency treatment, 290
Emergent literacy, 357
Employees
  needs and desires, 117–119
  probationary, 358
  reducing turnover, 121–122
Employer-assisted child care, 11, 216, 242
  forms of, 244–246

motivation for providing, 243–244
Environment, 254
  aesthetic, 255
  human-built, 36, 37, 254
  physical-biological, 36, 254
  social-cultural, 36, 38, 254, 410
  space, 254
Equilibrium, 40
Equipment
  child sized, 263
  companies, 278–279
  costs, 227
  criteria, 281
  lists, 227, 273–278
ERIC Clearinghouse, 183
Esteem needs, 118
Ethical dilemma, 65
Evaluation of center
  by children, 194
  food service, 205
  health and safety, 206
  management, 207
  money use, 204
  by parents, 200
  physical plant, 204
  programs, 193, 196, 360
  public relations, 206
  by staff, 195
Experience, of teachers, 135

Facility management, 254–278
Family
  functions, 376–377
  size, 5
  support system, 4
Family day care, 20
Fathers, child care needs, 6
Federal funding, 218
Field trips, 336
Financial decisions, 229
Financial economies, 236–239
Firing staff, 151
First Aid, 291
Floor plan, example of, 262
Food
  children, ages 1–12, 319
  cultural diversity, 320, 333
  federal subsidies, 316

infants, 318, 324
menu planning, 324, 326, 327, 329
personnel, 321
poisoning, prevention, 322
prescription diets, 298, 331
records, 325
safety, 320
service, 108, 320
vegetarian diets, 330
Four C (4-C), 296
Franchise centers, 216
Fringe benefits, 131
Funding, 214
federal, 218
grants, 221
in-kind, 221
proposals, 220
state, 219

Goal for program, 96
Goals, space usage, 257
Greater Minneapolis Day Care Association, 407
Group size, 102–104, 259, 344, 364
effects of, 103–104
Guidance techniques, 259–260

Handbook, information, 378
Handwashing, 299
Headstart, 11, 13, 218
standards, 191
teachers' requirements, 134
Health
children with disabilities, 293
of children, 286, 299
of employees, 292
parents' responsibility, 295
policies and practices, 283
policy board, 284
resources, 311–312
sleeping, 299, 302
standards, 285–286
system to meet requirements, 289
Health education, 303
Hepatitis B, 294
HighScope Curriculum, 33

HIV, AIDS, 294
Homeless families, 6
Home visits, 378
Hospitals and child care, 251
Human-built environment, 36, 37, 254
Human capital, 13, 37, 114
Human ecological system, 36
Human needs, 118
Human ratio, 105

IEP, 21, 269
IFSP, 21, 269
I-Messasges, 154
Immigrant families, 6
Immunization, 289
Inclusion, 21, 134, 268
Indirect guidance, 260
Indoor space, per child, 255
Industry and child care, 247–250
Infant care, 11
Information Service (NAEYC), 189, 314, 389
Insurance, 228
Interest centers, 261, 273–278
Internet, 183, 187
Inventory control, 236
I-Messages, 154
Isolation area, 277

Job
analysis, 123, 124–127
applications, 139, 140
charts, children, 109
classification, 128, 131
description, 123, 129
orientation, 148
performance, 150
specification, 128, 130
Journals, 184–187

Kids Count Data Book, 406
Kindergarten, 10

Labor, data, 6–7
Labor-management, 247
Latchkey children, 16
Laundry service, 111
Lead poisoning, 287

Leadership
and accreditation, 168
styles, 169
Leadership Effectiveness Training, 181
Leading, 55, 166
Learning centers, 261, 273–278
Legal rights, 398
Library, professional, 183
Licensing
agencies, 422–425
compared by state, 420–421
and quality of care, 387
requirements, 99, 285–286, 320
Life space, 257
Linkages with agencies, 387
Literacy, 357
Loans, 229

Maintenance service, 111
Management
approaches, 43–44
defined, 2
processes, 50
styles, 59
theories, 43
Management by objectives, 88
Manager's evaluation, 201–207
Manager's office, 272
Manager's role, 115, 344
Managing and leading, 166
Managing by walking around, 152
Marketing, 87, 373, 385
Maslow's Hierarchy of Needs, 118
Meals service, 331
Medical advice, 286
Medication permission, 291, 298
Mental health, 309
Menus, 327, 329
MESH formula, 225–226
Military child care, 251
Monetary decisions, 229
Monetary evaluation, 232
Monetary policies, 234
Money management, 214
Monitoring and controlling, 56–58, 190–211

Mothers
  poor, 11
  teenage, 6
  working, 8
Motivation, 119
Motor skills, 347–348
Multi-age groups, 106

NAEYC, 27, 71, 94, 113, 210,
    259, 288
  information service, 189, 314,
    389
  insurance, 228, 236, 241
Naptime, 277, 302
National Association of State
    Boards of Education, 23, 27
National Commission on
    Children, 392
National Council of Churches,
    85, 94
National Day Care Study,
    102–103, 134, 137, 231
National Fire Protection
    Association, 229
National Life Safety Fire Code,
    191
National Task Force on School
    Readiness, 392
Needs survey, 83, 84
Negotiations, 179
New business, 222, 224
  start up, 226–227
Newsletters, parents, 381
Nutrition
  education, 333
  goals, 315–316, 334
  requirements, 318, 319, 328

Office equipment, 107
Office services, 107
Office worker tasks, 101
Opportunity costs, 231
Organization plan, 99
Organizing, defined, 53, 96
Orientation for new families, 379
Outdoor play space, 255, 266

Paid planning time, 359
Parents
  concern for quality, 356

conferences, 379
cooperatives, 14, 216
evaluation, 200
functions, 376–377
home activities, 383
as human resources, 384
information handbook, 378
involvement, 372, 377
meetings, 382
newsletters, 379
Pedagogista, 137
Performance, 150
Personnel costs, 231
Petty cash, 235
Physical-biological environment,
    36, 254
Physiological needs, 299
PL 90-538, 21
PL 93-644, 21
PL 98-199, 21
PL 99-142, 21, 268
PL 99-457, 21, 268
PL 101-336, 21, 268
PL 101-576, 21
Planning
  categories, 74, 92
  daily, 354
  defined, 51, 74
  forecasts, 83
  importance, 79
  innovative, 88
  meal service, 316, 333
  needs survey, 83, 84
  steps, 53, 82–87
  time for, 79
  time block, 351
  time, paid, 79, 359
  time, scope, and cycling, 91
  types of, 87
  unit, 89
  weekly, 353
Play
  time for, 351
  space for, 410
Play yard, 266
Pledge to children, 416
Policies, 90, 230
Policy board, 75
Portfolios, 197, 381
Prepared environment, 31, 263

Prestige of center, 122
Primary caregiver, 287
Private schools, 216
Private speech, 32
Procedures, 90, 230
Professional development, 117,
    131, 156–160, 365
Professional resources
  internet, 183, 187
  journals, 184–187
  library, 183
  organizations, 184–186
  support, 182
  writing, 183, 387
Professionalism, 394, 402
Program evaluation, 360
Program for children, 349
Program guides, 349–351
Proposal for funding, 220, 223
Public policy, 220
Public relations, 389
Public school
  kindergartens, 10
  programs, 10, 14
  support for child care, 14
Publicity, 386
Purchasing, 237

Qualifications, staff, 358
Quality, monitoring and
    controlling defined, 190
Quality of programs, 190, 356

Record keeping, 107, 234, 286
References, staff, 139
Reggio Emilia, 33
Regulations, 99, 285–286, 320
Requests for Proposals (RFP),
    222
Research, professional, 183
Resource, defined, 224
  equipment, 227
  human energy, 227
  materials, 226
  required, 226–229
  space, 227, 256
Resource and referral, 246
Room arrangement, 261–262
"Rule of 72," 229
Rules, 90

Safety
  children's, 304–307
Salaries, 231
Sanitation, 320
Schedule, time blocks, 351, 352
School age child care, 16
Self-efficacy, 309
Services
  custodial, 111
  emergency, 111
  food, 108, 316–322
  transportation, 111
Sexual abuse, 307–308
  research, 268
Sick children, care for, 11,
  287–288, 296
Small Business Administration,
  224
Smoking, 152, 271
Snacks, 329
Social construction of
  knowledge, 32
Social-cultural environment, 36,
  38, 254, 410
Software, 235
Southern Association for
  Children Under Six,
  186
Space
  accessibility, 268
  allocation per child, 255
  bathroom design, 268
  cleaning, 263
  color use, 264
  costs, 227
  density, 259
  managing, 255
  mastery, 258
  open school, 265
  orientation, 264
  personal, 258
  play yard, 266
  room arrangement, 271
  rules for children, 259, 261
  safety, 260, 268
  scale, 259
  security, 267
  sexual abuse, 268
  special needs, 268–270
  for staff, 270

stimulation, 265
territoriality, 258
Space use, goals, 257
Span of control, 102
Special needs, 27, 268–270
Specialists, early childhood,
  131–137
  other staff, 137–138
Staff
  benefits, 131
  communication, 153
  compensation, principles of, 121
  development guides, 156–160
  educational requirements, 133
  evaluations, 150, 156
  meetings, 156
  needs, 117
  new, 119
  professional services, 137
  recruitment, 138
  relations, 151
  salaries, 231
  screening, 139, 141
  stability, 121–122
  stages of development, 136
  supervision, 136, 362, 366
  support, 364
Staffing
  civil rights, 146
  costs, 231
  defined, 55, 114
  interviewing, 144
  legal aspects, 142
  manager's role, 115
  manager's tasks, 358
  orientation, 148
  probationary, 358
  shortage, 120
Staff-child ratio, 104–105
Standards, 191, 320
State funding, 10, 17
  kindergartens, 10
Statistical data, 5, 6, 7, 9, 16, 18
Supervisory staff, 136
Supplemental care, 15
Support system for families, 4
Systems theory, 45

Task analysis, 97, 101
Tax support for centers, 217

Teacher
  certificates, 134
  preparation, 22
  qualifications, 133
Telephone etiquette, 374
Texas Child Care, 281, 282, 313,
  326, 341, 392
Theories, types of
  behaviorist, 33
  biogenetic, 34
  constructivist, 31
  developmental, 29, 30
  developmental-interactionist,
  34
  dialectical, 32
  ecological, 34
  environmentalist, 33
  functional, 34
  interactionist, 33
  management, 43
  maturationist, 33
Theory, defined, 28
Time management, 66–68
  usage, 238
Toilet training, 301
Total quality management,
  44–45
Toys, 273–278
Traffic flow, 261
Transportation
  safety, 308
  service, 111

U.N. Convention on the Rights
  of the Child, 401
UNICEF, 401
Unions and child care,
  247–250
Universal precautions, 294
U.S. Civil Service Commission,
  124–127
USDA requirements, 318, 319,
  328
U.S. Department of Agriculture,
  316, 319, 323, 328,
  341
U.S. Department of Commerce,
  4, 16
U.S. Department of Education,
  393

U.S. Department of Labor, 165,
    216, 218, 242, 246–250
U.S. Small Business Association,
    224

Values, 171
    constitutional, 172
    negotiations, 179

questionnaire, 175–177
Visits to center, 345, 375
Volunteers, 160, 238, 336, 364

Waldorf schools, 31
Workforce data, 216, 242
Working mothers, 6, 8

Writing
    advocacy, 402
    professional, 387
    selling, 403
    steps in, 387

Young Children, 69